# Unity Virtual Reality Projects
## *Second Edition*

Learn Virtual Reality by developing more than 10 engaging projects with Unity 2018

**Jonathan Linowes**

**BIRMINGHAM - MUMBAI**

# Unity Virtual Reality Projects
## *Second Edition*

**Commissioning Editor:** Kunal Chaudhari
**Acquisition Editor:** Reshma Raman
**Content Development Editor:** Onkar Wani
**Technical Editor:** Ralph Rosario
**Copy Editor:** Safis Editing
**Project Coordinator:** Devanshi Doshi
**Proofreader:** Safis Editing
**Indexer:** Aishwarya Gangawane
**Graphics:** Jason Monteiro
**Production Coordinator:** Deepika Naik

First published: September 2015
Second edition: May 2018

Production reference: 1180518

Published by Packt Publishing Ltd.
Livery Place
35 Livery Street
Birmingham
B3 2PB, UK.

ISBN 978-1-78847-880-9

www.packtpub.com

*This book is dedicated to Lisa—my wife, best friend, and soul mate—and the amazing family we created together: Rayna, Jarrett, Steven and Shira, who know in their hearts that the future is theirs to embrace*

`mapt.io`

Mapt is an online digital library that gives you full access to over 5,000 books and videos, as well as industry leading tools to help you plan your personal development and advance your career. For more information, please visit our website.

# Why subscribe?

- Spend less time learning and more time coding with practical eBooks and Videos from over 4,000 industry professionals

- Improve your learning with Skill Plans built especially for you

- Get a free eBook or video every month

- Mapt is fully searchable

- Copy and paste, print, and bookmark content

# PacktPub.com

Did you know that Packt offers eBook versions of every book published, with PDF and ePub files available? You can upgrade to the eBook version at `www.PacktPub.com` and as a print book customer, you are entitled to a discount on the eBook copy. Get in touch with us at `service@packtpub.com` for more details.

At `www.PacktPub.com`, you can also read a collection of free technical articles, sign up for a range of free newsletters, and receive exclusive discounts and offers on Packt books and eBooks.

# Contributors

## About the author

**Jonathan Linowes** founded Parkerhill Reality Labs, an immersive media indie studio and is the developer of the BridgeXR toolkit, Power Solitaire VR game, and the upcoming Chess Or Die game. He is a VR/AR evangelist, Unity developer, entrepreneur, and teacher. Jonathan has a BFA from Syracuse University and an MS from the MIT Media Lab. He held technical leadership positions at Autodesk and other companies. He authored Unity Virtual Reality Projects (first edition 2015), Cardboard VR Projects for Android (2016), and Augmented Reality for Developers (2017), all published by Packt.

# About the reviewer

**Krystian Babilinski** is an experienced Unity Developer with extensive knowledge in 3D design and has been developing professional AR/VR applications since 2015. He led Babilin Applications, a Unity Design group that promoted open source development and engaged with the Unity Community. Recently, Krystian published a how-to book on Augmented Reality, called *Augmented Reality for Developers*. Krystian now leads the development at Parkerhill Reality Labs, which publishes multiplatform VR games.

# Packt is searching for authors like you

If you're interested in becoming an author for Packt, please visit authors.packtpub.com and apply today. We have worked with thousands of developers and tech professionals, just like you, to help them share their insight with the global tech community. You can make a general application, apply for a specific hot topic that we are recruiting an author for, or submit your own idea.

# Table of Contents

# Preface

Today, we are witnesses to the burgeoning of **virtual reality** (**VR**), an exciting new technology and creative medium that promises to transform how we interact with our information, friends, and the world at large in a fundamental way.

Wearing a VR **head-mounted display** (**HMD**), you can view stereoscopic 3D scenes. You can look around by moving your head, walk around the space with room-scale tracking, and interact with virtual objects with positional hand controllers. With VR, you engage in fully immersive experiences. It's like you're really in some other virtual world.

This book takes a practical, project-based approach to teach you the specifics of virtual reality development using the Unity 3D game engine. We walk through a series of hands-on projects, step-by-step tutorials, and in-depth discussions using Unity 2018 and other free or open source software. While VR technology is rapidly advancing, we'll try to capture the basic principles and techniques you can use to make your own VR games and applications immersive and comfortable.

You will learn how to use Unity to develop VR applications that can be experienced with devices such as the Oculus Rift, Google Daydream, HTC VIVE, and others. We'll cover technical considerations that are especially important and possibly unique to VR. By the end of this book, you will be equipped to develop rich and interactive virtual reality experiences.

## About the author and this Second Edition

Years ago, I studied 3D computer graphics in college and user interface design in graduate school and then started a small software company developing a 3D graphics engine for managing AutoCAD engineering drawings. We sold the business to Autodesk. In the ensuing years, I focused on 2D web app development, blogged about my technical adventures, and pursued several new startups. Then, in the March of 2014, I read about Facebook purchasing Oculus for $2B; that certainly piqued my interest. I immediately ordered my first VR headset, the Oculus DK2 developer kit, and began developing small VR projects in Unity.

In February 2015, I had the idea to write a book on Unity VR development. Packt accepted my proposal right away, and suddenly I realized, "Oh no! I have to do this!" Within 6 months, in August 2015, the first edition of this book was published. That's a short time to go from proposal to outline to chapter drafts to review to final draft and publication. I was obsessed. At the time, I told my wife that I feel the book has a life of its own, "it's inside of me and struggling to get out, I just have to get out of its way." She replied, "It sounds like you're pregnant."

At the time of that writing, the Google Cardboard was a thing, but there were no consumer VR devices. The DK2 had no hand controllers, just an XBox game controller. Months after the book was released, in November 2015, the HTC Vive came to market with room scale and positionally tracked hand controllers. In March 2016, the Oculus Rift consumer version was released. Not until December 2016, almost a year and a half after the book came out, did Oculus release its positionally tracked Touch hand controllers.

Since the first edition of this book, many new VR devices have come to market, hardware and software features have improved, and the Unity game engine continues to add native VR SDK integrations and new features to support them. Oculus, Google, Steam, Samsung, PlayStation, Microsoft, and many others have joined the fray as the industry continues to accelerate and blossom.

Meanwhile, in 2016, I coauthored another book with Packt, *Cardboard VR Projects for Android*, a non-Unity VR book using Java and Android Studio to build Google Daydream and cardboard applications. (In that book, you build and use your own home-grown 3D graphics engine for mobile devices). Then in 2017, I coauthored a third book with Packt, *Augmented Reality for Developers*, an exciting and timely Unity-based projects' book for AR applications on iOS, Android, and HoloLens devices.

When the time came to begin this second edition of *Unity Virtual Reality Projects*, I expected it to be a relatively simple task of updating to the current version of Unity, adding support for positionally tracked hand controllers, plus a few tweaks here and there. Not so simple! While much of the fundamentals and advice in the first edition did not change, as an industry, we have learned a lot in these few short years. For example, it's really not a great idea to implement a trampoline in VR (one of our projects that got scrapped in this edition), as that can really cause motion sickness!

For this second edition, the book is significantly revised and expanded. Every chapter and project has been updated. We separated some topics into their own chapters with completely new projects, such as the audio fireball game (Chapter 8, *Playing with Physics and Fire*), animation (Chapter 11, *Animation and VR Storytelling*), and optimization (Chapter 13, *Optimizing for Performance and Comfort*). I sincerely hope you find this book fun, educational, and helpful, as we all aim to create great new VR content and explore this amazing new medium.

# Who this book is for

If you are interested in virtual reality, want to learn how it works, or want to create your own VR experiences, this book is for you. Whether you're a non-programmer and are unfamiliar with 3D computer graphics, or experienced in both but new to virtual reality, you will benefit from this book. Any experience in Unity is an advantage. If you are new to Unity, you too can pick up this book, although you might first want to work through some of Unity's own getting-started tutorials available on their website (https://unity3d.com/learn).

Game developers may already be familiar with the concepts in this book reapplied to the VR projects while learning many other ideas specific to VR. Mobile and 2D game designers who already know how to use Unity will discover another dimension! Engineers and 3D designers may understand many of the 3D concepts, but learn to use the Unity engine for VR. Application developers may appreciate the potential non-gaming uses of VR and may want to learn the tools to make that happen.

# What this book covers

Chapter 1, *Virtually Everything for Everyone*, is an introduction to the new technologies and opportunities in consumer virtual reality in games and non-gaming applications, including an explanation of stereoscopic viewing and head tracking.

Chapter 2, *Content, Objects, and Scale*, introduces the Unity game engine as we build a simple diorama scene and reviews importing 3D content created with other tools such as Blender, Tilt Brush, Google Poly, and Unity EditorXR.

Chapter 3, *VR Build and Run*, helps you set up your system and Unity project to build and run on your target device(s), including SteamVR, Oculus Rift, Windows MR, GearVR, Oculus Go, and Google Daydream.

Chapter 4, *Gaze-Based Control*, explores the relationship between the VR camera and objects in the scene, including 3D cursors and gaze-based ray guns. This chapter also introduces Unity scripting in the C# programming language.

Chapter 5, *Handy Interactables*, looks at user input events using controller buttons and interactable objects, using various software patterns including polling, scriptable objects, Unity events, and interactable components provided with toolkit SDK.

Chapter 6, *World Space UI*, implements many examples of user interface (UI) for VR using a Unity world space canvas, including a heads-up display (HUD), info-bubbles, in-game objects, and a wrist-based menu palette.

Chapter 7, *Locomotion and Comfort*, dives into techniques for moving yourself around a VR scene, looking closely at the Unity first-person character objects and components, locomotion, teleportation, and room-scale VR.

Chapter 8, *Playing with Physics and Fire*, explores the Unity physics engine, physic materials, particle systems, and more C# scripting, as we build a paddle ball game to whack fireballs in time to your favorite music.

Chapter 9, *Exploring Interactive Spaces*, teaches how to build an interactive art gallery, including the level design, artwork lighting, data management, and teleporting through space.

Chapter 10, *Using All 360 Degrees*, explains 360-degree media and uses them in a variety of examples, including globes, orbs, photospheres, and skyboxes.

Chapter 11, *Animation and VR Storytelling*, builds a complete VR storytelling experience using imported 3D assets and soundtrack, and Unity timelines and animation.

Chapter 12, *Social VR Metaverse*, explores multiplayer implementations using Unity Networking components as well as developing for Oculus platform avatars and VRChat rooms.

Chapter 13, *Optimizing for Performance and Comfort*, demonstrates how to use the Unity Profiler and Stats window to reduce latency in your VR app, including optimizing your 3D art, static lighting, efficient coding, and GPU rendering.

# To get the most out of this book

Before we get started, there are a few things that you'll need. Grab a snack, a bottle of water, or a cup of coffee. Besides that, you'll need a PC (Windows or Mac) with Unity 2018 installed.

You don't need a super powerful computer rig. While Unity can be a beast that can render complex scenes, and VR manufacturers like Oculus have published recommended specifications for PC hardware, you can actually get by with less; even a laptop will do for the projects in this book.

To get Unity, go to `https://store.unity.com`, select **Personal**, and download the installer. The free Personal version is fine.

We also optionally use the Blender open source project for 3D modeling. This book isn't about Blender, but we'll use it if you want. To get Blender, go to `https://www.blender.org/download/` and follow the instructions for your platform.

Access to a virtual reality **head-mounted display** (**HMD**) is strongly recommended in order to try out your builds and get first-hand experience of the projects developed in this book. Although not entirely required, you can use the emulation modes while working in Unity. Depending on your platform, you may need to install additional development tools. *Chapter 3, VR Build and Run*, goes into details of what you need for each device and platform, including SteamVr, Oculus Rift, Windows MR, GearVR, Oculus Go, Google Daydream, and others.

That should just about do it—a PC, the Unity software, a VR device, other tools described in *Chapter 3, VR Build and Run*, and we're good to go! Oh, some projects will be more complete if you download the associated assets from the Packt website, as follows.

# Download the project assets and example code files

You can download the project assets and example code files for this book from your account at `www.packtpub.com`. If you purchased this book elsewhere, you can visit `www.packtpub.com/support` and register to have the files emailed directly to you.

You can download the code files by following these steps:

1. Log in or register at `www.packtpub.com`.
2. Select the **SUPPORT** tab.
3. Click on **Code Downloads & Errata**.
4. Enter the name of the book in the **Search** box and follow the onscreen instructions.

Once the file is downloaded, please make sure that you unzip or extract the folder using the latest version of:

- WinRAR/7-Zip for Windows
- Zipeg/iZip/UnRarX for Mac
- 7-Zip/PeaZip for Linux

The code bundle for the book is also hosted on GitHub at `https://github.com/PacktPublishing/Unity-Virtual-Reality-Projects-Second-Edition`. In case there's an update to the code, it will be updated on the existing GitHub repository.

We also have other code bundles from our rich catalog of books and videos available at `https://github.com/PacktPublishing/`. Check them out!

# Download the color images

We also provide a PDF file that has color images of the screenshots/diagrams used in this book. You can download it here: https: `//www.packtpub.com/sites/default/files/downloads/B08826_UnityVirtual RealityProjectsSecondEdition_ColorImages.pdf`.

# Conventions used

There are a number of text conventions used throughout this book.

`CodeInText`: Indicates code words in text, database table names, folder names, filenames, file extensions, pathnames, dummy URLs, user input, and Twitter handles. Here is an example: "Mount the downloaded `WebStorm-10*.dmg` disk image file as another disk in your system."

A block of code is set as follows:

```
void Update () {
Transform camera = Camera.main.transform;
Ray ray;
RaycastHit hit;
GameObject hitObject;
```

When we wish to draw your attention to a particular part of a code block, the relevant lines or items are set in bold:

```
 using UnityEngine;
using UnityEngine.Networking;
public class AvatarMultiplayer : NetworkBehaviour
{
public override void OnStartLocalPlayer()
{
GameObject camera = Camera.main.gameObject;
transform.parent = camera.transform;
transform.localPosition = Vector3.zero;
GetComponent<OvrAvatar>().enabled = false;
}
}
```

**Bold**: Indicates a new term, an important word, or words that you see onscreen. For example, words in menus or dialog boxes appear in the text like this. Here is an example: "Select **System info** from the **Administration** panel."

Warnings or important notes appear like this.

Tips and tricks appear like this.

# Get in touch

Feedback from our readers is always welcome.

**General feedback**: Email feedback@packtpub.com and mention the book title in the subject of your message. If you have questions about any aspect of this book, please email us at questions@packtpub.com.

**Errata**: Although we have taken every care to ensure the accuracy of our content, mistakes do happen. If you have found a mistake in this book, we would be grateful if you would report this to us. Please visit www.packtpub.com/submit-errata, selecting your book, clicking on the Errata Submission Form link, and entering the details.

**Piracy**: If you come across any illegal copies of our works in any form on the Internet, we would be grateful if you would provide us with the location address or website name. Please contact us at copyright@packtpub.com with a link to the material.

**If you are interested in becoming an author**: If there is a topic that you have expertise in and you are interested in either writing or contributing to a book, please visit authors.packtpub.com.

# Reviews

Please leave a review. Once you have read and used this book, why not leave a review on the site that you purchased it from? Potential readers can then see and use your unbiased opinion to make purchase decisions, we at Packt can understand what you think about our products, and our authors can see your feedback on their book. Thank you!

For more information about Packt, please visit packtpub.com.

# 1
# Virtually Everything for Everyone

*This virtual reality thing calls into question, what does it mean to*
*"be somewhere"?*
*Before cell phones, you would call someone and it would make no sense to*
*say, "Hey, where are you?" You know where they are, you called their house,*
*that's where they are.*
*So then cell phones come around and you start to hear people say, "Hello. Oh, I'm at*
*Starbucks," because the person on the other end wouldn't necessarily know where you are,*
*because you became un-tethered from your house for voice communications.*
*So when I saw a VR demo, I had this vision of coming home and my wife has got the kids*
*settled down, she has a couple minutes to herself, and she's on the couch wearing goggles*
*on her face. I come over and tap her on the shoulder, and I'm like, "Hey, where are you?"*
*It's super weird. The person's sitting right in front of you, but you don't know where they*
*are.*

*-Jonathan Stark, mobile expert, and podcaster*

Welcome to **virtual reality (VR)**! In this book, we will explore what it takes to create virtual reality experiences on our own. We will take a walk through a series of hands-on projects, step-by-step tutorials, and in-depth discussions using the Unity 3D game engine and other free or open source software. Though the virtual reality technology is rapidly advancing, we'll try to capture the basic principles and techniques that you can use to make your VR games and applications feel immersive and comfortable.

In this first chapter, we will define virtual reality and illustrate how it can be applied not only to games but also many other areas of interest and productivity. This chapter discusses the following topics:

- What is virtual reality?
- Differences between virtual reality and augmented reality
- How VR applications may differ from VR games
- Types of VR experiences
- Technical skills that are necessary for the development of VR

# What is virtual reality to you?

Today, we are witnesses to the burgeoning consumer virtual reality, an exciting technology that promises to transform in a fundamental way how we interact with information, our friends, and the world at large.

What is virtual reality? In general, VR is the computer-generated simulation of a 3D environment, which seems very real to the person experiencing it, using special electronic equipment. The objective is to achieve a strong sense of being present in the virtual environment.

Today's consumer tech VR involves wearing an HMD (head-mounted display goggles) to view stereoscopic 3D scenes. You can look around by moving your head, and walk around by using hand controls or motion sensors. You are engaged in a fully immersive experience. It's as if you're really there in some other virtual world. The following image shows me, the author, experiencing an **Oculus Rift Development Kit 2 (DK2)** in 2015:

Virtual reality is not new. It's been here for decades, albeit hidden away in academic research labs and high-end industrial and military facilities. It was big, clunky, and expensive. Ivan Sutherland invented the first HMD in 1965 (see `https://amturing.acm.org/photo/sutherland_3467412.cfm`). It was tethered to the ceiling! In the past, several failed attempts have been made to bring consumer-level virtual reality products to the market.

In 2012, Palmer Luckey, the founder of Oculus VR LLC, gave a demonstration of a makeshift head-mounted VR display to John Carmack, the famed developer of the Doom, Wolfenstein 3D, and Quake classic video games. Together, they ran a successful **Kickstarter** campaign and released a developer kit called **Oculus Rift Development Kit 1** (**DK1**) to an enthusiastic community. This caught the attention of investors as well as Mark Zuckerberg, and in March 2014, Facebook bought the company for $2 billion. With no product, no customers, and infinite promise, the money and attention that it attracted helped fuel a new category of consumer products.

Concurrently, others also working on their own products which were soon introduced to the market, including Steam's HTC VIVE, Google Daydream, Sony PlayStation VR, Samsung Gear VR, Microsoft's immersive Mixed Reality, and more. New innovations and devices that enhance the VR experience continue to be introduced.

Most of the basic research has already been done and the technology is now affordable thanks in large part to the mass adoption of devices that work on mobile technology. There is a huge community of developers with experience in building 3D games and mobile apps. Creative content producers are joining in and the media is talking it up. At last, virtual reality is real!

Say what? *Virtual reality is real?* Ha! If it's virtual, how can it be... Oh, never mind.

Eventually, we will get past the focus on the emerging hardware devices and recognize that *content is king*. The current generation of 3D development software (commercial, free, and open source) that has spawned a plethora of indie, or independent, game developers can also be used to build non-game VR applications.

Though VR finds most of its enthusiasts in the gaming community, the potential applications reach well beyond that. Any business that presently uses 3D modeling and computer graphics will be more effective if it uses VR technology. The sense of immersive presence that is afforded by VR can enhance all common online experiences today, which includes engineering, social networking, shopping, marketing, entertainment, and business development. In the near future, viewing 3D websites with a VR headset may be as common as visiting ordinary flat websites today.

# Types of head-mounted displays

Presently, there are two basic categories of HMDs for virtual reality—**desktop VR** and **mobile VR**, although the distinctions are increasingly becoming blurred. Eventually, we might just talk about platforms as we do traditional computing, in terms of the operating system—Windows, Android, or console VR.

## Desktop VR

With desktop VR (and console VR), your headset is a peripheral to a more powerful computer that processes the heavy graphics. The computer may be a Windows PC, Mac, Linux, or a game console, although Windows is by far the most prominent PC and the PS4 is a bestseller in terms of console VR.

Most likely, the headset is connected to the computer with wires. The game runs on the remote machine and the HMD is a peripheral display device with a motion sensing input. The term *desktop* is an unfortunate misnomer since it's just as likely to be stationed in either a living room or a den.

The **Oculus Rift** (https://www.oculus.com/) is an example of a device where the goggles have an integrated display and sensors. The games run on a separate PC. Other desktop headsets include the **HTC VIVE**, Sony's **PlayStation VR**, and **Microsoft immersive Mixed Reality**.

Desktop VR devices rely on a desktop computer (usually via video and USB cables) for CPU and **graphics processing unit** (GPU) power, where more is better. Please refer to the recommended specification requirements for your specific device.

However, for the purpose of this book, we won't have any heavy rendering in our projects, and you can get by with minimum system specifications.

## Mobile VR

Mobile VR originated with **Google Cardboard** (https://vr.google.com/cardboard/), a simple housing device for two lenses and a slot for your mobile phone. The phone's display is used to show the twin stereoscopic views. It has rotational head tracking, but it has no positional tracking. The Cardboard also provides the user with the ability to click or *tap* its side to make selections in a game. The complexity of the imagery is limited because it uses your phone's processor for rendering the views on the phone display screen.

Google Daydream and Samsung GearVR improved the platforms by requiring more performant minimum specifications including greater processing power in the mobile phone. GearVR's headsets include motion sensors to assist the phone device. These devices also introduced a three-**degrees-of-freedom** (**DOF**) hand controller that can be used like a laser pointer within VR experiences.

The next generation of mobile VR devices includes all-in-one headsets, like Oculus Go, with embedded screens and processors, eliminating the need for a separate mobile phone. Newer models may include depth sensors and spatial mapping processors to track the user's location in 3D space.

The bottom line is, the projects in this book will explore features from the high end to the low end of the consumer VR device spectrum. But generally, our projects do not demand a lot of processing power nor do they require high-end VR capability, so you can begin developing for VR on any of these types of devices, including Google Cardboard and an ordinary mobile phone.

 If you are interested in developing VR applications for Google Daydream on Android directly in Java rather than through the Unity game engine, please also refer to another of the author's books, *Cardboard VR Projects for Android* from Packt Publishing (`https://www.packtpub.com/application-development/cardboard-vr-projects-android`).

# The difference between virtual reality and augmented reality

It's probably worthwhile to clarify what virtual reality is not.

A sister technology to VR is **augmented reality** (**AR**), which combines computer-generated imagery (CGI) with views of the real world. AR on smartphones has recently garnered widespread interest with the introduction of Apple's ARKit for iOS and Google ARCore for Android. Further, the Vuforia AR toolkit is now integrated directly with the Unity game engine, helping to drive even more adoption of the technology. AR on a mobile device overlays the CGI on top of live video from a camera.

The latest innovations in AR are wearable AR headsets, such as Microsoft's **HoloLens** and **Magic Leap**, which show the computer graphics directly in your field of view. The graphics are not mixed into a video image. If VR headsets are like closed goggles, AR headsets are like translucent sunglasses that combine the real-world light rays with CGI. A challenge for AR is ensuring that the CGI is consistently aligned with and mapped onto the objects in the real-world space and to eliminate latency while moving about so that they (the CGI and objects in the real-world space) stay aligned.

AR holds as much promise as VR for future applications, but it's different. Though AR intends to engage the user within their current surroundings, virtual reality is fully immersive. In AR, you may open your hand and see a log cabin resting in your palm, but in VR, you're transported directly inside the log cabin and you can walk around inside it.

We are also beginning to see hybrid devices that combine features of VR and AR and let you switch between modes.

 If you are interested in developing applications for AR, please also refer to the author's book *Augmented Reality for Developers* from Packt Publishing (`https://www.packtpub.com/web-development/augmented-reality-developers`).

# Applications versus games

Consumer-level virtual reality started with gaming. Video gamers are already accustomed to being engaged in highly interactive hyper-realistic 3D environments. VR just ups the ante.

Gamers are early adopters of high-end graphics technology. Mass production of gaming consoles and PC-based components in the tens of millions and competition between vendors leads to lower prices and higher performance. Game developers follow suit, often pushing the state of the art, squeezing every ounce of performance out of hardware and software. Gamers are a very demanding bunch, and the market has consistently stepped up to keep them satisfied. It's no surprise that many, if not most, of the current wave of VR hardware and software companies, are first targeting the video gaming industry. A majority of the VR apps on the Oculus Store such as Rift (`https://www.oculus.com/experiences/rift/`), GearVR (`https://www.oculus.com/experiences/gear-vr/`), and Google Play for Daydream (`https://play.google.com/store/search?q=daydreamc=apps hl=en`), for example, are games. And of course, the Steam VR platform (`http://store.steampowered.com/steamvr`) is almost entirely about gaming. Gamers are the most enthusiastic VR advocates and seriously appreciate its potential.

Game developers know that the core of a game is the **game mechanics**, or the rules, which are largely independent of the *skin*, or the thematic topic of the game. Gameplay mechanics can include puzzles, chance, strategy, timing, or muscle memory. VR games can have the same mechanic elements but might need to be adjusted for the virtual environment. For example, a first-person character walking in a console video game is probably going about 1.5 times faster than their actual pace in real life. If this wasn't the case, the player would feel that the game was too slow and boring. Put the same character in a VR scene and they will feel that it is too fast; it could likely make the player feel nauseous. In VR, you want your characters to walk at a normal, earthly pace. Not all video games will map well to VR; it may not be fun to be in the middle of a war zone when you're actually there.

That said, virtual reality is also being applied in areas other than gaming. Though games will remain important, non-gaming applications will eventually overshadow them. These applications may differ from games in a number of ways, with the most significant having much less emphasis on game mechanics and more emphasis on either the experience itself or application-specific goals. Of course, this doesn't preclude some game mechanics. For example, the application may be specifically designed to train the user in a specific skill. Sometimes, the **gamification** of a business or personal application makes it more fun and effective in driving the desired behavior through competition.

In general, non-gaming VR applications are less about winning and more about the experience itself.

Here are a few examples of the kinds of non-gaming applications that people are working on:

- **Travel and tourism**: Visit faraway places without leaving your home. Visit art museums in Paris, New York, and Tokyo in one afternoon. Take a walk on Mars. You can even enjoy Holi, the spring festival of colors, in India while sitting in your wintery cabin in Vermont.
- **Mechanical engineering and industrial design**: Computer-aided design software such as AutoCAD and SOLIDWORKS pioneered three-dimensional modeling, simulation, and visualization. With VR, engineers and designers can directly experience the end product before it's actually built and play with what-if scenarios at a very low cost. Consider iterating a new automobile design. How does it look? How does it perform? How does it appear when sitting in the driver's seat?

- **Architecture and civil engineering**: Architects and engineers have always constructed scale models of their designs, if only to pitch the ideas to clients and investors or, more importantly, to validate the many assumptions about the design. Presently, modeling and rendering software is commonly used to build virtual models from architectural plans. With VR, the conversations with stakeholders can be so much more confident. Other personnel, such as the interior designers, HVAC, and electrical engineers, can be brought into the process sooner.

- **Real estate**: Real estate agents have been quick adopters of the internet and visualization technology to attract buyers and close sales. Real estate search websites were some of the first successful uses of the web. Online panoramic video walkthroughs of for-sale properties are commonplace today. With VR, I can be in New York and find a place to live in Los Angeles.

- **Medicine**: The potential of VR for health and medicine may literally be a matter of life and death. Every day, hospitals use MRI and other scanning devices to produce models of our bones and organs that are used for medical diagnosis and possibly pre-operative planning. Using VR to enhance visualization and measurement will provide a more intuitive analysis. Virtual reality is also being used for the simulation of surgery to train medical students.

- **Mental health**: Virtual reality experiences have been shown to be effective in a therapeutic context for the treatment of **post-traumatic stress disorder** (**PTSD**) in what's called **exposure therapy**, where the patient, guided by a trained therapist, confronts their traumatic memories through the retelling of the experience. Similarly, VR is being used to treat arachnophobia (fear of spiders) and the fear of flying.

- **Education**: The educational opportunities for VR are almost too obvious to mention. One of the first successful VR experiences is **Titans of Space**, which lets you explore the solar system first-hand. In science, history, arts, and mathematics, VR will help students of all ages because, as they say, field trips are much more effective than textbooks.

- **Training**: Toyota has demonstrated a VR simulation of drivers' education to teach teenagers about the risks of distracted driving. In another project, vocational students got to experience the operating of cranes and other heavy construction equipment. Training for first responders, the police, and fire and rescue workers can be enhanced with VR by presenting highly risky situations and alternative virtual scenarios. The **National Football League** (**NFL**) and college teams are looking to VR for athletic training.

- **Entertainment and journalism**: Virtually attend rock concerts and sporting events. Watch music videos Erotica. Re-experience news events as if you were personally present. Enjoy 360-degree cinematic experiences. The art of storytelling will be transformed by virtual reality.

Wow, that's quite a list! This is just the low-hanging fruit.

The purpose of this book is not to dive too deeply into any of these applications. Rather, I hope that this survey helps stimulate your thinking and provides an idea of how virtual reality has the potential to be virtually anything for everyone.

# How virtual reality really works

So, what is it about VR that's got everyone so excited? With your headset on, you experience synthetic scenes. It appears 3D, it feels 3D, and maybe you even have a sense of actually being there inside the virtual world. The strikingly obvious thing is: VR looks and feels *really cool!* But why?

*Immersion* and *presence* are the two words used to describe the quality of a VR experience. The Holy Grail is to increase both to the point where it seems so real, you forget you're in a virtual world. *Immersion* is the result of emulating the sensory input that your body receives (visual, auditory, motor, and so on). This can be explained technically. *Presence* is the visceral feeling that you get being transported there—a deep emotional or intuitive feeling. You could say that immersion is the science of VR and presence is the art. And that, my friend, is cool.

A number of different technologies and techniques come together to make the VR experience work, which can be separated into two basic areas:

- 3D viewing
- Head-pose tracking

In other words, displays and sensors, like those built into today's mobile devices, are a big reason why VR is possible and affordable today.

Suppose the VR system knows exactly where your head is positioned at any given moment in time. Suppose that it can immediately render and display the 3D scene for this precise viewpoint stereoscopically. Then, wherever and whenever you move, you'll see the virtual scene exactly as you should. You will have a nearly perfect visual VR experience. That's basically it. *Ta-dah!*

Well, not so fast. Literally.

# Stereoscopic 3D viewing

Split-screen stereography was discovered not long after the invention of photography, like the popular stereograph viewer from 1876 shown in the following picture (B.W. Kilborn & Co, Littleton, New Hampshire; see `http://en.wikipedia.org/wiki/Benjamin_W._Kilburn`). A stereo photograph has separate views for the left and right eyes, which are slightly offset to create parallax. This fools the brain into thinking that it's a truly three-dimensional view. The device contains separate lenses for each eye, which let you easily focus on the photo close up:

Similarly, rendering these side-by-side stereo views is the first job of the VR-enabled camera in Unity.

Let's say that you're wearing a VR headset and you're holding your head very still so that the image looks frozen. It still appears better than a simple stereograph. Why?

The old-fashioned stereograph has relatively small twin images rectangularly bound. When your eye is focused on the center of the view, the 3D effect is convincing, but you will see the boundaries of the view. Move your eyes around (even with your head still), and any remaining sense of immersion is totally lost. You're just an observer on the outside peering into a diorama.

Now, consider what a VR screen looks like without the headset (see the following screenshot):

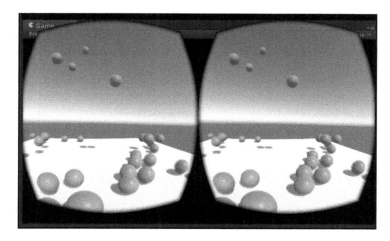

The first thing that you will notice is that each eye has a barrel-shaped view. Why is that? The headset lens is a very wide-angle lens. So, when you look through it, you have a nice wide field of view. In fact, it is so wide (and tall), it distorts the image (**pincushion effect**). The graphics software SDK does an inverse of that distortion (**barrel distortion**) so that it looks correct to us through the lenses. This is referred to as an **ocular distortion correction**. The result is an apparent **field of view** (**FOV**) that is wide enough to include a lot more of your peripheral vision. For example, the Oculus Rift has a FOV of about 100 degrees. (We talk more about FOV in Chapter 10, *Using All 360 Degrees*.)

Also, of course, the view angle from each eye is slightly offset, comparable to the distance between your eyes or the **Inter Pupillary Distance** (**IPD**). IPD is used to calculate the parallax and can vary from one person to the next. (The Oculus Configuration Utility comes with a utility to measure and configure your IPD. Alternatively, you can ask your eye doctor for an accurate measurement.)

It might be less obvious, but if you look closer at the VR screen, you will see color separations, like you'd get from a color printer whose print head is not aligned properly. This is intentional. Light passing through a lens is refracted at different angles based on the wavelength of the light. Again, the rendering software does an inverse of the color separation so that it looks correct to us. This is referred to as a **chromatic aberration correction**. It helps make the image look really crisp.

The resolution of the screen is also important to get a convincing view. If it's too low-res, you'll see the pixels, or what some refer to as a **screen-door effect**. The pixel width and height of the display is an oft-quoted specification when comparing the HMDs, but the **pixels per inch** (**PPI**) value may be more important. Other innovations in display technology such as **pixel smearing** and **foveated rendering** (showing higher-resolution details exactly where the eyeball is looking) will also help reduce the screen-door effect.

When experiencing a 3D scene in VR, you must also consider the **frames per second** (**FPS**). If the FPS is too slow, the animation will look choppy. Things that affect FPS include the GPU performance and the complexity of the Unity scene (the number of polygons and lighting calculations), among other factors. *This is compounded in VR because you need to draw the scene twice, once for each eye.* Technology innovations, such as GPUs optimized for VR, frame interpolation, and other techniques will improve the frame rates. For us, developers, performance-tuning techniques in Unity, such as those used by mobile game developers, can be applied in VR. (We will talk more about performance optimization in Chapter 13, *Optimizing for Performance and Comfort*.) These techniques and optics help make the 3D scene appear realistic.

Sound is also very important—more important than many people realize. VR should be experienced while wearing stereo headphones. In fact, when the audio is done well but the graphics are pretty crappy, you can still have a great experience. We see this a lot in TV and cinema. The same holds true in VR. Binaural audio gives each ear its own stereo *view* of a sound source in such a way that your brain imagines its location in 3D space. No special listening devices are needed. Regular headphones will work (speakers will not). For example, put on your headphones and visit the *Virtual Barber Shop* at https://www. youtube.com/watch?v=IUDTlvagjJA. True 3D audio provides an even more realistic spatial audio rendering, where sounds bounce off nearby walls and can be occluded by obstacles in the scene to enhance the first-person experience and realism.

Lastly, the VR headset should fit your head and face comfortably so that it's easy to forget that you're wearing it, and it should block out light from the real environment around you.

# Head tracking

So, we have a nice 3D picture that is viewable in a comfortable VR headset with a wide field of view. If this was it and you moved your head, it'd feel like you had a diorama box stuck to your face. Move your head and the box moves along with it, and this is much like holding the antique stereograph device or the childhood **View-Master**. Fortunately, VR is so much better.

The VR headset has a motion sensor (IMU) inside that detects spatial acceleration and rotation rates on all three axes, providing what's called the **six degrees of freedom**. This is the same technology that is commonly found in mobile phones and some console game controllers. Mounted on your headset, when you move your head, the current viewpoint is calculated and used when the next frame's image is drawn. This is referred to as **motion detection**.

The previous generation of mobile motion sensors was good enough for us to play mobile games on a phone, but for VR, it's not accurate enough. These inaccuracies (rounding errors) accumulate over time, as the sensor is sampled thousands of times per second and one may eventually lose track of where they were in the real world. This *drift* was a major shortfall of the older, phone-based Google Cardboard VR. It could sense your head's motion, but it lost track of your head's orientation. The current generation of phones, such as Google Pixel and Samsung Galaxy, which conform to the Daydream specifications, have upgraded sensors.

High-end HMDs account for drift with a separate *positional tracking* mechanism. The Oculus Rift does this with *inside-out positional tracking*, where an array of (invisible) infrared LEDs on the HMD are read by an external optical sensor (infrared camera) to determine your position. You need to remain within the *view* of the camera for the head tracking to work.

Alternatively, the Steam VR VIVE Lighthouse technology does outside-in positional tracking, where two or more dumb laser emitters are placed in the room (much like the lasers in a barcode reader at the grocery checkout), and an optical sensor on the headset reads the rays to determine your position.

Windows MR headsets use no external sensors or cameras. Rather, there are integrated cameras and sensors to perform spatial mapping of the local environment around you, in order to locate and track your position in the real-world 3D space.

Either way, the primary purpose is to accurately find the position of your head and other similarly equipped devices, such as handheld controllers.

Together, the position, tilt, and the forward direction of your head—or the *head pose*—are used by the graphics software to redraw the 3D scene from this vantage point. Graphics engines such as Unity are really good at this.

Now, let's say that the screen is getting updated at 90 FPS, and you're moving your head. The software determines the head pose, renders the 3D view, and draws it on the HMD screen. However, you're still moving your head. So, by the time it's displayed, the image is a little out of date with respect to your current position. This is called **latency**, and it can make you feel nauseous.

Motion sickness caused by latency in VR occurs when you're moving your head and your brain expects the world around you to change exactly in sync. Any perceptible delay can make you uncomfortable, to say the least.

Latency can be measured as the time from reading a motion sensor to rendering the corresponding image, or the *sensor-to-pixel* delay. According to Oculus's John Carmack:

> *A total latency of 50 milliseconds will feel responsive, but still noticeable laggy. 20 milliseconds or less will provide the minimum level of latency deemed acceptable.*

There are a number of very clever strategies that can be used to implement latency compensation. The details are outside the scope of this book and inevitably will change as device manufacturers improve on the technology. One of these strategies is what Oculus calls the **timewarp**, which tries to guess where your head will be by the time the rendering is done and uses that future head pose instead of the actual detected one. All of this is handled in the SDK, so as a Unity developer, you do not have to deal with it directly.

Meanwhile, as VR developers, we need to be aware of latency as well as the other causes of motion sickness. Latency can be reduced via the faster rendering of each frame (keeping the recommended FPS). This can be achieved by discouraging your head from moving too quickly and using other techniques to make yourself feel grounded and comfortable.

Another thing that the Rift does to improve head tracking and realism is that it uses a skeletal representation of the neck so that all the rotations that it receives are mapped more accurately to the head rotation. For example, looking down at your lap creates a small forward translation since it knows it's impossible to rotate one's head downwards on the spot.

Other than head tracking, stereography, and 3D audio, virtual reality experiences can be enhanced with body tracking, hand tracking (and gesture recognition), locomotion tracking (for example, VR treadmills), and controllers with haptic feedback. The goal of all of this is to increase your sense of immersion and presence in the virtual world.

# Types of VR experiences

There is not just one kind of virtual reality experience. In fact, there are many. Consider the following types of virtual reality experiences:

- **Diorama**: In the simplest case, we build a 3D scene. You're observing from a third-person perspective. Your eye is the camera. Actually, each eye is a separate camera that gives you a stereographic view. You can look around.

- **First-person experience**: This time, you're immersed in the scene as a freely moving avatar. Using an input controller (keyboard, game controller, or some other technique), you can walk around and explore the virtual scene.

- **Interactive virtual environment**: This is like the first-person experience, but it has an additional feature—while you are in the scene, you can interact with the objects in it. Physics is at play. Objects may respond to you. You may be given specific goals to achieve and challenges with the game mechanics. You might even earn points and keep score.

- **3D content creation**: In VR, create content that can be experienced in VR. **Google Tilt Brush** is one of the first blockbuster experiences, as is **Oculus Medium** and **Google Blocks** and others. Unity is working on **EditorXR** for Unity developers to work on their projects directly in the VR scene.

- **Riding on rails**: In this kind of experience, you're seated and being transported through the environment (or the environment changes around you). For example, you can ride a rollercoaster via this virtual reality experience. However, it may not necessarily be an extreme thrill ride. It can be a simple real estate walk-through or even a slow, easy, and meditative experience.

- **360-degree media**: Think panoramic images taken with **GoPro** on steroids that are projected on the inside of a sphere. You're positioned at the center of the sphere and can look all around. Some purists don't consider this *real* virtual reality, because you're seeing a projection and not a model rendering. However, it can provide an effective sense of presence.

- **Social VR**: When multiple players enter the same VR space and can see and speak with each other's avatars, it becomes a remarkable social experience.

In this book, we will implement a number of projects that demonstrate how to build each of these types of VR experience. For brevity, we'll need to keep it pure and simple, with suggestions for areas for further investigation.

# Technical skills that are important to VR

Each chapter of the book introduces new technical skills and concepts that are important if you wish to build your own virtual reality applications. You will learn about the following in this book:

- **World scale**: When building for a VR experience, attention to the 3D space and scale is important. One unit in Unity is usually equal to one meter in the virtual world.

- **First-person controls**: There are various techniques that can be used to control the movement of your avatar (first-person camera), gaze-based selection, tracked hand input controllers, and head movements.
- **User interface controls**: Unlike conventional video (and mobile) games, all user interface components are in world coordinates in VR, not screen coordinates. We'll explore ways to present notices, buttons, selectors, and other **user interface (UI)** controls to the users so that they can interact and make selections.
- **Physics and gravity**: Critical to the sense of presence and immersion in VR is the physics and gravity of the world. We'll use the Unity physics engine to our advantage.
- **Animations**: Moving objects within the scene is called *animation*—duh! It can either be along predefined paths or it may use AI (artificial intelligence) scripting that follows a logical algorithm in response to events in the environment.
- **Multi-user services**: Real-time networking and multi-user games are not easy to implement, but online services make it easy without you having to be a computer engineer.
- **Build**, **run and optimize**: Different HMDs use different developer kits SDK and assets to build applications that target a specific device. We'll consider techniques that let you use a single interface for multiple devices. Understanding the rendering pipeline and how to optimize performance is a critical skill for VR development.

We will write scripts in the C# language and use features of Unity as and when they are needed to get things done.

However, there are technical areas that we will not cover, such as realistic rendering, shaders, materials, and lighting. We will not go into modeling techniques, terrains, or humanoid animations. We also won't discuss game mechanics, dynamics, and strategies. All of these are very important topics that may be necessary for you to learn (or for someone in your team), in addition to this book, to build complete, successful and immersive VR applications.

So let's see what does this book actually covers and who does it caters to.

# What this book covers

This book takes a practical, project-based approach to teach the specifics of virtual reality development using the Unity 3D game development engine. You'll learn how to use Unity 2018 to develop VR applications, which can be experienced with devices such as the Oculus Rift or Google Cardboard and all kinds of devices in between.

However, we have a slight problem here—the technology is advancing very rapidly. Of course, this is a good problem to have. Actually, it's an awesome problem to have, unless you're a developer in the middle of a project or an author of a book on this technology! How does one write a book that does not have obsolete content the day it's published?

Throughout the book, I have tried to distill some universal principles that should outlive any short-term advances in virtual reality technology, which includes the following:

- Categorization of different types of VR experiences with example projects
- Important technical ideas and skills, especially the ones relevant to the building of VR applications
- General explanations on how VR devices and software works
- Strategies to ensure user comfort and to avoid VR motion sickness
- Instructions on using the Unity game engine to build VR experiences

Once VR becomes mainstream, many of these lessons will perhaps be obvious rather than obsolete, just like the explanations from the 1980s on *how to use a mouse* would just be silly today.

# Who are you?

If you are interested in virtual reality, want to learn how it works, or want to create VR experiences yourself, this book is for you. We will walk you through a series of hands-on projects, step-by-step tutorials, and in-depth discussions using the Unity 3D game engine.

Whether you're a non-programmer who is unfamiliar with 3D computer graphics, or a person with experience in both but new to virtual reality, you will benefit from this book. It could be your first foray into Unity, or you may have some experience, but you do not need to be an expert either. Still, if you're new to Unity, you can pick up this book as long as you realize that you'll need to adapt to the pace of the book.

Game developers may already be familiar with the concepts in the book, which are reapplied to the VR projects along with many other ideas that are specific to VR. Engineers and 3D designers may understand many of the 3D concepts, but they may wish to learn to use the game engine for VR. Application developers may appreciate the potential non-gaming uses of VR and want to learn the tools that can make this happen.

Whoever you are, we're going to turn you into a *3D software VR ninja*. Well, OK, this may be a stretch for this little book, but we'll try to set you on the way.

# Summary

In this chapter, we looked at virtual reality and realized that it can mean a lot of things to different people and can have different applications. There's no single definition, and it's a moving target. We are not alone, as everyone's still trying to figure it out. The fact is that virtual reality is a new medium that will take years, if not decades, to reach its potential.

VR is not just for games; it can be a game changer for many different applications. We identified over a dozen. There are different kinds of VR experiences, which we'll explore in the projects in this book.

VR headsets can be divided into those that require a separate processing unit (such as a desktop PC or a console) that runs with a powerful GPU and the ones that use your mobile technologies for processing.

We're all pioneers living at an exciting time. Because you're reading this book, you're one, too. Whatever happens next is literally up to you. *The best way to predict the future is to invent it.*

So, let's get to it!

In the next chapter, we'll jump right into Unity and create our first 3D scene and learn about world coordinates, scaling, and importing 3D assets. Then, in Chapter 3, *VR Build and Run*, we'll build and run it on a VR headset, and we'll discuss how virtual reality really works.

# 2
# Content, Objects, and Scale

You may remember building a diorama project for school from a shoebox as a child. We're going to make one today, using Unity. Let's assemble our first scene, which is composed of simple geometric objects. Along the way, we'll talk a lot about **world scale**. Then we'll explore various 3D content creation tools that developers and artists use for assets imported into Unity. In this chapter, we will discuss the following topics:

- A short introduction to the Unity 3D game engine
- Creating a simple diorama in Unity
- Making some measuring tools, including a unit cube and a grid projector
- Using **Blender** to create a cube with texture maps and importing it into Unity
- Using Google Tilt Brush to create a 3D sketch and importing it into Unity via Google Poly
- Using the experimental Unity EditorXR tools for editing scenes directly in VR

## Getting started with Unity

If you don't have the Unity 3D game engine application installed on your PC yet, do that now! The full-featured **Personal Edition** is free and runs on both Windows and Mac. To get Unity, go to `https://store.unity.com/`, select the version that you want, click on **Download Installer**, and continue following the instructions. This book assumes you have version 2017.2 or later of Unity.

For you beginners out there, we're going to take this first section nice and slow, with more hand-holding than what you'll get later on in the book. Furthermore, even if you already know Unity and have developed your own games, it may be worthwhile to revisit the fundamental concepts, since the rules are sometimes different when designing for virtual reality.

# Creating a new Unity project

Let's create a new Unity project named VR_is_Awesome, or whatever you'd like.

To create a new Unity project, launch Unity from your operating system and the **Open** dialog box will appear. From this dialog box, select **New**, which opens a **New Project** dialog box, as shown in the following screenshot:

Fill in the name of your project and verify that the folder location is what you want. Ensure that **3D** is selected (on the right). There is no need to add any extra asset packages at this time, as we'll bring them in later if we need them. Click on **Create project**.

 Unity 2018 introduced the Unity Hub tool for managing multiple Unity versions and projects. If you are using Unity Hub, you can choose the "3D" template, or one of the newer VR render pipeline templates for your project.

# The Unity editor

Your new project opens in the Unity editor, as shown in the following screenshot (where I arranged the window panels in a custom layout to facilitate this discussion and labeled the visible panels):

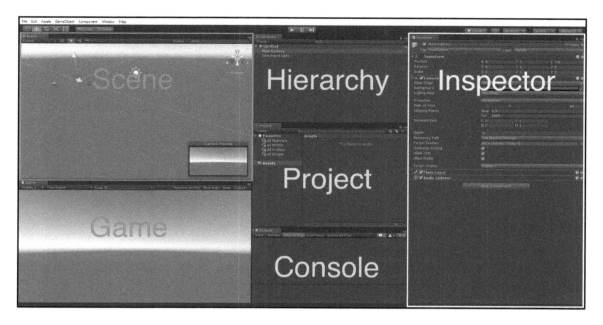

The Unity editor consists of a number of non-overlapping windows, or *panels*, which may be subdivided into *panes*. Here's a brief explanation of each panel that is shown in the preceding layout image (your layout may be different):

- The **Scene** panel on the upper left-hand side (highlighted) is where you can visually compose the 3D space of the current scene, including the placement of objects.

- Below the **Scene** panel is the **Game** view (lower left-hand side), which shows the actual game camera view (presently, it is empty with an ambient sky). When in **Play Mode**, your game runs in this panel.

- In the center, we have arranged the **Hierarchy**, **Project**, and **Console** panels (from the top to the bottom, respectively).

- The **Hierarchy** panel provides a tree view of all the *objects* in the current scene.

- The **Project** panel contains all the *reusable assets* for the project, including the ones imported as well as those that you'll create along the way.

- The **Console** panel shows messages from Unity, including *warnings and errors* from code scripts.

- On the right-hand side is the **Inspector** panel (highlighted), which contains the properties of the currently selected object. (Objects are selected by clicking on them in the **Scene**, **Hierarchy**, or the **Project** panel). The **Inspector** panel has separate panes for each component of the object.

- At the top is the main menu bar (on a Mac, this will be at the top of your screen, not at the top of the Unity window). There's a toolbar area with various controls that we'll use later on, including the **Play** (triangle icon) button that starts **Play** mode.

From the main menu bar's **Window** menu, you can open additional panels as needed. The editor's user interface is configurable. Each panel can be rearranged, resized, and tabbed by grabbing one of the panel tabs and dragging it. Go ahead, try it! On the upper right-hand side is a **Layout** selector that lets you either choose between various default layouts or save your own preferences.

# The default world space

A default empty Unity scene consists of a **Main Camera** object and a single **Directional Light** object, as listed in the **Hierarchy** panel and depicted in the **Scene** panel. The **Scene** panel also shows a perspective of an infinite reference ground plane grid, like a piece of graph paper with nothing on it yet. The grid spans across the *x* (red) and *z* (blue) axes. The *y* axis (green) is up.

 An easy way to remember the Gizmo axes colors is by keeping in mind that R-G-B corresponds to X-Y-Z.

The **Inspector** panel shows the details of the currently selected item. Select the **Directional Light** with your mouse, either from the **Hierarchy** list or within the scene itself, and look at the **Inspector** panel for each of the properties and components associated with the object, including its transform. An object's transform specifies its position, rotation, and scale in the 3D world space. For example, position (0, 3, 0) is 3 units above (in the Y direction) the center of the ground plane (X = 0, Z = 0). A rotation of (50, 330, 0) means that it's rotated 50 degrees around the *x* axis and 330 degrees around the *y* axis. As you'll see, you can change an object's transforms numerically here or directly with the mouse in the **Scene** panel.

Similarly, if you click on the **Main Camera**, it may be located at the (0, 1, -10) position with no rotation. That is, it's pointed straight ahead, towards the positive Z direction.

When you select the **Main Camera**, as shown in the preceding editor screenshot, a **Camera Preview** inset is added to the **Scene** panel, which shows the view that the camera presently sees. (If the **Game** tab is open, you'll see the same view there too). Presently, the view is empty and the reference grid does not get rendered, but a foggy horizon is discernible, with the grey ground plane below and the blue default ambient **Skybox** above.

# Creating a simple diorama

Now, we will add a few objects to the scene to set up the environment, including a unit cube, a flat plane, a red ball, and a photographic backdrop. Here is a photograph of a physical mock-up of the diorama we will build in VR:

# Adding a cube

Let's add the first object to the scene: a unit-sized cube.

Within the **Hierarchy** panel, use the **Create** menu and choose **3D Object | Cube**. The same selection can also be found in the main menu bar's **GameObject** drop-down menu.

A default white cube is added to the scene, centered on the ground plane at the (0, 0, 0) position, with no rotation, and a scale of one, as you can see in the **Inspector** panel. This is the **Reset** setting, which can be found in the object's **Transform** component of the **Inspector** panel.

The **Reset** values of the **Transform** component are **Position** (0, 0, 0), **Rotation** (0, 0, 0), and **Scale** (1, 1, 1).

If for some reason your cube has other Transform values, set these in the **Inspector** panel or locate the small *gear* icon in the upper right-hand side of the **Inspector** panel's **Transform** component, click on it, and select **Reset**.

This cube has the dimensions of one unit on each side. As we'll see later, one unit in Unity corresponds to one meter in world coordinates. Its local center is the center of the cube.

# Adding a plane

Now, let's add a ground plane object into the scene.

In the **Hierarchy** panel, click on the **Create** menu (or main **GameObject** menu) and choose **3D Object | Plane**.

A default white plane is added to the scene, centered on the ground plane at **Position** (0, 0, 0). (If necessary, select **Reset** from the **Inspector** panel's **Transform** component's *gear* icon). Rename it to GroundPlane.

Note that at a scale of (1, 1, 1), Unity's plane object actually measures 10 by 10 units in X and Z. In other words, the size of GroundPlane is 10 by 10 units and its transform's Scale is 1.

The cube is centered at **Position** (0, 0, 0), just like the ground plane. However, maybe it doesn't look like it to you. The **Scene** panel may show a **Perspective** projection that renders 3D scenes onto a 2D image. The **Perspective** distortion makes the cube not seem centered on the ground plane, but it is. Count the grid lines on either side of the cube. As you'll see, when it is viewed in VR and you're actually standing in the scene, it won't look distorted at all. This is shown in the following screenshot:

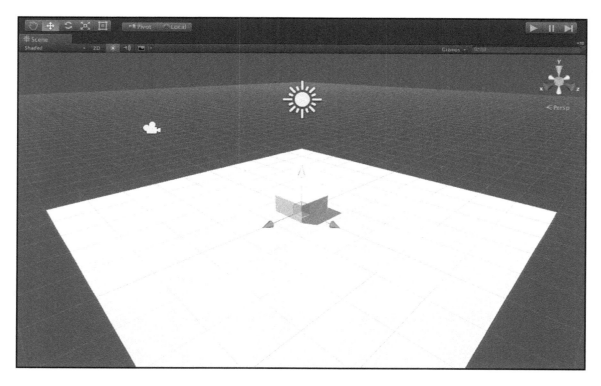

The cube is submerged in the ground plane because its local origin is at its geometric center—it measures 1 by 1 by 1 and its middle point is (0.5, 0.5, 0.5). This might sound obvious, but it is possible for the origin of a model to not be its geometric center (such as one of its corners). The **Transform** component's position is the world space location of the object's local origin. Let's move the cube as follows:

1. Move the cube onto the surface of the ground plane—in the **Inspector** panel, set its **Y** position to 0.5: **Position** (0, 0.5, 0).
2. Let's rotate the cube a bit around the *y* axis. Enter 20 into its **Y** rotation: **Rotation** (0, 0.5, 0).

Note the direction in which it rotates. That's 20 degrees clockwise. Using your left hand, give a thumbs-up gesture. See the direction your fingers are pointing? Unity uses a left-handed coordinate system. (There is no standard for the coordinate system *handedness*. Some software uses left-handedness, others use right-handedness).

Unity uses a left-handed coordinate system. And the *y* axis is up.

# Adding a sphere and some material

Next, let's add a sphere. Select **GameObject** | **3D Object** | **Sphere** from the menu.

Like the cube, the sphere has a radius of 1.0, with its origin at the center. (If necessary, select **Reset** from the **Inspector** panel **Transform** component's *gear* icon). It's hard to see the sphere as it is embedded in the cube. We need to move the sphere's position.

This time, let's use the **Scene** panel's **Gizmos** component to move the object. In the **Scene** view, you can select graphical controls, or Gizmos, to manipulate the objects transforms, as illustrated in the following screenshot from the Unity documentation (http://docs.unity3d.com/Manual/PositioningGameObjects.html):

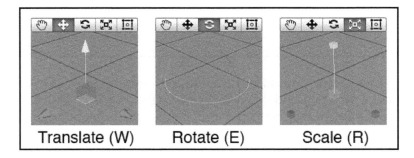

In the **Scene** panel, with the sphere selected, make sure that the **Translate** tool is active (second icon on the top-left icon toolbar) and use the arrows of the *x*, *y*, and *z* axes to position it. I left mine at **Position** (1.6, 0.75, −1.75).

A **Gizmo** is a graphical control that lets you manipulate the parameters of an object or a view. Gizmos have grab points or handles that you can click and drag with the mouse.

Before we go much further, let's save our work as follows:

1. From the main menu bar, select **File | Save Scene As...** and name it `Diorama`.
2. Also, navigate to **File | Save Project** for good measure. Note that in the **Project** panel, the new scene object was saved in the top-level **Assets** folder.

Let's add some color to the scene by making a couple of colored materials and applying them to our objects. Follow these steps:

1. In the **Project** panel, select the top-level **Assets** folder and select **Create | Folder**. Rename the folder to `Materials`.
2. With the `Materials` folder selected, select **Create | Material** and rename it to `Red Material`.
3. In the **Inspector** panel, click the white rectangle to the right of **Albedo**, which opens the **Color** panel. Choose a nice juicy red.
4. Repeat the preceding steps to make a `Blue Material` too.
5. Select **Sphere** from the **Hierarchy** (or **Scene**) panel.
6. Drag the `Red Material` from the **Project** panel into the **Inspector** panel for the sphere. The sphere should now look red.
7. Select **Cube** from the **Scene** (or **Hierarchy**) panel.
8. This time, drag the `Blue Material` from the `Project` panel into the scene and drop it onto the cube. It should now look blue.

Save your scene and save the project. Here's what my scene looks like now (yours might be a little different, but that's OK):

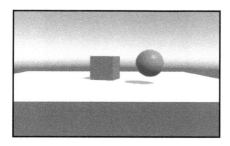

Note that we're using the folders in the Project panel `/Assets/` directory to organize our stuff.

# Changing the scene view

You can change the scene view any time in a number of ways, and this varies depending on whether you have a mouse with three-buttons, or two-buttons, or Mac with only one button. Read up on it in the Unity manual, which can be found at `http://docs.unity3d.com/Manual/SceneViewNavigation.html`, to find out what works for you.

In general, combinations of left/right mouse clicks with the *Shift* + *Ctrl* + *Alt* keys will let you perform the following actions:

- Drag the camera around.
- Orbit the camera around the current pivot point.
- Zoom in and out.
- Press *Alt* and right-click to swing the current eye orbit up, down, left, and right.
- When the **Hand** tool is selected (in the upper-left icon bar), the right mouse button moves the eye. The middle-click of the mouse does a similar thing.

In the upper right-hand side of the **Scene** panel, you have the **Scene View** Gizmo, which depicts the current scene view orientation as shown in the following screenshot. It may indicate, for example, a **Perspective** view, with **x** extending back to the left and **z** extending back to the right:

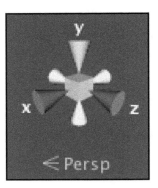

You can change the view to look directly along any of the three axes by clicking on the corresponding colored cone as shown in the following screenshot. Clicking on the small cube in the center changes the **Perspective** view to the **Orthographic** (non-distorted) view:

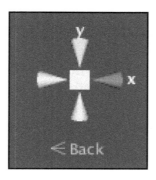

Before moving on, let's first align the scene view with the **Main Camera** direction. You may recall me saying that the default camera orientation, (0, 0, 0), is looking down the positive **z** direction (back to front). Follow the following steps:

1. Click on the white z cone on the Scene View Gizmo to adjust the view from the **Back** (back direction), looking forward.
2. Also, use the Hand tool (or the middle mouse button) to slide the view up a tad.

Now, when you select the **Main Camera** component (from the **Hierarchy** panel), you will see that the **Scene** view is roughly similar to the **Camera Preview**, looking in the same direction. (See the screen capture image shown in the following section for what the scene and preview looks like with this view direction after we add the photo.)

For a full list of Unity shortcut hotkeys, see `https://docs.unity3d.com/Manual/UnityHotkeys.html`.

# Adding a photo

Now, let's add a photo for the big-screen backdrop of our diorama.

In computer graphics, an image that is mapped onto an object is called a **texture**. While objects are represented in the **x**, **y**, and **z** world coordinates, textures are said to be in the U, V coordinates (such as pixels). We'll see that textures and UV maps can have their own scaling issues. Follow the following steps:

1.  Create a plane by navigating to **GameObject** | **3D Object** | **Plane** and rename it `PhotoPlane`.

2.  Reset the plane's transform. In the **Inspector** panel, find the *gear* icon on the upper right-hand side of the **Transform** panel. Click on this icon and select **Reset**.

3.  Next, rotate it by 90 degrees around the *z* axis (set its **Transform** component's **Rotation** value of **z** to -90). That's *minus 90*. So, it's standing up, perpendicular to the ground.

4.  Rotate it by 90 degrees around the *y* axis so that its front is facing us.

5.  Move it to the end of the ground plane at **Position** value of **z** = 5 and above, at **Position** value of **y** = 5 (you may recall that the ground plane is 10 x 10 units).

6.  Choose any photo from your computer to paste on this photo plane using Windows Explorer or Mac Finder. (Alternatively, you can use the `GrandCanyon.jpg` image that comes with this book).

7.  In the **Project** panel, select the top-level **Assets** folder and navigate to **Create** | **Folder**. Rename the folder to `Textures`.

8.  Drag the photo file into the `Assets/Textures` folder. It should automatically import as a texture object. Alternatively, you can right-click on the **Assets** folder, select **Import New Asset...**, and import the picture.

Select the new image **Texture** in the **Project** panel and review its settings in the **Inspector** panel. For Unity's rendering purposes, even if the original photo was rectangular, the texture is square now (for example, 2048 x 2048) and looks squished. When you map it onto a square-shaped face, it will be squished there too. Let's perform the following steps:

1.  Drag the photo texture from the **Project** panel onto the photo plane (in the **Scene** panel).

    Oops! In my case, the picture is rotated sideways—yours, too?

2.  Select `PhotoPlane` (the photo plane) and set the **Transform** component's **Rotation** value of **X** to 90 degrees.

OK, it's upright, but still squished. Let's fix this. Check the original resolution of your photo and determine its aspect ratio. My `Grand Canyon` image was 2576 x 1932. When you divide its width by its height, you get the 0.75 ratio.

3. In Unity, set the `PhotoPlane` plane **Transform** component's **Scale** value of **Z** to `0.75`.

   Because its scale origin is the center, we also have to move it back down a bit.

4. Set the **Position** value of **y** to `3.75`.

 Why 3.75? The height started at 10. So, we scaled it to 7.5. The scaling of objects is relative to their origin. So now, the half of the height is 3.75. We want to position the center of the backdrop 3.5 unit above the ground plane.

We have the size and position set up, but the photo looks washed out. That's because the ambient lighting in the scene is affecting it. You might want to keep it that way, especially as you build more sophisticated lighting models and materials in your scenes. But for now, we'll un-light it.

With `PhotoPlane` selected, note that the photo's **Texture** component in the **Inspector** panel has its default **Shader** component set as **Standard**. Change it to **Unlit | Texture**.

Here's what mine looks like; yours should be similar:

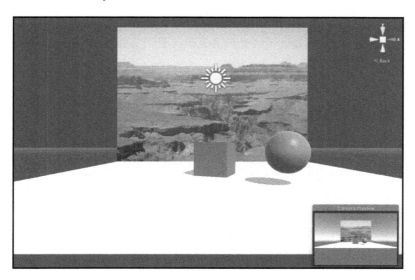

There! That looks pretty good. Save your scene and project.

 You may notice that Planes are only visible from their front. All surfaces in computer graphics have a front-facing direction (normal vector). The view camera must be towards the front face or else the object will not be rendered. This is a performance optimization. If you require a *plane* with faces on both sides, use a Cube scaled thinly, or two separate Planes facing away from each other.

Notice that if you check your Materials folder now, you'll find that Unity has automatically created a `GrandCanyon.mat` material for you that uses the `GrandCanyon.jpg` texture.

# Coloring the ground plane

If you want to change the ground plane color, create a new material (in the **Project** panel), name it `Ground`, and drag it onto the ground plane. Then, change its **Albedo** color. I suggest using the dropper (icon) to pick an earth tone from the image in your photo plane.

# Measurement tools

We've created a Unity scene, added a few primitive 3D objects, and created a couple of basic textures, including a photograph. Along the way, we learned about positioning and transforming objects in Unity's 3D world space. The problem is that the actual size of stuff in your scene is not always obvious. You could be zoomed up or you may be using either a **Perspective** or **Orthographic** view, or other features that affect the apparent size. Let's look at ways to deal with the scale.

# Keeping a unit cube handy

I suggest keeping a unit cube handy in your **Hierarchy** panel. When it's not needed, just disable it (uncheck the checkbox in the top left-hand side of the **Inspector** panel). It can be used like a measuring stick, or rather, a measuring block, when needed. I use one to estimate actual world sizes of objects, distances between objects, heights, and elevations, and so forth. Let's do it now.

Create a unit cube, name it `Unit Cube`, and place it somewhere out of the way for now, such as **Position** (-2, 0.5, -2).

Leave it enabled for the time being.

# Using a Grid Projector

I want to tell you about the **Grid Projector,** a handy tool that is used to visualize a scale in any Unity scene. It's one of the **Standard Assets** in the **Effects** package. So, you may need to import it into your project. To import, perform the following steps:

1. Select **Assets** in the main menu bar and then navigate to **Import Package | Effects**.
2. The **Import** dialog box pops up, containing a list of all the things that can get imported. Then select **Import**.

 If you cannot find the Effects package to import, you may not have installed Standard Assets when you installed Unity. To get them now, you will need to run the UnityDownloadAssistant again as described at the beginning of this chapter (and it may already be in your Downloads folder).

Now, we'll add a projector to the scene, as follows:

1. Find the Grid Projector prefab located in the **Project** panel by navigating to the Assets/Standard Assets/Effects/Projectors/Prefabs folder.
2. Drag a copy of the Grid Projector into your scene. Set the **y** value of the **Position** to 5 so that it's above the ground plane.

The default Grid Projector is facing downward (**Rotation** value of x = 90), which is usually what we want. In the **Scene** view, you can see the Orthographic projection rays. A Unity doc (http://docs.unity3d.com/Manual/class-Projector.html) explains a Projector as follows:

> *A Projector allows you to project a Material onto all objects that intersect its frustum.*

This means that the objects intersected by the projection rays will receive the projected material.

In this case, as you'd expect, the projector material (also named GridProjector) has a *grid* texture, which simply looks like a crosshair. (See for yourself, in the Assets/.../Projectors/Textures/Grid object).

By default, the projector shines the grid pattern as a light on the surface that it illuminates. In our scene, the `GroundPlane` plane is a light color. So, the grid may not show up. Now, follow the following steps:

With Grid Projector selected in the **Hierarchy** panel, locate the `GridProjector` material component in the **Inspector** panel and change its **Shader** from **Projector/Light** to **Projector/Multiply**.

It now paints the white gridlines black. To get a better feel of what's going on, change the scene view to a **Top** view orientation, as follows:

1. Click the green y cone on the **Scene View Gizmo** in the upper right-hand side of the **View** panel.
2. Also, click the little cube at the center of the Gizmo to change from the **Perspective** to the **Orthographic** (flattened) view.

You should now be looking straight down onto the ground plane. With the Grid Projector selected (make sure that the Translate tool is active, which is the second icon in the top-left icon toolbar), you can grab the **Translate Gizmo** attached to the **Projector** and move it from side to side. The grid line will move accordingly. You might leave it at **Position** (−2.5, 5, −0.5) and avoid the projector Gizmo blocking the directional light.

At this point, the built-in view reference grid might be confusing. So, turn it off in the following way:

1. In the **Scene** view panel, click on **Gizmos** (the menu with this name, which has options to control your Gizmos) and uncheck **Show Grid**.

   OK, so what does this get us? We can see that the default grid size measures half the edge of the unit cube. In **Inspector**, the Projector component's **Orthographic** size value is 0.25.

2. Change the Projector's **Orthographic** size value from 0.25 to 0.5.
3. Save the scene and the project.

Now we have a one-unit grid that can be turned on and projected onto the scene any time it is needed.

Let's leave it on for now because it looks kind of cool, as you can see in the following screenshot:

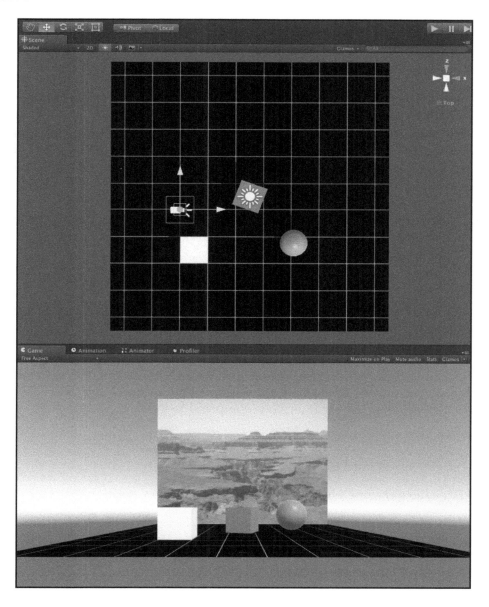

# Measuring the Ethan character

How big is an avatar? Unity comes with a third-person character named Ethan. Let's add him to our scene. He's one of the Standard Assets in the Characters package. So, you may need to import that into your project.

To import, perform the following steps:

1. Select **Assets** in the main menu bar and then navigate to **Import Package | Characters**.
2. The **Import** dialog box pops up, containing a list of all the things that can get imported. Click **All** and then **Import**. The ThirdPersonController is a prefab (pre-built asset) located in the **Project** panel. This can be found by navigating to the Assets/Standard Assets/Characters/ThirdPersonCharacter/Prefabs folder.
3. Drag a copy of ThirdPersonController into your scene. The exact **x** and **z** positions don't matter, but set **y** to 0 so that the character named Ethan is standing on GroundPlane. I left mine at (2.2, 0, 0.75).

Let's try it out:

1. Click on the *Play* icon at the top of the Unity window in the center, to start your game. Use the *W, A, S,* and *D* keys to move him around. *Run, Ethan! Run!*
2. Click on the *Play* icon again to stop the game and return to edit mode.

So, how big is Ethan? According to Google search, the average height of a human male is 5 foot 6 inches, or 1.68 meters (in the USA, the average adult male is more like 5' 10" or 1.77 meters tall). Let's see how tall Ethan is when compared to these:

- Slide the unit cube next to Ethan using the Translate Gizmo

  Alright, he's about 1.6 times its height

- Scale the unit cube's height (**y**) to 1.6 and center its **y** position to 0.8

Look again. As illustrated in the following screenshot, he's not quite 1.6. So, Ethan is a little shorter than the average male (unless you include his pointy hairdo). Swinging my view around, I'm looking Ethan right in the face, and by further adjusting the cube, the eye level is about 1.4 meters. Make a note of this:

1. Restore the unit cube's **Scale** (1,1,1) and **Position** (-2, 0.5, -2)
2. Save the scene and the project

The following screenshot shows the comparison of the unit cube and Ethan:

# Using third-party content

So far we have shown you how to use Unity and be productive creating a scene, but with pretty simple content. Inherently, Unity is not a 3D modeling or asset creation tool. Rather (as the name *Unity* suggests), it's a unified platform for pulling together content from a variety of sources to assemble and program a game or experience involving animation, physics, rendering effects, and so on. If you are a 3D artist you may know how to create content in other programs like Blender, 3D Studio Max, or Maya. If not, you can find a plethora of models on the web.

One terrific source is the **Unity Asset Store** (https://www.assetstore.unity3d.com/en/). Many asset packs are free, especially starter ones, with possible paid upgrades if you want more. If you are looking for a few things to get your learning and experimental projects going, here are some of my free favorites:

- Nature Starter Kit 1 and 2 (https://assetstore.unity.com/packages/3d/environments/nature-starter-kit-1-49962)
- Wispy Skybox (https://assetstore.unity.com/packages/2d/textures-materials/sky/wispy-skybox-21737)

- Planet Earth Free (`https://assetstore.unity.com/packages/3d/environments/sci-fi/planet-earth-free-23399`)
- Seamless Texture Pack (`https://assetstore.unity.com/packages/2d/textures-materials/seamless-texture-pack-21934`)
- And of course, Cute Snowman (`https://assetstore.unity.com/packages/3d/props/cute-snowman-12477`)

 In addition to 3D models, the Asset Store contains an amazing amalgamation of development tools, add-ons, audio, and more. The Asset Store, its active community of developers, and its huge amount of content is one of the things that has made Unity so successful.

The Asset Store is available directly within the Unity Editor. To access it, choose **Window | Asset Store** and begin exploring.

To add assets to your project using the Asset Store for example, simply find one and select **Download,** then choose **Import** to add it to your `Project Assets` folder. Asset packs often come with example scenes you can open to explore how it looks and works. After that, locate its `Prefab` folder and simply drag any prefabs into your own scene. An example is shown here:

Furthermore, there are many sites for sharing 3D models, both free and for a fee. Some are oriented towards higher-end 3D CAD for engineers. Others cater to 3D printing enthusiasts. No matter. Just be sure to look for FBX or OBJ file formats of the model so they can be imported into Unity. Some of the more popular resource sites include:

- 3D CAD Browser: `https://www.3dcadbrowser.com/`
- BlenderSwap: `http://www.blendswap.com/`
- CG Trader: `https://www.cgtrader.com/`
- Free3D: `https://free3d.com/`
- Google Poly: `https://poly.google.com/`
- Microsoft Remix 3D: `https://www.remix3d.com`
- Sketchfab: `https://sketchfab.com`
- TurboSquid: `http://www.turbosquid.com/`

We will use *Google Poly* later in this chapter.

# Creating 3D content with Blender

Unity offers some basic geometric shapes, but when it comes to more complex models, you'll need to go beyond Unity. As we discussed, the Unity **Asset Store** and many sites have tons of amazing models. Where do they come from? Will you run into problems while importing them into Unity?

I know that this book is about Unity, but we're going on a short side adventure right now. We're going to use Blender (version 2.7x), a free and open source 3D animation suite (`http://www.blender.org/`), to make a model and then import it into Unity. Grab a coffee and strap yourself in!

The plan is not to build anything very fancy right now. We'll just make a cube and a simple texture map. The purpose of this exercise is to find out how well a one-unit cube in Blender imports with the same scale and orientation into Unity.

Feel free to skip this section or try a similar experiment using your favorite modeling software (`https://en.wikipedia.org/wiki/List_of_3D_modeling_software`). If you prefer not to follow along or run into problems, a copy of the completed files created in this topic is available in the download package for this book.

# An introduction to Blender

Open the Blender application. Dismiss the opening splash screen. You will be in the Blender editor, which is similar to what's shown in the following screenshot:

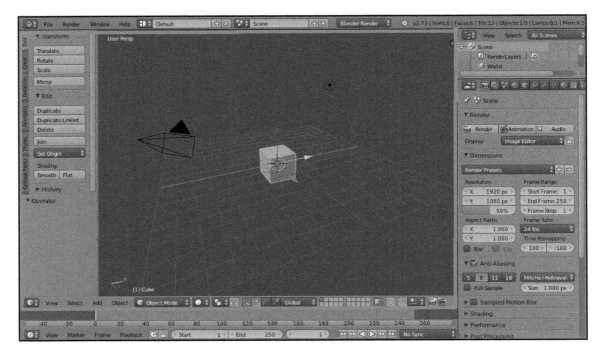

Like Unity, Blender consists of a number of non-overlapping windows, and their layout can be customized to suit your needs. However, the Blender interface can be more daunting, in part because it integrates a number of different editors that can be opened at the same time, in their own panels.

It's helpful to realize that the default view, as shown in the preceding screenshot, contains five different editors!

The most obvious editor is the large **3D View**, which I highlighted with a (red) rectangle. This is where you can view, move, and organize the objects in your Blender scene.

The following are the other editors that are opened:

- The **Info editor**, which can be seen along the top edge of the app, has global menus and information about the application
- The **Timeline editor**, which is present along the bottom edge of the app, is for animations
- The **Outliner editor**, on the upper right-hand side, has a hierarchical view of the objects in your scene
- The **Properties editor**, which can be seen to the right below the Outliner, is a powerful panel that lets you see and modify many properties of the objects in the scene

Each editor can have multiple panes. Let's consider the 3D View editor:

- The large area in the middle is the **3D Viewport**, where you can view, move, and organize the objects in your Blender scene.
- Just below the 3D Viewport is the editor **Header**, which is called so although it's at the bottom in this case. The Header is a row of menus and tools that provide great control over the editor, including view selectors, edit modes, transform manipulators, and layer management.
- On the left-hand side is the **Tool Shelf** containing various editing tools that can be applied to the currently selected object, which can be organized into tabbed groups. The **Tool Shelf** can be toggled open or closed by grabbing and sliding its edge or by pressing the key *T*.
- The 3D Viewport also has a **Properties** pane, which may be hidden by default and can be toggled open or closed by pressing the key *N*. It provides the property settings for the currently selected object.

In the upcoming instructions, we will ask you to change the **Interaction Mode** of the 3D View editor, say between the **Edit Mode** and **Texture Paint** mode. This is selected in the Header, as shown in the following screenshot:

The other editors also have the Header panes. The Info editor (at the top of the app) is only a Header! The outliner and Properties editors (on the right) have their Headers at the top of their panel rather than at the bottom.

Once you recognize this layout, it doesn't look so crowded and confusing.

The Properties editor Header has a wide set of icons, which act like tabs, to select the group of properties presented in the rest of the panel. Hovering your mouse over the icon (like any of the UI widgets here) will show a tooltip with a better hint in regards to what it's for. It's pictured in the following images (in a couple of pages) when we get to using it.

The Blender layout is very flexible. You can even change a panel from one editor to another. At the far left of each Header is the **Editor Type** selector. When you click on it, you can see all the options.

In addition to the plethora of things that you can click on in the Blender interface, you can use just about any command using a keyboard shortcut. If you forget where to find a selection, press the space bar and type in your best guess of the command name that you're looking for. It just might pop up!

The following is a screenshot showing the **Editor Type** selector available in Blender:

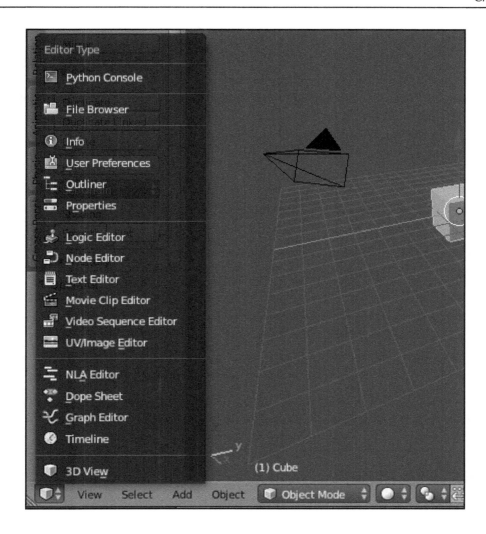

# A unit cube

Now, let's build a unit cube in Blender.

The default scene may already have objects, including a cube, camera, and a light source, as shown earlier in the default Blender window. (Your startup settings may be different since that can be configured.)

If your startup scene does *not* contain a unit cube, create one, as follows:

1. Make sure that the scene is empty by deleting whatever is in it (right-click to select, *X* on the keyboard to delete).
2. Set the 3D cursor to the origin (0,0,0) using *Shift + S* (opens the **Snap** options list) | **Cursor To Center**.
3. In the left **Tool Shelf** panel, choose the **Create** tab and under **Mesh** select **Cube** to add a cube.

OK, now we're all on the same page.

Note that in Blender, the reference grid extends in the *x* and *y* axes, and *z* is up (unlike Unity, where the *y* axis is up).

Furthermore, note that the default cube in Blender has a size of (2, 2, 2). We want a unit cube sitting on the ground plane at the origin. For this, follow the following steps:

1. Open the Properties pane with the keyboard *N* key
2. Navigate to **Transform** | **Scale** and set **X, Y, Z** to (0.5, 0.5, 0.5)
3. Navigate to **Transform** | **Location** and set **Z** to 0.5
4. Press the *N* key again to hide the pane
5. You can zoom in using the scroll wheel of the mouse

For our purposes, also ensure that the current renderer is **Blender Render** (in the drop-down selector on the Info editor—at the top of the app window in the center).

# UV Texture image

Let's paint the faces of our cube. 3D computer models in Unity are defined by *meshes*—a set of Vector3 points connected with edges, forming triangular-shaped facets. When building a model in Blender, you can unwrap a mesh into a flattened 2D configuration to define the mapping of texture pixels to the corresponding areas on the mesh surface (UV coordinates). The result is called a UV Texture image.

We will create a **UV Texture image** for our cube, as follows:

1. Go into **Edit Mode** using the Interaction Mode selector in the bottom Header bar.
2. Select *all* (press the *A* key on the keyboard twice) to make sure that all the faces are selected.
3. In the left **Tool Shelf** panel, select the **Shading/UVs** tab.
4. Under **UV Mapping** click on **Unwrap**, select **Smart UV Project** from the drop-down list, accept the default values, and click on **OK** (the result, shown in the following screenshot, also shows what the unwrapped cube looks like).
5. Now, go into the **Texture Paint** mode using the Interaction Mode selector in the bottom Header bar again.
6. We need to define a *paint slot* for our material. Click on **Add Paint Slot**, select **Diffuse Color**, name it CubeFaces, and press **OK**.

We can now start painting directly on the cube. Paint the front face first, as follows:

1. Make a smaller brush. In the left **Tool Shelf** panel, in the **Tools** tab, navigate to **Brush | Radius** and enter 8 px.
2. It may be easier to work in an orthographic view. From the menu bar at the bottom, navigate to **View | View Persp/Ortho**.
3. Then, navigate to **View | Front**.
4. You can zoom in or out using the mouse scroll wheel if needed.
5. With your best handwriting, write the word Front using the left-click of the mouse and draw.
6. Now, the back face.
7. From the menu bar at the bottom, navigate to **View | Back** and select this face with a right-click.
8. With your best handwriting, write Back.

Repeat the above process for the left, right, top, and bottom faces. If at some point it's not painting, make sure that there's a current face selected. Try right-clicking on the face to reselect it. The result should look something like this (shown side by side both in the **3D View** editor with an orthographic perspective and in the **UV/Image Editor**):

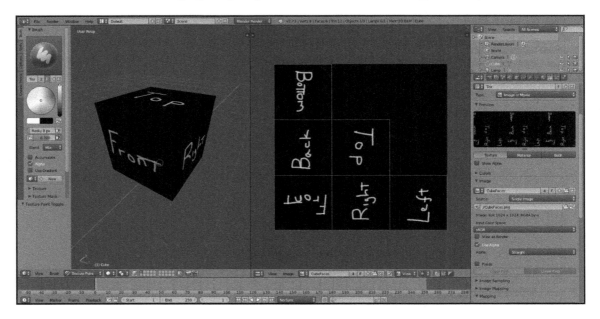

Now, we need to save the texture image and set up its properties, as follows:

1. Change the current **Editor Type** to **UV/Image Editor** using the selector on the far left of the Header at the bottom of the **3D View** editor.
2. Click on the **Browse Image to be linked** selector icon (just towards the left of the + icon) and choose CubeFaces from the list.
3. The Image menu item on the menu bar at the bottom now has an asterisk (**Image***) indicating that there's an unsaved image. Click on it, select **Save As Image**, and save it as CubeFaces.png. Use a folder outside the Unity project.

4. On the right-hand side, in the Properties editor panel, find the long row of icons in its Header and select the **Texture** one (third from the last.) It may be hidden if the panel isn't wide enough; you can scroll down with your mouse to show it, as shown in the following screenshot:

5. Within the Texture properties, change **Type** to **Image or Movie**.
6. Then, in the **Image** group of properties, click on the **Browse Image to be Linked** selector icon (as shown in the following screenshot) and choose CubeFaces:

7. You should see the labeled faces texture image in the **Preview** window.

Good! Let's save the Blender model, as follows:

1. Select **File** from the top main menu bar in the Info editor and click on **Save** (or press *Ctrl + S*).
2. Use the same folder as the one where you saved the texture image.
3. Name it UprightCube.blend and click on **Save Blender File**.

We should now have two files in a folder, UprightCube.blend and CubeFaces.png. I use a folder named Models/ in the root of my Unity project.

We recommend you then export the model as FBX format. This is a standard format for Unity. (Unity can import Blend files but may require you always have Blender installed on the same system). Use **File** | **Export** | **FBX** to save the .fbx version.

Wow, that was a lot. Don't worry if you didn't get it all. Blender can be daunting. However, Unity needs models. You can always download someone else's models from the Unity **Asset Store** and other 3D model sharing sites, or you can learn to make your own. Haha! Seriously, it's a good thing to start to learn. Actually, with VR, it's gotten a lot easier as we'll show you later in this chapter.

# Importing into Unity

Back in Unity, we now want to import both the files, UprightCube.fbx and CubeFaces.png, one at a time, as follows:

1. In the **Project** panel, select the top-level **Assets** folder, navigate to **Create** | **Folder**, and rename the folder to Models.

2. An easy way to import files into Unity is to just drag and drop the .fbx (or .blend) file from the Windows Explorer (or Mac Finder) window into the **Project** panel **Assets/Models** folder and drag and drop the .png file into the **Assets/Textures** folder (or you can use **Assets** | **Import New Asset...** from the main menu bar).

3. Add UprightCube to the scene by dragging it from the **Assets/Models** folder where it was just imported into the **Scene** view.

4. Set its position so that it's away from the other objects. I left mine at **Position** (2.6, 2.2, -3).

5. Drag the CubeFaces texture from the **Assets/Textures** folder into the **Scene** view, hovering over the just added UprightCube so that it receives the texture, and drop the texture onto the cube.

The scene should now look something like this:

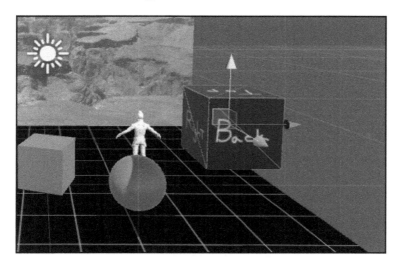

# A few observations

The back of the cube is facing us. Is that a mistake? Actually, it makes sense since the current viewpoint is looking forward. So, we should see the back of the cube. If you didn't notice already, the same goes for Ethan. It also seems like the cube has a one-unit dimension.

However, on closer examination, in the cube's **Inspector** panel, you'll see it imported with the scale that we gave it in Blender (0.5, 0.5, 0.5). Also, it has an **X** rotation of -90 (minus 90). Thus, if we reset the transform, that is, the scale to (1,1,1), it'll be 2 units in our world space and tipped over (so, don't reset it).

There's not much that we can do to compensate for the rotational adjustment without going back to Blender. But the scale can be adjusted in the model's Import Settings (in Inspector).

Blender's default up direction is **Z**, while Unity's is **Y**. Importing with a -90 **X** rotation adjusts for that. An imported scale can be adjusted in the object's **Inspector** panel's **Import Settings**.

We have more control when it comes to exporting FBX from Blender. As shown in the screenshot, during Export you can customize the settings, for example, making **Y** the up axis and **Z** the forward one and setting the scale factor for import:

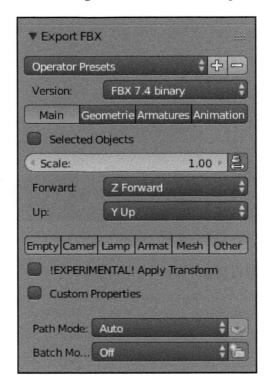

Before ending the preceding process, select UprightCube from the **Hierarchy** panel and drag it into the **Project** panel's **Assets** folder. (You may consider making an **Assets/Prefabs** subfolder and placing it into that.) This makes it a reusable prefab, texture image and all.

There are some important lessons in this exercise (other than having learned a little bit about Blender) that apply to any 3D Unity project, including the VR ones. Normally, you will be importing models that are much more complex than a cube. You will likely run into issues related to data conversion, scale, orientation, and UV texture images that might be confusing at best. If this happens, try to break the problem into smaller, more isolated scenarios. Do little tests to gain insight into how applications exchange data and to help you understand which parameter tweaks might be necessary.

# Creating 3D content in VR

In addition to traditional 3D modeling software like Blender (and ZBrush, 3D Studio Max, Maya, and so on) there is a new generation of 3D design apps that let you to directly create inside VR. After all, it's pretty awkward trying to use an inherently 2D desktop screen with a 2D mouse to form, sculpt, assemble, and manipulate 3D models. If only it could be more like real-life sculpture and construction. So, why not just do it directly in 3D? In VR!

Like other digital platforms, we can categorize VR apps into ones that present an experience, ones where you interact to engage with the environment, and ones where you actually create content, for yourself or for sharing. An example of the latter and one of the first to be widely successful is Google Tilt Brush (https://www.tiltbrush.com/) where you paint in 3D. This is one my favorite go-to apps when introducing VR to family and friends. Tilt Brush lets you paint in 3D in virtual reality.

Other VR 3D with sculpting and painting tools, to name just a few, include:

- **Google Blocks**: Low poly modeling (https://vr.google.com/blocks/)
- **Oculus Medium**: Sculpt, model, paint in VR (https://www.oculus.com/medium/)
- **Oculus Quill**: A VR illustration tool (https://www.facebook.com/QuillApp/)
- **Kudon**: Surface and volume sculpting (http://store.steampowered.com/app/479010/Kodon/)
- **MasterpieceVR**: VR sculpting and painting (https://www.masterpiecevr.com/)
- **Microsoft Paint 3D**: Easy 3D sculpting and painting bundled free with Windows (https://www.microsoft.com/en-us/store/p/paint-3d/9nblggh5fv99)

Making stuff and playing with it in VR is creative and fun, but to be useful and productive, you need to be able to share your creations outside of the app. Most VR sculpting tools let you export the models to share on the Internet, export in FBX file format, for example, and import them into Unity. There are two different workflows to do this:

- **Export/Import**: In the first workflow you make a model and export it to a compatible format, like FBX. This is akin to traditional 3D software like we did with Blender.
- **Publish/Import**: The second workflow is to upload it to a sharing service and subsequently download and install it into your Unity project.

In this section, we will use Tilt Brush as an example. Suppose you have Google Tilt Brush and a compatible VR rig. Further, suppose you have a creation you'd like to integrate with your VR app with Unity. Let's walk through each workflow process.

I opened Tilt Brush in VR and created a masterpiece using the Paper ribbon brush. I call it *TiltBox*, consistent with the cube theme we're using in this chapter. I know, it's beautiful.

 The Tilt Brush features and user interface presented here (at the time of writing) are considered by Google to be in beta or experimental and are subject to change by the time you read this.

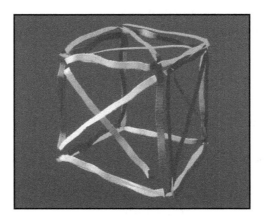

# Exporting and importing Tilt Brush models

We are going to export our model as FBX and then import it into Unity. This is an advanced topic so if you're new to Unity you may want to skip this topic for now and look at the *Publishing and importing with Google Poly* section instead.

In Tilt Brush, to export, go to the **Save** panel and choose the **More Options...** | **Labs** | **Export** menu. (Note the location of the **Export** option may change in a future release.)

The default folder where your files are saved in Windows is `Documents/Tilt Brush/Exports/[DrawingName]/`. If you turn your right-hand controller around you'll discover an Info panel on the back, which is a message console that reports the actual pathname of the drawing on your system, as shown here:

The folder will contain several files, including the .fbx of the model and the .png's of the brush textures (not used, as the Tilt Brush Toolkit also provides them).

To import into Unity you need the Tilt Brush Toolkit Unity package. The Google Poly package includes the toolkit (install from the Asset Store as described in the next topic). Or install it directly from GitHub, as follows:

1. Go to https://github.com/googlevr/tilt-brush-toolkit and use the download link for tiltbrush-UnitySDK-vNN.N.N.unitypackage (via https://github.com/googlevr/tilt-brush-toolkit/releases)

2. Import the toolkit in Unity using **Assets | Import Package | Custom Package…**, then press **Import**

You'll find that the toolkit includes assets for rendering brushes.

There is also a README file in the Exports folder with details about your Tilt Brush version and export capabilities, including how to use the CFG file for tweaking various options for advanced users.

Now we can import the drawing's FBX:

1. Drag the FBX file into your Project Assets (or use **Assets | Import New Asset...**).
2. Ignore any materials created by the import; we will use those provided in the toolkit. You can disable this in the model's Import settings **Materials | Import Materials** uncheck, and then click **Apply**.
3. You can now drag the model to your scene.
4. Locate the brush material for your sketch in `Assets/TiltBrush/Assets/Brushes/`. In our case, the sketch uses Paper brush strokes, located in the `Basic/Paper/` subfolder.
5. Drag the material onto your sketch strokes as needed.

Your scene now contains your Tilt Brush sketch. For more advanced features including audio reactive features, animations, and VR teleportation, please refer to the Tilt Brush documentation and example scenes.

That was not too difficult although a bit tedious. Other 3D modeling apps require a similar process to export models and import into Unity.

# Publishing and importing using Google Poly

Fortunately, Google has made things a whole lot easier with the introduction of Google Poly (`https://poly.google.com/`) as a place to publish, browse, and download free 3D objects created with Google Tilt Brush and Google Blocks (and other apps that create OBJ files with materials).

I don't mean to sound like a Google fanboy, but let's stick to the Tilt Brush theme. Within Tilt Brush, it is very easy to publish your sketches to Google Poly with the click of a button. And importing Poly models into Unity is equally easy with the Poly Toolkit Unity package available on the Asset Store. Let's go through it:

 Poly is not just for Unity developers. Google provides SDK for access from many platforms. See `https://developers.google.com/poly/`.

1. Within Tilt Brush, first, ensure that you are logged into your Google account (**My Profile**).
2. On the Save menu panel, choose the cloud upload option, as shown. This will upload your sketch to Poly.

3. Then complete the publishing step in your browser (out of VR), and press **Publish**.

Note that Poly Toolkit includes the Tilt Brush Toolkit. If you already imported the Tilt Brush toolkit into your project from the previous section, we suggest you delete it (and the third-party folders) first before importing Poly to avoid conflict.

In Unity:

1. Open the Asset Store panel (**Window** | **Asset Store**)
2. Search for `Poly Toolkit`, then **Download** and **Import** the Poly Toolkit asset package into your project (`https://assetstore.unity.com/packages/templates/systems/poly-toolkit-104464`)
3. Note that the toolkit installs a new Poly menu in the Unity menu bar. Choose **Poly** | **Browse Assets...** to open the Poly browser panel, as shown:

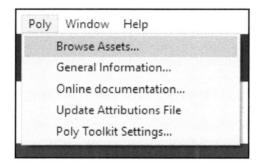

4. This panel can be docked in the Unity editor by dragging its tab
5. Before you can browse your own uploads, you must sign in using the Sign In button in the upper right
6. Then, in the Poly Toolkit panel's **Show** selection, choose **Your Uploads**
7. Locate the model you wish to import. Its page includes a number of import options, including scaling and recentering the model transform
8. Choose **Import Into Project**
9. By default, it will import the model into the `Project Assets/Poly/Assets/` folder as a prefab
10. Drag the model's prefab from the folder into your scene

That's it. You now have a world of 3D models at your fingertips: ones you created and published on Poly and others you've discovered on Poly, the Unity Asset store, or the plethora of other 3D model sites you can explore.

# Editing Unity in VR with EditorXR

In this chapter, we have learned about the Unity Editor—a tool for creating 3D scenes and projects on a 2D computer screen. We also learned a bit about Blender—a tool for creating 3D assets on at 2D computer screen. Then we progressed to the new generation of 3D asset creation tools in virtual reality including Tilt Brush and Poly. Now we'll explore creating VR scenes directly in virtual reality too!

**Unity EditorXR** (**EXR**) is a new experimental feature of Unity (at time of writing) where you can edit your 3D scenes directly in VR rather than on your 2D monitor. In this section, we may be getting ahead of ourselves in more ways than one. This is both an advanced topic and an experimental one. If you are just getting started with VR, or if you are just getting started with Unity, you may want to skip this topic for now and come back at a later time.

EXR is an advanced topic because it assumes you are comfortable with using the Unity Editor windows, are used to thinking in 3D, and are somewhat experienced in working with 3D assets. It also assumes you have a VR rig with tracking hand controllers, like Oculus Rift and HTC Vive. You will need a powerful PC with a high-end graphics card if you hope to have any chance of a smooth, comfortable experience. And last but not least, some of EXR's user interaction conventions take some learning and getting used to.

Despite that, EXR is a pretty sweet project that you could start using today to be productive. Especially if you're not afraid of software that is experimental. This also means that the UI we describe in this book is certainly subject to change. (For example, at this moment in time the package is being rebranded from EditorVR to EditorXR and EXR). Current links to information include:

- Getting started presentation: `https://docs.google.com/presentation/d/1THBAjLV267NVvZop9VLuUSNx1R2hyp8USgOc8110Nv8/edit#slide=id.g1e97811ad3_2_17`
- Getting started documentation: `https://docs.google.com/document/d/1xWunGC3NJoDRBBz44gxpMUAh3SmedtNK12LqACyy2L0/edit#heading=h.9hlhay6ebu98`

- EditorXR community forum: `https://forum.unity3d.com/forums/editorvr.126/`
- GitHub repository: `https://github.com/Unity-Technologies/EditorVR`

Another reason EXR is an advanced topic this early in this book is that we need to enable VR in our project, a topic we do not get to until the next chapter. But we'll walk you through it now quickly without a lot of explanation.

# Setting up EditorXR

To get started using EXR in your projects, download and install the Unity package. By the time you read this, it may already be bundled with the Unity Download Assistant or available in the Asset Store:

1. Download the EditorXR Unity package (`https://github.com/Unity-Technologies/EditorXR/releases`).
2. Import it into your project (**Assets** | **Import Package** | **Custom Package...**).
3. If you are using a version earlier than Unity 2018, download and import Text Mesh Pro from the Asset Store (`https://assetstore.unity.com/packages/essentials/beta-projects/textmesh-pro-84126`), a free asset from Unity Technologies.
4. If you are using VIVE, download and import the SteamVR Plugin from the Asset Store (`https://www.assetstore.unity3d.com/en/#!/content/32647`).
5. If you are using Oculus Rift with Touch controllers, download and import the Oculus Utilities for Unity (`https://developer3.oculus.com/downloads/`).
6. Set up your default VR platform in Player Settings (**Edit** | **Project Settings** | **Player**). Find the XR Settings section (at bottom of the Inspector panel) and check the Virtual Reality Supported checkbox.
7. Add the Virtual Reality SDKs for Oculus and/or OpenVR.
8. If you are using Oculus Rift with touch controllers, make sure the Oculus one comes first, as shown:

When you're ready to launch into EXR:

1. Select **Windows** | **EditorXR**
2. If necessary, press Toggle Device View to make the VR view active
3. Then put on your headset

Now you can access much of the same editing features found in Unity Editor but within VR.

# Using EditorXR

The user interaction in EXR is similar to Google Tilt Brush. One hand holds your menu palette and the other picks functions from it. Like a boxy glove, you can change menus with the flick of your thumb to rotate menu box faces. That's the starting point but EXR is ever more complex, as it needs to provide the rich set of Unity Editor features in your virtual workspace, compounded with the need to navigate the scene, organize your editor panels, and of course edit your scene game objects. We encourage you to watch a few demo videos before jumping in.

The hand controller selectors implement an innovative, simultaneous combination of laser pointers for picking distant objects and grabbing (via a *selection cone*) for objects within reach, as illustrated here:

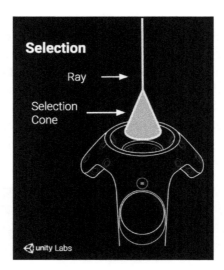

To manipulate objects, EXR has implemented robust 3D versions of the familiar scene editor widgets in the 2D Editor. They're really quite powerful and easy to use.

Without going into much further detail, here are the key features in EXR editor:

- **Selection**: Robust use of the hand controller thumbpad/stick, buttons, trigger, and grib
- **Menus**: Boxed glove menu panels, radial menu, shortcuts, and tools to organize panels in 3D
- **Navigation**: Move throughout your scene as you work, fly and blink modes, rotate in place, scale the world, use a mini-world view
- **Workspaces**: Correspond to windows in the 2D editor, for Project, Hierarchy, Inspector, Console, Profile, and more, can be opened and placed in the VR work area
- Other features include locked objects, snapping,

The following diagram shows how the manipulator Gizmo can be used for direct manipulation of the current selected object, in conjunction with the radial menu on your controller, to switch tools:

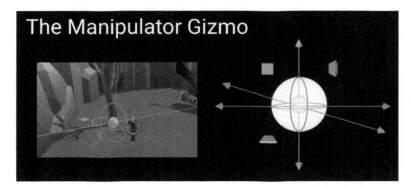

Perhaps one of the more challenging things to learn in EXR is what each of the hand controls do as they switch meaning depending on the current context. The following diagram shows the controller guides for the VIVE:

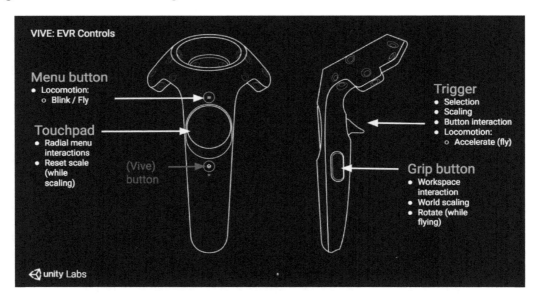

Controller guides for the Oculus touch are shown here:

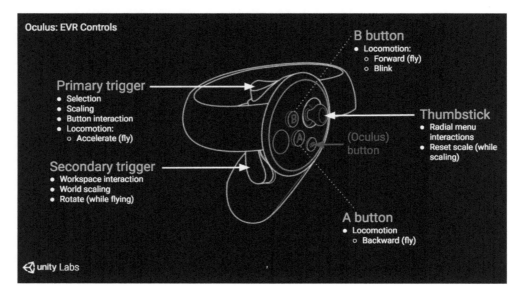

To wrap up this topic, you can even use Google Poly to find objects and insert them into your scene in VR. An example of the third-party extensions of the EditorXR interface and API, the Poly workspace is available in VR. If you have the Poly Toolkit installed (as discussed) and you are using EditorXR, then Poly is one of the available workspaces. Open it to browse and add 3D models from the cloud into your scene, as shown:

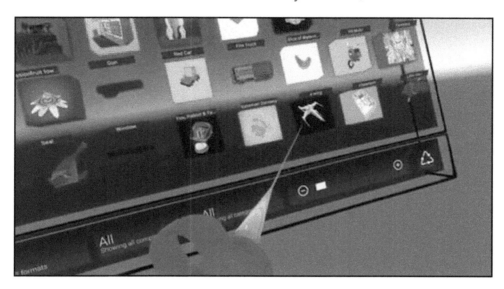

 To learn more about EditorXR and Google Poly see this debut blog post by Matt Schoen of Unity Labs: https://blogs.unity3d.com/2017/11/30/ learn-how-googles-poly-works-with-unity-editorxr/. As a side note, Schoen is a friend and the co-author of another book from Packt, *Cardboard VR Projects for Android* (2016): https://www.packtpub.com/ application-development/cardboard-vr-projects-android.

# Summary

In this chapter, we built a simple diorama, became more acquainted with the Unity editor, and learned about the importance of world scale in designing your scenes, including several in-game tools to help us work with scaling and positioning.

We then emphasized that Unity is not so much an asset creation tool. Developers typically use tools outside of Unity and then import their models. We introduced you to the free and open source Blender modeling app as well as Google Tilt Brush and showed you how to export assets and then import them into Unity, including cloud services like Google Poly.

One of the really cool things about developing for VR is how quickly things are changing. It's the burgeoning of a new industry, a new media, and new paradigms evolve year to year as VR comes into its own. New devices are being introduced every quarter. Unity is updated every month. New software tools are released every week. There are new things to do and learn every day. Of course, this can also be very frustrating. My advice is to not let this get to you, and rather embrace it.

One key to this is to continuously try new things. That's what we tried to usher you through in this chapter. Come up with an idea, then see if you can get it to work. Try out new software. Learn a new Unity feature. Do things one at a time so you don't become overwhelmed. Of course, that's what this book is about. The journey is a continuous and adventurous one.

In the next chapter, we'll set up your development system and Unity settings to build and run the project to play in your VR headset.

# VR Build and Run 3

*Yeah well, this is cool and everything, but where's my VR? I WANT MY VR!*

Hold on kid, we're getting there.

In this chapter, we are going to set up your system and configure your project to build and run with a virtual reality **head-mounted display** (**HMD**). We will be discussing the following topics:

- The levels of VR device integration software
- Enabling virtual reality for your platform
- Using device-specific camera rigs in your project
- Setting up your development machine to build and run VR projects from Unity

This chapter is very nuts and bolts. Although Unity aims to provide a unified platform for *create once, build many,* you are always going to need to do some system setup, project configuration, and include object components for your specific target devices. After the first couple of topics in this chapter, you can jump to the section(s) that most concern you and your target devices. This chapter includes cookbook instructions for the following:

- Building for SteamVR
- Building for Oculus Rift
- Building for Windows immersive MR
- Setting up for Android devices
- Building for GearVR and Oculus Go
- Building for Google VR
- Setting up for iOS devices

# Unity VR Support and Toolkits

Generally, as a developer, you spend your time working on your project scene. As we did for the diorama in the previous chapter, you'll add objects, attach materials, write scripts, and so on. When you build and run your project, the scene is rendered on a VR device and responds in real time to head and hand motions. The following diagram summarizes this Unity system VR architecture:

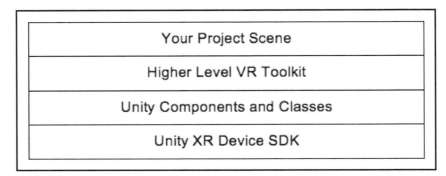

Within your scene, you may include a camera rig and other higher-level toolkit prefabs and components. All device manufacturers provide toolkits that are tuned to their specific devices. At a minimum, this includes the Unity Camera component for rendering the VR scene. It probably also includes a whole suite of prefabs and components, some required and some optional, which really help you create interactive, responsive, and comfortable VR experiences. We will go into detail throughout this chapter on how to set up your scene with these specific devices.

Unity has a growing library of built-in classes and components to support VR—what they call *XR*—and also to include augmented reality. Some are platform specific. But some are device independent. These include stereo rendering, input tracking, and audio spatializers, to name a few. For details, see the Unity Manual pages for `UnityEngine.XR` and `UnityEngine.SpatialTracking` (`https://docs.unity3d.com/ScriptReference/30_search.html?q=xr`).

At the lower level, any Unity project that runs on VR must set up the **XR Player Settings** with **Virtual Reality Supported**, and identify the specific low-level SDK the application should be used to drive the VR device. We will go into detail throughout this chapter on how to set up your project for specific devices.

So, as you can see, Unity is sandwiched between the app-level toolkit components and the device-level SDK. It provides a device-independent glue between device-specific API, tools, and optimizations.

 Strategically, the team at Unity Technologies is dedicated to delivering a unified development platform for 2D, 3D, VR, and AR games and apps. Important new components are under development at Unity (and may already be available by the time you read this book) including the VR Foundation Toolkit and new input system. These are not covered in this book.

Before jumping in, let's understand the possible ways to integrate our Unity project with virtual reality devices. Software for the integration of applications with VR hardware spans a spectrum, from built-in support and device-specific interfaces to device-independent and platform- independent ones. So, let's consider your options.

# Unity's built-in VR support

In general, your Unity project must include a camera object that can render stereoscopic views, one for each eye on the VR headset. Since Unity 5.1, support for VR headsets has been built into Unity for various devices across several platforms.

You can simply use a standard camera component, like the one attached to the default `Main Camera` when you create a new scene. As we'll see, you can have **Virtual Reality Supported** enabled in **XR Player Settings** for Unity to render stereoscopic camera views and run your project on a VR headset (HMD). In **Player Settings**, you then choose which specific virtual reality SDK(s) to use when the project is built. The SDK talks to the device runtime drivers and underlying hardware. Unity's support for VR devices is collected in the XR class, and is documented as follows:

- **XR Settings**: Global XR-related settings including a list of supported devices in the build, and eye textures for the loaded device. See `https://docs.unity3d.com/ScriptReference/XR.XRSettings.html`.
- **XR Device**: Query the capabilities of the current device such as the refresh rate and tracking space type. See `https://docs.unity3d.com/ScriptReference/XR.XRDevice.html`.
- **XR Input Tracking**: Access the VR positional tracking data including the position and rotation of individual *nodes*. See `https://docs.unity3d.com/ScriptReference/XR.InputTracking.html`.

Input controller buttons, triggers, touchpads, and thumbsticks can also map generically to Unity's Input system. For example, the OpenVR hand controller mappings can be found here: `https://docs.unity3d.com/Manual/OpenVRControllers.html`.

# Device-specific toolkits

While built-in VR support may be sufficient to get started, you are advised to also install the device-specific Unity package provided by the manufacturer. The device-specific interface will provide prefab objects, lots of useful custom scripts, shaders, and other important optimizations that directly take advantage of the features of the underlying runtime and hardware. The toolkits ordinarily include example scenes, prefabs, components, and documentation to guide you. Toolkits include:

- **SteamVR Plugin**: Steam's SteamVR toolkit (`https://assetstore.unity.com/packages/tools/steamvr-plugin-32647`) was originally released for HTC VIVE only. It now has support for several VR devices and runtimes that have positional-tracked left and right-hand controllers. This includes Oculus Rift and Windows Immersive MR. You build your project using the OpenVR SDK and the final executable program will decide at runtime which type of hardware you have attached to your PC and run that app on that device. This way, you don't need different versions of your app for VIVE, Rift, and IMR devices.
- **Oculus Integration Toolkit**: The Oculus Integration plugin for Unity (`https://assetstore.unity.com/packages/tools/integration/oculus-integration-82022`) supports Oculus VR devices including Rift, GearVR, and GO. In addition to the Touch hand controllers, it supports Oculus Avatar, Spatial Audio, and network Rooms SDK.
- **Windows Mixed Reality Toolkit**: The Windows MRTK plugin (`https://github.com/Microsoft/MixedRealityToolkit-Unity`) supports VR and AR devices in the Windows 10 UWP Mixed Reality family, including immersive HMD (like those from Acer, HP, and others) as well as the wearable HoloLens augmented reality headset.
- **Google VR SDK for Unity**: The GVR SDK for Unity plugin (`https://github.com/googlevr/gvr-unity-sdk/releases`) provides support for user input, controllers, and rendering for both Google Daydream and simpler Google Cardboard environments.

When you set up your VR projects in Unity, you will probably install one or more of these toolkits. We walk you through this later in this chapter.

# Application toolkits

If you require more device independence plus higher-level interactive features, consider the open source **Virtual Reality ToolKit** (**VRTK**) at `https://assetstore.unity.com/packages/tools/vrtk-virtual-reality-toolkit-vr-toolkit-64131` and **NewtonVR** (`https://github.com/TomorrowTodayLabs/NewtonVR`). These Unity plugins provide a framework for developing VR applications with support for multiple platforms, locomotion, interactions, and UI controls. NewtonVR focuses mostly on *physics interactions*. VRTK is built on top of the Unity built-in VR support plus the device-specific prefabs, so it's not *instead of* but is a wrapper on top of those SDKs.

It is worth mentioning at this point that Unity is working on its own toolkit, the **XR Foundation Toolkit** (**XRFT**) at `https://blogs.unity3d.com/2017/02/28/updates-from-unitys-gdc-2017-keynote/` which will include:

- Cross-platform controller input
- Customizable physics systems
- AR/VR-specific shaders and camera fades
- Object snapping and building systems
- Developer debugging and profiling tools
- All major AR and VR hardware systems

# Web and JavaScript-based VR

Important JavaScript APIs are being built directly into major web browsers, including special builds of Firefox, Chrome, Microsoft Edge, and other browsers like those from Oculus and Samsung for GearVR.

WebVR, for example, is like **WebGL** (the 2D and 3D graphics markup API for the web), adding VR rendering and hardware support. While Unity presently has support for WebGL, it does not support building VR apps for WebVR (yet). But we hope to see this happen one day soon.

The promise of Internet-based WebVR is exciting. The internet is the greatest content distribution system in the history of the world. The ability to build and distribute VR content just as easily as web pages will be revolutionary.

As we know, browsers run on just about any platform. So, if you target your game to WebVR or similar framework, you don't even need to know the user's operating system, let alone which VR hardware they're using! That's the idea anyway. Some of the tools and frameworks to watch include:

- **WebVR** (http://webvr.info/)
- **A-Frame** (https://aframe.io/)
- **Primrose** (https://www.primrosevr.com/)
- **ReactVR** (https://facebook.github.io/react-vr/)

## 3D worlds

There are a number of third-party 3D world platforms that provide multi-user social experiences in shared virtual spaces. You can chat with other players, move between rooms through *portals*, and even build complex interactions and games without having to be an expert. For examples of 3D virtual worlds, check out the following:

- **VRChat**: http://vrchat.net/
- **AltspaceVR**: http://altvr.com/
- **High Fidelity**: https://highfidelity.com/

While these platforms may have their own tools for building rooms and interactions, in particular, VRChat lets you develop 3D spaces and avatars in Unity. Then you export them using their SDK and load them into VRChat for you and others to share the virtual spaces you created over the internet in a real-time social VR experience. We will explore this in Chapter 13, *Social VR Metaverse*.

## Enabling Virtual Reality for your platform

The diorama scene we created in the previous chapter was a 3D scene using the Unity default Main Camera. As we saw, when you pressed **Play** in the Unity Editor you had the scene running in the **Game** window on your 2D computer monitor. The steps for setting up your project to run in VR include:

- Set the target platform for your project builds
- Enable Virtual Reality in the XR Player Settings in Unity and set the VR SDK

- Import the device toolkit for your target device into your project (optional but recommended) and use the prescribed prefabs instead of the default `Main Camera`
- Install the system tool required to build your target device
- Ensure your device's operating system is enabled for development
- Ensure your device's VR runtime is set up and running

If you are not sure, use the table to determine the target platform, virtual reality SDK, and Unity package to use for your VR device:

| Device | Target Platform | VR SDK | Unity Package |
|---|---|---|---|
| HTC Vive | Standalone | OpenVR | SteamVR Plugin |
| Oculus Rift | Standalone | OpenVR | SteamVR Plugin |
| Oculus Rift | Standalone | Oculus | Oculus Integration |
| Windows IMR | Universal Windows Platform | Windows Mixed Reality | Mixed Reality Toolkit Unity |
| GearVR/GO | Android | Oculus | Oculus Integration |
| Daydream | Android | Daydream | Google VR SDK for Unity and Daydream Elements |
| Cardboard | Android | Cardboard | Google VR SDK for Unity |
| Cardboard | iOS | Cardboard | Google VR SDK for Unity |

Links to the Unity packages for various integration toolkits are listed as follows:

- SteamVR Plugin: `https://assetstore.unity.com/packages/tools/steamvr-plugin-32647`
- Oculus Integration: `https://assetstore.unity.com/packages/tools/integration/oculus-integration-82022`
- MixedRealityToolkit-Unity: `https://github.com/Microsoft/MixedRealityToolkit-Unity`
- Google VR SDK for Unity: `https://github.com/googlevr/gvr-unity-sdk/releases`
- Google Daydream Elements: `https://github.com/googlevr/daydream-elements/releases`

Now, let's configure the project for your specific VR headset.

 As you know, installation and setup details are subject to change. We recommend you double-check with the current Unity manual and your device's Unity interface documentation for the latest instructions and links.

# Setting your target platform

New Unity projects normally default to targeting standalone desktop platforms. If this works for you, you do not need to change anything. Let's see:

1. Open the Build Settings window (**File** | **Build Settings...**) and review the Platform list
2. Choose your target platform. For example:
   - If you're building for Oculus Rift or HTC VIVE, for example, choose **PC, Mac & Linux Standalone**
   - If you're building for Windows MR, choose **Universal Windows Platform**
   - If you are building for Google Daydream on Android, choose **Android**
   - If you are building for Google Cardboard on iOS, choose **iOS**
3. Then press **Switch Platform**

# Setting your XR SDK

When your project is built with **Virtual Reality Supported** enabled in **Player Settings**, it renders stereoscopic camera views and runs on an HMD:

1. Go into Player Settings (**Edit** | **Project Settings** | **Player**).
2. In the Inspector window, find the **XR** Settings at the bottom and check the **Virtual Reality Supported** checkbox.
3. Choose the **Virtual Reality SDK** you will require for your target device. Refer to the previous table.

Depending on the target platform you are using, the Virtual Reality SDKs available in your Unity installation will vary. If your target VR is shown, then you're good to go. You can add others by pressing the ( + ) button in the list, and remove ones pressing the ( - ) button.

For example, the following screenshot shows the Virtual Reality SDKs selected for the Standalone platform. With Virtual Reality Supported enabled, the app will use Oculus SDK if it can. If the app cannot initialize the Oculus SDK at runtime, it will then try the OpenVR SDK.

At this point, by pressing **Play** in the Unity Editor you may be able to preview your scene in VR. Different platforms support Play mode in different ways. Some do not support Editor previews at all.

# Installing your device toolkit

Next, install your device-specific Unity package. If the toolkit is available in the Unity Asset Store, use the following steps:

1. Within Unity, open the Asset Store window (**Window | Asset Store**)
2. Search for the package you want to install
3. On the asset's page, press **Download**, and then click on **Install** to install the files in your `Project Assets/` folder

If you downloaded the package from the web separately, use the following steps:

1. Within Unity, select **Assets | Import Package | Custom Package**
2. Navigate to the folder containing the `.unitypackage` file you downloaded
3. Press **Open** and then click on **Install** to install the files into your `Project Assets/` folder

Feel free to explore the package contents files. Try opening and trying out any sample scenes included. And become familiar with any prefab objects (in a `Prefabs/` folder) that might be useful to you later in the book.

# Creating the MeMyselfEye player prefab

Most VR toolkits provide a preconfigured player camera rig as a prefab that you can insert into your scene. This rig replaces the default `Main Camera`. For this book, since we do not know which particular devices and platforms you are targeting, we will make our own camera rig. Let's called it `MeMyselfEye` (hey, this is VR!). This will be helpful later on, and it will simplify our conversations in this book, since different VR devices may use different camera assets. *Like an empty vessel for your VR soul...*

We will reuse this `MeMyselfEye` prefab in chapters throughout the book as a convenient generic VR camera asset in our projects.

A **prefab** is a reusable (prefabricated) object retained in your project's Assets folder that can be added one or more times into project scenes. Let's create the object using the following steps:

1. Open Unity and the project from the last chapter. Then, open the diorama scene by navigating to **File | Open Scene** (or double-click on the scene object in the **Project** panel, under **Assets**).

2. From the main menu bar, navigate to **GameObject | Create Empty**.

3. Rename the object `MeMyselfEye`.

4. Ensure it has a reset transform (in its **Inspector** window's **Transform** pane, choose the **gear icon** in upper-right and select **Reset**).

5. In the **Hierarchy** panel, drag the `Main Camera` object into `MeMyselfEye` so that it's a child object.

6. With the `Main Camera` object selected, reset its transform values (in the **Transform** panel, in the upper-right section, click on the *gear icon* and select **Reset**).

7. Then position yourself near the middle of the scene. Select `MeMyselfEye` again and set its **Position** (0, 0, -1.5).

8. On some VR devices, the player height is determined by the device calibration and sensors, that is, your height in real life, so leave the `Main Camera`'s Y-**Position** at 0.

9. On other VR devices, especially ones with no positional tracking, you need to specify the camera height. Select the `Main Camera` (or more specifically, the game object that has the Camera component on it) and set its **Position** (0, 1.4, 0)

The **Game** view should show that we're inside the scene. If you recall the Ethan experiment that we did earlier, I picked a Y-position of 1.4 so that we'll be at about the eye level with Ethan.

Now, let's save this as a reusable prefabricated object, or *prefab*, in the **Project** panel, under **Assets** so that we can use it again in the other scenes in the other chapters of this book:

1. In **Project** panel, under **Assets**, select the top-level `Assets` folder, right-click and navigate to **Create | Folder**. Rename the folder `Prefabs`.
2. Drag the `MeMyselfEye` prefab into the **Project** panel, under the `Assets/Prefabs` folder to create a prefab.

Your hierarchy with the prefab is shown here:

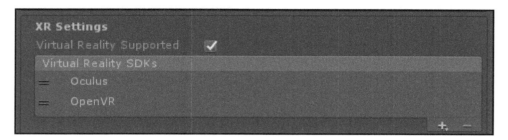

Now we will continue the discussion on how to build your project, on a per-platform basis. Please skip to the topic appropriate for your setup.

 If you want to try your projects on multiple platforms, say VIVE (Windows) and Daydream (Android), consider making separate prefabs for each target device, for example, `MeMyselfEye-SteamVR`, `MeMyselfEye-GVR`, and so on and then swap them in and out as needed.

# Building for SteamVR

To target your app to use *HTC VIVE* you will use the *OpenVR SDK*. This SDK also supports Oculus Rift with Touch controllers, and **Windows Immersive Mixed Reality** (**IMR**) devices:

1. Configure your Unity **Build Settings** to target the **Standalone** platform.
2. In **Player Settings**, under **XR Settings**, set Virtual Reality to Enabled
3. Ensure **OpenVR** is at the top of the **Virtual Reality SDKs** list.
4. Download and **Install** the SteamVR Plugin from the Asset Store, as instructed previously.

5. When you install **SteamVR** you may be prompted to accept recommended changes to your project settings. Unless you know better, we recommend you accept them.

Now we will add the SteamVR camera rig to the `MeMyselfEye` object in our scene:

1. Look in your **Project** window; under the `Assets` folder, you should have a folder named `SteamVR`.
2. Within that is a subfolder called `Prefabs`. Drag the prefab named `[CameraRig]` from the `Assets/SteamVR/Prefabs/` folder into your hierarchy. Place it as a child object of `MeMyselfEye`.
3. If necessary, reset its **Transform** to **Position** (0, 0, 0).
4. Disable the `Main Camera` object, also under `MeMyselfEye`; you can disable objects by unchecking the enable checkbox in the top-left of its Inspector window. Alternatively, you can just delete the `Main Camera` object.
5. Save the prefab by selecting `MeMyselfEye` in Hierarchy, then press its **Apply** button in the Inspector.

Note that the SteamVR camera rig Y position should be set to 0 as it will use the real-life height of the player to set the camera height in real time.

To test it out, make sure that the VR device is properly connected and turned on. You should have the SteamVR app opened on the Windows desktop. Click on the game **Play** button at the top-center of the Unity Editor. Put on the headset, and it should be awesome! Within VR, you can look all around—left, right, up, down, and behind you. You can lean over and lean in. Using the hand controller's thumb pad, you can make Ethan walk, run, and jump just like we did earlier.

Now you can build your game as a separate executable app using the following steps. Most likely, you've done this before, at least for non-VR apps. It's pretty much the same:

1. From the main menu bar, navigate to **File | Build Settings...**
2. If the current scene is not already in the **Scenes to Build** list, press **Add Open Scenes.**
3. Click on **Build** and set its name to `Diorama`.
4. I like to keep my builds in a subdirectory named `Build`; create one if you want to.
5. Click on **Save**.

An executable will be created in your Build folder. Run `Diorama` as you would do for any executable application: double-click on it.

 For more information on Unity support for OpenVR, see `https://docs.unity3d.com/Manual/VRDevices-OpenVR.html`.

# Building for Oculus Rift

To build for Oculus Rift you can use OpenVR. But if you plan to publish in the Oculus Store and/or use Oculus-specific SDK for other high-value features offered in the Oculus ecosystem, you will need to build to the Oculus SDK, as follows:

1. Configure your Unity **Build Settings** to target the **Standalone** platform
2. In **Player Settings**, under **XR Settings**, set **Virtual Reality Enabled**
3. Ensure **Oculus** is at the top of the **Virtual Reality SDKs** list.
4. Download and **Install** the Oculus Integration package from the Asset Store, as instructed previously

Now we will add the OVR camera rig to the `MeMyselfEye` object in our scene:

1. Look in your Project window, under the *Assets* folder you should have a folder named *OVR*.
2. Within that is a subfolder called `Prefabs`. Drag the prefab named `OVRCameraRig` from the `Assets/OVR/Prefabs/` folder into your Hierarchy. Place it as a child object of `MeMyselfEye`.
3. Set its Y position to 1.6 by setting its **Transform** to **Position** to (0, 1.6, 0).
4. Disable the `Main Camera` object, also under `MeMyselfEye`. You can disable objects by unchecking the enable checkbox in the top-left of its Inspector window. Alternatively, you can just delete the `Main Camera` object.
5. Save the prefab by selecting `MeMyselfEye` in Hierarchy, then press its **Apply** button in the Inspector.

Note that the OVR camera rig should be set to your desired height (1.6 in this case), which will be accommodated at runtime based on the height you configured in the Oculus runtime device configuration.

To test it out, make sure that the VR device is properly connected and turned on. You should have the Oculus runtime app opened on the Windows desktop. Click on the game **Play** button at the top-center of the Unity Editor. Put on the headset, and it should be awesome! Within VR, you can look all around—left, right, up, down, and behind you. You can lean over and lean in. Using the hand controller's thumbstick, you can make Ethan walk, run, and jump just like we did earlier.

Note that the Oculus package installs helpful menu items on the Unity Editor menu bar. We won't go into details here, and they are subject to change. We encourage you to explore the options and shortcuts they provide. See the screenshot:

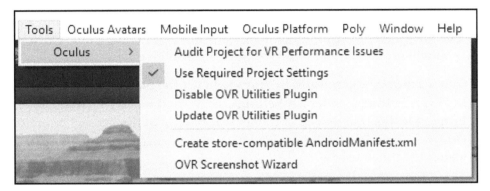

To include Oculus Dash support, you must use Oculus OVR version 1.19 or later (included with Unity 2017.3 or later). Then:

1. In **Player Settings, XR** panel, unfold the **Oculus SDK** for additional settings
2. Check the **Shared Depth Buffer** checkbox
3. Check the **Dash Support** checkbox:

For more information on Oculus Dash support in Unity, see `https://developer.oculus.com/documentation/unity/latest/concepts/unity-dash/`.

Now you can build your game as a separate executable app using the following steps. Most likely, you've done this before, at least for non-VR apps. It's pretty much the same:

1. From the main menu bar, navigate to **File | Build Settings...**
2. If the current scene is not already in the **Scenes to Build** list, press **Add Open Scenes**
3. Click on **Build** and set its name to `Diorama`
4. I like to keep my builds in a subdirectory named `Build`; create one if you want to
5. Click on **Save**

An executable will be created in your `Build` folder. Run `Diorama` as you would do for any executable application: double-click on it.

 For more information on Unity support for Oculus, see `https://developer.oculus.com/documentation/unity/latest/concepts/book-unity-gsg/`.

# Building for Windows Immersive MR

Microsoft's 3D media **Mixed Reality** strategy is to support the spectrum of devices and applications from virtual reality to augmented reality. This book and our projects are about VR. At the other end is the Microsoft HoloLens wearable AR device. The MixedRealityToolkit-Unity package that we will use includes support for both immersive MR headsets and HoloLens.

To allow your app to use a **Windows immersive Mixed Reality** (**IMR**) headset, you will use the Window Mixed Reality SDK, as follows:

1. Configure your Unity **Build Settings** to target the **Universal Windows Platform** platform.
2. In **Player Settings**, under **XR Settings**, set **Virtual Reality Enabled**
3. Ensure **Windows Mixed Reality** is at the top of the **Virtual Reality SDKs** list.
4. Download and install the **Mixed Reality Toolkit Unity**, as instructed previously.
5. We also recommend you install its sister examples unity package from the same location.

Now we will add the `MixedRealityCamera` rig to the `MeMyselfEye` object in our scene:

1. Look in your Project window; under the `Assets` folder, you should have a folder named `HoloToolkit` (or `MixedRealityToolkit`).
2. Within that is a subfolder called `Prefabs`. Drag the prefab named `MixedRealityCameraParent` from the `Assets/HoloToolkit/Prefabs/` folder into your Hierarchy. Place it as a child object of `MeMyselfEye`.
3. If necessary, reset its **Transform** to **Position** (0, 0, 0).
4. Disable the `Main Camera` object, also under `MeMyselfEye`. You can disable objects by unchecking the enable checkbox in the top-left of its Inspector window. Alternatively, you can just delete the `Main Camera` object.
5. Save the prefab by selecting `MeMyselfEye` in Hierarchy, then press its **Apply** button in the Inspector.

Note that the `MixedRealityCameraParent` rig y position should be set to 0 as it will use the real-life height of the player to set the camera height in real time.

To test it out, make sure that the VR device is properly connected and turned on. You should have the MR Portal app opened in the Windows desktop. Click on the game **Play** button at the top-center of the Unity Editor. Put on the headset, and it should be awesome! Within VR, you can look all around—left, right, up, down, and behind you. You can lean over and lean in. Using the hand controller's thumb pad, you can make Ethan walk, run, and jump just like we did earlier.

# Setting up Windows 10 Developer mode

For Windows MR, you must be developing on Windows 10, with Developer mode enabled. To set Developer mode:

1. Go to **Action Center** | **All Settings** | **Update & Security** | **For Developers**.
2. Select **Developer mode**, as shown:

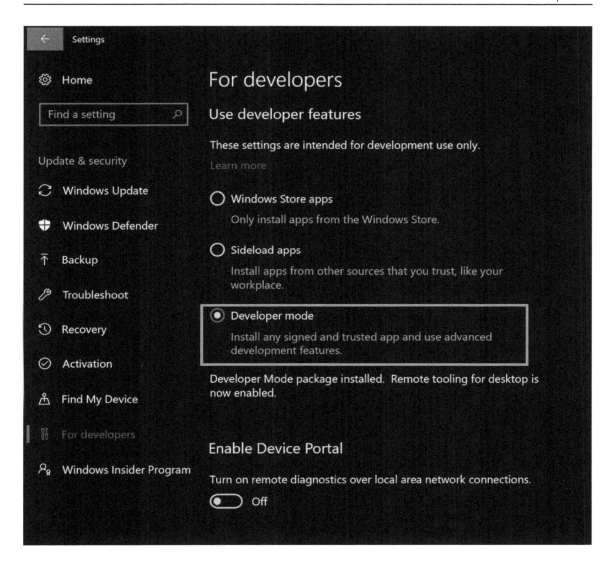

# Installing UWP support in Visual Studio

When you install Unity, you have the option to install *Microsoft Visual Studio Tools for Unity* as the default script editor. It's a great editor and debugging environment. However, this edition installed with Unity is not a full version of Visual Studio. To target your build as a separate UWP app, you will need to use a full version of Visual Studio.

Visual Studio is a powerful **integrated developer environment** (IDE) for all kinds of projects. When we build for UWP from Unity we will actually build a Visual Studio-ready project folder that you can then open in VS to complete the compile, build and deploy process, to run the app on your device.

Visual Studio comes in three editions, *Community, Professional,* and *Enterprise;* any of these are sufficient for us. The Community version is *free* and can be downloaded from here: https://www.visualstudio.com/vs/.

Once the installer is downloaded, open it to choose which components to install. Under the **Workloads** tab we have selected:

- **Universal Windows Platform development**
- **Game development with Unity**

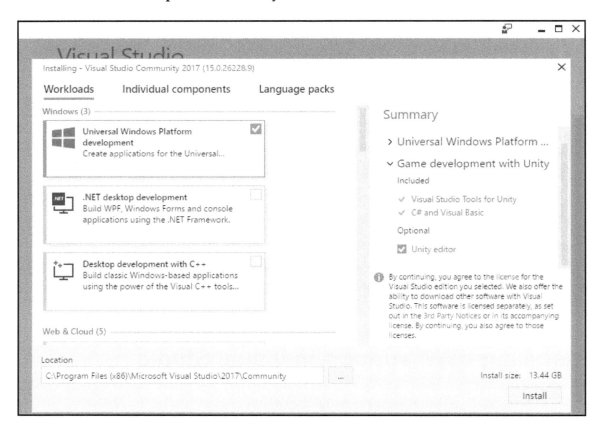

Also, select the **Game development with Unity** options, as follows:

We can now go into Unity. First, we should make sure Unity knows we're using Visual Studio:

1. Go to **Edit | Preferences**
2. In the **External Tools** tab, make sure **Visual Studio** is selected as your **External Script Editor**, like so:

# UWP build

Now, you can build your game as a separate executable app using the following steps:

1. From the main menu bar, navigate to **File | Build Settings...**
2. If the current scene is not already in the **Scenes to Build** list, press **Add Open Scenes**

3. On the right side of the dialog are options:
    - **Target Device: PC**
    - **Build Type: D3D**
    - **SDK: Latest Installed** (for example, 10.0.16299.0)
4. Click on **Build** and set its name
5. I like to keep my builds in a subdirectory named Build; create one if you want to
6. Click on **Save**

Note that the Mixed Reality ToolKit provides shortcuts to these and other settings and services, as shown:

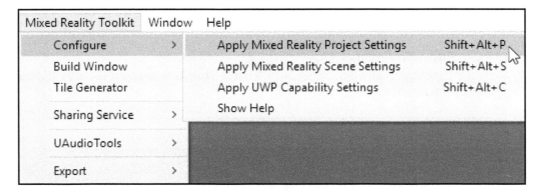

Now open the project in Visual Studio:

1. An easy way is to navigate to the Build folder in File Explorer and look for the `.sln` file for the project (SLN is the Microsoft VS *solution* file). Double-click it to open the project in Visual Studio.
2. Choose the solution configuration: **Debug, Master** or **Release.**
3. Set the target to **x64.**
4. Press **Play Local Machine** to build the solution.

For more information on Unity support for Windows Mixed Reality, see `https://github.com/Microsoft/MixedRealityToolkit-Unity`, including the link to the Getting Started page.

# Setting up for Android devices

To develop VR apps that will run on Google Daydream, Cardboard, GearVR, Oculus GO, or other Android devices, we will need to set up a development machine for Android development.

This section will help you set up your Windows PC or Mac. The requirements are not specific to virtual reality; these are the same steps required by anyone building any Android app from Unity. The process is also well documented elsewhere, including the Unity documentation at `https://docs.unity3d.com/Manual/android-sdksetup.html`.

The steps include:

- Install Java Development Kit
- Install Android SDK
- Install USB device drivers and debugging
- Configure the Unity External Tools
- Configure the Unity Player Settings for Android

OK, let's get going.

# Installing the Java Development Kit (JDK)

You may already have Java installed on your machine. You can check by opening a terminal window and running the command `java-version`. If you do not have Java or need to upgrade, follow the steps:

1. Browse on over to the Java SE Downloads web page at `http://www.oracle.com/technetwork/java/javase/downloads/index.html` and get it. Look for the **JDK** button icon, which takes you to the downloads page.
2. Choose the package for your system. For example, for Windows choose **Windows x64**. After the file downloads, open it and follow the installation instructions.
3. Make a note of the installation directory for later reference.
4. Once installed, open a fresh terminal window and run `java -version` once more to verify.

Whether you just installed the JDK or it was already there, please make a note of its location on your disk. You will need to tell Unity this information in a later step.

On Windows, the path is probably something like Windows: `C:\Program Files\Java\jdk1.8.0_111\bin`.

If you can't find it, open Windows Explorer, navigate to the `\Program Files` folder, look for **Java**, and drill down until you see its **bin** directory, as the following screenshot shows:

On OS X, the path is probably something like: `/Library/Java/JavaVirtualMachines/jdk1.8.0_121.jdk/Contents/Home`.

If you can't find it, from a terminal window, run the following command: `/usr/libexec/java_home`.

# Installing Android SDK

You also need to install the Android SDK. Specifically, you need the **Android SDK Manager**. This is available by itself as a command-line tool or part of the full Android Studio IDE. If you can afford the disk space I recommend just installing Android Studio, as it provides a nice graphical interface for SDK Manager.

To install Android Studio IDE, go to `https://developer.android.com/studio/install.html` and click Download Android Studio. When the download is done, open it and follow the installation instructions.

You will be prompted for the locations of the Android Studio IDE and the SDK. You can accept the default locations or change them. Please make a note of the SDK path location; you will need to tell Unity this information in a later step:

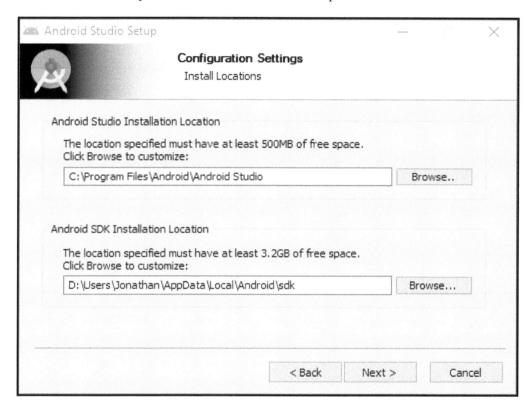

Personally, I have more room on my `D:` drive so I installed the app into `D:\Programs\Android\Android Studio`. And I like to keep the SDK near the Android Studio program files, as it's easier to find again that way, so I change the Android SDK Installation Location to `D:\Programs\Android\sdk`.

# Via Command Line Tools

Unity really only needs the command-line tools to build projects for Android. If you prefer, you can install just that package and save disk space. Scroll to the section named **Get just the command line tools** at the bottom of the downloads page. Select the package for your platform:

---

**Get just the command line tools**

If you do not need Android Studio, you can download the basic Android command line tools below. You can use the included sdkmanager to download other SDK packages.

These tools are included in Android Studio.

| Platform | SDK tools package | Size | SHA-1 checksum |
|---|---|---|---|
| Windows | tools_r25.2.3-windows.zip | 292 MB (306,745,639 bytes) | b965decb234ed793eb9574bad8791c50ca574173 |
| Mac | tools_r25.2.3-macosx.zip | 191 MB (200,496,727 bytes) | 0e88c0bdb8f8ee85cce248580173e033a1bbc9cb |
| Linux | tools_r25.2.3-linux.zip | 264 MB (277,861,433 bytes) | aafe7f28ac51549784efc2f3bdfc620be8a08213 |

See the SDK tools release notes.

---

This is a ZIP file; uncompress it to a folder and please remember its location. As mentioned, on Windows I like to use `D:\Programs\Android\sdk`. This will contain a `tools` subfolder.

The ZIP is only the tools, not the actual SDK. Use the `sdkmanager` to download the packages you'll need. See `https://developer.android.com/studio/command-line/sdkmanager.html` for details.

To list the installed and available packages, run `sdkmanager --list`. You can install multiple packages by listing them in quotes, delimited with a semicolon as follows:

```
sdkmanager "platforms;android-25"
```

As of writing, the minimum Android API levels are as follows (check the current documentation for changes):

**Cardboard**: API Level 19 (Android 4.4 *KitKat*)
**GearVR**: API Level 21 (Android 5.0 *Lollipop*)
**Daydream**: API Level 24 (Android 7.0 *Nougat*)

---

# About your Android SDK root path location

If you already had Android installed, or if you forget where the SDK is installed, you can find the root path by opening the SDK Manager GUI. While Android Studio is open, navigate to the main menu and **Tools | Android | SDK Manager**. You can find the path near the top:

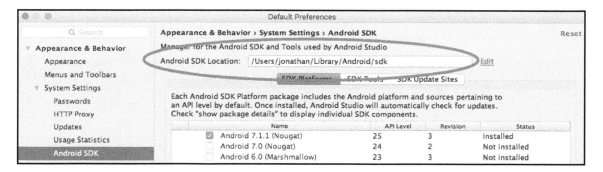

On Windows, the path is probably something like:

- **Windows**: `C:\Program Files\Android\sdk`, or `C:/Users/Yourname/AppData/Local/Android/Sdk`

On OS X, the path is probably something like:

- **OS X**: `/Users/Yourname/Library/Android/sdk`

# Installing USB device debugging and connection

The next step is to enable USB debugging on your Android device. This is part of the **Developer Options** in your Android **Settings**. But Developer Options may not be visible and has to be enabled:

1. Find the **Build number** property in **Settings | About** on the device. Depending on your device you may even need to drill down another level or two (such as **Settings | About | Software Information | More | Build number**).
2. Now for the magic incantation. Tap on the build number seven times. It'll count down until the **Developer Options** are enabled, and will now appear as another choice in the Settings.
3. Go to **Settings | Developer** options, find **USB debugging**, and enable it.
4. Now connect the device to your development machine via USB cable.

The Android device may automatically be recognized. If you are prompted to update the drivers, you can do this through the Windows Device Manager.

On Windows, if the device is not recognized, you may need to download the Google USB Driver. You can do this through the SDK Manager, under the SDK Tools tab. For more information see https://developer.android.com/studio/run/win-usb.html. The following screenshot, for example, shows the SDK Manager's SDK Tools tab with the Google USB Driver selected:

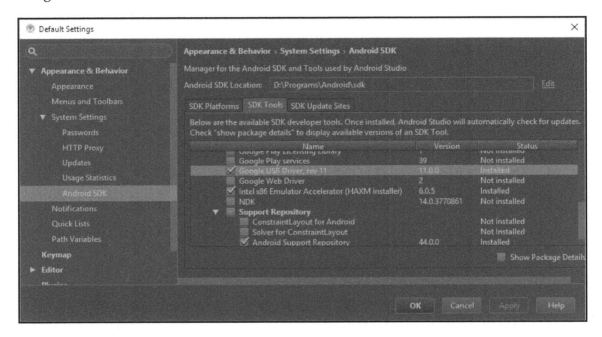

Great job so far!

# Configuring the Unity External Tools

Armed with all the stuff we need and the paths to the tools we installed, we can now go back into Unity. We need to tell Unity where to find all the Java and Android stuff. Note that if you skip this step, then Unity will prompt you for the folders when building the app:

1. On Windows, navigate to main menu and to **Edit | Preferences**, then select the **External Tools** tab on the left. On OS X it's in **Unity | Preferences**.
2. In the **Android SDK** text slot, paste the path of your Android SDK.

3. In the **Java JDK** text slot, paste the path of your Java JDK.

The Unity Preferences with my SDK and JDK are shown here:

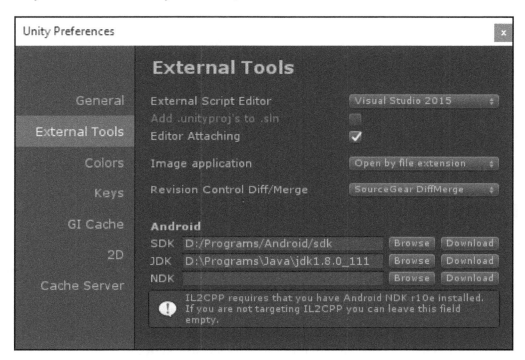

# Configuring Unity Player Settings for Android

We now will configure your Unity project to build for Android. First, ensure **Android** is your target platform in **Build Settings**. Unity provides a great deal of support for Android, including configuration and optimization for runtime features and the capabilities of mobile devices. These options can be found in **Player Settings**. We only need to set a couple of them now. The minimum required to build our demo project are Bundle Identifier and Minimum API Level:

1. In Unity, navigate to **File** | **Build Settings** and examine the **Platform** pane.
2. If Android is not presently selected, select it now and press **Switch Platform**.
3. If you have the **Build Settings** window open, press the **Player Settings...** button. Or, you can get there from the main menu and **Edit** | **Project Settings** | **Player**.

4. Look across at the **Inspector** panel, which now contains the Player Settings.
5. Find the **Other Settings** group of parameters, and click the header bar (if it's not already opened) to find the **Identification** variables
6. Set the **Bundle Identifier** to a unique name for your product that resembles a traditional Java package name. An ID is required for all Android apps. Typically it is in the format `com.CompanyName.ProductName`. It must be unique on the target device, and eventually, unique in the Google Play store. You can choose whatever name you want.
7. Set a **Minimum API Level** for your target platform (as listed earlier).

Again, there are many other options in the Player Settings but we can use their defaults for now.

# Building for GearVR and Oculus Go

To build for Samsung GearVR and Oculus Go mobile devices, you will use the Oculus SDK. These are both Android-based devices so you must set up your development machine for Android development as described previously (Oculus Go is binary and compatible with GearVR). Then complete the following steps in Unity:

1. Configure your Unity **Build Settings** to target the **Android** platform.
2. In `Player Settings`, under **XR Settings**, set **Virtual Reality Enabled**
3. Ensure **Oculus** is at the top of the **Virtual Reality SDKs** list.
4. Download and **Install** the Oculus Integration package from the Asset Store, as instructed previously.

Now we will add the OVR camera rig to the MeMyselfEye object in our scene. These steps are like the Standalone Oculus Rift setup described previously. In this case, you can use the same MeMyselfEye prefab for both Rift and GearVR.

1. Look in your Project window; under the *Assets* folder you should have a folder named OVR.
2. Within that is a subfolder called `Prefabs`. Drag the prefab named `OVRCameraRig` from the `Assets/OVR/Prefabs/` folder into your Hierarchy. Place it as a child object of `MeMyselfEye`.
3. Set its height to 1.6 by setting its **Transform** to **Position** to (0, 1.6, 0).

4. Disable the `Main Camera` object also under `MeMyselfEye`. You can disable objects by unchecking the enable-checkbox in the top-left of its Inspector window. Alternatively, you can just delete the `Main Camera` object.

5. Save the prefab by selecting `MeMyselfEye` in Hierarchy, then press its **Apply** button in the Inspector.

Now, you can build your game as a separate executable app using the following steps:

1. From the main menu bar, navigate to **File | Build Settings...**
2. If the current scene is not already in the **Scenes to Build** list, press **Add Open Scenes**
3. Click on **Build and Run** and set its name to `Diorama`
4. I like to keep my builds in a subdirectory named Build; create one if you want to.
5. Click on **Save**

An Android APK file will be created in your Build folder and uploaded to your attached Android device.

For more information on Unity support for Oculus SDK, see `https:// docs.unity3d.com/Manual/VRDevices-Oculus.html`.

# Building for Google VR

The Google VR SDK supports both Daydream and Cardboard. **Daydream** is the higher-end version limited to faster, more capable Daydream-ready Android phones. **Cardboard** is lower end and supported on many more mobile devices including Apple iOS iPhones. You can build projects in Unity that target both.

## Google Daydream

To build for *Google Daydream* on mobile Android devices, you will use the Daydream SDK. You must set up your development machine for Android development as described above. Then complete the following steps:

1. Configure your Unity **Build Settings** to target the **Android** platform
2. In **Player Settings**, under **XR Settings**, set **Virtual Reality Enabled**

3. Ensure **Daydream** is at the top of the **Virtual Reality SDKs** list
4. Download and **Install** the Google VR SDK package, as instructed previously

We will now build the `MeMyselfEye` camera rig for our scene. At the present time, the best example we have is the **GVRDemo** example scene provided with the Google VR SDK (can be found in the `Assets/GoogleVR/Demos/Scenes/` folder):

1. In your scene Hierarchy, create an empty game object under the `MeMyselfEye` (select the `MeMyselfEye` object, right-click, select **Create Empty**). Name it `MyGvrRig`.
2. Set its height to 1.6 by setting its **Transform** to **Position** to (0, 1.6, 0).
3. From the Project folders, locate the provided prefabs (`Assets/GoogleVR/Prefabs`).
4. Drag a copy of each of the following prefabs from the Project folder to Hierarchy as a child of `MyGvrRig`:
   - Headset/GvrHeadset
   - Controllers/GvrControllerMain
   - EventSystem/GvrEventSystem
   - GvrEditorEmulator
   - GvrInstantPreviewMain
5. Leave the `Main Camera` object under `MeMyselfEye` and enable it. The GoogleVR uses the existing `Main Camera` object.
6. Save the prefab by selecting `MeMyselfEye` in Hierarchy, then press its **Apply** button in the Inspector.

The `GvrHeadset` is a VR camera properties manager. The `GvrControllerMain` provides support for the Daydream 3DOF hand controller. We will use `GvrEventSystem` in later chapters; it provides a drop-in replacement for Unity's Event System object. The `GvrEditorEmulator` is not actually part of your app but enables previewing your scene in the Unity Editor when you press Play. Likewise, adding `GvrInstantPreviewMain` lets you preview your app on your phone when you press Play in the editor.

These are the prefabs that we know we're going to want to use. Certainly, go ahead and explore the other prefabs provided in the SDK. See `https://developers.google.com/vr/unity/reference/`.

We also recommend you take a look at Google Daydream Elements which provides additional demos and scripts "for developing high-quality VR experiences." We introduce this in the next chapter. See `https://developers.google.com/vr/elements/overview`.

When you're ready, you can build your game as a separate executable app using the following steps:

1. From the main menu bar, navigate to **File** | **Build Settings...**.
2. If the current scene is not already in the **Scenes to Build** list, press **Add Open Scenes**.
3. Click on **Build and Run** and set its name to `Diorama`.
4. I like to keep my builds in a subdirectory named Build; create one if you want to.
5. Click on **Save**.

An Android APK file will be created in your Build folder and uploaded to your attached Android phone.

# Google Cardboard

Building for Google Cardboard is similar, but simpler, than Daydream. Also, Cardboard apps can run on iPhones. You must set up your development machine for Android development as described. Or if you're developing for iOS, see the next section for details. Then set up your project as follows:

1. Configure your Unity Build Settings to target **Android** or **iOS** platform.
2. In Player Settings, under **XR Settings**, set **Virtual Reality Enabled**, and
3. Ensure Cardboard is in the **Virtual Reality SDKs** list.
4. Download and **Install** the Google VR SDK package, as instructed previously.

We will now build the `MeMyselfEye` camera rig for our scene.

1. In your scene Hierarchy, create an empty game object under the `MeMyselfEye` (select the `MeMyselfEye` object, right-click, select **Create Empty**). Name it `MyGvrRig`.
2. Set its height to 1.6 by setting its **Transform** to **Position** to (0, 1.6, 0).
3. From the Project folders, locate the provided prefabs (`Assets/GoogleVR/Prefabs`).

4. Drag a copy of each of the following prefabs from the Project folder to Hierarchy as a child of MyGvrRig:
   - Headset/GvrHeadset
   - GvrEditorEmulator

5. Leave the `Main Camera` object under `MeMyselfEye` and enable it. The GoogleVR uses the existing `Main Camera` object.

6. Save the prefab by selecting `MeMyselfEye` in Hierarchy, then press its **Apply** button in the Inspector

When you're ready, you can build your game as a separate executable app using the following steps:

1. From the main menu bar, navigate to **File | Build Settings....**
2. If the current scene is not already in the **Scenes to Build** list, press **Add Open Scenes**.
3. Click on **Build and Run** and set its name to `Diorama`.
4. I like to keep my builds in a subdirectory named Build; create one if you want to.
5. Click on **Save**.

An Android APK file will be created in your Build folder and uploaded to your attached Android phone.

# Google VR Play Mode

When your project is configured for Google VR (Daydream or Cardboard), and you press Play in Unity can you preview the scene and use keyboard keys to emulate device motion:

- Use *Alt* + mouse-move to pan and tilt forward or backwards.
- Use *Ctrl* + mouse-move to tilt your head from side to side.
- Use *Shift* + mouse control the Daydream hand controller (Daydream only).
- Click the mouse to select.

For more details, see `https://developers.google.com/vr/unity/get-started`.

With Daydream, you also have the option to use Instant Preview which allows you to test your VR app instantly on your device. Follow the instructions in the Google VR docs (`https://developers.google.com/vr/tools/instant-preview`) to set up your project and device to take advantage of this feature.

For more information on Unity support for Google VR SDK for Daydream, see `https://docs.unity3d.com/Manual/VRDevices-GoogleVR.html`.

# Setting up for iOS devices

This section will help set up your Mac for iOS development from Unity for iPhones. The requirements are not specific to virtual reality; these are the same steps required by anyone building any iOS app from Unity. The process is also well documented elsewhere, including the Unity documentation at `https://docs.unity3d.com/Manual/iphone-GettingStarted.html`.

A requirement of Apple's closed ecosystem is you must use a Mac as your development machine to develop for iOS. That's just the way it is. The upside is the setup process is very straightforward.

At the time of writing, the only VR apps that will run on iOS are Google Cardboard.

The steps include:

- Have an Apple ID
- Install Xcode
- Configure the Unity Player Settings for iOS
- Build And Run

OK, let's take a bite of this apple.

# Have an Apple ID

To develop for iOS you need a Mac computer to develop on, and an Apple ID to log into the App Store. This will permit you to build iOS apps that run on your personal device.

It is also recommended that you have an Apple Developer account. It costs $99 USD per year but is your admission ticket to the tools and services including setup provisioning profiles needed to share and test your app on other devices. You can find out more about the Apple Developer Program here: `https://developer.apple.com/programs/`.

# Install Xcode

Xcode is the all-in-one toolkit for developing for any Apple devices. It is free to download from the Mac App Store here: `https://itunes.apple.com/gb/app/xcode/id497799835?mt=12`. Beware: it is quite big (over 4.5 GB as of writing). Download it, open the downloaded `dmg` file, and follow the installation instructions.

# Configuring the Unity Player Settings for iOS

We now will configure your Unity project to build for iOS. First, ensure *iOS* is your target platform in Build Settings. Unity provides a great deal of support for iOS, including configuration and optimization for runtime features and the capabilities of mobile devices. These options can be found in Player Settings. We only need to set a couple of them now (the minimum required to build our projects):

1. In Unity, navigate to **File | Build Settings** and examine the **Platform** pane. If iOS is not presently selected, select it now and press **Switch Platform**.
2. If you have the **Build Settings** window open, press the **Player Settings...** button. Or, you can get there from the main menu: **Edit | Project Settings | Player**. Look across at the Inspector panel, which now contains the Player Settings.
3. Find the **Other Settings** group of parameters, and click the header bar (if it's not already opened) to find the Identification variables.
4. Set the **Bundle Identifier** to a unique name for your product that resembles a traditional Java package name. An ID is required for all iOS apps. Typically, it is in the format `com.CompanyName.ProductName`. It must be unique on the target device, and eventually, unique in the App Store. You can choose whatever name you want.
5. Set the **Automatic Signing Team ID** to your Signing Team setup in Xcode, and check the **Automatically Sign** checkbox.

 To configure your Apple ID with Xcode, in Xcode go to **Preferences | Accounts** and add an Apple ID by tapping +.

# Build And Run

Xcode consists of an **integrated development environment** (IDE) that hosts your Xcode projects. When you build for iOS from Unity, it doesn't actually build an iOS executable. Rather, Unity builds an Xcode-ready project folder that you then open in Xcode to complete the compile, build, and deploy process, and to run the app on your device. Let's go!

1. Be sure your device is turned on, connected, and you grant permission for the Mac to access.
2. In the Build Settings, press the **Build And Run** button to begin building.
3. You will be prompted for a name and location of the build files. We recommend you create a new folder in your project root named `Build` and specify the file or subfolder name under that, as needed.

If all goes well, Unity will create an Xcode project and open it in Xcode. It will attempt to build the app, and if successful, upload it to your device. You now have a running VR app on your device you can show off to your friends and family!

# Summary

In this chapter, we helped you set up your system for VR development and built your project for your target platform and devices. We discussed the different levels of device integration software and then installed software that was appropriate for your target VR device onto your development machine and asset packages into your Unity project. While we have summarized the steps, all of these steps are well documented on the device manufacturers sites and in the Unity manual and we encourage you to look at all the relevant documentation.

At this point, you should be able to preview your VR scene in Unity Editor's Play mode. And you should be able to build and run your project and install and run it as a binary directly on your device.

In the next chapter, we'll work more on the diorama scene and explore techniques to control objects in virtual reality. From a third-person perspective, we'll interact with objects in the scene (Ethan, the zombie) and implement look-based control.

# 4
# Gaze-Based Control

Right now, our diorama is a third-person virtual reality experience. When you go into it, you're like an observer or a third-person camera. Sure, you can look around and add controls that let you move the camera's viewpoint. However, any action in the scene is from a third-person perspective.

In this chapter, we'll pretty much stay in the third-person mode, but we'll get a little more personally involved. We will explore techniques that can be used to control objects in your virtual world by looking and staring. Our character, Ethan, will be under your control, responding to where you look. Furthermore, we'll start programming the Unity scripts. Along the way, we will discuss the following topics:

- Adding **AI** (short for **artificial intelligence**) and **NavMesh** to our third-person character, Ethan
- Unity programming in C#
- Using our gaze to move a 3D cursor
- Shooting and killing Ethan, the zombie, to good effect

Most intros to Unity development tip-toe you through the easy stuff and maybe never even get to the more interesting, although more complex, things. We're going to mix things up in this chapter, throwing you into a few different 3D graphics topics, some a little advanced. If it's new to you, think of this as a survey tutorial. Nonetheless, we go through it step by step so you should be able to follow along and have a lot of fun too!

## Ethan, the walker

Gaming is a common application of virtual reality. So, we might as well start out from there, too! We are going to give our character, Ethan, a life of his own. Well, sort of (or not), because he's going to become a zombie!

We left off at the diorama, with Ethan hanging out. You can make him run around the scene if you have a hand controller with a thumbstick or touchpad, but that is not guaranteed on some VR devices. In fact, if you're viewing the scene with a Google Cardboard, it's pretty unlikely that you'll have a handheld controller (notwithstanding the Bluetooth game controllers). In the next chapter, Chapter 5, *Handy Interactables*, we will go into handheld input controllers. For now, we will consider another way to make him move around, using the direction of your gaze while wearing your VR headset.

Before we attempt this, we'll first transform Ethan into a zombie and have him walk around aimlessly without any user control. We'll do this by giving him some AI and writing a script that sends him to random target locations.

*AI controllers* and *NavMesh* are somewhat advanced topics in Unity, but we're going to throw you into it just for fun. Besides, it's not as scary as zombies.

# Artificially intelligent Ethan

To start, we want to replace the ThirdPersonController prefab that we used initially with Unity's AI character, AIThirdPersonController, using the following steps. Unity uses the word *artificial intelligence* loosely to mean *script-driven*. Perform the following steps:

1. Open the Unity project from the previous chapters with the Diorama scene, and have the Characters package imported from Standard Assets.
2. In the **Project** panel, open the Standard Assets/Characters/ThirdPersonCharacter/Prefabs folder and drag AIThirdPersonController into the scene. Name it Ethan.
3. In the **Hierarchy** panel (or in **Scene**), select the previous ThirdPersonController, (the old Ethan). Then, in the **Inspector** panel's **Transform** pane, choose the *gear* icon on the upper right of the **Transform** pane and select **Copy Component**.
4. Select the new Ethan object (from the **Hierarchy** panel or **Scene**). Then, in the **Inspector** panel's **Transform** pane, choose the *gear* icon and select **Paste Component Values**.
5. Now, you can delete the old Ethan object by selecting it from the **Hierarchy** panel, right-clicking to open options, and clicking on **Delete**.

**TIP**

If you cannot find the `Characters` package to import, you may not have installed `Standard Assets` when you installed Unity. To get them now, you will need to run the `UnityDownloadAssistant` again as described at the beginning of `Chapter 2`, *Content, Objects, and Scale* (and it may already be in your Downloads folder).

Note that this controller has a `NavMesh Agent` component and an `AICharacterControl` script. The NavMesh Agent has parameters for how Ethan will move around the scene. The `AICharacterControl` script takes a target object where Ethan will walk to. Let's populate that, as follows:

1. Add an empty game object to the **Hierarchy** panel, and rename it `WalkTarget`.
2. Reset its **Transform** values to position (0,0,0) (using the gear icon in upper-right of the Transform pane).
3. Select Ethan and drag `WalkTarget` into the **Target** property in the **Inspector** panel's **AI Character Control** pane, as shown here:

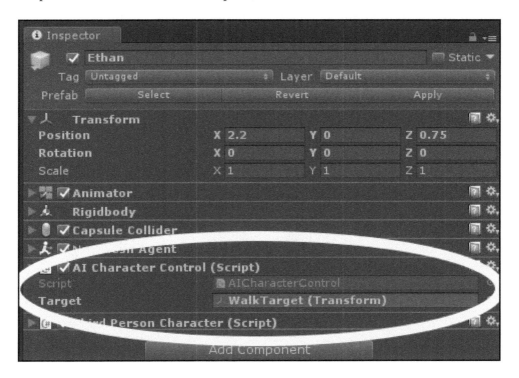

At this point, we have an AI character in the scene (`Ethan`), an empty game object that will be used as a navigation target (`WalkTarget`) initially in the center of our scene, and we told the AI Character Controller to use this target object. When we run the game, wherever `WalkTarget` is, Ethan will go there. But not yet.

# The NavMesh bakery

Ethan cannot just go walking around without being told where he's allowed to roam! We need to define a *NavMesh*-a simplified geometrical plane that enables a character to plot its path around obstacles.

In our scene, Ethan is an agent. Where he's allowed to walk is the *navmesh*. Note that he has a **NavMesh Agent** component and an `AICharacterControl` script. The NavMesh Agent has parameters for how Ethan will move around the scene.

Create a `NavMesh` by first identifying the objects in the scene that affect navigation by marking them **Navigation Static**, and then baking the NavMesh, as follows:

1. Select the **Navigation** panel. If it's not already a tab in your editor, open the **Navigation** window from the main menu by navigating to **Window** | **Navigation**.
2. Select its **Object** tab.
3. Select the **Ground Plane** in **Hierarchy**, then in the **Navigation** window's Object pane, check the **Navigation Static** checkbox. (Alternatively, you can use the object's Inspector window Static dropdown list.)
4. Repeat step 3 for each of the objects that should get in his way: the cubes and the sphere. An example is shown for the sphere.
5. In the Navigation window, select the **Bake** tab, and click on the **Bake** button at the bottom of the panel:

The **Scene** view should now show a blue overlay where the NavMesh is defined, as shown in the following screenshot:

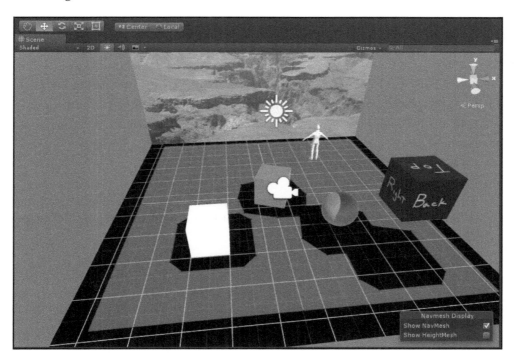

Let's test this out. Ensure that the **Game** panel's **Maximize on Play** is deselected. Click on the *Play* mode button (the triangle at the top of editor). In the **Hierarchy** panel, select the WalkTarget object and ensure that the Translate gizmo is active in the **Scene** panel (press the W key on keyboard). Now, drag the red (**x**) and/or the blue (**z**) arrow handles on the WalkTarget object to move it around the floor plane. As you do, Ethan should follow! Click on *Play* again to stop **Play Mode**.

# A random walker in the town

Now, we'll write a script that moves the WalkTarget object to random places.

Writing scripts is an important part of developing with Unity. If you've done anything more that tinker with Unity, you've probably already written at least some scripts. We're going to use the C# programming language.

 If you are new to programming, don't panic! We provide a more detailed introduction to Unity scripting at the end of this chapter. You can skip to that now and come back, or just follow along.

For this first script, we'll take it slow. We will attach the script to the WalkTarget object, as follows:

1. Select the WalkTarget object in the **Hierarchy** panel or the **Scene** view.
2. In its **Inspector** panel, click on the **Add Component** button.
3. Select **New Script** (you many need to scroll down to find it).
4. Name it RandomPosition.
5. Ensure that the **C Sharp** language is selected.
6. Click on **Create and Add**.
7. This should create a script component on the WalkTarget object. Double-click on the RandomPosition script in the slot to the right of **Script** in the **Inspector** pane to open it in your code editor.

# The RandomPosition script

We want to move the `WalkTarget` object to a random location so that Ethan will head in that direction, wait a few seconds, and move the `WalkTarget` object again. That way, he'll appear to be wandering around aimlessly. We can do this with a script. Rather than developing the script incrementally, I'm presenting the finished version first, and we'll go through it line by line. The `RandomPosition.cs` script looks like this:

```
using UnityEngine;
using System.Collections;

public class RandomPosition : MonoBehaviour {

  void Start () {
    StartCoroutine (RePositionWithDelay());
  }

  IEnumerator RePositionWithDelay() {
    while (true) {
      SetRandomPosition();
      yield return new WaitForSeconds (5);
    }
  }

  void SetRandomPosition() {
    float x = Random.Range (-5.0f, 5.0f);
    float z = Random.Range (-5.0f, 5.0f);
    Debug.Log ("X,Z: " + x.ToString("F2") + ", " +
      z.ToString("F2"));
    transform.position = new Vector3 (x, 0.0f, z);
  }
}
```

This script defines a `MonoBehaviour` sub-class named `RandomPosition`. The first thing we do when defining the class is declare any variables that we'll be using. A variable is a placeholder for a value. The value can be initialized here or assigned elsewhere, just as long as it has a value before the script uses it.

The meat of the script is further down, the function named `SetRandomPosition()`. Let's see what that does.

If you recall, the `GroundPlane` plane is 10 units square, with the origin in the middle. So, any (x, z) location on the plane will be within a range from −5 to 5 along each axis. The line `float x = Random.Range (-5.0f, 5.0f)` picks a random value within the given range and assigns it to a new `float x` variable. We do the same thing to get a random **z** value. (Usually, I discourage *hardcoding* constant values like this instead of using variables, but I'm keeping things simple for illustration purposes.)

The line `Debug.Log ("X,Z: " + x.ToString("F2") + ", " + z.ToString("F2"))` prints the x and z values in the **Console** panel when the game is running. It'll output something like `X, Z: 2.33, -4.02` because `ToString("F2")` says round up to two decimal places. Note that we're using plus signs to combine the parts of the output string together.

We actually move the target to the given location with the line `transform.position = new Vector3 (x, 0.0f, z);`. We're setting the transform position of the object that this script is attached to. In Unity, values that have an X, Y, and Z are represented by the `Vector3` objects. So, we create a new one with the `x` and `z` values that we generated. We give y=0 so that it sits on `GroundPlane`.

Each `MonoBehaviour` class has a built-in variable called `this`, which refers to the object that the script is attached to. That is, when the script is a component of an object and appears in its **Inspector** panel, the script can refer to its object as `this`. In fact, `this` is so obvious, if you want to call functions on the `this` object, you don't even need to say it. We could have said `this.transform.position = ...`, but the `this` object is implied and is normally omitted. On the other hand, if you had a variable for some other object (for example, `GameObject` that;), then you'd need to say that when you set its position, like `that.transform.position = ...`.

The last mysterious bit is how we handle time delays in Unity, using co-routines. This is a somewhat advanced coding technique, but very handy. In our case, the transform position should get changed once every five seconds. It's solved in several parts:

1. In the `Start()` function, there's the line `StartCoroutine (RePositionWithDelay());`. A **co-routine** is a piece of code that runs separately from the function from which it was called. So, this line kicks off the `RePositionWithDelay()` function in a co-routine.
2. Inside that, there's a `while (true)` loop, which as you might guess, runs forever (as long as the game is running).
3. It calls the `SetRandomPosition()` function, which actually repositions the object.

4. Then, at the bottom of this loop, we do a `yield return new WaitForSeconds (5);` statement, which basically says to Unity, *hey, go do what you want for five seconds and then come back here so that I can go through my loop again.*

5. For all of this to work, the `RePositionWithDelay` co-routine must be declared as the `IEnumerator` type (because the documentation says so).

This co-routine/yield mechanism, although an advanced programming topic, is a common pattern in time-sliced programs such as Unity.

Our script should be saved to a file named `RandomPosition.cs`.

We are now good to go. In the Unity editor, click on *Play*. Ethan is running from one place to another like a madman!

# "Zombie-ize" Ethan!

OK, that's pretty random. Let's adjust the NavMesh steering parameters to slow him down to a nice zombie-like pace. For that, perform the following steps:

1. Select `Ethan` in the **Hierarchy** panel
2. Navigate to **Inspector** | **Nav Mesh Agent** | **Steering** and set the following:
   - **Speed**: `0.3`
   - **Angular Speed**: `60`
   - **Acceleration**: `2`

Play again. He has slowed down. That's better.

One more finishing touch: let's turn him into a zombie. I have a texture image named `EthanZombie.png` that will help (included with this book). Perform the following steps:

1. From the **Assets** tab on the main menu, select **Import New Asset...**. Navigate to the files folder with the assets that came with this book.
2. Select the `EthanZombie.png` file.
3. Click on **Import**. For tidiness, ensure that it resides in the `Assets/Textures` folder. (Alternatively, you can just drag and drop the file from Windows Explorer into the **Project** panel Assets/Textures folder.)
4. In the **Hierarchy** panel, unfold the `Ethan` object (click on the triangle) and select `EthanBody`.

5. In the `Inspector` panel, unfold the `EthanGray` shader by clicking on the triangle icon to the left of **Shader**.
6. Select the `EthanZombie` texture from the `Project Assets/Textures` folder.
7. Drag it onto the **Albedo** texture map. It's a small square just to the left of the **Albedo** label under **Main Maps**.
8. In the **Hierarchy** panel, select `EthanGlasses` and uncheck it to disable glasses in the **Inspector** panel. After all, zombies don't need glasses!

His portrait is featured below. *What'd you say? That's not a scary enough zombie??* Well, maybe he's just recently turned. Go ahead and make a better one yourself. Use Blender, Gimp, or Photoshop and paint your own (or even import a whole different zombie humanoid model to replace `EthanBody` itself):

Now, build the project and try it in VR.

We're looking from a third-person perspective. You can look around and watch what's going on. It's kind of fun, and it's pretty interesting. And it's passive. Let's get more active.

# Go where I'm looking

In this next script, instead of being random, we'll send Ethan to wherever we look. In Unity, this is accomplished by using **ray casting.** It's like shooting a ray from the camera and seeing what it hits (for more information, visit `http://docs.unity3d.com/Manual/CameraRays.html`).

We're going to create a new script, which will be attached to WalkTarget like before, as follows:

1. Select the WalkTarget object in the **Hierarchy** panel or the **Scene** view.
2. In its **Inspector** panel, click on the **Add Component** button.
3. Select **New Script**.
4. Name it LookMoveTo.
5. Ensure that the **C Sharp** language is selected.
6. Click on **Create** and **Add**.

This should create a script component on the WalkTarget object. Double-click on it to open it in your code editor.

> This LookMoveTo script replaces the RandomPosition one we created before. Disable the RandomPosition component of WalkTarget before proceeding.

# The LookMoveTo script

In our script, each time Update() is called, we'll read where the camera is pointing (by using its transform position and rotation), cast a ray in that direction, and ask Unity to tell us where it hits the ground plane. Then, we'll use this location to set the WalkTarget object's position.

Here's the full LookMoveTo.cs script:

```
using UnityEngine;
using System.Collections;

public class LookMoveTo : MonoBehaviour {
  public GameObject ground;

  void Update () {
    Transform camera = Camera.main.transform;
    Ray ray;
    RaycastHit hit;
    GameObject hitObject;

    Debug.DrawRay (camera.position,
      camera.rotation * Vector3.forward * 100.0f);
```

```
    ray = new Ray (camera.position,
      camera.rotation * Vector3.forward);
    if (Physics.Raycast (ray, out hit)) {
      hitObject = hit.collider.gameObject;
      if (hitObject == ground) {
        Debug.Log ("Hit (x,y,z): " + hit.point.ToString("F2"));
        transform.position = hit.point;
      }
    }
  }

}
```

Let's go through the script a bit at a time.

```
    public GameObject ground;
```

The first thing the script does is declare a variable for the GroundPlane object. Since it's public, we can use the Unity editor to assign the actual object:

```
    void Update () {
      Transform camera = Camera.main.transform;
      Ray ray;
      RaycastHit hit;
      GameObject hitObject;
```

Inside Update(), we define a few local variables, camera, ray, hit, and hitObject, which have datatypes that are required by the Unity functions that we're going to use.

Camera.main is the current active camera object (that is, tagged as MainCamera). We get its current transform, which will be assigned to the camera variable:

```
    ray = new Ray (camera.position,
      camera.rotation * Vector3.forward);
```

Ignoring the handy Debug statements for a moment, we first determine the ray from the camera using new Ray().

A **ray** can be defined by a starting position in the **x**, y, and z space and a direction vector. A **direction vector** can be defined as the relative offsets from a 3D starting point to some other point in space. The forward direction, where **z** is positive, is (0, 0, 1). Unity will do the math for us. So, if we take a unit vector (Vector3.forward), multiply it by a three-axis rotation (camera.rotation), and scale it by a length (100.0f), we'll get a ray pointing in the same direction as the camera, measuring 100 units long:

```
    if (Physics.Raycast (ray, out hit)) {
```

Then, we cast the ray and see if it hit anything. If so, the `hit` variable will now contain more details about what was hit, including the specific object in `hit.collider.gameObject`. (The `out` keyword means that the `hit` variable value is filled in by the `Physics.Raycast()` function.)

```
if (hitObject == ground) {
  transform.position = hit.point;
}
```

We check whether the ray hit the `GroundPlane` object and if so, we'll assign that as the position to move the `WalkTarget` object to the `hit` location.

> The ==compare operator should not to be confused with =, which is the assignment operator.

This script contains two `Debug` statements, which are a useful way to monitor what's going on while a script is running in Play Mode. `Debug.DrawRay()` will draw the given ray in the **Scene** view so that you can actually see it, and `Debug.Log()` will dump the current hit position to the console if and when there's a hit.

Save the script, switch into the Unity editor, and perform the following steps:

1. With `WalkTarget` selected, in the `Inspector` panel, the `LookMoveTo` script component now has a field for the `GroundPlane` object.
2. From the **Hierarchy** panel, select and drag the `GroundPlane` game object onto the **Ground** field.

Save the scene. The script pane looks like this:

Then, click the *Play* button. Ethan should follow our gaze (at his own pace).

In projects with more than a few objects with colliders, in order to optimize the performance of your raycast, it is advised to place the objects on a specific layer (for example, named "Raycast") and then add that layer mask to the Raycast call. For example, if "Raycast" is layer 5, `int layerMask = 1 << 5,` then `Physics.Raycast(ray, out hit, maxDistance, layerMask);`. See https://docs.unity3d.com/ScriptReference/Physics.Raycast.html and https://docs.unity3d.com/Manual/Layers.html for details and examples.

# Adding a feedback cursor

Given it's not always obvious where your gaze is hitting the ground plane, we'll now add a cursor to the scene. It's really easy because what we've been doing is moving around an invisible, empty `WalkTarget` object. If we give it a mesh by using the following steps, it'll be visible:

1. In the **Hierarchy** panel, select the `WalkTarget` object.
2. Right-click on the mouse and navigate to **3D Object | Cylinder**. This will create a cylindrical object parented by `WalkTarget`. (Alternatively, you can use the **GameObject** tab on the main menu bar, and then drag and drop the object onto `WalkTarget`.)
3. Ensure that we're starting with the reset values of transform by clicking on **Reset** from the *gear* icon menu in the **Transform** pane.
4. Select the new cylinder and in its **Inspector** panel, change the **Scale** to (`0.4, 0.05, 0.4`). This will create a flat disk with a diameter of `0.4`.
5. Disable its **Capsule Collider** by unchecking that checkbox.
6. As a performance optimization, in **Mesh Renderer** you can also disable **Cast Shadows**, **Receive Shadows**, **Use Light Probes**, and **Reflection Probes**.

Now, try to play again. The cursor disk follows our gaze.

If you want, decorate the disk better with a colored material. Better yet, find an appropriate texture. For example, we used a grid texture in *Chapter 2*, *Content, Objects, and Scale*, for the `GridProjector` file (`Standard Assets/Effects/Projectors/Textures/Grid.psd`). The `CircleCrossHair.png` file is provided with the files for this book. Drop the texture onto the cylinder cursor. When you do, set its **Shader** to **Standard**.

# Observing through obstacles

In this project, we got Ethan to follow where we're looking by moving the `WalkTarget` object to a position on the ground plane determined by raycasting from the camera and seeing where it intersected that plane.

You may have noticed that the cursor seems to get *stuck* when we slide our gaze over the cube and sphere. That's because the **physics engine** has determined which object is hit first, never getting to the ground plane. In our script, we have the conditional statement `if (hitObject == ground)` before moving `WalkTarget`. Without it, the cursor would float over any object in 3D space where the cast ray hits something. Sometimes, that's interesting, but in our case, it is not. We want to keep the cursor on the ground. However now, if the ray hits something other than the ground, it doesn't get repositioned and seems *stuck*. Can you think of a way around it? Here's a hint: look up `Physics.RaycastAll`. Alright, I'll show you. Replace the body of `Update()` with the following code:

```
Transform camera = Camera.main.transform;
Ray ray;
RaycastHit[] hits;
GameObject hitObject;
Debug.DrawRay (camera.position, camera.rotation *
    Vector3.forward * 100.0f);
ray = new Ray (camera.position, camera.rotation *
    Vector3.forward);
hits = Physics.RaycastAll (ray);
for (int i = 0; i < hits.Length; i++) {
  RaycastHit hit = hits [i];
  hitObject = hit.collider.gameObject;
  if (hitObject == ground) {
    Debug.Log ("Hit (x,y,z): " +
        hit.point.ToString("F2"));
    transform.position = hit.point;
  }
}
```

On calling `RaycastAll`, we get back a list, or an array, of hits. Then, we loop through each one looking for a ground hit anywhere along the path of the ray vector. Now our cursor will trace along the ground, whether or not there's another object in between.

 **Extra challenge**: Another more efficient solution is to use the *layer system*. Create a new layer, assign it to the plane, and pass it as an argument to `Physics.raycast()`. Can you see why that's much more efficient?

# If looks could kill

We got this far. We might as well try to kill Ethan (haha!). Here are the specifications for this new feature:

- Looking at Ethan hits him with our line-of-sight raygun
- Sparks are emitted when the gun hits its target
- After 3 seconds of being hit, Ethan is killed
- When he's killed, Ethan explodes (we get a point) and then he respawns at a new location

# The KillTarget script

This time, we'll attach the script to a new empty `GameController` object by performing the following steps:

1. Create an empty game object and name it `GameController`.
2. Attach a new C# script to it, using **Add Component**, named `KillTarget`.
3. Open the script in MonoDevelop.

Here's the completed `KillTarget.cs` script:

```
using UnityEngine;
using System.Collections;

public class KillTarget : MonoBehaviour {
  public GameObject target;
  public ParticleSystem hitEffect;
  public GameObject killEffect;
  public float timeToSelect = 3.0f;
  public int score;

  private float countDown;

  void Start () {
    score = 0;
    countDown = timeToSelect;
  }

void Update () {
    Transform camera = Camera.main.transform;
    Ray ray = new Ray (camera.position, camera.rotation *
      Vector3.forward);
```

```
        RaycastHit hit;
        if (Physics.Raycast (ray, out hit) && (hit.collider.gameObject
            == target)) {
          if (countDown > 0.0f) {
            // on target
            countDown -= Time.deltaTime;
            // print (countDown);
            hitEffect.transform.position = hit.point;
            hitEffect.Play ();
          } else {
            // killed
            Instantiate( killEffect, target.transform.position,
              target.transform.rotation );
            score += 1;
            countDown = timeToSelect;
            SetRandomPosition ();
          }
        } else {
          // reset
          countDown = timeToSelect;
          hitEffect.Stop ();
        }
      }

      void SetRandomPosition () {
        float x = Random.Range (-5.0f, 5.0f);
        float z = Random.Range (-5.0f, 5.0f);
        target.transform.position = new Vector3 (x, 0.0f, z);
      }
    }
```

Let's go through this. First, we declare a number of public variables, as follows:

```
public GameObject target;
public ParticleSystem hitEffect;
public GameObject killEffect;
public float timeToSelect = 3.0f;
public int score;
```

Like we did in the previous LookMoveTo script, our target will be Ethan. We're also adding a hitEffect particle emitter, a killEffect explosion, and a start value for the countdown timer, timeToSelect. Lastly, we'll keep track of our kills in the score variable.

The Start() method, which is called at the start of the gameplay, initializes the score to zero and sets the countDown timer to its starting value.

Then, in the `Update()` method, like in the `LookMoveTo` script, we cast a ray from the camera and check whether it hits our target, Ethan. When it does, we check the `countDown` timer.

If the timer is still counting, we decrement its value by the amount of time that's gone by since the last time `Update()` was called, using `Time.deltaTime`, and make sure that `hitEffect` is emitting at the hit point.

If the ray is still on its target and the timer is done counting down, Ethan is killed. We explode, bump up the score by one, reset the timer to its starting value, and move (respawn) Ethan to a random new location.

For an explosion, we'll use one of Unity's standard assets found in the `ParticleSystems` package. To activate it, `killEffect` should be set to the prefab named `Explosion`. Then, the script *instantiates* it. In other words, it makes it an object in the scene (at a specified transform), which kicks off its awesome scripts and effects.

Lastly, if the ray did not hit Ethan, we reset the counter and turn off the particles.

Save the script and go into the Unity Editor.

 **Extra challenge**: Refactor the script to use co-routines to manage the delay timing, like we did in the `RandomPosition` script at the start of this chapter.

# Adding particle effects

Now, to populate the `public` variables, we will perform the following steps:

1. First, we need the `ParticleSystems` package that comes with Unity standard assets. If you do not have them, navigate to **Assets** | **Import Package** | **ParticleSystems**, choose **All**, and then click on **Import**.
2. Select `GameController` from the **Hierarchy** panel and go to the **Kill Target (Script)** pane in the **Inspector** panel.
3. Drag the `Ethan` object from the **Hierarchy** panel onto the **Target** field.
4. From the main menu bar, navigate to **GameObject** | **Effects** | **Particle System** and name it `SparkEmitter`.

5. Reselect `GameController` and drag `SparkEmitter` onto the **Hit Effect** field.
6. In the **Project** panel, find the `Explosion` prefab in `Assets/Standard Assets/ParticleSystems/Prefabs` and drag the `Explosion` prefab onto the **Kill Effect** field.

The script pane looks like the following screenshot:

We created a default particle system that will be used as the spark emitter. We need to set that up to our liking. I'll get you started, and you can play with it as you desire, as follows:

1. Select `SparkEmitter` from the **Hierarchy** panel.
2. And in its **Inspector** panel, under **Particle System**, set the following values:
   - **Start Size**: `0.15`
   - **Start Color**: pick a red/orange color
   - **Start Lifetime**: `0.3`
   - **Max Particles**: `50`
3. Under **Emission**, set **Rate over Time**: `100`
4. Under **Shape**, set **Shape**: **Sphere** and **Radius**: `0.01`

Here's what my **Scene** view looks like as I run Play Mode and zap Ethan in the chest:

When Ethan is shot, the `hitEffect` particle system is activated. After 3 seconds (or whatever value you set in the `TimeToSelect` variable), his *health* is depleted, the explosion effect is instantiated, the score is incremented, and he respawns at a new location. In `Chapter 6`, *World Space UI*, we'll see how we can show the current score to the player.

## Cleaning up

One last thing before we're done: let's clean up the `Assets` folder a bit and move all the scripts into an `Assets/Scripts/` subfolder. Select the Project Assets folder in Project, create a folder, name it Scripts, and drag all your scripts into it.

# Short intro to Unity C# programming

As we just saw, Unity does a lot of things: it manages objects, renders them, animates them, calculates the physics of those objects, and so on. Unity itself is a program. It's made of code. Probably a lot of good code written by some very smart people. This internal Unity code can be accessed by you, the game developer, through the Unity Editor point-and-click interface that we've already been using. Within the Unity Editor, scripts are manifested as configurable components. However, it's also made more directly accessible to you through the Unity scripting API.

**API** (short for **Application Programming Interface**), refers to published software functions that you can access from your own scripts. Unity's API is very rich and nicely designed. That's one reason why people have written amazing applications and plugin add-ons for Unity.

There are many programming languages in the world. Unity has chosen to support the C# language from Microsoft. Computer languages have a specific syntax that must be obeyed. Otherwise, the computer will not understand your script. In Unity, script errors (and warnings) appear in the **Console** panel of the editor as well as in the bottom footer of the app window.

The default script editor for Unity is an integrated development environment, or an IDE, called **MonoDevelop**. You can configure a different editor or an IDE if you want, such as Microsoft's Visual Studio. MonoDevelop has some nice features such as autocompletion and pop-up help that understand the Unity documentation. C# scripts are text files that are named with a .cs extension.

In a Unity C# script, some of the words and symbols are a part of the C# language itself, some come from the Microsoft .NET Framework, and others are provided by the Unity API. And then there's the code that you write.

An empty default Unity C# script looks like this:

```
using UnityEngine;
using System.Collections;

public class RandomPosition : MonoBehaviour {

  // Use this for initialization
  void Start () {

  }

  // Update is called once per frame
  void Update () {

  }
}
```

Let's dissect it.

The first two lines indicate that this script needs some other stuff to run.
The `using` keyword belongs to the C# language. The line using `UnityEngine` says that we'll be using the `UnityEngine` API. The line using `System.Collections` says that we also might use a library of functions named `Collections` to access lists of objects.

In C#, each line of code ends with a semicolon. Double slashes (//) indicate comments in the code, and anything from there to the end of that line will be ignored.

This Unity script defines a class named `RandomPosition`. **Classes** are like code templates with their own properties (variables) and behavior (functions). Classes derived from the `MonoBehaviour` base class are recognized by Unity and used when your game runs. For example, in the first script we wrote at the top of this chapter, the line `public class RandomPosition : MonoBehaviour` basically says *we are defining a new public class named* `RandomPosition`," *which inherits all the abilities of the* `MonoBehaviour` *Unity base class,* including the capabilities of the `Start()` and `Update()` functions. The body of the class is enclosed in a pair of curly braces ({ }).

When something is `public`, it can be seen by other code outside this specific script file. When it's `private`, it can only be referenced within this file. We want Unity to see the `RandomPosition` class.

Classes define variables and functions. A **variable** holds data values of a specific type, such as `float`, `int`, `boolean`, `GameObject`, `Vector3`, and so on. **Functions** implement logic (step-by-step instructions). Functions can receive *arguments*-variables enclosed in a parenthesis used by its code-and can return new values when it's done.

Numeric `float` constants, such as `5.0f`, require an `f` at the end in C# to ensure that the data type is a *simple* floating point value and not a *double-precision* floating point value.

Unity will automatically call some special functions if you've defined them `Start()` and `Update()` are two examples. Empty versions of these are provided in the default C# script. The datatype in front of a function indicates the type of value returned. `Start()` and `Update()` do not return values, so they're `void`.

Each `Start()` function from all `MonoBehaviour` scripts in your game is called before the gameplay begins. It's a good place for data initialization. All the `Update()` functions are called during each time slice, or frame, while the game is running. This is where most of the action lies.

Once you've written or modified a script in the MonoDevelop or Visual Studio editor, save it. Then, switch to the Unity Editor window. Unity will automatically recognize that the script has changed and will reimport it. If errors are found, it will report them right away in the **Console** panel.

This is just a cursory introduction to Unity programming. As we work through the projects in this book, I will explain additional bits as they're introduced.

# Summary

In this chapter, we explored the relationship between the VR camera and objects in the scene. We first made Ethan (the zombie) walk randomly around the scene and enabled him to move by using a NavMesh, but then we directed his wanderings using a 3D cursor on the **x, z** ground plane. This cursor follows our gaze as we look around the scene in virtual reality. Lastly, we also used our gaze to shoot a ray at Ethan, causing him to lose health and eventually explode.

These look-based techniques can be used in non-VR games, but in VR, it's very common and almost essential. We'll be using them more in the later chapters of this book too.

In the next chapter, we will use our hands to interact with the virtual scene. We will learn about Unity Input events, as well as input systems for SteamVR, Oculus, and Windows Mixed Reality, to name a few. As this can get complicated, we'll write our own VR input event system to keep our application independent of the specific VR devices.

# Handy Interactables

**5**

You're in a virtual world with all this cool stuff; it is our nature to try to reach out and touch something. While gaze-based selection, as we saw in the previous chapter, is a good first step for interacting with virtual scenes, most people intuitively want to use their hands. Most VR devices provide a hand controller to select, grab, and interact with virtual objects in the scene.

In this chapter, we introduce practices for capturing user input in Unity, illustrating how to use them in a simple VR scene. Everyone loves balloons, so in this project we will make balloons. We may even pop a few. We will continue from the previous chapter, using C# programming for basic scripting, and explore several software design patterns for user input. We will discuss the following topics:

- Polling for input device data
- Using scriptable data objects for storing and retrieving input state
- Invoking and subscribing to input events
- Using interactable components provided with device-specific Unity packages

An important lesson we will learn in this chapter is there is not just one way to handle user input for your VR application. There isn't even one *best way*. Unity includes several mechanisms for handling user input and, in general, messaging between objects. VR device manufacturers provide their own input controller objects and scripts for their SDK.

Furthermore, VR manufacturers and others offer convenient framework toolkits with higher-level components and prefabs. We recommend you become familiar with the toolkits provided for your target device. Study the demo scenes to see how the components work and their recommended practices, as we will do at the end of this chapter.

That said, in this chapter we will start with the very simple button press input, and progress from there, showing various design patterns. You won't always want to roll your own, but you should have an understanding of how things work.

# Setting up the scene

To begin our exploration of input mechanisms, let's set up our scene. The plan is to let players create balloons. Everyone loves balloons!

For this scene, you could start with a new scene (**File** | **New Scene**) and then add the **MyMyselfEye** prefab we built in the previous chapter. Instead, I've decided to start with the Diorama scene created in the previous chapter, and remove all but the GroundPlane and PhotoPlane, as follows:

1. Open the **Diorama** scene
2. Remove all the objects, except for **MyMyselfEye, Directional Light, GroundPlane** and **PhotoPlane**
3. Position the **MeMyselfEye** at the scene origin, **Position** (0, 0, 0)
4. Select **File** | **Save Scene As** and give it a name, such as "Balloons"

# Creating a balloon

For the balloon, you can simply use a standard Unity sphere 3D primitive if you choose. Or you can find an object in the Unity Asset Store or elsewhere. We are using a low poly balloon object that we found on Google Poly (`https://poly.google.com/view/a01Rp51l-L3`) and which is provided with the download files for this chapter.

Either way, please parent the object so its origin (pivot point) is at the bottom, as follows:

1. In **Hierarchy**, create an empty object (**Create** | **Create Empty**) and name it "Balloon".
2. Reset its transform (**Transform** | **gear-icon** | **Reset**), then **Position** it at (0, 1, 1).
3. Drag the balloon prefab into the Hierarchy as a child object of Balloon (mine is found in the `Assets/Poly/Assets/` folder).
4. If you do not have a balloon model, use a sphere (**Create** | **3D Object** | **Sphere**). And add a material, like the "Blue Material" we created in the previous chapter.
5. Set the child object's **Position** to (0, 0.5, 0) so its origin (pivot point) is at its bottom when referenced from the parent.

The scene should look something like this:

# Making it a prefab

Our intent is to instantiate new balloons from a prefab when your player presses a button on their controller. And when the button is released, the balloon gets released and it floats away.

Let's scale and position the balloon initially in the scene at a starting size and workable distance. We will also give it some physics properties by adding a `RigidBody` component:

> We discuss RigidBodies and Unity physics in more detail in `Chapter 8`, *Playing with Physics and Fire*.

1. Select your Balloon object in **Hierarchy**
2. In **Inspector**, set its **Transform Scale** to (0.1, 0.1, 0.1)

3. Set its **Position** to (0, 1, 1)
4. Use **Add Component** to add a **Rigid Body**
5. Uncheck the **Use Gravity** checkbox

My balloon object now has the following properties:

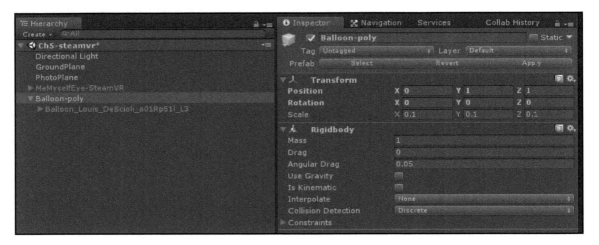

Make it a prefab as follows:

1. Drag the balloon object into your `Prefabs/` folder to make it a prefab object
2. Delete the original balloon object from your Hierarchy

Okay. Now let's play around with controller buttons.

If you ever want to modify a prefab, drag an instance of it back into the scene. Make the changes you want. Then, use the **Apply** button to save the changes back onto the prefab of the object. Delete the temporary instance from the Hierarchy if it's no longer needed in the scene.

# Basic button input

Unity includes a standard Input Manager for accessing traditional game controller, keyboard, mouse, and mobile touchscreen input. This can include specific button presses, joystick axes, and the device accelerometer, for example. It also supports input from VR and AR systems.

The Input Manager provides an abstraction layer over the physical input devices. For example, you can reference logical inputs, such as the `Fire1` button, which is mapped to a physical button. The mappings for your project can be set up and modified in **Edit** | **Project Settings** | **Input**.

 For a general overview and details of Unity Input Manager, see `https://docs.unity3d.com/Manual/ConventionalGameInput.html`. For scripting the Input class, see `https://docs.unity3d.com/ScriptReference/Input.html`. Input mapping for various VR devices can be found at `https://docs.unity3d.com/Manual/vr-input.html`.

Let's take a look. To start, we will write a test script to get a specific button state and see how the Unity Input class works. A common logical button is the one named "Fire1." Let's see which button your input device uses for "Fire1."

# Using the Fire1 button

We will now write a script, `MyInputController`, to detect when your user has pressed the `Fire1` button. Add the script to your `MeMyselfEye` object as follows:

1. In **Hierarchy**, select the **MyMyselfEye** object
2. In **Inspector**, click **Add Component**, then **New Script**
3. Name it `MyInputController` and press **Create And Add**
4. Double-click the `MyInputController` script to open it for editing

Edit the script as follows:

```
public class MyInputController : MonoBehaviour
{
  void Update ()
  {
    ButtonTest();
  }

  private void ButtonTest()
  {
    string msg = null;

    if (Input.GetButtonDown("Fire1"))
      msg = "Fire1 down";

    if (Input.GetButtonUp("Fire1"))
```

```
        msg = "Fire1 up";

    if (msg != null)
        Debug.Log("Input: " + msg);
    }
}
```

In this script, in each frame Update, we call a private function, `ButtonTest`. This function builds a message string named `msg` that reports whether the `Fire1` button has just been pressed down or released. The call to `Input.GetButtonDown("Fire1")`, for example, will return a Boolean (true or false) value, which we check in the `if` statement. When either of these situations are true, the `msg` string is not empty (null) and gets printed to the Unity Console window:

1. Press **Play** in the Unity editor to run the scene
2. When you press the Fire1 button on your input controller, you will see the **Input: Fire1 down** message as output
3. When you release the Fire1 button, you will see the **Input: Fire1 up** message, as shown here:

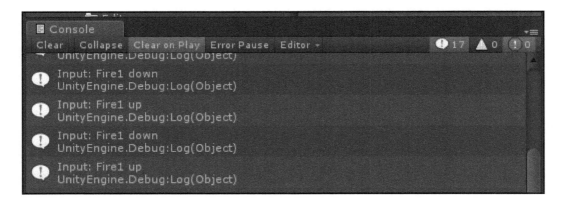

You can use even use this script to identify which physical button on your input controller maps to the logical `Fire1` button. Using OpenVR, for example, `Fire1` is triggered with the menu button on a Vive controller or the **B** button on the Oculus Touch controller ("Button.Two") as shown on the Unity Input System Mappings section in the Input for OpenVR Controllers page of the Unity manual (`https://docs.unity3d.com/Manual/OpenVRControllers.html`). Feel free to experiment with using other logical input names, and/or modifying the mappings using the Input project settings (**Edit** | **Project Settings** | **Input**).

Instead of using Unity logical inputs, it is also common to access the device directly through SDK components. Let's look into that in the next section.

# OpenVR trigger button

If you have a VR device supported by OpenVR (HTC Vive, Oculus Rift, or Windows MR), let's modify the `ButtonTest` function to check for a pull and release of the trigger button.

To implement this, we need to provide our script with the specific input component that we want to query. In OpenVR, this is represented by the `SteamVR_TrackedObject` component, as shown in the following variation of our script:

```
public class MyInputController : MonoBehaviour
{
  public SteamVR_TrackedObject rightHand;

  private SteamVR_Controller.Device device;

  void Update ()
  {
    ButtonTest();
  }

  private void ButtonTest()
  {
    string msg = null;

    // SteamVR
    device = SteamVR_Controller.Input((int)rightHand.index);
    if (device != null &&
      device.GetPressDown(SteamVR_Controller.ButtonMask.Trigger))
    {
      msg = "Trigger press";
      device.TriggerHapticPulse(700);
    }
    if (device != null &&
      device.GetPressUp(SteamVR_Controller.ButtonMask.Trigger))
    {
      msg = "Trigger release";
    }

    if (msg != null)
      Debug.Log("Input: " + msg);
  }
}
```

After saving this script, we need to populate the `rightHand` variable:

1. In Unity, select **MeMyselfEye** so you can see the **My Input Controller** in the **Inspector**
2. In the **Hierarchy**, unfold the **[CameraRig]** object
3. Click the **Controller (Right)** child object and drag it onto the **My Input Controller**'s Right Hand slot in the **Inspector**

Given the `rightHand` object, we reference its `SteamVR_TrackedObject` component directly. In the `ButtonTest` function, we get the *device* data using the right hand's device ID (`rightHand.index`), and check specifically for the trigger press status. As a bonus, I've shown you how to also provide a haptic buzz pulse on the device when the trigger is pressed.

Now when you press **Play**, pulling the controller trigger will be recognized.

Using the SDK components like this, you can access other inputs specific to the device not supported by the Unity Input Manager. The trigger on some controllers are not just pressed/unpressed but can return a percentage of press, represented as a value between 0.0 and 1.0. Another example is the touch-sensitive grips, buttons, and thumb pad on the Oculus Touch controllers and other controllers.

Try modifying the script to recognize the controller `Grip` button instead, or other inputs. Hint: try *SteamVR_Controller.ButtonMask.Grip*.

# Daydream controller clicks

Google Daydream VR on Android may not respond, by default, to `Fire1` events. The following code shows how to access controller clicks directly:

```
private void ButtonTest()
{
  string msg = null;

  if (GvrControllerInput.ClickButtonDown)
    msg = "Button down";
  if (GvrControllerInput.ClickButtonUp)
    msg = "Button up";

  if (msg != null)
```

```
        Debug.Log("Input: " + msg);
    }
}
```

In this case, we call the `GvrControllerInput` class static functions `ClickButtonDown` and `ClickButtonUp`. There is no need to identify a specific controller object because `GvrControllerInput` is a *singleton*. That is why we're guaranteed to have only one instance of it in the scene, so we can reference its data directly. This makes sense because on Daydream there will only be one hand controller, whereas on OpenVR there will be two.

# Polling for clicks

The simplest way to obtain user input is just *get* the current data from an input component. We've already seen this using the Input class and VR SDK. Presently, we will write our own input component that maps the Unity (or SDK) input to our own simple API in `MyInputController`. Then, we'll write a `BalloonController` that polls the input, as illustrated:

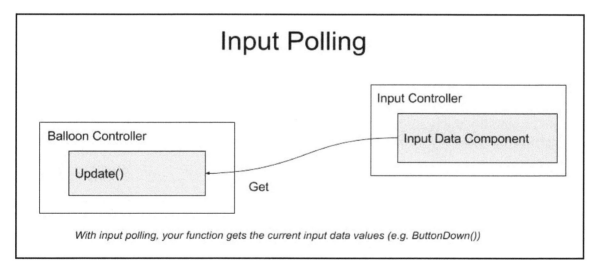

# Our own button interface functions

You may recall that the `MeMyselfEye` player rig may have device-specific toolkit child objects for a particular VR SDK. The version for OpenVR, for example, has their **[CameraRig]** prefab. The version for Daydream has the Daydream **Player** prefab. It makes sense to add our `MyInputController` component to `MeMyselfEye`, as it may make device-specific SDK calls. In this way, should you want to maintain camera rig prefabs for a variety of platforms, and swap them in and out as you build the project for a different VR target, the API that is exposed to the rest of your application will be consistent and independent of the specific device toolkit.

Our input controller will expose two custom API Functions, `ButtonDown` and `ButtonUp`. The implementation of these functions will be hidden from the components that call them. For example, we could write it to handle `Fire1` button presses as first but later change it to use a trigger press instead, or make a version for Daydream that does not use `Fire1`. Let's update the `MyInputController` by adding the following code:

```
public bool ButtonDown()
{
  return Input.GetButtonDown("Fire1");
}

public bool ButtonUp()
{
  return Input.GetButtonUp("Fire1");
}
```

Or you can modify the preceding code to use the button interface that works for you. For example, for Daydream you might use this instead:

```
public bool ButtonDown()
{
  return GvrControllerInput.ClickButtonDown;
}

public bool ButtonUp()
{
  return GvrControllerInput.ClickButtonUp;
}
```

Now, we'll use our little `ButtonUp/ButtonDown` input API.

# Creating and releasing balloons

Let's now create a `BalloonController` that will be the application component that creates and controls balloons. It will reference our `MyInputController`. Follow these steps:

1. In **Hierarchy**, create an empty game object, reset its Transform, and name it `BalloonController`

2. Create a new script on the object named `BalloonController` and open it for editing as follows:

```
public class BalloonController : MonoBehaviour
{
  public GameObject meMyselfEye;

  private MyInputController inputController;

  void Start ()
  {
    inputController =
meMyselfEye.GetComponent<MyInputController>();
  }

  void Update ()
  {
    if (inputController.ButtonDown())
    {
      NewBalloon()
    }
    else if (inputController.ButtonUp())
    {
      ReleaseBalloon();
    }
    // else while button is still pressed, grow it
  }
```

This is the skeleton of the controller. Given a reference to the `MeMyselfEye` object, the `Start()` function gets its `MyInputController` component and assigns it to the `inputController` variable.

`Update()` is called each frame while your game is running. It will call `inputController.ButtonDown` or `ButtonUp` to see if the user has changed their input, and in response, either create or release a balloon. We'll write the functions next.

Note that we've also included a placeholder (as a comment) where we'll add the `GrowBalloon` function too.

Given the balloon prefab, the `BalloonController` can create new instances of it in our scene, by calling the Unity `Instantiate` function. Add the following `public` variable declaration at the top of your controller class for the balloon prefab:

```
public GameObject balloonPrefab;
```

And add a `private` variable to hold the current instance of the balloon:

```
private GameObject balloon;
```

Now, the `NewBalloon` function, which is called when the player presses the button, references the prefab and instantiates it as follows:

```
private void NewBalloon()
{
  balloon = Instantiate(balloonPrefab);
}
```

The `ReleaseBalloon` function is called when the player releases the button. It will apply a gentle upward force on the balloon so it floats skyward. We'll define a floatStrength variable and apply it to the object's RigidBody (the Unity physics engine and RigidBodies are explained in a later chapter):

```
public float floatStrength = 20f;
```

And,

```
private void ReleaseBalloon()
{
  balloon.GetComponent<Rigidbody>().AddForce(Vector3.up * floatStrength);
  balloon = null;
}
```

Notice that we also clear the balloon variable (setting it to null), getting it ready for the next button press.

Save the file and in Unity:

1. Drag the **MeMyselfEye** object from **Hierarchy** onto the BalloonController's **Me Myself Eye** slot in **Inspector**
2. Drag the **Ballon** prefab from the Project's `Assets` folder onto the BalloonController's **Balloon Prefab** slot in **Inspector**

When you're ready, press **Play**. Inside VR, when you press the `Fire1` button (or whichever you programmed), a new balloon is instantiated. When you release it, the balloon floats upwards. In the following game window, I have pressed the button multiple times in succession, creating a series of balloons:

Here is the Hierarchy of the same game state, showing the cloned balloons in the **Hierarchy** (my prefab's name is `Balloon-poly`):

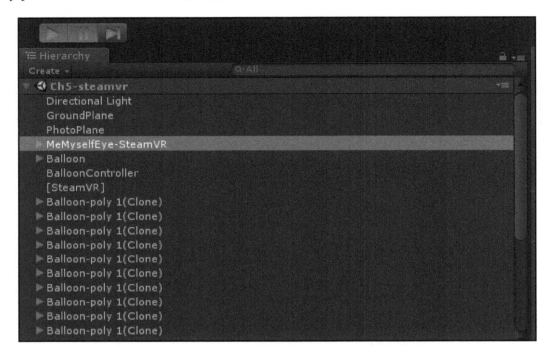

## Inflating a balloon while pressed

The next thing we want to do is inflate the balloon while you're still holding the button. We can do this by checking whether there's a current balloon instance from a button press, and modifying its scale each update by a specified grow rate. Let's define that first, to grow by 150% each second the button is held down (1.5 times):

```
public float growRate = 1.5f;
```

Now, modify the Update function with a third `else if` condition as follows:

```
else if (balloon != null)
{
  GrowBalloon();
}
```

And add the `GrowBalloon` function like this:

```
private void GrowBalloon()
{
   balloon.transform.localScale += balloon.transform.localScale * growRate
* Time.deltaTime;
}
```

The `GrowBalloon` function will modify the balloon's local scale by a percentage of its current size. `growRate` is the rate of growth per second. So, we multiply that by the current fraction of a second in this frame (`Time.deltaTime`).

Press **Play** in Unity. When you press the controller button, you'll create a balloon, which continues to inflate until you release the button. Then the balloon floats up. Wow, that's actually pretty fun!

Next, we're going to refactor our code to use a different software pattern for getting user input, using scriptable objects.

No one writes code without expecting to change it. Programming is a dynamic art as you rethink how to do things, as requirements grow, and problems get fixed. Sometimes, these changes are not necessarily to add a new feature or fix a bug but to make the code cleaner, easier to use, and easier to maintain. This is called **refactoring**, when you change or rewrite parts of a program but do not necessarily change how the feature works from the player's perspective.

# Using scriptable objects for input

In this example, we will further decouple our application from the underlying input device using a technique called **scriptable objects.** These are data objects used for holding information such as game state, player preferences, or any other data that is not necessarily graphical. Scriptable objects are instantiated during runtime, much like MonoBehaviour ones, but do not live in the Hierarchy, have no Transform, nor other physics and rendering behaviors.

It's useful to think of scriptable objects as *data containers* in your projects.

In the previous implementation, `BalloonController` requires a reference to the `MeMyselfEye` object to use its `MyInputController` component. Although the input controller component does separate you from the underlying SDK calls, if you modify your application to use a different `MeMyselfEye` (for example, from OpenVR to Daydream), you will need to find and replace all references to one `MeMyselfEye` in the scene and replace them with the new one. Here's will have the input controller populate a scriptable object, and then our `BalloonController` reference that object for the data, as illustrated here:

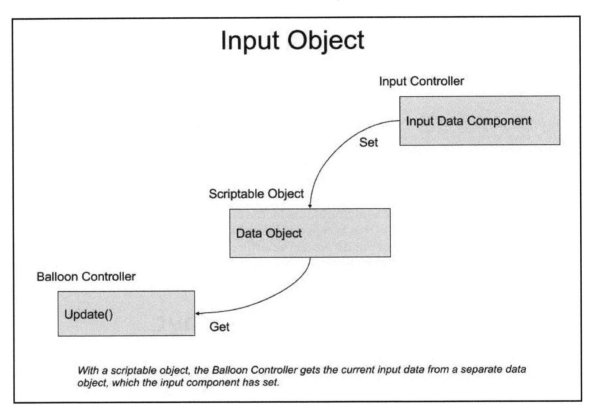

With a scriptable object, the Balloon Controller gets the current input data from a separate data object, which the input component has set.

The process of implementing scriptable objects is a little more involved than game objects with components. But not much. Let's go!

Keep in mind this is just one example how to use scriptable objects and serves as an introduction to this powerful design pattern in Unity. For more information, see the Unity Tutorial *Introduction to scriptable objects* at `https://unity3d.com/learn/tutorials/modules/beginner/live-training-archive/scriptable-objects`. Also, see `Chapter 9`, Exploring Interactive Spaces, for another example of scriptable objects for data management in a project.

# Creating the scriptable object

In this example, our object will just have one variable, for the current button action. We'll say the button can have one of three possible values: `PressedDown`, `ReleasedUp`, or `None`. We'll define the action as having occurred current during the current `Update`, then it's cleared to `None`. That is, rather than record the current button state (for example, is pressed), we are capturing the current button action (was just pressed), to be consistent with other examples in this chapter.

It's useful to keep scriptable objects in their own folder in the Project `Assets`:

1. In the **Project** window, create a new folder under *Assets* named `ScriptableObjects`
2. In the new folder, right-click and select **Create | C# Script**
3. Name the script `MyInputAction`
4. Then, open the `MyInputAction.cs` script for editing

Edit the `MyInputAction.cs` script as follows:

```
[CreateAssetMenu(menuName = "My Objects/Input Action")]
public class MyInputAction : ScriptableObject {
  public enum ButtonAction { None, PressedDown, ReleasedUp };
  public ButtonAction buttonAction;
}
```

Rather than inheriting from `MonoBehaviour`, we will define the class as a `ScriptableObject`. We represent the action using an enum to restrict its possible values to the selection list.

"The **enum** keyword is used to declare an enumeration, a distinct type that consists of a set of named constants called the enumerator list." - `https://docs.microsoft.com/en-us/dotnet/csharp/language-reference/keywords/enum`

Notice the first line of the preceding script. We provide a *property attribute* which generates a menu item in the Unity Editor for our object. Since scriptable objects are not added to the scene Hierarchy, we need a way to create them in the project. Using this attribute makes it easy, as follows:

1. Save the script and return to Unity.
2. In the Unity editor main menu, navigate to **Assets | Create**.
3. You will see a new item, **My Objects**, with a submenu with an item **Input Action**, as directed in the `CreateAssetsMenu` property attribute in our script. The menu is shown next.
4. Choose **Input Action** to create an instance. By default, it will be created in the currently selected Project Assets folder. So if you have the `ScriptableObjects` folder open, it will be created there.
5. Rename the object `My Input Action Data`.

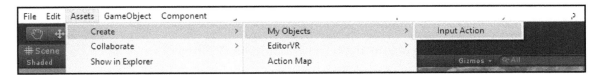

If you select the new `My Input Action Data` object in your `ScriptableObjects/` folder, you can see its properties in the **Inspector**. In the following screen capture, I have clicked the **Button Action** drop-down list to reveal the possible enum values we've specified in our code:

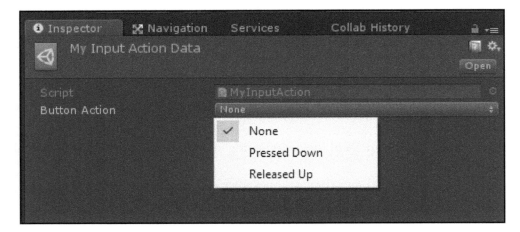

# Populating the input action object

The next step is to change `MyInputController.cs` to populate the input data object, using a reference to the object, as follows:

```
public MyInputAction myInput;

void Update ()
{
  if (ButtonDown())
  {
    myInput.buttonAction = MyInputAction.ButtonAction.PressedDown;
  } else if (ButtonUp())
  {
    myInput.buttonAction = MyInputAction.ButtonAction.ReleasedUp;
  } else
  {
    myInput.buttonAction = MyInputAction.ButtonAction.None;
  }
}
```

The script uses its own `ButtonDown` and `ButtonUp` functions to set the `buttonAction` as appropriate. These could even be changed from *public* to *private* to further encapsulate it.

Save the script. Then in Unity:

1. Select **MeMyselfEye** object in Hierarchy
2. Find the **My Input Action Data** object in your `ScriptableObjects` folder
3. Drag it onto the **My Input** slot of the **My Input Controller (Script)** component, as shown here for my Steam version of `MeMyselfEye`:

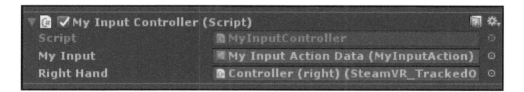

# Accessing the input action object

Now the `BalloonController` can access the input data object rather than `MeMyselfEye`. Otherwise is very similar and a simple refactor. Modify `BalloonController.cs` as follows.

First, we can remove any references to `MeMyselfEye` in the `BalloonController`, including the public variable and the entire `Start()` function (we do not need the `GetComponent<MyInputController>`).

Add a variable for the input data object:

```
public MyInputAction myInput;
```

And reference it in the `Update` conditions:

```
void Update()
{
  if (myInput.buttonAction == MyInputAction.ButtonAction.PressedDown)
  {
    NewBalloon();
  }
  else if (myInput.buttonAction == MyInputAction.ButtonAction.ReleasedUp)
  {
    ReleaseBalloon();
  }
  else if (balloon != null)
  {
    GrowBalloon();
  }
}
```

Save the script. Then in Unity, as we did previously for `MyInputController`:

1. Select the **BalloonController** object in **Hierarchy**
2. Find the **My Input Action Data** object in your `ScriptableObjects` folder
3. Drag it onto the **My Input** slot of the **Balloon Controller** component

Press **Play**. The app should work just like before. Press the button to create a balloon, hold the button to inflate it, and release the button to release the balloon.

# Simulation testing with scriptable objects

An interesting advantage of this architecture is how it facilitates testing. Having completely decoupled our application objects from the input device, we can simulate input actions without actually using physical input controllers. For example, try this:

1. Select **MeMyselfEye** in **Hierarchy**. Then in **Inspector**, temporarily disable the **My Input Controller** component by unchecking its checkbox.
2. Select the **My Input Action Data** object in the Project `ScriptableObjects/` folder
3. Press **Play.**
4. While the game is running, in **Inspector**, change the **Button Action** from **None** to **PressedDown.**
5. The **BalloonController** thinks a **PressedDown** action has occurred. It creates a new balloon and begins inflating it.
6. In **Inspector**, change the **Input Action** to **PressedUp**.
7. The **BalloonController** sees a **PressedUp** action has occurred and releases the current balloon.

When you're done testing, don't forget to re-enable the input controller component!

This kind of manual setup of object states for development and testing can be very helpful, especially as your project grows and gets more complex.

# Using Unity events for input

The third software pattern we will explore using Unity Events. Events allow decoupling of the source of the event from the consumer of the event. Basically, events are a messaging system where one object triggers an event. Any other objects in the project can listen for the event. It can subscribe a specific function to be called when the event occurs.

You can set this up using drag-and-drop via the Unity Inspector. Or you can subscribe listener functions in scripts. In this example, we will minimize the scripting involved, and use the Unity editor to subscribe to events.

Events are a very rich topic and we can only introduce them here. For more information on using Unity Events, there are a lot of good references online, including the Unity tutorials `https://unity3d.com/learn/tutorials/topics/scripting/events` and `https://unity3d.com/learn/tutorials/topics/scripting/events-creating-simple-messaging-system`.

The following diagram illustrates the relationship between our input controller, which invokes events, and the balloon controller, which subscribes to the events:

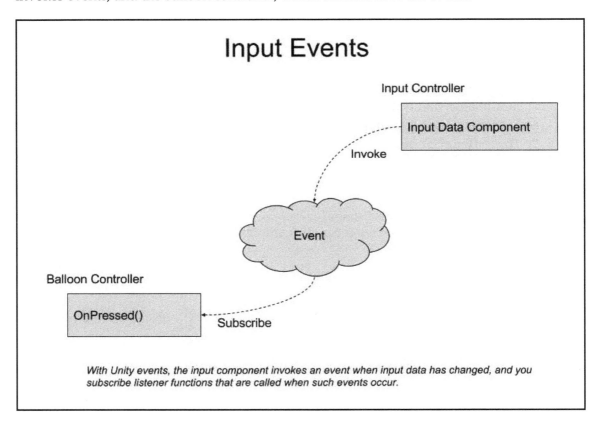

*With Unity events, the input component invokes an event when input data has changed, and you subscribe listener functions that are called when such events occur.*

It's important to note that, unlike normal events, these events do not need to be unsubscribed.

 If you are a developer and familiar with .NET, it may help to know that Unity Events are delegates. As explained in the Unity Manual, "UnityEvents can be added to any MonoBehaviour and are executed from code like a standard .net delegate. When a UnityEvent is added to a MonoBehaviour it appears in the Inspector and persistent callbacks can be added."

# Invoking our input action events

To implement our example using events, we'll first have the `MyInputController` trigger events when a button is pressed and another event when the button is released.

First, at the top of the script we need to declare that we are using the Unity event API. The we declare the two UnityEvents we will invoke. The `Update()` function only needs to invoke one event or the other as they happen.

The entire `MyInputController.cs` is as follows:

```
using UnityEngine;
using UnityEngine.Events;

public class MyInputController : MonoBehaviour
{
 public UnityEvent ButtonDownEvent;
 public UnityEvent ButtonUpEvent;

 void Update()
 {
   if (ButtonDown())
     ButtonDownEvent.Invoke();
   else if (ButtonUp())
     ButtonUpEvent.Invoke();
 }

 private bool ButtonDown()
 {
   return Input.GetButtonDown("Fire1");
 }

 private bool ButtonUp()
 {
```

```
      return Input.GetButtonUp("Fire1");
  }
}
```

That's it for this side of the equation.

# Subscribing to input events

Using events, `BalloonController` does not need to check for input actions each frame Update. All that conditional logic can be bypassed. Instead, we'll drag and drop the components to subscribe them to events. The `Update` function now only needs to grow the balloon if it's already instantiated.

The entire `BalloonController.cs` now looks like this. Aside from being less code, please note that we changed the `NewBalloon` and `ReleaseBalloon` functions from `private` to `public` so we can reference them in the Inspector:

```
public class BalloonController : MonoBehaviour
{
  public GameObject balloonPrefab;
  public float floatStrength = 20f;
  public float growRate = 1.5f;

  private GameObject balloon;

  void Update()
  {
    if (balloon != null)
      GrowBalloon();
  }

  public void NewBalloon()
  {
    balloon = Instantiate(balloonPrefab);
  }

  public void ReleaseBalloon()
  {
    balloon.GetComponent<Rigidbody>().AddForce(Vector3.up * floatStrength);
    balloon = null;
  }

  private void GrowBalloon()
  {
    balloon.transform.localScale += balloon.transform.localScale * growRate
```

```
*  Time.deltaTime;
   }
}
```

To wire up the input events to our balloon controller:

1. Select **MeMyselfEye** and look at its **Inspector** window
2. You will see the **My Input Controller** component now has two event lists, as we declared in its script
3. On the **Button Down Event** list, press the + in the lower-right to create a new item.
4. Drag the **BalloonController** from **Hierarchy** into the empty Object slot
5. In the function select list, choose **BalloonController** | **NewBalloon**

Repeat the process for the Button Up Event as follows:

1. On the **Button Up Event** list, press the + in the lower-right to create a new item
2. Drag the **BalloonController** from **Hierarchy** into the empty Object slot
3. In the function select list, choose **BalloonController** | **ReleaseBalloon**

The component should now look like this:

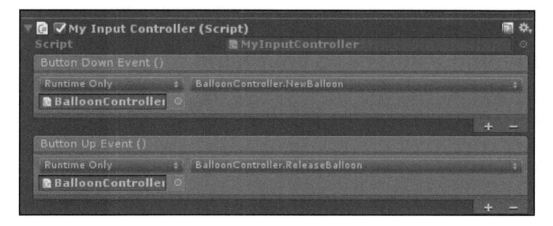

Now when you press **Play** and press a button, the input controller invokes an event. The *NewBalloon* function is listening for these events and gets called. Likewise for the Button Up event.

This wiring can also be done entirely with scripting. We will not go into it here. As a developer, we more often are "users" of event systems set up by others. As your experience grows, you may find yourself implementing your own custom events.

 For another detailed example of using Unity Events for user interface, consider *Augmented Reality for Developers*, a Unity projects book from Packt Publishing co-authored by the author of this book, Jonathan Linowes, and Krystian Babilinski.

# Really using your hands

The last couple of things we'll explore in the chapter involve getting your hands even more into virtual reality. In addition to buttons and touch pads, VR hand controllers can be tracked in 3D space along with your head. PC- and console-based VR, such as Rift, Vive, MR, and PSVR, are really very good at this, with full positionally tracked hand controllers for both left and right hands. Lower-end mobile VR, such as Daydream, has a single hand controller with limited tracking, but better than nothing.

To start, we'll take advantage of positional tracking by simply parenting the balloon to your hand model. On VR, without actual positional tracking, like Daydream, the location of your hand controller is approximated by the SDK software, but useful enough.

## Parenting balloons to your hand

Suppose when you press the button, rather than creating the new balloon at a fixed position in space, it spawns and grows from your hand position. One way to accomplish this is to make the balloon instance a child of your hand controller object.

The BalloonController will need to know which hand pressed the button and parent the balloon to that controller object. Specifically, we'll pass the hand Game Object to the `NewBalloon` function as follows:

```
public void NewBalloon(GameObject parentHand)
{
  if (balloon == null)
  {
    balloon = Instantiate(balloonPrefab);
    balloon.transform.SetParent(parentHand.transform);
    balloon.transform.localPosition = Vector3.zero;
  }
}
```

Note that in this function we added an extra test for (`balloon == null`), just to make sure we haven't called `NewBalloon` twice in a row without releasing the first one yet.

Like before, we instantiate a new balloon from the prefab.

Then, we set its parent to the `parentHand` object. This is comparable to dragging one object to become a child of another in the Hierarchy. The parent-child relationships between game objects are handled by the built-in *Transform* component so the API functions are on the transform.

Lastly, we reset the local position of the balloon. If you recall, the prefab was positioned at (0, 1, 1) or something like that. As a child of the hand, we want it attached directly at the pivot point of the hand model. (Alternatively, you could offset the balloon origin to a different attachment point as needed.)

Worth noting, there are variations of the *Instantiate* function that let you specify the parent and transforms all in one call. See `https://docs.unity3d.com/ScriptReference/Object.Instantiate.html` .

Likewise, the `ReleaseBalloon` detaches the balloon from the hand before send it on its way, as follows:

```
public void ReleaseBalloon()
{
  if (balloon != null)
  {
    balloon.transform.parent = null;
    balloon.GetComponent<Rigidbody>().AddForce(Vector3.up *
floatStrength);
  }
  balloon = null;
}
```

How do we pass the hand game object to NewBalloon? Assuming your project is presently using the Unity Events we setup in the previous topic, it's very easy. In **Inspector** we need to update the **Button Down Event** function, since it now requires the game object argument:

1. In Unity editor, select the **MeMyselfEye** object
2. In the **Button Down Event** list, the function may now say something like `Missing BalloonController.NewBalloon`
3. Select the **function** dropdown and choose **BalloonController | NewBalloon(GameObject)**

4. Unfold the **MeMyselfEye** object in **Hierarchy** and look for the hand model, then drag it onto the empty Game Object slot
5. If you are using OpenVR, the hand will be called **Controller (right)**
6. If you are using Daydream, the hand will be called **GvrControllerPointer**

Here is a screenshot of me generating a bunch of balloons flying "over" the Grand Canyon, fun!

# Popping balloons

To be honest, it's really hard to think about creating balloons without also wanting to pop them! For fun, let's do a quick implementation. You can come up with your own ideas how to improve on it.

The Unity physics engine can detect when two object collide. To do this, each object must have a *Collider* component attached. You can then have the collision trigger an event. And we can subscribe that event to make something else happen, like play an explosion effect. This gets set up on the balloon prefab. So when two balloons collide, they'll explode. Let's do that:

1. Drag a copy of your Balloon prefab from Project `Assets prefabs` folder into the scene **Hierarchy.**
2. Select **Add Component** I **Physics** I **Sphere Collider.**
3. To scale and center the collider into position, click the **Edit Collider** icon in its component.
4. In the **Scene** window, the green collider outline has small anchor points you can click to edit. Note that the *Alt* key pins the center position and *Shift* locks the scale ratio.
5. Or, you can edit the **Center** and **Radius** values directly. I like **Radius** 0.25 and **Center** (0, 0.25, 0) on my balloon.

Now, we will add a script to handle the collision events.

1. **Add Component** to create a new C# script,
2. Name it `Poppable`
3. And open it for editing

The `Poppable` script will provide a callback function for `OnCollisionEnter` events. When another object with a collider enters this object's collider, our function will get called. At that point, we'll call `PopBalloon` which instantiates the explosion and destroys the balloon:

```
public class Poppable : MonoBehaviour
{
 public GameObject popEffect;

 void OnCollisionEnter(Collision collision)
 {
   PopBalloon();
 }

 private void PopBalloon()
 {
   Instantiate(popEffect, transform.position, transform.rotation);
   Destroy(gameObject);
 }
}
```

You can see that the `OnCollisionEnter` gets a `Collision` argument with information including what game object collided with it. We will ignore this here but you might explore it more: `https://docs.unity3d.com/ScriptReference/Collision.html`.

Save the script. Now, back in Unity:

1. Select a particle system prefab from **Project** Assets, such as `Assets/Standard Assets/ParticleSystems/Prefabs/Explosion` (this is the one we used to kill Ethan in `Chapter 4`, *Gaze-Based Control*)
2. Drag the **effects** prefab onto the Poppable's `Pop Effect` slot
3. Save these changes back to the prefab by pressing **Apply**
4. You can now delete the **Balloon** from the **Hierarchy**

Alright, let's try it. Press **Play**. Create a balloon. Then, reach out and push the button again so a new balloon collides with that one. Does it explode? Yikes!

# Interactable items

Directly interacting with objects in VR, such as grabbing items and using them to perform other actions, is a bit more complex. And, it can be tricky to get right. So it doesn't make sense, especially in this book, to grow our own interaction system. Unfortunately, there is not a single standard toolkit either. But, there are more than a few very good toolkits you can use, albeit most are specific to individual target platforms.

Generally, the architecture is similar among these solutions:

- Provides prefabs for the player camera rig
- Camera rig includes objects for your hands, including input controller components
- Hand objects include components that trigger events when interactions occur
- An interactable component is added to any objects in the scene that can be interacted with using input events
- Additional components and options extend the interactable behaviors

Toolkits will include a number of demo scenes which provide rich examples how to use the particular toolkit. Often, it is more informative to study the demos to see how to use the toolkits than the actual documentation.

In this section, we introduce a grabbing and throwing mechanic using two toolkits, the *SteamVR InteractionSystem* and the *Daydream VR Elements*. The technique is similar for other platforms.

 For Oculus SDK (without OpenVR), you will need to integrate the Oculus Avatar SDK (see `Chapter 12`, *Social VR Metaverse*, for details on Oculus Avatars). Also, here's a quick video showing how to add an `OVR Grabber` component to your `OVRCameraRig` controllers: `https://www.youtube.com/watch?v=sxvKGVDmYfY`.

# Interactables using SteamVR Interaction System

The SteamVR Unity package includes an Interaction System, originally developed and used for minigames and scenes from Steam's impressive demo VR application, *The Lab* (`http://store.steampowered.com/app/450390/The_Lab/`). It can be found in the `Assets/SteamVR/InteractionSystem/` folder. We recommend you explore the example scenes, prefabs, and scripts.

The Interaction System includes its own **Player** camera rig which replaces the default **[CameraRig]** we have been using. The Player hierarchy is shown here:

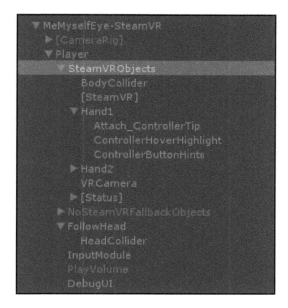

It includes a *VRCamera*, two hands (*Hand1* and *Hand2*), and other useful objects. Each hand includes an attach point (*Attach_ControllerTip*), a hover highlight (*ControllerHoverHighlight*), and a tooltips object (*ControllerButtonHints*).

1. Locate the **Player** prefab in `SteamVR/InteractionSystem/Core/Prefabs` and drag it as a child of **MyMyselfEye** in your scene **Hierarchy**
2. Delete or disable the **[CameraRig]** object

For compatibility with the current scene, we also need to update the **NewBalloon** argument in **Button Down Event**:

1. Unfold the **Player** object in **Hierarchy** so you can see the **Hand1** and **Hand2** objects
2. Select the **MeMyselfEye** in **Hierarchy**
3. Drag **Hand2** (or **Hand1**) from **Hierarchy** onto the **GameObject** argument slot in the **Button Down Event** on the **My Input Controller** component

Next, for interactable objects there is a large collection of components available. Review the `SteamVR/InteractionSystem/Core/Scripts` folder contents. We will use the *Throwable* one.

First, lets try this on a basic Cube. Then, we'll make the balloons grabbable and throwable too:

1. In Hierarchy, create a cube (**Create** | **3D Object** | **Cube**).
2. Scale and position it within reaching distance of the Player. For example, **Scale** (0.3, 0.3, 0.3) and **Position** (-0.25, 1.3, -0.25) may work.
3. With the Cube selected, **Add Component** `Throwable` from the Interaction System.
4. Notice this will automatically add other required components, including the base Interactable and a RigidBody.
5. On the **RigidBody** component, uncheck the **Use Gravity** checkbox, so it hangs in the air rather than falling to the ground when you play.

Now when you press **Play**, reach out to the Cube so your controller penetrates (collides) it. Then, using the Trigger on your controller, grab the Cube and throw it *outta here*!

To make the balloons throwable, we modify the prefab:

1. Drag a copy of the **Balloon** prefab from the **Project** window into the scene **Hierarchy**
2. **Add Component** the Steam **Throwable**
3. Press **Apply** to save the prefab
4. And delete the Balloon from the Hierarchy

Press **Play**. Press the **Fire1** button to create and inflate a balloon. Release it. Then, grab it with the trigger. Throw the balloon. If you implemented the *Poppable* explosion earlier, it'll even explode like a projectile when it hits something, like the ground or the photo plane!

# Interactables using Daydream VR Elements

The base GoogleVR package does not include interactables, but you can find them in the Daydream Elements package. This package is a collection of demo scenes, components, and prefabs for using Daydream VR from the engineers at Google. To get the package:

1. Visit the Daydream Elements' Github Releases page at `https://github.com/googlevr/daydream-elements/releases`
2. Download `DaydreamElements.unitypackage`
3. Import it into your project using **Assets | Import Package | Custom Package...**

The package includes a prefab named `ObjectManipulationPointer` which is a drop-in replacement for the `GvrControllerPointer` we have been using:

1. In **Hierarchy,** unfold your **MeMyselfEye** and drill down to the **Player** object
2. Select **GvrControllerPointer** and disable it in Inspector
3. In the **Project** window, navigate to the `Assets/DaydreamElements/Elements/ObjectManipulationDemo/Prefabs/UI/` folder
4. Drag the **ObjectManipulationPointer** prefab into **Hierarchy** as a sibling of **GvrControllerPointer**

For compatibility with the current scene, we also need to update the **NewBalloon** argument in **Button Down Event**:

1. Select the **MeMyselfEye** in **Hierarchy**
2. Drag **ObjectManipulationPointer** from **Hierarchy** onto the **GameObject** argument slot in the **Button Down Event** on the **My Input Controller** component

Next, for interactable objects we add a `MoveablePhysicsObject` component, found in `Assets/DaydreamElements/Elements/ObjectManipulationDemo/Scripts/`.

 Additional information on Daydream Elements object manipulation can be found at `https://developers.google.com/vr/elements/object-manipulation`.

First, lets try this on a basic Cube. Then, we'll make the balloons grabbable and throwable too:

1. In **Hierarchy**, create a cube (**Create | 3D Object | Cube**).
2. Scale and position it within reaching distance of the Player. For example, **Scale** (0.25, 0.25, 0.25) and **Position** (-0.4, 0.75, -0.3) may work.
3. With the Cube selected, **Add Component** `MoveablePhysicsObject`.
4. Notice this will automatically add a `RigidBody` component if not present.
5. On the `RigidBody` component, uncheck the **Use Gravity** checkbox, so it hangs in the air rather than falling to the ground when you play.

Now when you press **Play**, use your controller so its laser beam hits the cube. Then, press the clicker button on your controller to grab it. Move it around and press again to release it.

Since the app is presently using the same button to create new balloons and manipulate the laser pointer, we get a balloon each time we use the button. Consider that a bug in your application. We will leave this as an exercise for you to implement the logic, for example, to tell *MyInputController* to not invoke events if the *MoveablePhysicsObject* is busy moving something.

 Hint: you could add a script component to Cube that checks the MoveablePhysicsObject state and disables MyInputController actions when the object is Selected. This is not well documented but look at the source code for MoveablePhysicsObjects.cs and its base class, BaseInteractiveObjects.cs.

To make the balloons throwable, we modify the prefab:

1. Drag a copy of the **Balloon** prefab from the **Project** window into the scene **Hierarchy**
2. **Add Component** the **MoveablePhysicsObject**
3. Click **Apply** to save the prefab
4. And delete the Balloon from Hierarchy

Press **Play**. Press the button to create and inflate a balloon. Release it. Then, try to grab it with the laser pointer. If you implemented the *Poppable* explosion earlier, it'll even explode like a projectile when it hits something!

# Summary

In this chapter, we explored a variety of software patterns for handling user input for your VR projects. The player uses a controller button to create, inflate, and release balloons into the scene. First, we tried the standard Input class for detecting logical button clicks, like the "Fire1" button, and then learned how to access device-specific SDK input, such as the OpenVR trigger button with haptic feedback.

In our scene, we implemented a simple input component for polling the button actions. Then, we refactored the code to use scriptable objects to hold the input action data. In the third implementation, we used Unity Events to message input actions to listening components. We also enhanced the scene to attach the balloon to your virtual hand position, and added the ability to pop the balloons as explosive projectiles! Lastly, we used an interactable framework (for SteamVR and Daydream) to implement grabbing and throwing mechanics, using components provided in given toolkits rather than attempting to write our own.

In the next chapter, we will further explore user interactions, using the Unity UI (user interface) system for implementing information canvases, buttons, and other UI controls.

# 6
# World Space UI

In the previous chapter, we discovered how to interact with game objects in the world space scene. Not only can these objects can be balls and toys, or tools and weapons, but they can be buttons you interact with and other user interface widgets. Furthermore, Unity includes a user interface canvas system for building menus and other UI.

**Graphical user interface** (**GUI**) or just UI, usually refers to on-screen two-dimensional graphics, which overlay the main gameplay and present information to the user with status messages, gauges, and input controls such as menus, buttons, sliders, and so on.

In Unity, UI elements always reside on a **canvas**. The Unity manual describes the `canvas` component as follows:

> *The* `canvas` *component represents the abstract space in which the UI is laid out and rendered. All UI elements must be children of a* `GameObject` *that has a* `canvas` *component attached.*

In conventional video games, UI objects are usually rendered in a **screen space** canvas as an overlay. The screen space UI is analogous to a piece of cardboard pasted on your TV or monitor, overlaying the game action behind it.

However, that doesn't work in VR. If you attempt to use screen space for UI in virtual reality, you'll run into issues. Since there are two stereographic cameras, you need separate views for each eye. While conventional games may co-opt the edges of the screen for UI, *virtual reality has no screen edges*!

Instead, in VR, we use various approaches that place the user interface elements in **World Space** rather than screen space. In this chapter, I characterize a number of these types. We'll define these types in detail and show you examples of them throughout this chapter:

- **Visor heads-up display**: In a visor **heads-up display** (**HUD**), the user interface canvas appears at the same spot in front of your eyes regardless of your head movement

- **Reticle cursors**: Similar to visor HUD, a crosshair or a pointer cursor is used to choose things in the scene
- **Windshield HUD**: This is a pop-up panel floating in 3D space like a windshield in a cockpit
- **Game element UI**: The canvas is in the scene as a part of the gameplay, like a scoreboard in a stadium
- **Info bubble**: This is a UI message that is attached to objects in the scene, like a thought bubble hovering over a character's head
- **In-game dashboard**: This is a control panel that is a part of the gameplay, usually at waist or desk height
- **Wrist-based menu palette**: With two-handed input controllers, one hand can hold a menu palette while the other makes selections and uses the selected tool

The differences in these UI techniques basically comes down to where and when you display the canvas and how the user interacts with it. In this chapter, we're going to try each of these in turn. Along the way, we'll also continue to explore user input with head movement and gestures as well as button clicks.

Note that some of the exercises in this chapter use the scene completed in Chapter 4, *Gaze-Based Control*, but are separate and not directly required by the other chapters in this book. If you decide to skip any of it or not save your work, that's OK.

# Studying VR design principles

Before we get into the implementation details, I would like to introduce the topic of designing 3D user interfaces and VR experiences. A lot of work has been done over the past few decades, and more so in the past few years.

With consumer VR devices so readily available, and powerful development tools like Unity, it's not surprising there are many people inventing and trying new things, innovating continuously, and producing really excellent VR experiences. You are probably one of them. But the context of today's VR is not a vacuum. There is a history of research and development that feeds into present-day work. The book *3D User Interfaces: Theory and Practice* (Bowman et al), for example, is a classic academic survey of 3D user interaction for consumer, industrial, and scientific applications and research. Originally published in 2004, the second edition was published in 2017 (LaViola et al) and is an up-to-date review of academic theory and practical principles.

Current writings for VR design are more accessible. An easy to read but practical introduction to VR user experience design is the Medium article *Get started with VR: user experience design* (https://medium.com/vrinflux-dot-com/get-started-with-vr-user-experience-design-974486cf9d18) by Adrienne Hunter, co-creator of the popular VR physics package, NewtonVR. She identifies some important core principles, including It's like theatre in the round, drawing attention with to objects, lighting, and audio cues, and designing space for height and accessibility.

Another great article is *Practical VR: A Design Cheat Sheet* (https://virtualrealitypop.com/practical-vr-ce80427e8e9d). This is intended to be a living primer with VR design guidelines, process, tools and other resources the author intends to maintain and update.

One of my favorite studies of design for VR is the *VR Interface Design Pre-Visualization Methods* produced by Mike Algers as a grad student in 2015. His inspiring video at https://vimeo.com/141330081 presents an easily digestible thesis of design principles, especially for seated VR experiences, based on established ergonomics of workspaces and visual perception. We'll use some of these ideas in this chapter. Algers also explores button design for VR, mockup workflows, and concepts for VR operating system design. (Algers presently works in the Google VR development group.)

In his thesis, Algers establishes a set of comfort zones radially around the user's first-person location, as shown:

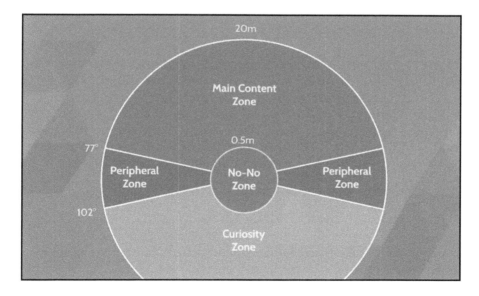

Anything closer than **0.5 m** is too close for comfort; you might have to cross your eyes just to focus and follow objects at that range. Beyond **20 m** is too far way to have meaningful interactions, and is also too far for depth perception with parallax. Your **Peripheral Zones** (**77–102** degrees) should not contain primary content and interactions but can have secondary ones. Behind you he calls the **Curiosity Zone**, you'd need to stretch (or swivel your chair or turn around) to see what's going on there so it'd better be important yet not imperative. The **Main Content Zone** is your normal workspace. Then, accounting for arm reach (forward, up, and down) and other normal human movement in a workspace, Algers defines the optimal virtual work zone for seated VR experience as shown:

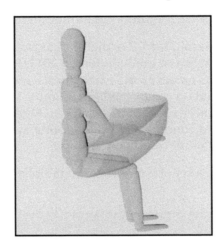

For standing and room-scale VR, the workspace is different. When standing, it may be much easier (and expected) to be able to turn around to access things all around you. With room-scale, you can walk around (and jump, duck, and crawl, for that matter). Alex Schwartz and Devin Reimer of Owlchemy Labs (since acquired by Google), in their talk at Oculus Connect 2 ( https://www.youtube.com/watch?v=hjc7AJwZ4DI), discuss the challenges of designing standing VR experiences for their popular Job Simulator, including accommodation for real-world ergonomics and varied height experiences.

Some other great resources on designing for virtual reality include:

- Oculus's series of articles on VR design best practices, including on user input (https://developer.oculus.com/design/latest/concepts/bp-userinput/) which includes recommendations on movement, button mapping, menus, and using your hands in VR.

- Leap Motion (we do not cover its hand-recognition technology in this book) has some great writings on VR design, which can be found at `https://developer.leapmotion.com/explorations`, including very good articles on interactive design (`http://blog.leapmotion.com/building-blocks-deep-dive-leap-motion-interactive-design/`) and user Interface Design (`http://blog.leapmotion.com/beyond-flatland-user-interface-design-vr/`).
- Google has produced a number of seminal examples, including *Daydream Labs: Lessons Learned from VR Prototyping - Google I/O 2016* (`https://www.youtube.com/watch?v=lGUmTQgbiAY`) and Daydream Elements (`https://developers.google.com/vr/elements/overview`).

Of course, this just scratches the surface; more is being published every day. Google it. A curated, living list of resources on user Interface Design and user experience in virtual reality can be found at The UX of VR site (`https://www.uxofvr.com/`).

Have fun reading and watching videos. Meanwhile, let's get back to work. It's time to implement some VR UI ourselves.

# A reusable default canvas

Unity's UI canvas provides lots of options and parameters to accommodate the kinds of graphical layout flexibility that we have come to expect not only in games but also from web and mobile apps. With this flexibility comes additional complexity. To make our examples in this chapter easier, we'll first build a reusable prefab canvas that has our preferred default settings.

Create a new canvas and change its **Render Mode** to **world space** as follows:

1. Navigate to **GameObject | UI | Canvas**
2. Rename the canvas as `DefaultCanvas`
3. Set **Render Mode** to **World Space**

The **Rect Transform** component defines the grid system on the canvas itself, like the lines on a piece of graph paper. It is used for the placement of UI elements on the canvas. Set it to a convenient `640 x 480`, with a `0.75` aspect ratio. The `Rect Transform` component's width and height are different from the world space size of the canvas in our scene. Let's configure the `Rect Transform` component using the following steps:

1. In `Rect Transform`, set the **Width** to `640` and the **Height** to `480`.

2. In **Scale**, set **X, Y, Z** to (0.00135, 0.00135, 0.00135). This is the size for one of our pixels in world space units.

3. Now, position the canvas centered on the ground plane one unit above (0.325 is half of 0.75). In **Rect Transform**, set **Pos X, Pos Y, Pos Z** to (0, 1.325, 0).

Next, we will add an empty Image element (with a white background) to help us visualize the otherwise transparent canvas and provide an opaque background for the canvas when we need one (we can also use a Panel UI element):

1. With DefaultCanvas selected, navigate to **GameObject | UI | Image** (ensure that it's created as a child of DefaultCanvas; if not, move it under DefaultCanvas).

2. With the **Image** selected, on the upper left of its **Rect Transform** pane, there is an **anchor presets** button (shown in the following screenshot). Selecting it opens the **anchor presets** dialog box. Press and hold the *Alt* key to see the **stretch** and **position** options and choose the one in the bottom-right corner (**stretch-stretch**). Now, the (blank) image is stretched to fill the canvas:

3. Double-check your **Image** settings based on the default properties for the `Image` child of the `DefaultCanvas` as shown in the following screenshot:

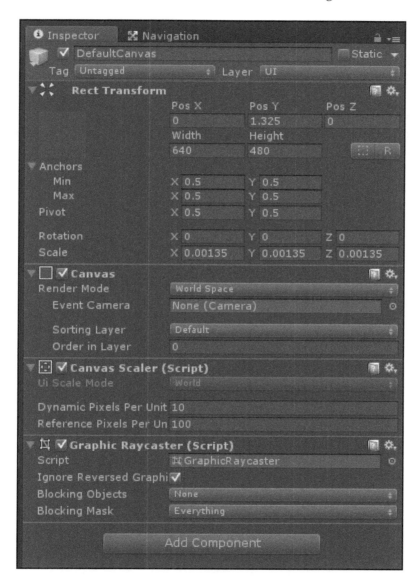

Add a `Text` element with useful default settings, as follows:

1. With `DefaultCanvas` selected, navigate to **GameObject | UI | Text** (ensure that it's created as a child of `DefaultCanvas` (if not, move it under `DefaultCanvas`). The words `New Text` should appear on the canvas.
2. With the **Text** selected, set **Alignment** to **Center Align** and **Middle Align** and set **Vertical Overflow** to **Overflow**. Set the **Scale** to (4, 4, 4).
3. Set its **anchor presets** button to (**stretch - stretch**) using the widget on the upper left of its **Rect Transform** pane.
4. Double-check your **Text** settings based on the default properties for the `Text` child of the `DefaultCanvas` as shown in the following screenshot:

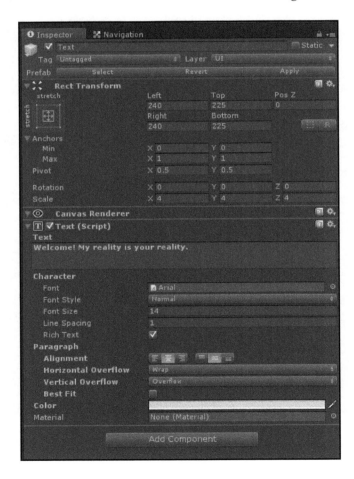

Increase the pixel resolution to give cleaner text fonts by keeping `DefaultCanvas` selected and setting the **Canvas Scaler | Dynamic Pixels Per Unit** to `10`.

Finally, save your work as a prefab asset that you can reuse throughout the chapter in the following manner:

1. If necessary, in **Project Assets**, create a new folder named `Prefabs`.
2. Drag the `DefaultCanvas` object into the `Project Assets/Prefabs` folder to create a prefab.
3. Delete the `DefaultCanvas` instance in the **Hierarchy** panel now.

OK, glad we got that out of the way! Now we can use the `DefaultCanvas` prefab with different VR user interfaces.

> A canvas has a `Rect Transform` component, which defines the grid system on the canvas itself, like the lines on a piece of graph paper. It is used for the placement of UI elements on the canvas. This is different from the size and position of a canvas object in world space.

# Visor HUD

A heads-up display, or HUD, is a floating canvas in your field of view that overlays the gameplay scene. In VR vernacular, there are two variations of HUDs. I'll call these variations the *visor HUD* and the *windshield HUD*. This section looks at the first one.

In visor HUD, the UI canvas is attached to the camera. It doesn't appear to respond to your head movement. When you move your head, it appears to be *stuck to your face*. Let's look at a nicer way of visualizing it. Suppose you're wearing a helmet with a visor, and the UI appears projected onto the surface of that visor. There may be contexts where this is OK in virtual reality, but it is likely to break the sense of immersion. So, it should generally only be used either when the visor is a part of the gameplay, or if the intent is to take you out of the scene, such as the utility menus for the hardware or the system.

Let's make a visor HUD with a welcome message as follows, and see for ourselves how it feels:

1. In the **Hierarchy** panel, unfold the `MeMyselfEye` object and then drill down to the `Main Camera` object (for OpenVR that might be `[CameraRig]/Camera (head)`; for Daydream, it may be `Player/Main Camera/`).

2. From the **Project** panel, drag the `DefaultCanvas` prefab onto the camera object so that it becomes a child of it.

3. In the **Hierarchy** panel, with the canvas selected, rename the canvas to `VisorCanvas`.

4. In the **Inspector** panel for the canvas, change the `Rect Transform` component's **Pos X, Pos Y, Pos Z** to (0, 0, 1).

5. Unfold `VisorCanvas` and select the child `Text` object.

6. In the **Inspector** panel, change the text from **Default Text** to **Welcome! My reality is your reality**. (You can enter line breaks in the input text area.)

7. Change the text color to something bright, such as green.

8. Disable the `Image` object so that only the text shows by unchecking its **Enable** checkbox in **Inspector**.

9. Save the scene, and try it in VR.

Here's a capture of the Rift screen with the `VisorCanvas`:

In VR, when you move your head around, the text follows along as if it's attached to a visor in front of your face.

A visor HUD canvas and reticle cursor canvas are set as a child object of the camera.

Now, go ahead and either disable `VisorCanvas` or just delete it (in the **Hierarchy** panel, right-click on it and click on **Delete**) because we're going to display the welcome message in a different way in a later section. Next, we'll look at a different application of this technique.

# The reticle cursor

A variant of the visor HUD that is essential in first-person shooter games is a *reticle* or crosshair cursor. The analogy here is that you're looking through a gun-sight or an eyepiece (rather than a visor) and your head movement is moving in unison with the gun or turret itself. You can do this with a regular game object (for example, Quad + texture image), but this chapter is about UI. So, let's use our canvas, as follows:

1. Find your **Main Camera** object in the **Hierarchy** panel as we did previously.
2. From the **Project** panel, drag the `DefaultCanvas` prefab onto the camera object so that it becomes a child of the camera. Name it `ReticleCursor`.
3. Set the **Rect Transform** component's **Pos X**, **Pos Y**, **Pos Z** to (0, 0, 1).
4. Delete its child objects: `Image` and `Text`. This will *break* the prefab association; that's OK.
5. Add a raw image child by selecting it from the main menu bar, navigating through **GameObject | UI | Raw Image** and making sure that it's a child of `ReticleCursor`.
6. In the **Raw Image** panel's **Rect Transform**, set **Pos X**, **Pos Y**, **Pos Z** to (0, 0, 0) and the **Width** and **Height** to (22, 22). Then, choose a noticeable **Color** such as red in the **Raw Image** (**Script**) properties.
7. Save the scene and try it in VR.

If you'd like a nicer-looking reticle, in the **Raw Image** (**Script**) properties, populate the **Texture** field with a cursor image. For example, click on the tiny *circle* icon on the far right of the **Texture** field. This opens the **Select Texture** dialog. Find and select a suitable one, such as the `Crosshair` image. (A copy of `Crosshair.gif` is included with this book.) Just be sure to change the **Width** and **Height** to the size of your image (`Crosshair.gif` is 22 x 22 in size) and ensure that the **Anchor** is set to **middle-center**.

We set the canvas position **Pos Z** to `1.0` so that the reticle floats in front of you at a 1-meter distance. A fixed distance cursor is fine in many UI situations, like when you're picking something from a flat canvas that is also at a fixed distance from you.

However, this is world space. If another object is between you and the reticle, the reticle will be obfuscated.

Also, if you look at something much farther away, you'll refocus your eyes and have trouble viewing the cursor at the same time. To emphasize this problem, try moving the cursor closer. For example, if you change the **Pos Z** of the `ReticleCursor` to `0.5` or less, you might have to go cross-eyed to see it! To compensate for these issues, we can ray cast and move the cursor to the actual distance of the object that you're looking at, resizing the cursor accordingly so that it appears to stay the same size. Here's a cheap version of this idea:

1. With `ReticleCursor` selected, click on **Add Component** | **New Script**, name it `CursorPositioner` and click on **Create** and **Add**.
2. Open the script in MonoDevelop by double-clicking on the name.

Here's the `CursorPositioner.cs` script:

```
using UnityEngine;
using UnityEngine.EventSystems;
using System.Collections;

public class CursorPositioner : MonoBehaviour {
  private float defaultPosZ;

  void Start () {
    defaultPosZ = transform.localPosition.z;
  }

  void Update () {
    Transform camera = Camera.main.transform;
    Ray ray = new Ray (camera.position, camera.rotation *
      Vector3.forward);
    RaycastHit hit;
```

```
    if (Physics.Raycast (ray, out hit)) {
      if (hit.distance <= defaultPosZ) {
        transform.localPosition = new Vector3(0, 0, hit.distance);
      } else {
        transform.localPosition = new Vector3(0, 0, defaultPosZ);
      }
    }
  }
}
```

The **Rect Transform** component's **Pos Z** is found in the script in `transform.localPosition`. This script changes it to `hit.distance` if it's less than the given **Pos Z**. Now, you can also move the reticle to a more comfortable distance, such as **Pos Z** = 2.

An excellent tutorial by @eVRydayVR shows how to implement both distance and size compensated world space reticles. You can visit `https://www.youtube.com/watch?v=LLKYbwNnKDg`, which is a video titled Oculus Rift DK2 - Unity Tutorial: Reticle.

We just implemented our own cursor reticle, but many VR SDKs now also provide cursors. For example, in Google VR, the `GvrReticlePointer.cs` script is a more thorough implementation. Another example, the Oculus OVR package, includes a `Cursor_Timer` prefab you can use as a Loading... indicator cursor.

# The windshield HUD

The term *heads-up display*, or HUD, originates from its use in aircrafts, where a pilot is able to view information with their head positioned in such a way that they are looking forward rather down at their instrument panels. Owing to this usage, I'll refer it as *windshield HUD*. Like visor HUD, the information panel overlays the gameplay, but it isn't attached to your head. Instead, you can think of it as being attached to your seat while you are in a cockpit or at the dentist.

A visor HUD is like the UI canvas—it is attached to your head. A windshield HUD is like it's attached to a glass dome around you.

Let's create a simple windshield HUD by performing the following steps:

1. From the **Project** panel, drag the `DefaultCanvas` prefab onto the `MeMyselfEye` object in the **Hierarchy** panel so that it becomes an immediate child of `MeMyselfEye` (not under the camera this time).
2. Rename it to `WindshieldCanvas`.
3. With `WindshieldCanvas` selected, set the **Rect Transform** component's **Pos X**, **Pos Y**, **Pos Z** to (0, 1.4, 1).

4. Now, we'll set the **Text** component. With **Text** under `WindshieldCanvas` selected, change the text to **Welcome! My reality is your reality**. Also, change the color to something bright, such as green.
5. This time, we'll make the panel translucent. Select the image from **Image** under `WindshieldCanvas` and select its color swatch. Then in the **Color** dialog, modify the `Alpha ("A")` channel from `255` to about `115`.

That's pretty straightforward. When you view it in VR, the canvas starts out just in front of you, but as you look around, its position seems to remain stationary and relative to the other objects in the scene, as shown in the following screenshot:

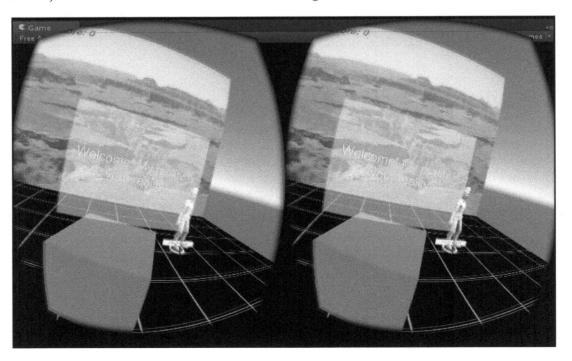

As we'll see in the next chapter, Chapter 7, *Locomotion and Comfort*, when a first-person character moves through the scene, the HUD canvas will stay in front of you, at the same relative position to your body object, MeMyselfEye. You can try it now in the editor:

1. Select MeMyselfEye in **Hierarchy**.

2. Press **Play**.

3. Then in the **Scene** window, using the **Move gizmo**, move the MeMyselfEye position. In VR, you'll see the HUD follows along like it's part of your body or a spaceship's cockpit.

You might have realized that it's possible for objects in the scene to obfuscate the HUD panel since they're all occupying the same world space. If you need to prevent this, you have to ensure that the canvas is always rendered last so that it appears in front of any other objects regardless of its position in 3D space. In a conventional monoscopic game, you can do this by adding a second camera for the UI and changing its render priority. In stereoscopic VR, you have to accomplish this differently, possibly by writing a custom shader for your UI object or doing per-layer occlusion culling. This is an advanced topic; see the *World Space canvas on top of everything?* discussion thread for details: https://answers.unity.com/questions/878667/world-space-canvas-on-top-of-everything.html.

A variant of this HUD is to turn the canvas so that it's always facing you, while its position in 3D space is fixed. See the *Info bubble* section of this chapter to learn how to code this.

For kicks, let's write a script that removes the welcome message canvas after 15 seconds, as follows:

1. With WindshieldCanvas selected, click on **Add Component | New Script**, name the script as DestroyTimeout, and click on **Create** and **Add**.
2. Open the script in MonoDevelop.

Here's the DestroyTimeout.cs script:

```
using UnityEngine;

public class DestroyTimeout : MonoBehaviour
{
    public float timer = 15f;
```

```
  void Start ()
  {
    Destroy (gameObject, timer);
  }
}
```

The `WindshieldCanvas` will disappear after the timer runs out when the game starts up.

 A windshield HUD canvas is set as a child object of the first-person avatar, a sibling object of the camera.

In this example, we start to move further towards a first-person experience. Imagine sitting in a car or the cockpit of an aircraft. The HUD is projected on the windshield in front of you, but you're free to move your head to look around. In the scene's **Hierarchy** panel, there's a first-person object (`MeMyselfEye`) that contains the camera rig, possibly your avatar body, and the other furnishings surrounding you. When the vehicle moves in the game, the entire cockpit moves in unison, including the camera rig and the windshield. We'll work with this more later in this chapter and `Chapter 7`, *Playing with Physics and Fire*.

# The game element UI

When Ethan gets killed in the Diorama scene from `Chapter 4`, *Gaze-Based Control*, the score value in the `GameController` object's `KillTarget` script is updated, but we don't show the current score to the player (set up in that chapter). We'll do this now, adding a scoreboard into the scene at the top-left corner of the backdrop `PhotoPlane` image:

1. From the **Project** panel, drag the `DefaultCanvas` prefab directly into the **Scene** view
2. Rename it `ScoreBoard`
3. With `ScoreBoard` selected, set the **Rect Transform** component's **Pos X, Pos Y, Pos Z** to (-2.8, 7, 4.9) and the **Width** and **Height** to (3000, 480)
4. With **Text** under `ScoreBoard` selected, set the **Font Size** to 100 and choose a noticeable color such as red for the **Text**
5. Enter the **Score: 0** sample string for **Text**
6. Disable **Image** under `ScoreBoard` by unchecking the **Enable** check box or deleting it

We have added another canvas to the scene, sized and placed it where we want, and formatted the text for display. It should look like this:

Now, we need to update the `KillTarget.cs` script, as follows:

- We may be using the UnityEngine UI classes:

```
using UnityEngine.UI;
```

- Add a public variable for `scoreText`:

```
public Text scoreText;
```

- Add a line to `Start()` to initialize the score text:

```
scoreText.text = "Score: 0";
```

- And add a line to `Update()` to change the score text when the score changes:

```
score += 1;
scoreText.text = "Score: " + score;
```

After saving the script file, go back into the Unity editor, select `GameController` in the **Hierarchy** panel, and then drag and drop the **Text** object under `ScoreBoard` from **Hierarchy** onto the **Score Text** field in **Kill Target (Script)**.

Run the scene in VR. Each time you kill Ethan (by staring at him), your score will be updated on the `ScoreBoard` on the upper left of `PhotoPlane`.

A game element UI canvas is a part of the scene like any other game object.

This was an example of using an object that's a part of the scene for information display. Our example is pretty simplistic. You might want to make a nicer modeled scoreboard, like the one you'd see in a stadium or something. The point is, it's a part of the scene and to see the message you might have to actually turn your head and, well, look at it.

# Using TextMeshPro

To make a billboard glow like a neon sign, you can use TextMesh Pro which presently comes included free with Unity. For instance:

1. With `ScoreBoard` selected in Hierarchy, create a new `TextMesh` text element (right-click **UI | TextMeshPro - Text**).
2. This replaces our standard UI text element, so disable the `Text` object.
3. On the TMP text, set its **Font Asset** to **Bangers SDF**.
4. For its **Material Preset**, use **Bangers SDF Glow**.
5. Scroll to **Glow** settings to adjust the colors and other settings as you desire.

You can even write a script that cyclically modifies the glow settings to make a flashing, glowing sign!

If you choose to try this, be sure to update the GameController's `KillTarget` script to use the TMP object rather than the UI one. Modify `KillTarget.cs` as follows:

We may be using the UnityEngine TextMesh Pro classes:

```
using TMP;
```

Replace the data type of the `scoreText` variable with `TMP_Text`:

```
public TMP_Text scoreText;
```

Drag the TMP text item onto the slot in the Inspector. The rest of the script is unchanged since `TMP_Text` has a `text` property just as the UI text one has.

**TextMesh Pro** is a great tool for text formatting and layout in Unity. It is a replacement for Unity's UI Text, with added advanced text rendering, custom shaders, typographic controls such as paragraph spacing and kerning, and a lot more. It was a third-party plugin and is now included free with Unity. Documentation can be found here: `http://digitalnativestudios.com/textmeshpro/docs/`.

Here is a screenshot of the scoreboard text using a glow effect with TextMesh Pro and its Inspector settings:

# Info bubble

In a comic book, when a character says something, it's shown in a *speech bubble*. In many online social VR worlds, participants are represented by avatars and, hovering above someone's avatar, their name is displayed. I'll call this type of user interface an *info bubble*.

Info bubbles are located in world space at a specific 3D position, but the canvas should always be facing the camera. We can ensure this with a script.

In this example, we'll display the **X, Z** location of the `WalkTarget` object (set up in Chapter 4, *Gaze-Based Control*), controlled by the `LookMoveTo.cs` script. To add the info bubble, perform the following steps:

1. From the **Project** window, drag the `DefaultCanvas` prefab directly into the **Hierarchy** window so that it's a child of `WalkTarget`.
2. Rename it to `InfoBubble`.
3. With `InfoBubble` selected, set the **Rect Transform** component's **Pos X, Pos Y, Pos Z** to (0, 0.2, 0).
4. With **Text** under `InfoBubble` selected, set the **Rect Transform** component's **Pos X, Pos Y, Pos Z** to (0, 0, 0) and **Right** and **Bottom** to 0, 0.
5. With **Image** under `InfoBubble` selected, set **Scale** to (0.7, 0.2, 1).
6. Enter the `X:00.00, Z:00.00` sample string for **Text**.

Verify that the canvas and text look roughly the right size and position and adjust the text as you please. (In my scene, there's a cube at the origin so I temporarily disable it to see the WalkTarget also at the origin.)

Now, we will modify the `LookMoveTo.cs` script to show the current `WalkTarget` **X, Z** position. Open the script in the MonoDevelop editor and add the following code:

```
using UnityEngine;
using UnityEngine.UI;

public class LookMoveTo : MonoBehaviour
{
  public GameObject ground;
  public Transform infoBubble;

  private Text infoText;

  void Start ()
  {
    if (infoBubble != null)
    {
      infoText = infoBubble.Find ("Text").GetComponent<Text> ();
    }
  }

  void Update ()
  {
    Transform camera = Camera.main.transform;
    Ray ray;
    RaycastHit[] hits;
```

```
GameObject hitObject;

ray = new Ray (camera.position, camera.rotation * Vector3.forward);
hits = Physics.RaycastAll (ray);
for (int i=0; i < hits.Length; i++)
{
  RaycastHit hit = hits [i];
  hitObject = hit.collider.gameObject;
  if (hitObject == ground)
  {
    if (infoBubble != null)
    {
      infoText.text = "X: " + hit.point.x.ToString("F2") +
                      "Z: " + hit.point.z.ToString("F2");

      infoBubble.LookAt (camera.position);
      infoBubble.Rotate (0, 180f, 0);
    }
    transform.position = hit.point;
  }
}
}
}
```

The line `using UnityEngine.UI;` states that this script will need access to the Unity UI API. We defined a `public Transform infoBubble` variable, which will be set to the `WalkTarget/InfoBubble` object. We also defined a `private Text infoText` variable, which gets set to the `InfoBubble` object's **Text** object. The script assumes that the given `InfoBubble` has a child **Text** UI object.

Unfortunately, the overuse of the word *text* can be confusing. The `infoText` *text* object has a *text* component, which has a *text* string property! You can see what I mean in Unity editor. If you examine the Inspector panel while `InfoBubble/Text` is selected, you'll see that it contains a **Text** (**Script**) component, which has a **Text** field. This **Text** field is where we write our messages. So in `Setup()`, we find the `WalkTarget/InfoBubble/Text` object, assigning the **Text** object to `infoText`, and then in `Update()`, we set the string value of `infoText.text` so that the score is shown on the bubble canvas.

Also, in `Update()`, we transformed the `infoBubble` canvas so that it's always facing us using `infoBubble.LookAt()` and passing it the camera position. The result of `LookAt()` has the canvas facing away from us. So, we also need to rotate it around the *y* axis by 180 degrees.

Save the script and drag the `InfoBubble` object from **Hierarchy** onto the **Info Bubble** slot in the **Look Move To** (**Script**) component. If you don't assign the `InfoBubble` canvas, the script will still run because we test for `null` objects before we reference them.

 An info bubble UI canvas is attached to other game objects, moving when they move and always facing the camera (like a billboard).

Run the scene in VR and you'll see that `WalkTarget` has a little info bubble telling us about its **X**, **Z** position.

 Extra challenge: Want to try something else? Implement a health meter bar for Ethan. Use the `countDown` variable in the `KillTarget` script to determine his percentage of health and to display a health meter (horizontal bar) above his head when it's not at 100 percent.

Info bubbles are useful when you need to display UI messages that belong to specific objects in the scene and may move in concert with the objects.

# An in-game dashboard with input events

An in-game dashboard or control panel is a UI display that is integrated into the game itself. A typical scenario is an automobile or a spaceship, where you are seated in a cockpit. At waist level (desk level) is a panel with a set of controls, gauges, information displays, and so on. Dashboards generally feel more natural in a seated VR experience.

A few pages back, we discussed windshield HUDs. Dashboards are pretty much the same thing. One difference is that the dashboard may be more obviously part of the level environment and not simply an auxiliary information display or a menu.

In fact, dashboards can be a very effective mechanism to control VR motion sickness. Researchers have found that when a VR user has a better sense of being grounded and has a consistent *horizon line* in view, he's much less likely to experience nausea while moving around a virtual space. In contrast, being a floating one-dimensional eyeball with no sense of self or grounding is asking for trouble! (See the *Oculus Best Practices* for this, and other great tips, by visiting
https://developer.oculus.com/documentation/intro-vr/latest/concepts/bp_intro/).

In this example, we'll make a simple dashboard with Start/Stop buttons. For now, the buttons will operate a water hose in the scene to help fend off the zombies. (*Why not?*) Like other examples in this chapter, this project uses the scene created in `Chapter 4`, *Gaze-Based Control*.

This project is a bit more complicated than you might expect. However, if you've ever had to build anything in Minecraft, you know that even the simple things may require assembling multiple parts. Here's what we will do:

- Create a dashboard canvas with two functional buttons—Start and Stop
- Add a water hose to the scene and wire it to the buttons
- Write a simple version of the script that activates the buttons
- Highlight a button by looking at it
- Improve the script to activate the button only if it's highlighted

So let's get to it.

# Creating a dashboard with buttons

First, let's create a dashboard with a Start and a Stop button, as follows:

1. From the **Project** window, drag the `DefaultCanvas` prefab onto the `MeMyselfEye` object in the **Hierarchy** panel so that it becomes a child.
2. Rename it to `Dashboard`.
3. With `Dashboard` selected, set the **Rect Transform** component's **Pos X, Pos Y, Pos Z** to (0, 0.6, 0.6) and its **Rotation** to (60, 0, 0). Feel free to adjust the position for preferred comfort zone and your specific VR device camera rig.
4. Disable or delete the **Text** child object of `Dashboard`.

This places the dashboard 1 m below your eyes and a little out in front.

For a *work-in-progress* look, if you'd like, I've included an image sketch of a vehicle dashboard that you can use, as follows:

1. Import the `DashboardSketch.png` file into your **Project** (such as the `Assets/Textures` folder).
2. Add a new **GameObject | UI | Raw Image** as a child of `Dashboard`.
3. Drag the `DashboardSketch` texture from the **Project** panel onto the **Texture** field of the **Raw Image** component.

4. Set its **Rect Transform** component's **Pos X, Pos Y, Pos Z** to (0,0,0), **Width** to 140, and **Height** to 105.

5. It should be **Anchored** at **middle-center** (0.5,0.5) in **X**, **Y**, and **Pivot**, with **Rotation** (0,0,0).

6. Set **Scale** to (4.5,4.5,4.5).

Next, we will add the Start and Stop buttons. They can go anywhere you'd like on the canvas, but the sketch has two nice spaces predefined for them:

1. Add a new **GameObject | UI | Button** as a new child of Dashboard. Name it StartButton.

2. Set its **Rect Transform** component's **X, Y, Z** to (-48, 117, 0), the **Width** and **Height** to (60, 60), and **Anchored** to **center-middle** (0.5). No **Rotation** and **Scale** of 1.

3. In the button's **Image (Script)** component pane, for **Source Image**, click on the tiny circle on the far right to open the **Select Sprite** picker and choose ButtonAcceleratorUpSprite (which you may have imported into the Assets/Standard Assets/CrossPlatformInput/Sprites folder).

4. In the button's **Button (Script)** component pane, for the **Normal Color**, I used RGB (89,154,43) and set **Highlighted Color** to (105, 255, 0).

5. Similarly, create another button named StopButton with the **Rect Transform** component's **X, Y, Z** (52, 118, 0) and set the **Width** and **Height** to (60, 60). For **Source Image**, select ButtonBrakeOverSprite, then choose the **Normal Color** (236, 141, 141) and **Highlighted Color** (235, 45, 0).

The result should look like this:

One last thing. If you're using the `ReticleCursor` that was created earlier in this chapter with the `CursorPositioner.cs` script, we want the dashboard itself to have a collider for the script. We can achieve this by performing the following steps:

1. With `Dashboard` selected, right-click for options, and navigate to **3D Object | Plane**.
2. Set its **Position** to (0,0,0), **Rotation** to (270,0,0), and **Scale** to (64,1,48).
3. Disable its **Mesh Renderer** (but leave its **Mesh Collider** enabled).

Now the dashboard has a plane child that isn't rendered, but its collider will be detected when `CursorPositioner` does its ray cast. We do this to see your gaze on this dashboard panel rather than the ground below even when not looking directly at a button.

Having a single toggle button with pressed and released states might be better than separate **Start** and **Stop** buttons. When you're done with this chapter, go ahead and figure out how to do it!

We just created a world space canvas that should appear in VR at waist or desk level. We decorated it with a dashboard sketch and added two UI buttons. Now, we'll wire up the buttons to specific events.

# Linking the water hose to the buttons

Let's first give the buttons something to do, such as the action of turning on a water hose. If we aim it strategically, it might even fend off rogue zombies. Coincidentally, the Unity **Particle Systems** under **Standard Assets** which we imported earlier has a water hose that we can use. Add it to the scene as follows:

1. If you haven't done so already, import the **Particle Systems** standard asset from the main menu bar by navigating to **Assets | Import Package | ParticleSystems**.
2. In the **Project** window, find the `Assets/Standard Assets/Particle Systems/Prefabs/Hose` prefab and drag it into the **Hierarchy** window.
3. Set its **Transform** component's **X, Y, Z** to (–3, 0, 1.5) and **Rotation** to (340, 87, 0).
4. Ensure that **Hose** is enabled (check its **Enable** checkbox).
5. Unfold the **Hose** in **Hierarchy** so that you can see its child **WaterShower** particle system. Select it.
6. In **Inspector**, in the **Particle System** properties pane, look for **Play On Awake** and uncheck it.

Note that the **Hose** object in **Hierarchy** has a `WaterShower` child object. This is the actual particle system that we will control with the buttons. It should start as *off*.

The **Hose** prefab itself comes with mouse-driven script that we don't want to use, so disable it as follows:

1. With **Hose** selected, disable (uncheck) its **Hose (Script)**.
2. Also, disable (uncheck) the **Simple Mouse Rotator (Script)** component.

Now we will wire up `StartButton` to the **WaterShower** particle system by telling the buttons to listen for the `OnClick()` events, as follows:

1. Unfold the **Hose** in **Hierarchy** so that you can see its child **WaterShower** particle system.
2. In **Hierarchy**, select `StartButton` (under `MeMyselfEye/Dashboard`).
3. Note that in the **Inspector,** the **On Click()** pane of the `Button` component is empty. Click on the *Plus* (+) icon on the lower right of that pane to reveal a new field labeled **None (Object)**.
4. Drag the **WaterShower** particle system from **Hierarchy** onto the **None (Object)** field.
5. Its function selector, the default value, is **No Function**. Change it to **ParticleSystem | Play()**.

OK. The steps are similar for the `StopButton`, as follows:

1. In **Hierarchy**, select `StopButton`.
2. Click on the *Plus* (+) icon on the lower right of it's **On Click()** pane.
3. Drag the **WaterShower** from **Hierarchy** onto the **None (Object)** field.
4. Its function selector, the default value, is **No Function**. Change it to **ParticleSystem | Stop()**.

The Start and Stop buttons *listen for* `OnClick()` *events*, and when one comes, it will call the **WaterShower** particle system's `Play()` and `Stop()` functions respectively. To make it work, we need to press the buttons.

# Activating buttons from the script

Before we give the user a way to press the buttons, let's see how we can do this from a script. Create a new script on GameController, as follows:

1. With GameController selected in Hierarchy, press **Add Component** | **New Script** to create a script named ButtonExecuteTest.
2. Open the script in MonoDevelop.

In the following script, we turn the hose on and off in five-second intervals, as follows:

```
using UnityEngine;
using UnityEngine.UI;

public class ButtonExecuteTest : MonoBehaviour
{
  public Button startButton;
  public Button stopButton;

  private bool isOn = false;
  private float timer = 5.0f;
  void Update ()
  {
    timer -= Time.deltaTime;
    if (timer < 0.0f)
    {
      isOn = !isOn;
      timer = 5.0f;

      if (isOn)
      {
        stopButton.onClick.Invoke();
      } else
      {
        startButton.onClick.Invoke();
      }
    }
  }
}
```

The script manages a Boolean isOn value, which says if the hose is on or off. And it has a timer which counts down from 5 seconds on each update. We use the private keyword for variables that are only used within this script, whereas the public ones can be viewed and modified via the Unity editor and other scripts. For startButton and stopButton, you'll drag and drop them in the Unity editor.

In this script, we use the `UnityEngine.UI`. As we saw in the previous chapter, *Events* are a way for different components to talk to one another. When an event occurs, such as a button press, a function in another script may get called. In our case, we're going to trigger an event corresponding to the start button press, and another corresponding to the stop button press, as we set up in the Inspector.

Save the script and click on **Play**. The hose should turn on and off every five seconds.

Now that we have tested the event system connection between the button clicks and the hose, we can disable this script before moving on to the next one:

1. With `GameController` selected,
2. Disable the `ButtonExecuteTest` component by unchecking its **Enable** checkbox, or remove the component.

 Breaking down a complex feature into bite-sized pieces and testing them separately is an excellent implementation strategy.

# Look to highlight a button

Meanwhile, let's detect when the user is looking at a button and highlight it. Although **Button** is a Unity UI object, it needs to be detected with a ray cast. There may be other ways to accomplish this, as discussed later in this chapter, but here we will add a game object sphere to each button and cast a ray to detect it. First, add the spheres by performing the following steps:

1. In the **Hierarchy** panel, select `StartButton` (under `MeMyselfEye/Dashboard`), right-click for options, and navigate to **3D Object | Sphere**.
2. Set its **Transform** component's **Scale** to (52, 52, 52) so that it fits the button size.
3. Disable the sphere's **Mesh Renderer** by unchecking the **Mesh Renderer** checkbox.

Also, repeat these steps for `StopButton`. A shortcut is to duplicate the sphere, as follows:

1. Right-click the Sphere and choose **Duplicate**.
2. Drag the duplicated item (`Sphere (1)`) into `StopButton`.
3. Reset it **Position** to (0,0,0).

Now, create a new script on StartButton, as follows:

1. With StartButton selected, navigate to **Add Component** | **New Script** to create a script named RespondToGaze.
2. Open the script for editing.

In the following RespondToGaze.cs script, we tell the button to become highlighted when you look at it, using the child Sphere object's collider:

```csharp
using UnityEngine;
using UnityEngine.UI;

public class RespondtoGaze : MonoBehaviour
{
  public bool highlight = true;
  private Button button;
  private bool isSelected;

  void Start ()
  {
    button = GetComponent<Button>();
  }

  void Update ()
  {
    isSelected = false;
    Transform camera = Camera.main.transform;
    Ray ray = new Ray(camera.position, camera.rotation * Vector3.forward);
    RaycastHit hit;
    if (Physics.Raycast (ray, out hit) &&
        (hit.transform.parent != null) &&
        (hit.transform.parent.gameObject == gameObject)
    {
      isSelected = true;
    }

    if (isSelected)
    {
      if (highlight)
        button.Select();
    }
    else {
UnityEngine.EventSystems.EventSystem.current.SetSelectedGameObject(null);
    }
  }
}
```

In this script, on each update, we cast a ray from the camera. If it hits this button's sphere collider, then the hit object's parent should be this button. So (after checking that the hit object has a parent), we compare the parent gameObject to this button's gameObject.

If the gaze has selected this button, we trigger the button's **Select** to make it highlight. The highlighting is done within Unity's EventSystem. While the EventSystem has all this implemented for mouse clicks and screen touches, we have to manually tell the button it's been selected by calling button.Select().

Unhighlighting the button is not so obvious. The EventSystem maintains a currently selected object across your runtime scene. We clear it by passing null to SetSelectedGameObject().

Save the script and *Play*. When you gaze at a button, it should highlight, and when you gaze away from it, it should remove the highlight.

This is also an example of a reusable component script. We just wrote and tested it for the StartButton. We can use the same script for the StopButton:

1. Select the **StopButton** from the **Hierarchy**.
2. Drag the **RespondToGaze** script from the **Project Assets** onto the button, or
3. Select **Add Component | Scripts | RespondToGaze**.

Test the project one more time. Both buttons should highlight when you gaze at them.

 If you are using Google VR for Cardboard or Daydream, you can include the GvrEventSystem prefab in your scene. Then this RespondToGaze script becomes unnecessary and redundant. The Daydream component already supports gaze-based select, highlight, and clicking with the input controller. But I encourage you to follow along with this project nonetheless to experience how this functionality can be implemented. If so, temporarily disable GvrEventSystem in your scene.

# Looking and then clicking to select

To be a functional dashboard, the buttons should operate when they're clicked. In Chapter 5, *Handy Interactables*, we explored the Unity Input system, including the "Fire1" event and other hand controller buttons. You may want to review that now. And choose which code snippet you want to use, if not the basic Input.GetButtonDown("Fire1").

The changes to make to the `RespondToGaze.cs` script are pretty simple. At top of the class, add the following public variables:

```
public bool clicker = true;
public string inputButton = "Fire1";
```

At the bottom of `Update()`, make the following changes:

```
...
if (isSelected)
{
  if (highlight)
      button.Select();
  if (clicker && InputGetButtonDown("Fire1"))
      button.onClick.Invoke();
}
```

When the controller `"Fire1"` button is pressed, it will trigger a click of the UI button.

The component gives you the option to enable highlights and/or clicking with the input controller. You can also choose the logical input button that will trigger the click events.

We now have an in-game dashboard with buttons that respond to user input, which controls the behavior of an object (water hose) in the scene.

# Looking and starting to select

Instead of using a clicker, we can use a time-based selection to click on the button. To make this work, we'll keep a countdown timer while staring at a button, much like the one that we used to kill Ethan in the previous chapter.

Change the `RespondToGaze.cs` script. At top of the class, add the following variables:

```
public bool timedClick = true;
public float delay = 2.0f;

private float timer = 0f;
```

In `Update()`, make the following changes:

```
...
  if (isSelected)
  {
    if (highlight)
        button.Select();
```

```
    if (clicker && Input.GetButtonDown("Fire1"))
       button.onClick.Invoke();
    if (timedClick)
    {
      timer += Time.deltaTime;
      if (timer >= delay)
        button.onClick.Invoke();
  }
  else {
 UnityEngine.EventSystems.EventSystem.current.SetSelectedGameObject(null);
    timer = 0f;
  }
```

Now, not only will a button click get involved on `Input.GetButtonDown`, but also if you gaze at the button long enough (when `timedClick` is `true`). We begin a timer when the button is selected (highlighted) and count up. When the timer expires the click event is invoked. If the button is deselected before then, the timer is reset to zero.

*Does it work for you? Woohoo!*

So this was a relatively complex project. The goal was to create a dashboard with buttons that turn a hose on and off. We broke it down into discrete steps, added the objects and components a step at a time, and tested each step to make sure that it worked as expected before moving on. If you tried to implement this all at once or blew through it without testing, things can (and will) go wrong, and it'll be much harder to figure out where the problem cropped up.

 Extra challenge: This feature can be further enhanced for different purposes. For example, it can be used to give the user the information that the countdown is running, perhaps by animating a spinner cursor. Also, further feedback can be given when the click event is executed. For example, the Button UI object has a Transition option called Animation that might be helpful. Also, consider audio cues.

# Pointing and clicking with VR components

As we have seen, while Unity provides UI elements such as canvas text, buttons, and other controls that are specially tuned for conventional screen space UI and mobile app, using them in World Space and tying them together with VR user input can get pretty involved. World space interactions assume some physics, colliders, and ray casts to detect interaction events.

Fortunately, VR device-specific toolkits may provide components that take care of some of this work already. As we saw in previous chapters, device manufacturers provide toolkits built atop their Unity SDK with convenient scripts, prefabs, and demo scenes that illustrate how to use them.

In this case, we're looking for components that let you design scenes using Unity UI elements on a canvas, take advantage of all their EventSystem interactivity goodness, use world space 3D models, and input controllers or laster pointers. For example, consider these:

- Oculus Rift and GearVR: OVRInputModule; see `https://developer.oculus.com/blog/unitys-ui-system-in-vr/`
- SteamVR: Steam InteractionSystem; see the `/Assets/SteamVR/InteractionSystem/` folder after installing the SteamVR package
- Daydream:
- VRTK open source toolkit: `https://github.com/thestonefox/VRTK`

Lastly, you might consider purchasing a package from the Unity Asset Store. The Curved UI package ($25), for example, lets you make VR-ready curved canvases and supports Vive, Oculus Touch, Daydream controllers, and gaze input, as depicted:

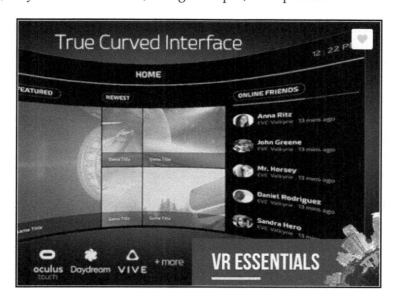

# Using Unity UI and SteamVR

We introduced the SteamVR InteractionSystem in Chapter 5, *Handy Interactables*. It is intended as an example of how to use the SteamVR SDK but includes some very useful components and demo scenes. Using the Interaction System, it's very easy to convert your Dashboard into a control panel you can operate directly with your positionally tracked hand controllers.

The Interaction System includes its own `Player` camera rig which replaces the default `[CameraRig]` we have been using. It includes a VRCamera, two hands (Hand1 and Hand2), and other useful objects.

1. Locate the `Assets/SteamVR/InteractionSystem/Core/Prefabs` folder in the **Project** window
2. Drag the `Player` prefab as a child of `MyMyselfEye` into your scene **Hierarchy**
3. Delete or disable the `[CameraRig]` object

To make the `StartButton` and `StopButton` interactable, add the `Interactable` component. Also add the UI `Element` component to handle **OnHandClick** events, as follows:

1. Select the `StartButton` object in **Hierarchy** (child of `Dashboard`).
2. In **Inspector**, select **Add Component | Scripts | Valve.VR.InteractionSystem | Interactable** (tip: use the **Search** field for "Interactable").
3. Select **Add Component | Scripts | Valve.VR.InteractionSystem | UI Element.**
4. In **Inspector** on the **UI Element** component, press the "+" to add an **On Hand Click** handler.
5. Drag the `WaterShower` particle system (child of `Hose` object) from **Hierarchy** onto the **GameObject** field, like we did for the standard **Button OnClick** event.
6. Select the **ParticleSystem | Play()** function.
7. Optionally, disable the `RespondToGaze` component.

Similarly, repeat these steps for the `StopButton`, but choose function **ParticleSystem | Stop().**

You may also need to move the `Dashboard` closer to yourself so the buttons are within comfortable reach when you're in VR. When you press **Play** you can now reach to touch a button; it highlights. Pull the trigger to press it, as shown in the screenshot, and it turns on the hose:

# Using Unity UI and Daydream

Let's now take a look at how to do this on a mobile VR device using Google Daydream. In this case, we won't actually reach out and press the button but use the 3DOF hand controller laser pointer. The solution is as simple as replacing the `GvrReticlePointer` (if you had been using it) with a `GvrControllerPointer`.

1. Under your MeMyselfEye `GVR Camera Rig/ Player / Main Camera /`, if there is a GvrReticlePointer, disable it.
2. Locate the GvrControllerPointer in the `GoogleVR/Prefabs/Controller/` folder.
3. Drag the prefab under Player (as a sibling of Main Camera).

Then set up the Dashboard canvas to accept raycasts:

1. Select the Dashboard object in Hierarchy.
2. Add the GvrPointerGraphicRaycaster component.

Press Play. You can now use the Daydream controller to press the buttons.

Explore the component options for the GvrControllerPointer, its child Laser object, and other Gvr object provided with the package. There's some pretty interesting and useful configurations available, including settings for laser color, end color, and max distance. There's even a checkbox to Draw Debug Rays in the Editor Scene window during Play mode.

# Building a wrist-based menu palette

Some VR applications, designed for two-handed setups such as Oculus Rift, HTC Vive, and Windows MR, give you a virtual menu palette attached to one wrist while the other hand selects buttons or items from it. Let's see how that is done. *This scenario will assume you have a two hand controller VR system.* We'll describe it using the SteamVR camera rig, involving attaching the controls to your left hand and selecting them with your right.

Converting our dashboard control panel into a wrist palette is not too difficult. We just need to scale it appropriately and attach it to the hand controller.

Given you've built the scene up to the point described in the previous *Using Unity UI and SteamVR* section, including the SteamVR `Player` rig (instead of `[CameraRig]`), we'll duplicate and repurpose the `Dashboard` to use it on your left wrist:

1. In Hierarchy, right-click the Dashboard and Duplicate.
2. Rename the new one to "Palette".
3. Disable the old Dashboard.
4. Drag the Palette as a child of the Player/Hand1 object.

Now we'll modify the Palette graphics as follows. Feel free to change for what works for you:

1. On the Palette itself, set its Pos X,Y,Z to (0, 0.1, -0.1); Rotation to (90, -150, -115); Scale (X,Y,Z) to 0.0005;
2. Unfold the Palette and disable or delete the Raw Image object.
3. Enable the Image child object (if it's missing, create a new Image with Anchor Presets to stretch-stretch).
4. Set the Image Scale (X,Y,Z) to 0.5.
5. Set the Image Color Alpha to 75 so it's translucent.
6. Enable the Text child object. Set its Rect Transform Top to 100, Font Size to 18, and Text to "Hose".
7. Move the StartButton Pos Y to 0.
8. Move the StopButton Pos Y to 0.

That's it! All of the click wiring we set up for the Dashboard works without change. Shown here is a screenshot of using the Palette attached to the left-hand controller, and selecting the start button on it with the right-hand controller:

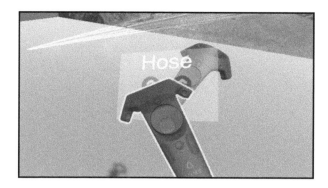

Naturally, the palette can be extended with other buttons and input controls. If you had multiple panels arranged as the sides of cube (like the TiltBrush menu), you could use the thumb pad to scroll or rotate between the various menus. And that's how it's done.

# Summary

In Unity, user interfaces that are based on a canvas object and the event system include buttons, text, images, sliders, and input fields, which can be assembled and wired to objects in the scene.

In this chapter, we took a close look at various world space UI techniques and how they can be used in virtual reality projects. We considered ways in which UI for VR differs from UI for conventional video games and desktop applications. Also, we implemented over a half-dozen of them, demonstrating how each can be constructed, coded, and used in your own projects. Our C# scripting got a little more advanced, probing deeper into the Unity Engine API and modular coding techniques.

You now have a broader vocabulary to approach UI in your VR projects. Some of the examples in this chapter can be directly applicable in your own work. However, not all need to be home-grown. VR UI tools are increasingly being provided in VR headset SDKs, open source VR middleware projects, and third-party Unity Assets Store packages.

In the next chapter, we will add a first-person character controller to our scene. We'll learn about avatars and methods to control navigation in VR so that we can comfortably move around inside the virtual world. Also, we'll learn about managing one of the negative aspects of virtual reality experiences—VR motion sickness.

# 7
# Locomotion and Comfort

Up to this point in this book, the player's point-of-view camera has been stationary. In this chapter, we'll start to move around as we consider various techniques for locomotion and teleportation. First, we'll dig deeper into the Unity standard character components, and then we move ourselves into a controllable first-person character and explore techniques to move around in the virtual world. We'll also discuss practices for managing motion sickness and sense of self within VR.

In this chapter, we will discuss the following topics:

- Unity's character objects and components
- Glide locomotion
- Comfort mode locomotion
- Teleportation
- Issues around VR motion sickness

 Note that the projects in this chapter are separate and not directly required by the other chapters in this book. If you decide to skip any of it or not save your work, that's OK.

## Understanding Unity characters

A first-person character is such a key asset in a VR project that we really should understand its components inside out. So, before we go about building one for our project, it would be a good idea to take a close look at the built-in components and standard assets that Unity provides.

# Unity components

As you probably know, each Unity game object contains a set of associated **components**. Unity includes many types of built-in components, which you can see by browsing the **Component** menu in the main menu bar. Each component adds properties and behaviors to the object that it belongs to. A component's properties are accessible via the Unity editor's **Inspector** panel and scripts. A script attached to a game object is also a type of a component and may have properties that you can set in the **Inspector** panel.

The component types used to implement first-person characters include the **Camera**, **Character Controller**, and/or **Rigidbody**, and various scripts. Let's review each of these standard components.

## The Camera component

The Camera component specifies the viewing parameters that are used to render the scene on each frame update. Any object with a Camera component is considered a `camera` object. Naturally, we've been using a camera in our scenes since we started, and we've been accessing it in the scripts that we've written.

A stereographic VR camera object renders two views, one for each eye. In VR, the camera controller scripts read data from the headset's motion sensors and positional tracking to determine the current head pose (position, direction, and rotation) and set the camera's transform appropriately.

## The Rigidbody component

When you add a Rigidbody component to any Unity game object, it will benefit from the calculations that are performed by the **physics engine**. Rigidbody components have parameters for gravity, mass, and drag, among others. During gameplay, the physics engine calculates each rigid object's *momentum* (mass, speed, and direction).

Rigid objects interact with other rigid objects. For example, if they collide, they'll bounce off each other and the parameters of the interaction can be controlled with a **physic material** with properties such as friction and bounciness factors.

Rigidbodies can be flagged as *kinematic*, which is usually only used when the object is driven by animation or scripts. Collisions will not affect kinematic objects, but they will still affect the motion of other rigidbodies. It's mostly used when objects are chained together with *joints*, like the ones connecting a humanoid's bones or a swinging pendulum.

Any rigid object, given a child camera object, becomes a rigid first-person character. Then, you can add scripts to handle user input to move, jump, look around, and so on.

# The Character Controller component

Like a Rigidbody, the **Character Controller** (**CC**) is used for *collision detection* and *character movement*. It needs scripts to handle the user input to move, jump, and look around, too. However, it doesn't automatically have the physics built in.

The CC component is specifically designed for character objects because characters in a game often are not really expected to behave the same as other physics-based objects. It can be used instead of, or in addition to, a Rigidbody.

The CC component has a built-in **Capsule Collider** behavior to detect collisions. However, it doesn't automatically use the physics engine to *respond* to the collision.

For example, if a CC object hits a rigid object such as a wall, it will just stop. It won't bounce. If a rigid object, such as a flying brick, hits a CC object, the brick will get deflected (bounce) based on its own properties, but the CC object will not be affected. Of course, if you want to include behavior like this on the CC object, you can program that in your own scripts.

The CC component does have an especially good support for one force in its scripting API-*gravity*. Built-in parameters are specifically related to keeping the object's feet on the ground. For example, the **Step Offset** parameter defines how tall a step the character can hop onto rather than being an obstacle that blocks his way. Similarly, the **Slope Limit** parameter says how big an incline is too steep and whether it should be treated like a wall. In your scripts, you can use the `Move()` method and the `IsGrounded` variable to implement character behavior.

Unless you script it, a CC object has no momentum and can stop on a dime. It feels very precise, but this could also lead to a jerky movement. The opposite is true for Rigidbody objects, which feel more fluid because they have momentum, acceleration/deceleration, and obey the laws of physics. In VR, we'd ideally like some combination of the two, if we use it at all.

Using physics to move yourself through a VR scene is not always best. As we'll see, alternative locomotion techniques may not use physics at all, such as *teleportation*.

# Unity Standard Assets

The **Characters** package in Unity **Standard Assets** comes with a number of third- and first-person character prefab objects. These prefab objects are compared in the following table:

| Prefab | Components |
|---|---|
| | 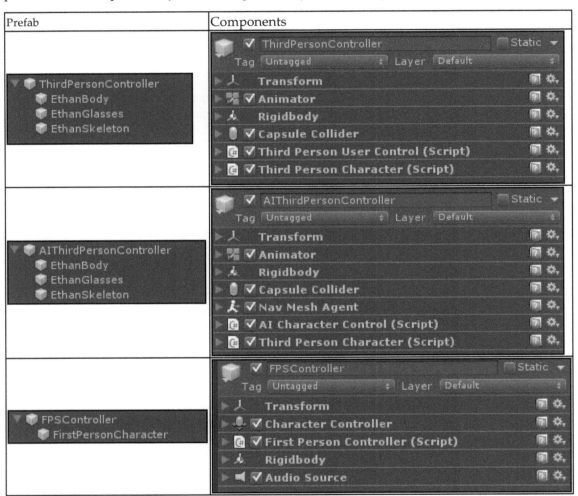 |

Let's discuss this in more detail.

# ThirdPersonController

We've already used both of the third-person prefabs, `ThirdPersonController` and `AIThirdPersonController`, in `Chapter 2`, *Content, Objects, and Scale,* and `Chapter 4`, *Gaze-Based Control,* respectively.

The `ThirdPersonController` prefab has child objects that define the character's body, namely our friend Ethan. He is a rigged avatar (from the `.fbx` file), which means that humanoid animations can be applied to make him walk, run, jump, and so on.

The `ThirdPersonController` prefab uses a Rigidbody for physics and Capsule Collider for collision detection.

It has two scripts. A `ThirdPersonUserControl` script takes user input, such as thumbstick presses, and tells the character to move, jump, and so on. A `ThirdPersonCharacter` script implements physics movements and calls the animations that are needed for running, crouching, and so on.

# AIThirdPersonController

The `AIThirdPersonController` prefab is identical to the `ThirdPersonController` prefab, but the former adds a `NavMeshAgent` and an `AICharacterControl` script, which constrains where and how the character can move around the scene. If you recall, in `Chapter 4`, *Gaze-Based Control,* we used the `AICharacterController` to make Ethan walk around the scene and avoid bumping into objects.

# First-person FPSController

The FPSController prefab is a first-person controller that uses both a CC component and a Rigidbody. It has a child camera attached to it. When the character moves, the camera moves with it.

The core distinction between third-person controller prefabs and first-person controller prefabs is the **child object**. Third-person controller prefabs have a rigged humanoid child object, while first-person controller prefabs have a camera child object.

Its body mass is set to a low value (1) and IsKinematic is enabled. This means that it will have limited momentum and does not react to other rigid objects, but it can be driven by animations.

Its FirstPersonController script offers a plethora of parameters for running, jumping, audio footsteps, and more. The script also includes parameters and animations for a *head bob*, which bounces the camera in a natural way when the character is moving. If you use the FPSController script in your VR project, *be sure to disable any head bob features* or you might need to clean the puke off your keyboard!

# RigidBodyFPSController

The RigidBodyFPSController prefab is a first-person controller with a Rigidbody but no CC component. Like FPSController, it has a child camera object. When the character moves, the camera moves with it.

A RigidBodyFPSController prefab's body mass is more substantial, set to 10, and is not kinematic. That is, it *can* get bounced around when it collides with other objects. It has a separate Capsule Collider component with the ZeroFriction physic material. The RigidBodyFirstPersonController script is different from the FPSController one, but the former has a lot of similar parameters.

**Why am I going through all of this detail here?**
If you've built any non-VR projects in Unity, then you've most likely used these prefabs. However, you might not have paid much attention to how they're assembled. Virtual reality is experienced from the first-person perspective. Our implementation toolbox is Unity. It is important to understand Unity's tools that manage and control this first-person experience.

# Using glide locomotion

For our locomotion features in this chapter, let's take an *agile* approach to development. This means (in part) that we'll start by defining our new feature, or story, with a set of requirements. Then, we'll incrementally build and test this feature, one requirement at a time, by iterating and refining our work as we go along. Experimentation is not only allowed, it's encouraged.

 **Agile software development** is a broad term for methodologies that encourage small incremental and iterative development in a fashion that's easy to respond to changing and refined requirements. See the Agile Manifesto at `http://agilemanifesto.org/`.

The feature we want to implement is this: as a first-person character, when I start walking, I will move through the scene in the direction I am looking until I indicate to stop walking. Here are the requirements to achieve this feature:

- Move in the direction you're looking
- Keep your feet on the ground
- Don't pass through solid objects
- Don't fall off the edge of the world
- Step over small objects and handle uneven terrain
- Start and stop moving by clicking an input button

This sounds reasonable.

To begin, if you have a saved version of the scene from `Chapter 4`, *Gaze-Based Control*, you can start with that. Or, build a similar simple new scene containing a ground plane, some 3D objects as obstacles, and a copy of your `MeMyselfEye` prefab.

## Move in the direction you're looking

We already have a `MeMyselfEye` object containing the camera rig. We're going to turn it into a first-person controller. Our first requirement is to move about the scene in the direction you're looking. Add a script named `GlideLocomotion`. Keeping it simple, let's start by performing the following steps:

1. Select the `MeMyselfEye` object in the **Hierarchy** panel
2. In the **Inspector** panel, select **Add Component | New Script** and name it `GlideLocomotion`

Then, open the script and code it, as follows:

```
using UnityEngine;

public class GlideLocomotion : MonoBehaviour
{
    public float velocity = 0.4f;

    void Update ()
    {
        Vector3 moveDirection = Camera.main.transform.forward;
        moveDirection *= velocity * Time.deltaTime;
        transform.position += moveDirection;
    }
}
```

The normal walking speed for humans is about 1.4 meters per second. In VR, that could make you feel sick. Let's travel a lot slower than that, at 0.4 m/s. During `Update()`, we check the current direction in which the player is looking (`camera.transform.forward`) and move the `MeMyselfEye` transform position in this direction at the current velocity.

Note the coding shortcuts for the self-modification of a variable (`*=` and `+=`). The last two lines of the preceding code could have been written out like this:

```
moveDirection = moveDirection * velocity * Time.deltaTime;
transform.position = transform.position  + moveDirection;
```

Here, I used the `*=` and `+=` operators instead. Save the script and the scene and try it in VR.

When you look forward, you move forward. Look left, move left. Look right, move right. It works!

Look up... *Whoa!! Did you expect that?! We're freakin' flying!* You can move up, down, and all around as if you're Superman or piloting a drone. Presently, `MeMyselfEye` has no mass and physics and does not respond to gravity. Nonetheless, it meets our requirement to move in the direction you're looking. So, let's continue.

# Keep your feet on the ground

The next requirement wants you to keep your feet on the ground. We know that `GroundPlane` is flat and positioned at **Y** = 0. So, let's just add this simple constraint to the `GlideLocomotion` script, as follows:

```
void Update ()
```

```
{
    Vector3 moveDirection = Camera.main.transform.forward;
    moveDirection *= velocity * Time.deltaTime;
    moveDirection.y = 0f;
    transform.position += moveDirection;
}
```

Save the script and try it in VR.

Not bad. Now, we can move around the **Y** = 0 plane.

On the other hand, you're like a ghost, readily passing through the cube, sphere, and the other objects.

# Don't pass through solid objects

The third requirement states *don't pass through solid objects*. Here's an idea. Give it a Rigidbody component, a collider, and let the physics engine take care of it. Follow these steps:

1. Select the `MeMyselfEye` object in the **Hierarchy** panel
2. In the **Inspector** panel, navigate to **Add Component** | **Physics** | **Rigidbody**
3. Then **Add Component** | **Physics** | **Capsule Collider**
4. Set the Capsule Collider **Height** to **2**
5. If your Character Controller's capsule collider (green mesh in the Scene window) extends through the ground plane, adjusts its **Center Y** to 1

Try it in VR.

*Whoa!! What the...?* It was going fine there for a second, but as soon as you knock into the cube, you go spinning out of control in wild directions, like a spacewalk gone bad in the movie *Gravity*. Well, that's a Rigidbody for you. Forces are being applied in all directions and axes. Let's add some constraints as follows.

In the **Inspector** panel's **Rigidbody** pane, check off the checkboxes for **Freeze Position: Y** and **Freeze Rotation: X** and **Z**.

Try it in VR.

Now that's pretty nice! You're able to move by looking in a direction, you're not flying (**Y** position constrained), and you don't pass through solid objects. Instead, you slide past them since only the **Y** rotation is allowed.

If your `KillTarget` script is still running (from `Chapter 2`, *Content, Objects, and Scale*), you should be able to stare at Ethan until he explodes. Do it, make Ethan explode... *Whoa!* We just got blown out of here by the explosion, spinning out of control in wild directions again. Maybe we're just not ready for this powerful physics engine yet. We can probably address this in the scripting, but for the time being, let's abandon the Rigidbody idea. We'll come back to it in the next chapter.

You may recall that CC includes a Capsule Collider and supports movement that is constrained by collisions. We'll try that instead, as follows:

1. In the **Inspector** panel, click on the **Rigidbody** pane's *gear* icon and select **Remove Component**
2. Also, remove its **Capsule Collider** component
3. In the **Inspector** panel, navigate to **Add Component | Physics | Character Controller**
4. If your Character Controller's capsule collider (green mesh in the Scene window) extends through the ground plane, adjusts its **Center Y** to 1

Modify the `GlideLocomotion` script, as follows:

```
using UnityEngine;

public class GlideLocomotion : MonoBehaviour
{
  public float velocity = 0.4f;

  private CharacterController character;

  void Start ()
  {
    character = GetComponent<CharacterController>();
  }

  void Update ()
  {
    Vector3 moveDirection = Camera.main.transform.forward;
    moveDirection *= velocity * Time.deltaTime;
    moveDirection.y = 0.0f;
    character.Move(moveDirection);
  }
}
```

Instead of updating `transform.position` directly, we called the built-in `CharacterController.Move()` function and let it do it for us. It knows that the characters should behave with certain constraints.

Save the script and try it in VR.

This time, when we bump into objects (a cube or sphere), we kind of go over it and then remain in the air. The `Move()` function does not apply gravity to the scene for us. We need to add that to the script, which isn't so hard (see the Unity API docs at `http://docs.unity3d.com/ScriptReference/CharacterController.Move.html`).

However, there is a simpler way. The `CharacterController.SimpleMove()` function applies gravity to the move for us. Just replace the whole `Update()` function with the following one-liner:

```
void Update ()
{
    character.SimpleMove(Camera.main.transform.forward * velocity);
}
```

The `SimpleMove()` function takes care of gravity and also handles `Time.deltaTime`. So, all that we need to give it is the movement direction vector. Also, since it's introducing gravity, we don't need the **Y** = 0 constraint either. Much simpler.

Save the script and try it in VR.

Awesome! I think we've met all the requirements so far. *Just don't go walking off the edge...*

> The exercises in this section assume you're using VR in seated or standing mode, not room-scale. We're modifying the whole MyMyselfEye rig as we move the player. In room-scale, that's moving the play area bounds as well. Since we're attaching the collider to the MyMyselfEye position, if you physically step away from the center of the play area, the collider will not be aligned with your actual body position. Later on, we will address issues of locomotion with room-scale VR.

# Don't fall off the edge of the world

Now that we have gravity, if we walk off the edge of the ground plane, you'll fall into oblivion. Fixing this isn't a first-person character thing. Just add some railings to the scene.

Use cubes, scaling them to the desired thickness and length and moving them into position. Go ahead and do it. I won't give you the step-by-step instructions for it. For example, I used these transforms:

- **Scale**: 0.1, 0.1, 10.0
- Railing 1: **Position**: –5, 1, 0
- Railing 2: **Position**: 5, 1, 0
- Railing 3: **Position**: 0, 1, –5; **Rotation**: 0, 90, 0
- Railing 4: **Position**: 0, 1, 5; **Rotation**: 0, 90, 0

Try it in VR. Try to walk through the railings. Whew! This is safer.

# Stepping over small objects and handling uneven terrain

While we're at it, add a few things to walk on and over, such as a ramp and other obstacles. The result will look like this:

Try it in VR. Walk up the ramp and step off the cube. Hey, this is fun!

The CC component is taking care of the requirement to step over small objects and handle uneven terrain. You might want to tinker with its **Slope Limit** and **Step Offset** settings.

**Caution**: Glide locomotion can cause motion sickness, especially for players who are susceptible. Please use it with caution in your apps. This may become especially noticeable as you glide up the ramp and then jump off the block onto the ground plane. On the other hand, some people love rollercoaster VR! Also, giving the player control of the locomotion through a mechanic as simple as a button press can go a long way in helping reduce queasiness and motion sickness, which we'll add next.

# Starting and stopping movement

The next requirement is *to start and stop moving by clicking an input button*. We'll look for a button press using the logical "Fire1" button. If you want to use a different button, or if you're targeting a platform that does not have a mapping to "Fire1" please refer to Chapter 5, *Handy Interactables*, under the topic *Basic button input*.

Modify the GlideLocomotion script as follows:

```
using UnityEngine;

public class GlideLocomotion : MonoBehaviour
{
  public float velocity = 0.7f;

  private CharacterController controller;
  private bool isWalking = false;

  void Start()
  {
    controller = GetComponent<CharacterController> ();
  }

  void Update () {
    if (Input.GetButtonDown("Fire1"))
        isWalking = true;
    else if (Input.GetButtonUp("Fire1"))
        isWalking = false;

    if (isWalking) {
      controller.SimpleMove (Camera.main.transform.forward * velocity);
    }
  }
}
```

On Daydream, you may call `GvrControllerInput.ClickButtonDown` and `ClickButtonUp` instead.

By adding a Boolean `isWalking` flag, we can switch the forward movement on and off, which can be signaled by a key press.

# Adding comfort mode locomotion

We have mentioned the potential of motion sickness several times already in this chapter, and earlier in this book. In general, the more control you give the player in moving around within VR the better off she'll be and reduce the risk of feeling queasy. Offering a button to start/stop motion is one step, as we just saw. Another is what's commonly referred to as *comfort mode*.

It's been discovered that using glide locomotion around curves is worse that simply going in a straight line. So, one technique for getting around in a VR scene is only allow forward motion, regardless of which direction the player is looking, and then use the thumbstick to change direction. Also, rather than allow the thumbstick to change the direction angle continuously, we limit it to fixed angle steps of 30 degrees, for example. We'll add this to our `GlideLocomotion` script as follows.

At the top of the class, add the following variables:

```
public float comfortAngle = 30f;
private bool hasRotated = true;
```

Then in `Update()`, add the following statements:

```
void Update()
{
  if (Input.GetButtonDown("Fire1"))
    isWalking = true;
  else if (Input.GetButtonUp("Fire1"))
    isWalking = false;

  if (isWalking)
    character.SimpleMove(transform.forward * velocity);

  float axis = Input.GetAxis("Horizontal");
  if (axis > 0.5f)
  {
    if (!hasRotated)
      transform.Rotate(0, comfortAngle, 0);
```

```
    hasRotated = true;
  }
  else if (axis < -0.5f)
  {
    if (!hasRotated)
      transform.Rotate(0, -comfortAngle, 0);
    hasRotated = true;
  }
  else
  {
    hasRotated = false;
  }
}
```

Now, when the `"Fire1"` button is pressed and `isWalking` is true, we move the `MeMyselfEye` forward in the direction indicated in its transform, rather than the `Camera` look directions, changing the line to `character.SimpleMove(transform.forward * velocity)`.

When the user pushes the thumbstick to the right, that is, the logical `"Horizontal"` axis is positive, we will rotate the rig clockwise by 30 degrees (`comfortAngle`). When the thumbstick is pressed left, we rotate counter-clockwise. We check for greater than 0.5 rather than exactly 1.0 so the player does not need to jam the stick all the way to the edge.

We don't want to keep rotating, again and again, each update while the joystick is pressed, so we set a flag, `hasRotated`, and then ignore the axis until it comes to rest at the zero position. Then, we'll allow the player to press it again.

The result is a comfortable navigation mechanic where one button moves you forward and another lets you change direction in large increments.

For your reference, some button mappings used in this mechanic are as follows:

- In OpenVR on HTC VIVE, `"Fire1"` is the menu button on one controller, `"Horizontal"` is touching the touchpad on the other controller.
- In OpenVR on Oculus, `"Fire1"` is the right controller's **B** button, `"Horizontal"` is the left controller thumbstick.

- On Daydream, you should modify the code to use `GvrControllerInput`. To detect horizontal clicks on the touchpad, call `GvrControllerInput.TouchPosCentered`, which returns a `Vector2`, and check x for values between −1 and 1. For example, replace the call to GetAxis with the following:

```
Vector2 touchPos = GvrControllerInput.TouchPosCentered;
float axis = touchPos.x;
if (axis > 0.5f) ...
```

You're encouraged to extend the `ButtonTest()` function used in the beginning of Chapter 5, *Handy Interactables*, to determine which button mappings, axes, and SDK functions work best for your target VR device.

We just implemented glide locomotion, where you move forward smoothly in the direction you're looking, or with comfort mode, in the direction your body is facing, while your head can look around. Comfort mode reduces the chance of motion sickness by having you change the direction you're facing in jumps of 30-degree angles. But even that may not be comfortable enough, and some developers (and players) prefer no gliding at all, and instead let you just *teleport* from one location to another.

# Other locomotion considerations

If you want to offer your players a VR ride, you can define a predefined *track* to glide along, like a guided tour of a building or art gallery. Tracks can be 3D, moving you up and down too, with gravity, such as VR roller coasters, or without gravity, such as a space tour. We do not recommend this mechanic except for the most hardcore thrill seekers as it has a good chance of causing motion sickness.

Another technique for comfort during locomotion is **Tunneling**. During the movement, the camera is cropped with a vignette and simple background, like a grid, is displayed in the player's peripheral vision, so the user only sees what is directly before them. Eliminating peripheral vision while moving can reduce the chance of motion sickness.

For vertical locomotion, apps have implemented a climbing mechanic, using your hands to reach, grab, and pull yourself up. Mountain climbing simulation games such as The Climb (http://www.theclimbgame.com/) takes this idea to the next level (literally!), providing a number of different reach mechanics and grip types to grab onto.

Other apps have also tried using your hands, not for climbing, but for walking. For example, reaching and pulling like a rope, or swinging your arms like a runner, or even a circular pulling motion like you're operating a wheelchair.

Of course, there are hardware devices, such as that implement locomotion mechanisms using your feet to walk and run. Examples include:

- VR treadmills such as Virtuix Omni (`http://www.virtuix.com/`) and VR Virtualizer (`https://www.cyberith.com/`), where you walk in place with your feet and legs to walk and run in VR.
- Exercise bikes such as VirZoom (`https://www.virzoom.com/`) where you can bike and even hang glide in VR.
- Body tracking sensors can be used not just for player locomotion but also motion capture for creating character animations. Devices include Optitrack (`http://optitrack.com/motion-capture-virtual-reality/`), Perception Neuron (`https://neuronmocap.com/`), ProVR (`http://www.vrs.org.uk/virtual-reality-gear/motion-tracking/priovr.html`), and others.

You probably need to write your app specifically for that device as there are no standards for these body tracking devices, but they're certainly a lot of fun.

# Techniques for teleportation

**Pointer teleportation** is a mechanic where you point to a location you want to go to, and you jump there. No gliding. You just teleport to the new location. A laser beam or arc may be drawn, along with a teleport location receptacle to indicate where you may go.

As we've seen in previous chapters, we can make our own scripts. But since this is a core feature of VR applications, teleportation components are often included with device SDK toolkits. We'll write our own and consider some provided ones afterward.

To begin, if you have a saved version of the scene from `Chapter 4`, *Gaze-Based Control*, you can start with that. You may disable a few objects that we do not need, including `Ethan` and `WalkTarget`. Or, build a similar simple new scene containing a ground plane, some 3D objects as obstacles, and a copy of your `MeMyselfEye` prefab.

# Looking to teleport

The mechanic we'll implement for our homegrown teleportation will work on any VR platform, using gaze-based pointing. Similar to how we controlled Ethan the zombie in `Chapter 4`, *Gaze-Based Control*, we'll cast a ray from the player's camera view to the ground plane to choose a move-to location.

In our script, we'll use button press to initiate the teleport and release to jump there if you've selected a valid location. Alternatively, you could consider other input such as a forward push of the thumbstick using `Input.GetAxis(`*vertical*`)`.

First, let's create a teleport marker (similar to the WalkTarget one), as follows:

1. Add an empty game object to the **Hierarchy** panel, and rename it `TeleportMarker`.
2. Reset its **Transform** values to position (0,0,0) (using the gear icon in the upper-right of the Transform pane).
3. Right-click on the mouse and navigate to **3D Object** | **Cylinder**. This will create a cylindrical object parented by `TeleportMarker`.
4. Reset its transform and change the **Scale** to (`0.4, 0.05, 0.4`). This will create a flat disk with a diameter of `0.4`.
5. Disable or remove its **Capsule Collider**.

For now, we'll use the default material. Or, you could decorate your marker with another material. (For example, if you have Steam `InteractionSystem` installed, try the `TeleportPointVisible` material. If you have Daydream Elements installed, try the `TeleportGlow` material.)

Now, let's write the script:

1. Select the `MeMyselfEye` object in the **Hierarchy** panel
2. Disable or remove the `GlideLocomotion` component, if present
3. Select **Add Component** | **New Script** and name it `LookTeleport`

Write the script as follows:

```
using UnityEngine;

public class LookTeleport : MonoBehaviour
{
    public GameObject target;
    public GameObject ground;
```

```
void Update()
{
    Transform camera = Camera.main.transform;
    Ray ray;
    RaycastHit hit;

    if (Input.GetButtonDown("Fire1"))
    {
        // start searching
        target.SetActive(true);
    }
    else if (Input.GetButtonUp("Fire1"))
    {
        // done searching, teleport player
        target.SetActive(false);
        transform.position = target.transform.position;
    }
    else if (target.activeSelf)
    {
        ray = new Ray(camera.position, camera.rotation *
Vector3.forward);
        if (Physics.Raycast(ray, out hit) &&
            (hit.collider.gameObject == ground))
        {
            // move target to look-at position
            target.transform.position = hit.point;
        }
        else
        {
            // not looking a ground, reset target to player position
            target.transform.position = transform.position;
        }
    }
}
```

The script works as follows:

- When the player clicks, targeting begins, and the target marker is made visible (SetActive(true)).
- While targeting, we identify what the player is looking at (Raycast). And if it's the ground, we position the target there (hit.point). Otherwise, the target is reset to the player's position.
- When the player stops pressing the button, the target is hidden. And we position the player to the target's current position, thus completing the teleportation.

Notice that we are using the `TeleportMarker` target to store the state of our teleport mechanic while in targeting mode. When the target is active, we're targeting. When we exit targeting, we use the target's position as the new player position.

Save the script and in Unity:

1. Drag the `GroundPlane` object onto the Ground slot
2. Drag the `TeleportMarker` object onto the Target slot

Press **Play**. Pressing the input button will activate the target marker, which moves as you look. On releasing the button, you teleport to that position. You can cancel the teleport by looking at something other than the ground and releasing the button.

# Teleporting between surfaces

In the previous script, we're using a plain Raycast to determine where to place the `TeleportMarker`. This really only works on Plane objects. For any other 3D object, the hit point might be any surface, not just the topside walkable one.

An alternative approach is to use NavMesh to identify surfaces you can teleport to within the scene. Back in `Chapter 4`, *Gaze-Based Control*, we generated a NavMesh for Ethan's `AIThirdPersonController` to control where he's allowed to roam. This time, we also use the NavMesh to determine where we (`MeMyselfEye`) can go. Feel free to go back and review our conversations about NavMesh.

The advantage of this approach is the available teleportation locations can be a subset of the ground plane. There can be can be multiple other object surfaces and even complex terrains. The teleportation locations will be limited to valid flat or slightly sloped surfaces.

In case you skipped that section, or if you've rearranged objects in your scene since then, we will regenerate the NavMesh now:

1. Select the **Navigation** panel. If it's not already a tab in your editor, open the Navigation window from the main menu by navigating to **Window | Navigation**.
2. Select its **Object** tab.
3. Select the **Ground Plane** in **Hierarchy**, then in the **Navigation** window's **Object** pane, check the **Navigation Static** checkbox. (Alternatively, you can use the object's **Inspector** window **Static** drop-down list.)
4. Repeat step 3 for each of the objects that should block your possible teleportation locations: the cubes, sphere, and so on.

For demonstration, we will now also add a second story platform:

1. In **Hierarchy**, create a new 3D **Cube** and name it Overlook
2. Set its **Scale** to (2.5, 0.1, 5) and its **Position** to (4, 2.5, 0.5)
3. In the **Navigation** window, select the **Object** tab and check **Navigation Static** for the overlook, then
4. Select the **Bake** tab and click on the **Bake** button at the bottom of the panel

Note that its height (**Y Scale**) of the platform is greater than **Agent Height** (2) in the **Navigation** Bake settings. This will ensure the player can go both beneath the platform and on top of it. In the **Scene** window, you can see the areas in blue defined by the NavMesh, shown next, including a nice lookout area on the second story platform:

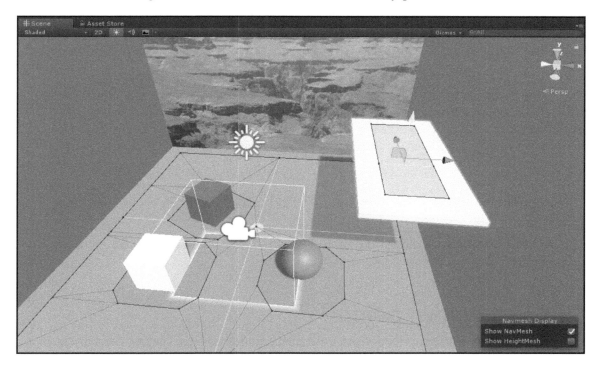

We can now modify the script to find our teleport target position on the NavMesh rather than the ground plane. Unfortunately, Unity does not provide a Raycast function for directly finding a hit point on the NavMesh. Instead, we find a hit point, as usual, using Physics colliders (which may be on the side or bottom of an object, not just the walkable surface), and then call NavMesh.SamplePosition to find the hit point position on the NavMesh. Modify the LookTeleport script as follows.

Add the following line at the top of your script to access the NavMesh API:

```
using UnityEngine.AI;
```

Now, modify `Update()` as follows:

```
if (Physics.Raycast(ray, out hit))
{
  NavMeshHit navHit;
  if (NavMesh.SamplePosition(hit.point, out navHit, 1.0f,
NavMesh.AllAreas))
    target.transform.position = navHit.position;
}
```

The call to `NavMesh.SamplePosition` takes the `hit.point` and finds the closest point on the NavMesh, within a given radius (we gave 1.0).

Press **Play**. Now, you can set the `TeleportMarker` not only on the walkable surface of the `GroundPlane` but also on top of the Overlook!

One more thing. Doing a `Physics.Raycast` can get quite expensive, especially in scenes with a lot of objects. You can limit the Raycast search by providing a layer mask. For example, create a layer named `Teleport` and set this layer for both `GroundPlane` and Overlook game objects. Then, modify the Raycast call as follows:

```
if (Physics.Raycast(ray, out hit, LayerMask.GetMask("Teleport")))
```

This will limit our Raycast to just the surfaces overlaid by the NavMesh, namely the ground plane and overlook.

The next scenario we'll consider is not permitting free roaming at all, but setting up a limited set of teleportation locations.

# Teleport spawn points

It is very common in VR applications to limit teleportation to only specific predefined locations within the scene. In that case, you would not need any free-roaming glide locomotion or arbitrary teleportation targets. Instead, you can define the specific teleportation spawn points. Let's see how to do this.

First, let's create a `TeleportSpawn` prefab to mark our locations:

1. In Hierarchy, create a 3D **Sphere** and name it `TeleportSpawn`
2. Reset its transform (**gear icon | Reset**)
3. Set its **Scale** to `0.4, 0.4, 0.4`
4. Set its **Position** to something like (2, 0, 3)
5. Create a new layer named `TeleportSpawn` from **Inspector | Layers | Add Layer** and fill in the name in an empty slot
6. Select the `TeleportSpawn` object in Hierarchy again, and now set its layer (**Layers | TeleportSpawn**) to the one we just defined

Let's quickly make a material:

1. In your Materials folder, right-click to **Create** a new **Material** and name it `Teleport Material`
2. Set its **Rendering Mode** to **Transparent**
3. Set its **Albedo** color and give it a low alpha (such as 30) so it's translucent, such as our pale green (70, 230, 70, 30)
4. Drag the material onto the `TeleportSpawn` object

For this exercise, we'll replace the `LookTeleport` component on `MeMyselfEye` with a new `LookSpawnTeleport` one:

1. In Hierarchy, select `MeMyselfEye`
2. Disable the `LookTeleport` component, if present
3. Add **Component | New Script** and name it `LookSpawnTeleport`

Write the new script as follows:

```
using UnityEngine;

public class LookSpawnTeleport : MonoBehaviour
{
  private Color saveColor;
  private GameObject currentTarget;

   void Update()
   {
       Transform camera = Camera.main.transform;
       Ray ray;
       RaycastHit hit;
       GameObject hitTarget;
```

```
        ray = new Ray(camera.position, camera.rotation *
        Vector3.forward);
        if (Physics.Raycast(ray, out hit, 10f,
            LayerMask.GetMask("TeleportSpawn")))
        {
            hitTarget = hit.collider.gameObject;
            if (hitTarget != currentTarget)
            {
                Unhighlight();
                Highlight(hitTarget);
            }

            if (Input.GetButtonDown("Fire1"))
            {
                transform.position = hitTarget.transform.position;
            }
        }
        else if (currentTarget != null)
        {
            Unhighlight();
        }
    }
}
```

The `Update()` function does a Raycast to see if any of the spawn point objects is selected. If so, the object is highlighted (unhighlighting any previous ones). Then, if the `Fire1` button is pressed, it teleports the player to that location.

We add a couple of private helper functions, `Highlight()` and `Unhighlight()`. The first highlights an object by modifying its material color, making it more opaque (alpha 0.8). Unhighlight restores the original color when you look away:

```
private void Highlight(GameObject target)
{
    Material material = target.GetComponent<Renderer>().material;
    saveColor = material.color;
    Color hiColor = material.color;
    hiColor.a = 0.8f; // more opaque
    material.color = hiColor;
    currentTarget = target;
}

private void Unhighlight()
{
    if (currentTarget != null)
    {
      Material material =
```

```
currentTarget.GetComponent<Renderer>().material;
        material.color = saveColor;
        currentTarget = null;
    }
  }
```

OK, now let's place a few of the markers around the scene:

1. Drag the `TeleportSpawn` object from Hierarchy to your `Prefabs` folder in the **Project Assets**
2. Duplicate `TeleportSpawn` three times
3. **Position** one of them at (0, 0, -1.5) (the default `MeMyselfEye` position)
4. Move the others to suitable locations, such as (2, 0, 3), (-4, 0, 1), and if you have the Overlook, (3.5, 2.5, 0)

Alright! Press **Play**. When you look at a spawn point, it highlights. When you press the `Fire1` button, you teleport to the location.

It may be useful to add a reticle (small cursor) at the center of your camera view to help focus the player's attention on the teleport objects, as we did in `Chapter 6`, *World Space UI*, under the topic *The reticle cursor*.

Although the teleport works, it may be nice if it also sets your view direction. One way to do this is to carefully place the `TeleportSpawn` objects facing the direction we want the player to face, and setting the player's transform rotation, in addition to position.

To give a visual clue for the direction the spawn point is facing, we'll add a graphic. We have included an image file, `flip-flops.png`, with this book. Otherwise, use anything that indicates a forward direction. Perform the following steps:

1. Import the `flip-flops.png` texture by dragging it into your `Project Textures` folder (or navigating to **Import New Asset...**).
2. Create a new material in the Material folder and name it `FlipFlops`.
3. Drag the `flip-flops` texture onto the `FlipFlops` material's **Albedo** map and choose **Rendering Mode** as **Cutout**.
4. Select the `TeleportSpawn` object in **Hierarchy**.
5. Create a child **Quad** object (right-click **Create** I **3D Object** I **Quad**).
6. Drag the `FlipFlops` material onto the `Quad`.
7. Set the Quad's **Transform Position** to (0, .01, 0) and its **Rotation** to (90, 0, 0) so that it lies flat on the ground plane.

8. Select the parent `TeleportSpawn` object and in Inspector, press **Apply** to save these changes to the prefab. Now all the spawns will have feet.

9. Note that for the one up on the Overlook, you can adjust its Quad so it's visible from below, such as **Position** (`0`, `-0.2`, `0`) and **Rotation** (`-90`, `0`, `180`)

The modification to our script to apply the rotation is trivial:

```
if (Input.GetButtonDown("Fire1"))
{
    transform.position = hitTarget.transform.position;
    transform.rotation = hitTarget.transform.rotation;
}
```

There it is, a gaze-based teleportation system with predefined spawn points, as shown here in the **Scene** window:

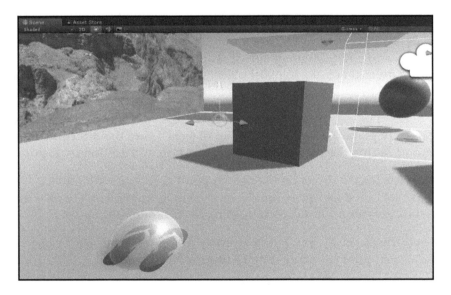

# Other teleport considerations

There's a lot more that can be said and done with teleportation. You may prefer to select the location using hand controllers rather than gaze. It is common to show the teleport pointer using an arced laser beam (using a Bezier curve). The teleport spawn point is often rendered using a glow or fiery effect. Many of these features have already been built and provided using higher-level VR toolkits (see next topic).

Blink teleport is a technique that does a fade-out fade-in between the change in player position. It is said to provide an additional degree of comfort. We won't show the code here, but there are several techniques for implementing fades for VR, such as creating a screen-space canvas that covers the entire camera with a black panel, and lerping its alpha channel as it fades (see `https://docs.unity3d.com/ScriptReference/Mathf.Lerp.html`). Some have even found fading with a literal blink effect is quite natural, where you rapidly fade out from top to bottom, and fade in bottom to top, like an eyelid closing and opening.

Another technique is to provide a third-person view of the scene from above, sometimes called a **mini-map**, **god view**, or **dollhouse view**. From this perspective, the player could point to a new location to teleport. This mini version of the scene could be an object the player uses as a tool in the main scene, or you transition to this view mode during the teleportation selection process.

You can also teleport to a different scene. Combined with the blink fade in/out, you call `SceneManager.LoadScene("OtherSceneName")` rather than simply changing the transform position. Note, you must add the other scene to the **Build Settings Scenes to Build** list (see `https://docs.unity3d.com/ScriptReference/SceneManagement.SceneManager.LoadScene.html`).

Clever use of teleportation and the player's direction can lead to efficient use of limited play space and give the perception of the VR space being much larger than actually in real life. For example, in room-scale VR, if you have the player walk toward the edge of the play space and enter an elevator (teleport), she could be facing the back of the elevator going in and must turn around when the doors open on the new level and can now physically walk forward. In fact, infinite corridors and connected rooms could be implemented this way while maintaining player immersion.

# Teleportation toolkits

We have explored several different locomotion and teleportation mechanics. All of them use your gaze direction for selection. This is sometimes the best choice. Sometimes it's not. It certainly is the lowest common denominator between various VR devices, from high-end HTC VIVE and Oculus Rift to the low-end Google Cardboard, gaze-based selection with a simple click will always be available.

It is likely you will prefer to use the hand controller for selection. High-end systems include two positionally tracked controllers, one for each hand. Lower-end devices, such as Google Daydream, include a single 3DOF "laser pointer" controller. Another reason we avoided implementing with controllers so far is the coding varies greatly from one device to the next. Also, the device-specific toolkits often come with components and prefabs that implement this mechanic, optimized for their particular platform, including high-performance shaders for rendering arced laser beams and teleportation markers.

In this section, we will show how to implement teleportation using these higher-level components, using SteamVR Interaction System and Google Daydream Elements. If you're not using one of these, please see the toolkits project with your target device, or consider a generalized toolkit such as the open source VRTK (`https://github.com/thestonefox/VRTK`).

# Teleporting with SteamVR Interaction System

The SteamVR Interaction System we first introduced in `Chapter 5`, *Handy Interactables* includes easy to use teleport components. If you are using SteamVR SDK, it can be found in the `Assets/SteamVR/InteractionSystem/Teleport/` folder. The teleport tools include a lot of extras we didn't get a chance to implement ourselves, including materials, models, prefabs, scripts, shaders, sounds, textures, haptics, oh my!

Specifically, the teleport toolkit includes:

- `Teleporting` prefab: Teleportation controller, add one per scene
- `TeleportPoint` prefab: Locations you want to teleport to, add one for each location
- `TeleportArea` component: Add to a game object, such as a Plane, to allow teleporting anywhere on that area

Interaction System includes its own `Player` camera rig which replaces the default `[CameraRig]` we have been using, as follows:

1. Locate the `Player` prefab in `SteamVR/InteractionSystem/Core/Prefabs`
2. Drag it as a child of `MeMyselfEye` in your scene **Hierarchy**
3. Delete or disable the `[CameraRig]` object

4. Drag a copy of `Teleporting` prefab from Project `Assets/SteamVR/InteractionSystem/Teleport/Prefabs` as a child of `MeMyselfEye` (this controller can actually go anywhere in the scene)
5. Select the **Player** in **Hierarchy**, and drag its parent `MeMyselfEye` onto its **Tracking Origin Transform** slot

This last step is important. The toolkit's teleportation components change the position of the `Player` object by default. We want to teleport the Player parent, `MeMyselfEye`, when we teleport. This might also be used if in your game, for example, the player is sitting in the cockpit of vehicle and you intend to teleport the whole vehicle, not just the Player itself.

If you followed the projects earlier in this chapter, disable the things we won't be using here:

1. On `MyMyselfEye`, disable or remove the **Look Teleport** and **Look Spawn Teleport** components
2. Disable or delete each of the `TeleportSpawn` objects

Now, for each teleport location:

1. Drag a copy of the `TeleportPoint` prefab from Project `Assets/SteamVR/InteractionSystem/Teleport/Prefabs` into the Hierarchy
2. Place one where you want in the scene. As previously, we used (0, 0, -1.5), (2, 0, 3), (-4, 0, 1), and on the Overlook (3.5, 2.5, 0)

That's it! Press **Play**. The teleport points do not show until you press the button on your controller, then they glow, a dashed laser arc lets you choose one, and you go there. In the Game window shown here, I am teleporting to the Overlook location:

Please review the many options on the Teleport component. You can modify or replace materials used for highlighting teleport points, sounds, and other effects. The Teleport Arc component has options for rendering the laser arc, and the `TeleportPoints` themselves can each be modified separately.

# Teleporting with Daydream Elements

The Google Daydream Elements package we first introduced in Chapter 5, *Handy Interactables* includes some teleport components. If you are targeting Google Daydream, you can install the separate Daydream Elements download from GitHub (`https://github.com/googlevr/daydream-elements/releases`). And documentation can be found on the Elements site (`https://developers.google.com/vr/elements/teleportation`).

Once imported into your project, it can be found in the `Assets/DaydreamElements/Elements/Teleport/` folder. There is a demo scene, **Teleport**, and associated materials, models, prefabs, scripts, shaders, and textures.

Out of the box, the tools are pretty generic and very customizable. The primary prefab is `TeleportController`, which does all the work. The user input used to trigger teleport behavior can be configured in the Unity Editor by filling the component slots, as shown here:

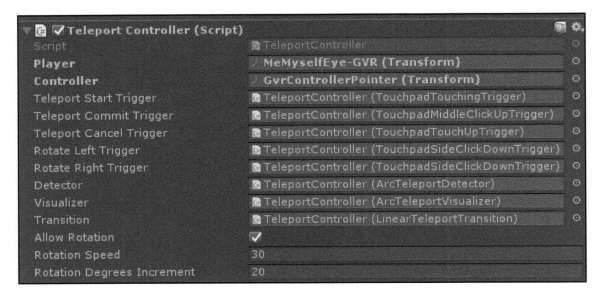

You can extend the teleporter by changing its *detector*, *visualizer*, and *transition* classes.

- **Detector**: Such as the `ArcTeleportDetector` does a curved arc Raycast to find objects in the scene and limits the hit to horizontal surfaces with adequate space to "fit" the player, so you do not teleport into walls.
- **Visualizer**: Such as the `ArcTeleportVisualizer`, renders the arc when teleport is triggered.
- **Transition**: Such as `LinearTeleportTransition`, animates the player to the new location. This could be modified to implement a blink effect, for example.

To add it to your scene:

1. Drag the `TeleportController` prefab into your **Hierarchy** as child of **Player** (for us that `MeMyselfEye` | **GVRCameraRig** | **Player**)
2. Reset its **Transform**, if necessary
3. Drag the `MeMyselfEye` object onto the `TeleportController` component's **Player** transform slot
4. Drag `GvrControllerPointer` (or whichever controller game object you're using) onto the **Controller** transform slot

Press **Play** and you can teleport all around your scene. There is no need to place specific teleport targets.

By default, the `TeleportController` will work by letting you land on any object in the scene that has a collider. You can limit the objects considered by the detector's Raycast by specifying the layer(s). Also, if you want arbitrarily shaped target areas that are not necessarily game objects in your scene, you can add sets of objects with just colliders, no renderers. This is how the teleport areas on the islands are implemented in the Daydream Elements teleport demo.

# Resetting center and position

Sometimes in VR, the view presented in the headset is not quite in sync with your body's orientation. Device SDKs provide functions to reset the orientation of the headset with respect to the real-world space. This is often referred to as the **recentering** of the view.

Unity provides an API call that maps to the underlying device SDK to recenter the device, `UnityEngine.VR.InputTracking.Recenter()`. This function will center tracking to the current position and orientation of the HMD. It only works with seated and standing experiences. Room scale experiences are not affected.

At the time of this writing, Recenter does not work in SteamVR, even for seated configuration. The solution is to call the following code instead:

```
Valve.VR.OpenVR.System.ResetSeatedZeroPose();
Valve.VR.OpenVR.Compositor.SetTrackingSpace(Valve.VR.ETrackingUniverseOrigi
n.TrackingUniverseSeated);
```

The Daydream controller has reset built into the underlying system (press and hold the system button). This is because unwanted drift is so common on mobile VR devices. Also, for Cardboard (and Daydream users without a controller), there is a standard floor canvas menu you should include in your player rig (as we did in Chapter 3, *VR Build and Run*), that includes a reset and recenter buttons.

On other systems, you can choose a button that triggers a call to Recenter as needed.

# Supporting room scale teleportation

As mentioned, the Unity Recenter function does not have any affect on room scale setups. We assume that room scale players are standing and mobilized, so they can just turn themselves to face "forward" within the VR scene.

When teleporting, however, we are moving the player to a new location, and possibly to an entirely different scene. When we reposition MyMyselfEye or any parent of the positionally tracked camera, the player is not necessary located at origin of that rig. If the player teleports to a new location, his whole play space should be ported and the player should end up standing on the virtual location he specifically chose.

The following function will compensate the teleport transform to the player's relative pose within the playspace. As written, it assumes it is a component on the MeMyselfEye player root object:

```
private void TeleportRoomscale( Vector3 targetPosition )
{
    Transform camera = Camera.main.transform;
    float cameraAngle = camera.eulerAngles.y;
    transform.Rotate( 0f, -cameraAngle, 0f);
    Vector3 offsetPos = camera.position - transform.position;
    transform.position = targetPosition.position - offsetPos;
}
```

To use it in our previous teleport script examples, replace the `transform.position = target.transform.position;` line with a call to `TeleportRoomscale( target.transform.position )` instead.

# Managing VR motion sickness

VR motion sickness, or simulator sickness, is a real symptom and a concern for virtual reality. Researchers, psychologists, and technologists with a wide array of specializations and PhDs are studying the problem to better understand the underlying causes and find solutions.

A cause of VR motion sickness is a lag in screen updates, or latency, when you're moving your head. Your brain expects the world around you to change exactly in sync. Any perceptible delay can make you feel uncomfortable, to say the least.

Latency can be reduced by faster rendering of each frame, keeping to the recommended frames per second. Device manufacturers see this as their problem to solve, in both hardware and device driver software. GPU and chip manufacturers see it as a processor performance and throughput problem. We will undoubtedly see leaps and bounds of improvements over the coming years.

At the same time, as VR developers, we need to be aware of latency and other causes of VR motion sickness. Developers need to look at it like it's our problem too because ultimately, it comes down to performance and ergonomics. With an ongoing dichotomy of mobile VR versus desktop VR, there will always be upper bounds on the performance of devices that our players will be using. In `Chapter 13`, *Optimizing for Performance and Comfort*, we dive into the technical details of the rendering pipeline and performance.

But it's not just technology. I can get nauseous riding a real-world roller coaster. So, why wouldn't a VR one have a similar effect? Things to consider that help improve your players' comfort and safety include game mechanics and user experience design such as the following:

- **Don't move fast**: When moving or animating a first-person character, don't move too fast. High-speed first-person shooter games that work on gaming consoles and desktop PCs may not work out so well in VR.
- **Look forward**: When moving through a scene, if you're looking to the side rather than straight ahead, you're more likely to feel nauseous.

- **Don't turn your head too fast**: Discourage users from turning their head quickly with the VR headset on. The latency in updating the HMD screen is aggravated by larger changes in the viewport in small time slices.

- **Offer comfort mode**: When a scene requires you to quickly turn yourself a lot of times, provide a ratcheted rotation mechanism, also known as comfort mode, which lets you change the direction in which you look in larger increments.

- **Use fade or blink** cuts during teleportation and scene changes. When fading, go to a dark color, as white can be startling.

- **Use tunneling** or other techniques during locomotion. Reduce what is visible in the peripheral vision by masking the camera except what is just in front of you.

- **Use a third-person camera**: If you have high-speed action but you don't necessarily intend to give the user a thrill ride, use a third-person camera view.

- **Stay grounded**: Provide visual cues that help the user stay grounded, such as horizon lines, nearby objects in your field of view, and relative fixed-position objects, such as dashboards and body parts.

- **Provide an option to recenter the view**: Mobile VR devices, in particular, are subject to drift and the need to be recentered on occasion. With wired VR devices, it helps you avoid getting tangled in HMD wires. As a safety issue, recentering your view relative to the real world may help you avoid hitting furniture and walls in the physical space.

- **Don't use cut scenes**: In traditional games (and movies), a technique that can be used to transition between levels is to show a 2D cutscene movie. This does not work in VR if the head motion detection is disabled. It breaks the immersion and can cause nausea. An alternative is to simply fade to black and then open the new scene.

- **Optimize rendering performance**: It behooves all VR developers to understand the underlying causes of latency-specifically rendering performance-and what you can do to optimize it, such as lowering the poly count and choosing lighting models carefully. Learn to use performance monitoring tools in order to keep the frames per second within the expected and acceptable limits. More on this will be discussed in `Chapter 10`, *Using All 360 Degrees*.

- **Encourage users to take breaks**: Alternatively, you can maybe just provide a puke-bag with your game! Or not.

# Summary

In this chapter, we explored many different ways of moving around within your virtual environments. We started by examining Unity's components that support conventional third-person and first-person characters and quickly realized most of those capabilities are not too useful in VR. For instance, we don't want the app to bob our head up and down as we walk, and we don't necessarily want to go jumping off buildings either. Moving around is important, but player comfort is more so. You don't want to induce motion sickness.

Locomotion is moving smoothly and linearly across the scene, akin to walking. Using gaze-based mechanics, we implemented moving in the direction you're looking and used input buttons to start and stop. Then, we separated the locomotion from head direction, always moving "forward" and using a separate input (thumbpad) to change the angle our body is facing. With this *comfort mode*, you can locomote and still look around.

Jumping to a new location is called teleportation. We started again with a gaze-based mechanic, letting you select a teleport location where you're looking. We implemented a couple ways of constraining where you are allowed to teleport, using NavMesh and using teleport spawn points. Then, we looked at some teleportation toolkits, from SteamVR and Google Daydream, which provide a rich set of capabilities, as well as a juicy user experience that is not trivial to implement from scratch. If you're targeting a different platform, such as Oculus, there are similar tools.

In the next chapter, we'll explore the Unity physics engine more and implement some interactive games.

# 8
# Playing with Physics and Fire

In this chapter, we will use physics and other Unity features to build variations of an interactive ball game. Along the way, we explore managing objects, Rigidbody physics, and adding more interactivity to the virtual experience. You will see how properties and materials based on physics can be added to objects, as well as more on C# scripting, particle effects, and music.

In this chapter, you will learn about the following topics:

- The Unity physics engine, the Unity Rigidbody component, and Physic Materials
- Using velocity and gravity
- Managing object lifetime and object pooling
- Interacting with objects in VR using your head and hands
- Building a fireball using particle effects
- Synchronizing with music

Note that the projects in this chapter are separate and are not directly required by the other chapters in this book. If you decided to skip any of it or not save your work, that's OK.

## Unity physics

In Unity, the behavior of an object that is based on physics is defined separately from its mesh (shape), materials (UV texture), and the renderer properties. The items that play into physics include the following:

- **Rigidbody**: Enables the object to act under the control of the physics engine, receive forces and torque to move in a realistic way
- **Collider**: Defines a simplified, approximated shape of the object used for calculating collisions with other objects

- **Physic Material**: Defines friction and bounce effects of colliding objects
- **Physics Manager**: Applies global settings for 3D physics for your project

Basically, physics (in this context) is defined by the positional and rotational forces that affect the transform of an object, such as gravity, friction, momentum, and collisions with other objects. It is not necessarily a perfect simulation of physics in the real world because it's optimized for performance and separation of concerns to facilitate animation. Besides, virtual worlds might just need their own laws of physics that aren't found in our God-given universe!

Unity integrates the **NVIDIA PhysX** engine, a real-time physics calculation middleware, which implements classical Newtonian mechanics for games and 3D applications. This multiplatform software is optimized to utilize fast hardware processors when present. It is accessible via the Unity scripting API.

A key to physics is the Rigidbody component that you add to objects. Rigidbodies have parameters for gravity, mass, and drag, among others. Rigidbodies can automatically react to gravity and collisions with other objects. No extra scripting is needed for this. During gameplay, the engine calculates each rigid object's momentum and updates its transform position and rotation.

Details on Rigidbodies can be found at
`http://docs.unity3d.com/ScriptReference/Rigidbody.html`.

Unity projects have a global gravity setting, found in the project's Physics Manager by navigating to **Edit | Project Settings | Physics**. As you might expect, the default gravity setting is a **Vector3** with values (0, -9.81, 0) that apply a downward force to all Rigidbodies. Gravity is in meters per second squared.

Rigidbodies can automatically react to gravity and collisions with other objects. Extra scripting is not needed for this.

In order to detect a collision, both the colliding objects must have a `Collider` component. There are built-in colliders with basic geometric shapes such as a cube, sphere, cylinder, and a capsule. A mesh collider can assume an arbitrary shape. If you can, it's best to use one or more basic collider shapes that approximately fit the actual object, rather than a mesh collider to reduce the expense of calculating the actual collisions during gameplay. Unity requires that if your object will be used in physics and has a Rigidbody, then its mesh collider must be marked as convex and be limited to 255 triangles.

When rigid objects collide, the forces pertinent to each object in the collision are applied to the others. The values of the resulting forces are calculated based on the objects' current velocity and body mass. Other factors are also taken into consideration, such as gravity and drag (that is, resistance). Furthermore, you have options to add constraints to freeze the position or rotation of a given object in any of its *x*, *y*, and *z* axes.

The calculations can be further affected when a Physic Material is assigned to the object's collider, which adjusts the friction and the bounciness effects of the colliding objects. These properties will be applied only to the object that owns the Physic Material. (Note that it's really spelled *Physic Material* rather than *Physics Material* for historical reasons.)

So, let's say that Object A (Ball) hits Object B (Brick). If Object A has bounciness and Object B does not, Object A will have an impulse applied in the collision, but Object B will not. However, you have options to determine how their friction and bounciness combine, as we'll see next. It's not necessarily an accurate simulation of real-world physics. It's a game engine, not a computer-aided engineering modeler.

From a scripting point of view, Unity will trigger events when objects collide (`OnTriggerEnter`), each frame while objects are colliding (`OnTriggerStay`), and when they've stopped colliding (`OnTriggerExit`).

If this sounds daunting, read on. The rest of this chapter breaks it down into understandable bits and pieces.

# Bouncy balls

The feature we'll implement here is, when a ball drops from mid-air and hits the ground, it bounces back up and down, and up again, diminished over time.

We are going to start simply with a new scene that consists of a ground plane and a sphere. Then, we'll add physics to it, a bit at a time, as follows:

1. Create a new scene by navigating to **File | New Scene.**
2. Then, navigate to **File | Save Scene As...** and name it `BallsFromHeaven`.
3. Create a new plane by navigating to **GameObject | 3D Object | Plane** and reset its transform using the `Transform` component's *gear* icon **| Reset.**
4. Create a new sphere by navigating to **GameObject | 3D Object | Sphere** and rename it `BouncyBall`.
5. Set its **Scale** to (`0.5, 0.5, 0.5`) and **Position** to (0, 5,0) so that it's above the center of the plane.
6. Drag the **Red** material from **Project Assets** (created in `Chapter 2`, *Content, Objects and Scale*) onto it so that it looks like a bouncy ball.

The new Unity scene defaults come with **Directional Light** and **Main Camera**. It's OK to use this **Main Camera** for the time being.

Click on the *Play* button. Nothing happens. The ball just sits in mid-air and doesn't move.

Now, let's give it a Rigidbody, as follows:

1. With `BouncyBall` selected, in **Inspector**, navigate to **Add Component | Physics | Rigidbody.**
2. Click on the *Play* button. It drops like a lead balloon.

Let's make it bounce, as follows:

1. In the **Project** panel, select the top-level **Assets** folder, navigate to **Create | Folder**, and rename it to `Physics`
2. With the `Physics` folder selected, create a material by navigating to **Assets | Create | Physic Material** (or right-click within the folder)
3. Name it `Bouncy`
4. Set its **Bounciness** value to 1
5. With the `BouncyBall` sphere selected in **Hierarchy**, drag the `Bouncy` asset from **Project** onto the sphere's **Collider** material field in **Inspector**

Click on the *Play* button. It bounces, but it does not go very high. We used the maximum value for **Bounciness** as 1.0. What's slowing it down? It's not the **Friction** settings. Rather, the **Bounce Combine** is set to **Average**, which determines how much of the bounciness of the ball (1) is mixed with that of the plane (0). So, it diminishes rapidly over time. We want the ball to retain all its bounciness. We will accomplish this, as follows:

1. Change the Bouncy object's **Bounce Combine** to **Maximum**.
2. Click on the *Play* button.

Much better. Actually, too much better. The ball keeps bouncing back up to its original height, ignoring gravity. Now, change the **Bounciness** to 0.8. The bounces diminish, and the ball will eventually come to a stop.

Let's check it out in VR, as follows:

1. Delete the default **Main Camera** from the **Hierarchy** root.
2. Drag the MeMyselfEye prefab from **Project Assets** into the scene. Set its **Position** to (0, 0, −4).

Run it in VR. Pretty neat! Even the simplest things look impressive in VR.

Unity's Standard Assets package includes a handful of example physic materials, including Bouncy, Ice, Meta, Rubber, and Wood.

OK, let's have some fun. Make it rain bouncy balls! To do this, we'll make the ball a prefab and write a script that instantiates new balls, dropping them from random positions, as follows:

1. Drag the BouncyBall object from **Hierarchy** into the Project Assets/Prefabs folder, making it a prefab.
2. Delete the BouncyBall object from the **Hierarchy**, since we'll be instantiating it with a script.
3. Create an empty game controller object to attach the script to by navigating to **GameObject** | **Create Empty**. Rename it GameController.
4. In **Inspector**, navigate to **Add Component** | **New Script**, name it BallsFromHeaven, and open the script for editing.

Edit the script so that it looks like this:

```
using UnityEngine;

public class BallsFromHeaven : MonoBehaviour
{
  public GameObject ballPrefab;
  public float startHeight = 10f;
  public float interval = 0.5f;

  private float nextBallTime = 0f;

  void Update ()
  {
    if (Time.time > nextBallTime)
    {
      nextBallTime = Time.time + interval;
      Vector3 position = new Vector3( Random.Range (-4f, 4f),
        startHeight, Random.Range (-4f, 4f) );
      Instantiate( ballPrefab, position, Quaternion.identity );
    }
  }
}
```

The script drops a new ball from `startHeight` at the rate of every `interval` seconds (an interval of 0.5 means that a new ball is dropped every half second). The new ball position is at a random **X-Z** coordinate between -4 and 4. The `Instantiate()` function adds a new ball into the scene **Hierarchy**.

Save the script. We now need to populate the **Ball** field with the `BouncyBall` prefab, as follows:

1. With `GameController` selected in **Hierarchy**, drag the `BouncyBall` prefab from the `Project Assets/Prefabs` folder onto the **Ball Prefab** slot in the **Balls From Heaven (Script)** panel in **Inspector**.
2. Be sure to use the `BouncyBall` prefab from **Project Assets** so that can be instantiated.
3. Save the scene. Run it in VR. Fun!

This is what I get:

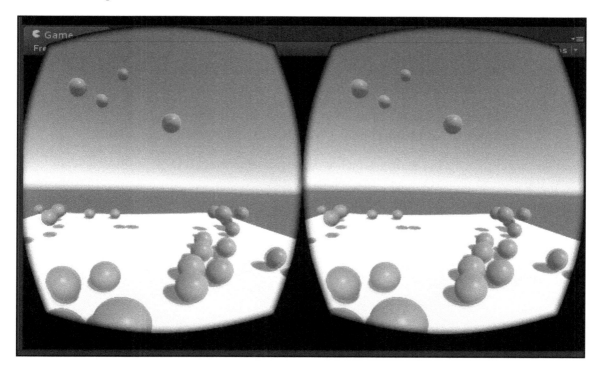

In summary, we created a sphere with a Rigidbody and added a Physic Material with a **Bounciness** property of 0.8 and **Bounce Combine** to **Maximum**. Then, we saved the BouncyBall as a prefab and wrote a script to instantiate new balls that drop from above.

# Managing game objects

Whenever you have a script that instantiates objects, you must be aware of the life cycle of the object and possibly arrange to destroy it when it is no longer needed. You can destroy game objects, for example, after it is no longer visible in the scene, or after a specific life duration, or limit the scene to a maximum number of balls.

# Destroying fallen objects

In our scene, we have a limited size ground plane and as balls hit one another, some will fall off the plane into oblivion. At that point, we can remove the fallen ball from the scene. Watch the **Hierarchy** panel as new balls are instantiated. Note that some balls end up bouncing off the plane platform but remain in the **Hierarchy** panel. We need to clean this up by adding a script that destroys the balls that are out of play, as follows:

1. Select the `BouncyBall` prefab in `Project Assets/Prefabs`
2. Navigate to **Add Component | New Script** and name it `DestroyBall`

Here's a `DestroyBall.cs` script, which will destroy the object if its **Y** position is well below the ground plane (**Y** = 0):

```
using UnityEngine;
using System.Collections;

public class DestroyBall : MonoBehaviour
{
  void Update ()
  {
    if (transform.position.y < -5f)
    {
      Destroy (gameObject);
    }
  }
}
```

# Setting a limited lifetime

Another strategy for managing object life cycle is to limit their duration. This is especially effective for things like projectiles (bullets, arrows, bouncyballs) or other objects that the player cares most when its instantiated and then isn't paying attention to as gameplay moves on.

To implement, you could put a timer on the object prefab itself to destroy itself when time runs out.

Modify the `DestroyBall.cs` script to destroy the object after `delay` seconds:

```
public float timer = 15f;

void Start ()
```

```
{
    Destroy (gameObject, timer);
}
```

When you play, notice that the ground plane remains substantially less crowded than before. Each BouncyBall will be destroyed after 15 seconds or when it has fallen off the plane, whichever comes first.

# Implementing an object pool

If your `GameController` Interval is 0.5 seconds and the destroy timer is 15, then (do the math) there will be at most 30 balls in play at a time. Or less, if some have fallen over the edge. In that case, we do not need to make our app continuously allocate new memory for a new instance of BouncyBall, only to delete that object up to 15 seconds later. Too much instantiation and destroying of objects results in fragmented memory. Unity will periodically go through and clean this up, a computationally expensive process called **garbage collection** (**GC**) that is best to be avoided whenever possible.

Object pooling is when you create a list of reusable objects to be used in your game, rather than continuously instantiating new ones. You will activate/deactivate the objects instead of instantiate/destroy.

To implement this, we will write a generic object pooler and add it to the `GameController` in the scene.

For this, we are also introducing you to the concept of lists in C#. As the name indicates, a list is an ordered collection of objects, like an array. Lists can be searched, sorted, and otherwise manipulated (see the documentation here: https://msdn.microsoft.com/en-us/library/6sh2ey19.aspx). We will use them simply to hold our pre-instantiated objects. Let's name the script `ObjectPooler`:

1. Select the `GameController` in Hierarchy
2. Navigate to **Add Component** | **New Script** and name it `ObjectPooler`

Open for editing. Let's start by declaring several variables at the top:

```
using System.Collections.Generic;
using UnityEngine;

public class ObjectPooler : MonoBehaviour
{
    public GameObject prefab;
    public int pooledAmount = 20;
```

```
        private List<GameObject> pooledObjects;

    }
```

The public `prefab` will get the prefab object we want to instantiate, namely `BouncyBall`. And `pooledAmount` says how many objects to initially instantiate. The actual list is held in `pooledObjects`.

Now, when the scene starts, we initialize the list as follows:

```
    void Start () {
        pooledObjects = new List<GameObject>();
        for (int i = 0; i < pooledAmount; i++)
        {
            GameObject obj = (GameObject)Instantiate(prefab);
            obj.SetActive(false);
            pooledObjects.Add(obj);
        }
    }
```

We allocate a new list and populate it in the `for` loop, by instantiating our prefab, initially making it inactive, and adding it to the list.

Now when we want a new object, we'll call `GetPooledObject`, which looks for one in the list that is presently not active. If all of them are active and none is available for reuse, we return `null`:

```
    public GameObject GetPooledObject()
    {
        for (int i = 0; i < pooledObjects.Count; i++)
        {
            if (!pooledObjects[i].activeInHierarchy)
            {
                return pooledObjects[i];
            }
        }

        return null;
    }
```

That's it.

We can also enhance the script to optionally grow the list so it never returns null. Add the option at the top:

```
        public bool willGrow = true;
```

And add the following statements to `GetPooledObject` after the `for` loop:

```
...
if (willGrow)
{
    GameObject obj = (GameObject)Instantiate(prefab);
    pooledObjects.Add(obj);
    return obj;
}

return null;
}
```

Save the script, attach it to `GameController`, and drag the `BouncyBall` prefab onto the **Prefab** slot for the component.

Now we need to modify our `BallsFromHeaven` script to call `GetPooledObject` from `ObjectPooler` instead of `Instantiate`. The updated `BallsFromHeaven` script is as follows:

```
using UnityEngine;

[RequireComponent(typeof(ObjectPooler))]
public class BallsFromHeaven : MonoBehaviour
{
    public float startHeight = 10f;
    public float interval = 0.5f;

    private float nextBallTime = 0f;
    private ObjectPooler pool;

    void Start()
    {
        pool = GetComponent<ObjectPooler>();
        if (pool == null)
        {
            Debug.LogError("BallsFromHeaven requires ObjectPooler
component");
        }
    }

    void Update()
    {
        if (Time.time > nextBallTime)
        {
            nextBallTime = Time.time + interval;
            Vector3 position = new Vector3(Random.Range(-4f, 4f),
```

```
startHeight, Random.Range(-4f, 4f));
            GameObject ball = pool.GetPooledObject();
            ball.transform.position = position;
            ball.transform.rotation = Quaternion.identity;
            ball.GetComponent<RigidBody>().velocity = Vector3.zero;
            ball.SetActive(true);
        }
    }
}
```

Note that we added a directive, [RequireComponent(typeof(ObjectPooler)], to ensure the object has an ObjectPooler component (and we also double-check in the Start function).

It's important to note that since we're not instantiating new objects but reusing them, you may need to reset any object properties to their starting values. In this case, we reset not just the transform but the RigidBody's velocity to zero.

The last part is we modify DestroyBall to just disable (deactivate) the object rather than literally destroying it. Initially, handle the *fallen off the ground plane* case as follows:

```
using UnityEngine;

public class DestroyBall : MonoBehaviour {

    void Update () {
        if (transform.position.y < -5f)
        {
            DisableMe();
        }
    }

    private void DisableMe()
    {
        gameObject.SetActive(false);
    }
}
```

Instead of calling Destroy, we changed Update to call a new function, DisableMe, which simply deactivates the object, returning it to the pool of available objects.

For the timed destroy, there's a number of different ways to implement this. Earlier, we called Destroy(gameObject, timer) from Start(). We can do something similar, using OnEnable instead of Start, since that's when this instance starts. And it calls Invoke(), instead of destroy directly:

```
void OnEnable()
{
    Invoke("DisableMe", timer);
}

void OnDisable()
{
    CancelInvoke();
}
```

We also provide an OnDisable to cancel the Invoke, since the object could be disabled should the ball fall over the edge before the timer is done and potentially re-enabled, we should make sure it's not being invoked twice at the same time.

Now when you press **Play**, you can see in Inspector that new BouncyBalls are instantiated at the start to initialize the list, and then as it plays the objects are disabled and reactivated as they are returned to the pool and reused, as shown here (deactivated **BouncyBall(Clone)** objects are dimmer than the activated ones):

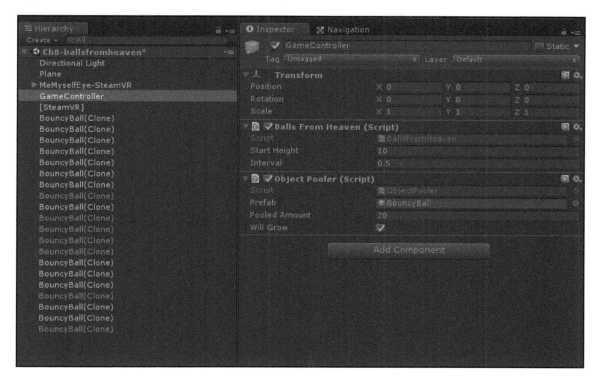

# Headshot game

Wouldn't it be fun to actually play with these bouncy balls? Let's make a game where you aim the ball at a target using headshots. For this game, balls drop one at a time from above and bounce off your forehead (face), aiming for a target.

The feature we'll implement here is, when a ball drops from above your head, you bounce it off your face and aim for a target.

To implement this, create a cube as a child of the camera object (much like we did for the reticle cursor in Chapter 6, *World Space UI*). This provides a collider parented by the VR camera, so our head pose will move the face of the cube. I decided a cube-shaped collider will be better for this game than a sphere or capsule because it provides a flat face that will make the bounce direction more predictable. Balls will drop out of the sky. For a target, we'll use a flattened cylinder. We'll add audio cues to indicate when a new ball has been released and when a ball hits the target.

Create a new scene or, more simple, start here by doing a Save As, and implement the head as follows:

1. Navigate to **File | Save Scene As** and name it BallGame
2. Delete the BallsFromHeaven script component attached to GameController using the *gear* icon **Remove Component**. We won't need it
3. In **Hierarchy**, unfold MeMyselfEye, drilling down to the Camera object and selecting it (for OpenVR that might be [CameraRig]/Camera (head); for Daydream, it may be Player/Main Camera/)
4. Create a new **3D Object | Cube**
5. With GameController selected, navigate to **Add Component | Audio | Audio Source**
6. Click on the small *circle-shaped* icon on the far right of the **AudioClip** field of **Audio Source** to open the **Select AudioClip** dialog box and choose the clip named Jump
7. With GameController selected, navigate to **Add Component | New Script**, name it BallGame, and open it for editing

You can decide to disable the cube's **Mesh Renderer**, but I think it's cool to watch it in the Scene window as you play. Since the camera is inside the cube, the player will not see it (since only the outward facing surfaces are rendered in the game view).

We'll play the `Jump` sound clip (provided with the `Characters` package of Unity's **Standard Assets**) to indicate when a new ball is dropped. You might try another, perhaps more interesting, effect.

Here's the `BallGame.cs` script. It looks a lot like the `BallsFromHeaven` one with just a few differences:

```
using UnityEngine;

public class BallGame : MonoBehaviour
{
    public Transform dropPoint;
    public float startHeight = 10f;
    public float interval = 3f;

    private float nextBallTime = 0f;
    private ObjectPooler pool;
    private GameObject activeBall;
    private AudioSource soundEffect;

    void Start()
    {
        if (dropPoint == null)
        {
            dropPoint = Camera.main.transform;
        }
        soundEffect = GetComponent<AudioSource>();
        pool = GetComponent<ObjectPooler>();
    }

    void Update()
    {
        if (Time.time > nextBallTime)
        {
            nextBallTime = Time.time + interval;
            soundEffect.Play();
            Vector3 position = new Vector3(
                dropPoint.position.x,
                startHeight,
                dropPoint.position.z);

            activeBall = pool.GetPooledObject();
            activeBall.transform.position = position;
```

```
                         activeBall.transform.rotation = Quaternion.identity;
                         activeBall.GetComponent<RigidBody>().velocity = Vector3.zero;
                         activeBall.SetActive(true);
               }
        }
    }
```

We instantiate a new ball every 3 seconds ( `interval` ) from a `startHeight` position above the current head position.

The drop point defaults to directly above the player's head position, as defined by the VR camera. That may feel uncomfortable on your neck, so let's extent it in front a little, 0.2 units:

1. As a child of `MeMyselfEye` (or as a child of your head or main camera object), create an empty game object and name it `Drop Point`
2. Set its Position to (0, 0, 0.2)
3. Drag this `Drop Point` onto the `GameController`'s Ball Game Drop Point slot

On positionally tracked VR rigs, if your drop point is relative to the camera, it will follow the player around. If it's relative to `MeMyselfEye`, it will be relative to your play space while the player can move around.

Try it in VR.

When you hear the ball, look up and aim the angle of your face to direct the bounce of the ball. *COOOL!*

Now, we need the target. Perform the following steps:

1. Create a flat cylinder for the target, navigate to **Game Object | 3D Object | Cylinder**, and name it `Target`.
2. Set its **Scale** to (3, 0.1, 3) and **Position** to (1, 0.2, 2.5) so that it's out in front of you on the ground.
3. Drag the `Blue` material from the `Project Assets/Materials` folder (created in `Chapter 2`, *Content, Objects and Scale*) onto it, or make a new one.
4. Note that its default Capsule Collider is domed, and it really won't do. On the Capsule Collider, select its *gear* icon | **Remove Component**.

5. Then, navigate to **Add Component | Physics | Mesh Collider**.

6. In the new **Mesh Collider**, enable the **Convex** checkbox and the **Is Trigger** checkbox too.

7. Add an audio source by navigating to **Add Component | Audio | Audio Source**.

8. With the `Target` selected, click on the small *circle* icon on the far right of the **AudioClip** field to open the **Select AudioClip** dialog box, and choose the clip named `Land` (found in Standard Assets).

9. Uncheck the **Play On Awake** checkbox.

10. And a new script, navigate to **Add Component | New Script**, name it `TriggerSound`, and open it in MonoDevelop.

Since we enabled Is Trigger, when something hits the collider, the `OnTriggerEnter` and other event handlers will get a call when present on the target object. The following `TriggerSound.cs` script will play a sound clip when you hit the target with a ball:

```
using UnityEngine;
using System.Collections;

public class TriggerSound : MonoBehaviour {
  public AudioSource hitSound;

  void Start() {
    hitSound = GetComponent<AudioSource> ();
  }

  void OnTriggerEnter(Collider other) {
    hitSound.Play ();
  }
}
```

The ball enters the target's collider and the physics engine invokes a trigger enter event. The script uses the `OnTriggerEnter()` handler to play the audio clip.

For a full list of the collider properties and trigger events, including `OnTrggerEnter` and `OnTriggerExit`, see the documentation at `https:/ /docs.unity3d.com/ScriptReference/Collider.html`.

Try it in VR. It's a VR game! The following image shows the scene with the first person's colliders and a ball bouncing off the cube collider towards the target:

 **Extra challenge**: Keep score. Provide an aiming reticle. Add a backboard. Add other features to make the game more challenging. For instance, you can vary the fire interval or increase the initial ball velocity.

Up to this point, we assigned **Bounciness** through a Physic Material attached to a sphere object. When the ball collides with another object, the Unity physics engine considers this bounciness to determine the ball's new velocity and direction. In the following section, we'll look at how one can transfer a bounce force from one object to another.

# Paddle ball game

Next, we'll add hand controlled paddles to hit the ball. To keep things somewhat generic, our game paddles will be simple objects parented by the hand controllers in your camera rig. We'll move the target to be on a wall instead of the floor, and serve the balls a little further out in front of you so they're reachable

To set up the scene, you can Save As a new name and we'll work from here. I'll name my `PaddleBallGame`.

1. Select **File** | **Save Scene As** and name it `PaddleBallGame`
2. Disable the head **Cube** we previously added as child of the camera, if present

First, let's create a paddle. We'll construct a very simple model using cylinders. You can find better ones, shaped and textured, online.

1. In the **Hierarchy** root, **Create** | **Create Empty**, name it `Paddle`, and reset its **Transform**
2. Add a child cylinder object (**Create** | **3D Object** | **Cylinder**) and name it `Handle`
3. Set the Handle's **Scale** to (`0.02, 0.1, 0.02`)
4. Add another **Cylinder** as a sibling of Handle and name it `Pad`
5. Set the pad's **Scale** to (`0.2, 0.005, 0.2`), **Rotation** (`90, 0, 0`), and **Position** (`0, 0.2, 0`)
6. In your Project Materials folder, create a new material (**Create** | **Material**) and name it `Paddle Material`
7. Give the material **Albedo** a wooden color, such as (`107, 79, 54, 255`), then drag the material onto the **Handle** and **Pad** objects

Now, modify the colliders:

1. Select the **Handle**, and delete its **Capsule Collider**
2. Select the **Pad**, and delete its **Capsule Collider**
3. With Pad selected, add a Mesh Collider (**Add Component** | **Physics** | **Mesh Collider**)
4. Check the **Convex** checkbox

Save the paddle as a prefab:

1. Drag the **Paddle** into your Project Prefabs folder
2. Delete the **Paddle** from your Hierarchy

We want to parent the Paddle to your hands. This is platform-specific. If you are using OpenVR, for example, that may be `MeMyselfEye / [CameraRig] / Controller` *(right)*. On Daydream, that might be `MeMyselfEye / Player / GvrControllerPointer`.

1. In **Hierarchy**, select the hand controller within `MeMyselfEye` (such as Controller (right). or `GvrControllerPointer`)
2. Create **Empty** child game object and name it `Hand` (reset its **Transform** if needed)
3. Create another **Empty** child beneath **Hand** and name it `Attach Point` (and reset its Transform if needed)
4. Drag the **Paddle** prefab from Project into **Hierarchy** as a child of **Attach Point**

Now, we can adjust the paddle's relative position and rotation so its grip feels natural within your hand. The follow values seem to work for me:

- In OpenVR, use the attach point **Rotation** (`20, 90, 90`)
- In Daydream, use **Position** (`0, 0, 0, 05`) and **Rotation** (`0, 90, 90`)

On Daydream, the `GvrControllerPointer` includes a `GvrArmModel` component that can be configured for simulating arm, elbow, and wrist movement with the simple 3DOF controller. Setting this up yourself can be confusing. Fortunately, a bunch of examples are provided in the **ArmModelDemo** scene the Daydream Elements package (in the `DaydreamElements/Elements/ArmModels/Demo/` folder) including prefabs with some preconfigured arm models. Let's add one. If you are on Daydream:

1. Find the `Elements/ArmModels/Prefabs` folder in Project Assets
2. Drag the `SwingArm` prefab into `MeMyselfEye / Player` as a sibling of `GvrControllerPointer`
3. Move `GvrControllerPointer` as a child of **SwingArm**

This will give more arm extension for using the paddle. You can further adjust the settings as needed, including try moving the SwingArm transform **Position** further in front (`0, 0, 0.3`).

Lastly, you might want to extend the ball drop location a little further out in front of you so it's more readily within hand reach. In the earlier version of the project, we defined a **Drop Point**; modify its position as desired (for example, z = `0.6`).

The paddle in play using HTC Vive is shown here:

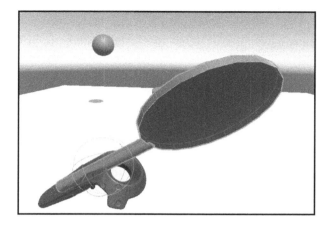

# Deflector versus paddle

As implemented, our paddle acts more like a deflector shield than a paddle. The ball will bounce off the paddle's Pad in a direction based on the Pad's surface normal orientation. But if you whack the ball, that doesn't transfer any physics. We can change this by adding a RigidBody to the Pad, as follows:

1. Select the **Pad** of your **Paddle**
2. **Add Component | Physics | RigidBody**
3. Uncheck **Use Gravity** checkbox
4. Check the **Is Kinematic** checkbox
5. Click the **Apply** button at top of Inspector to save your changes in the prefab

By making it kinematic, our Pad will apply physics to objects colliding with it, but will not react to collisions itself. This is good, otherwise, the paddle would shatter when hit by a ball.

One important lesson in this project is the use of attach points for defining relative positions for specific behaviors. We used a Drop Point to mark the X, Z position where balls are dropped from. We used an Attach Point to mark the relative position and rotation of the paddle in your hand. We could have added a Grip Point to the paddle itself to specify its relative origin. And so on.

# Shooter ball game

For the next iteration of this project, we'll shoot balls at the player and you have to hit them at a target on a wall. There's not a lot of innovation in this version, but it shows how you can take an existing mechanic and turn it on its side (both literally and figuratively).

To begin, lets make a wall and put the target on it:

1. In the **Hierarchy** root, create an **Empty** game object named `TargetWall` and
2. **Position** it at (0, 0, 5)
3. Create a child **Cube** and name it `Wall`
4. Set the Wall **Scale** to (10, 5, 0.1) and **Position** (0, 2.5, 0)
5. Create a new Material named `Wall Material`
6. Set its **Rendering Mode** to **Transparent**, and its **Albedo** color to (85, 60, 20, 75) so it's a translucent glassy color
7. Move the **Target** to a child of `TargetWall`
8. Modify the Target **Transform Scale** to (1.5, 0.1, 1.5), **Rotation** (90, 0, 0), and **Position** (0, 2.5, -0.25) so it's smaller and just in front of the wall itself

Next, instead of serving balls by dropping them out of the sky and relying on gravity, we'll shoot balls at you from a source on the wall:

1. Create a **Sphere** game object as a child of `TargetWall`, named `Shooter`
2. Set its **Scale** to (0.5, 0.5, 0.5) and **Position** (4, 2.5, -0.25)
3. Disable or remove its **Sphere Collider** component
4. Create a new Material named `Shooter Material`, with **Albedo** color (45, 22, 12, 255)

We'll add a gun barrel to the shooter:

1. Create another **Sphere** object as a child of Shooter, named `Barrel`
2. Set its **Scale** (0.1, 0.1, 0.1), **Rotation** (90, 0, 0), and **Position** (0, 0, -0.25)

Duplicate the Shooter and set the second one's **Position** to (-4, 2.5, -0.25) so there's one on either side of the Target. Here is a capture of the Scene view of the `TargetWall` with its sexy shooters:

The game controller script is similar to the BallGame one we have, but sufficiently different we should create a new one:

1. In **Hierarchy**, select GameController and disable or remove the BallGame component
2. Create a new C# script named ShooterBallGame and open it for editing

Write the ShooterBallGame script as follows. We give it two shooters and the script alternates between them to shoot balls in the direction of a shootAt location. We play a sound effect each time a ball is shot. First, let's define the public and private variable we will need:

```
using UnityEngine;

[RequireComponent(typeof(ObjectPooler))]
public class ShooterBallGame : MonoBehaviour
{
    public Transform shootAt;
    public Transform shooter0;
    public Transform shooter1;
    public float speed = 5.0f;
    public float interval = 3f;
```

```
    private float nextBallTime = 0f;
    private ObjectPooler pool;
    private GameObject activeBall;
    private int shooterId = 0;
    private Transform shooter;

    private AudioSource soundEffect;
}
```

The Start function initializes the variable we get at runtime:

```
void Start()
{
    if (shootAt == null)
    {
        shootAt = Camera.main.transform;
    }
    soundEffect = GetComponent<AudioSource>();
    pool = GetComponent<ObjectPooler>();
    if (pool == null)
    {
        Debug.LogError("BallGame requires ObjectPooler component");
    }
}
```

And the Update function shoots the balls at specified intervals, alternating between the two shooter locations:

```
void Update()
{
    if (Time.time > nextBallTime)
    {
        if (shooterId == 0)
        {
            shooterId = 1;
            shooter = shooter1;
        }
        else
        {
            shooterId = 0;
            shooter = shooter0;
        }

        nextBallTime = Time.time + interval;
        ShootBall();
    }
}
```

Finally, here's the `ShootBall()` code we extracted into its own function:

```
    private void ShootBall()
    {
        soundEffect.Play();
        activeBall = pool.GetPooledObject();
        activeBall.transform.position = shooter.position;
        activeBall.transform.rotation = Quaternion.identity;
        shooter.transform.LookAt(shootAt);
        activeBall.GetComponent<Rigidbody>().velocity = shooter.forward *
speed;
        activeBall.GetComponent<Rigidbody>().angularVelocity =
Vector3.zero;
        activeBall.SetActive(true);
    }
```

`ShootBall` grabs a new ball from the object pool and initializes its position based on the shooter position. It then rotates the shooter to be pointing at the `shootAt` position (using `transform.LookAt`) and uses its forward vector to define the ball's RigidBody velocity vector.

Back in Unity, we need to populate the public variable slots:

1. Drag the `Shooter` object (child of `TargetWall`) on to the **Shooter 0** slot
2. Drag the other `Shooter` object on to the **Shooter 1** slot

Leave the **Shoot At** slot empty for now, so it will default to the player's live head position.

Press **Play**. *Not bad*. The balls are too big and heavy. Let's create new ball prefabs with different properties:

1. Drag the `BouncyBall` prefab from `Project` folder into the **Hierarchy**
2. Rename it `ShooterBall`
3. Set its **Scale** to (0.25, 0.25, 0.25)
4. Uncheck the **Use Gravity** checkbox (alternatively, you could play with its RigidBody **Mass** property)
5. Drag the **ShooterBall** from **Hierarchy** into your `Prefabs` folder, creating a new prefab for it
6. Delete the **ShooterBall** from the **Hierarchy**
7. Select `GameController` in Hierarchy, and drag the **ShooterBall** onto its **Object Pooler Prefab** slot

Now, the object pool will instantiate a collection of the new prefab objects.

Press **Play**. *Oh yeah!* The game is now much more challenging. Also, try modifying the **Interval** and **Speed** settings.

It may be awkward that the ball is always shooting towards your head, especially on Daydream where you have limited hand control. You can adjust the scene, for example, positioning the **ShootAt** empty game object, as child of `MeMyselfEye`, at **Position** (0, 0.9, 0.6), and setting it into the `GameController`'s **ShootAt** slot.

Some obvious gameplay improvement ideas should come to mind. You could make a moving target, perhaps in a predictable oscillating motion, or completely random. You could introduce some random variation in the ball velocity direction and speed or the intervals between shots. You could keep score, using `OnTriggerEnter` on the Target. You could disqualify bank shots that bounce first on the floor (using `OnTriggerEnter` on the ground plane).

# Juicing the scene

Having the basic mechanics implemented, we can now *juice it*! One of my favorite VR games is the popular Audio Shield (`http://audio-shield.com/`). We're almost there building our own, we just need to add fireballs, a compelling environment scene, and synchronizing the fireball shots with music!

The term *juice it* for game design was popularized by Jonasson and Purho in their presentation talk from 2012, *Juice it or lose it - a talk by Martin Jonasson & Petri Purho* (`https://www.youtube.com/watch?v=Fy0aCDmgnxg`). *A juicy game feels alive and responds to everything you do, tons of cascading action and response for minimal user input.*

# Great balls of fire

In the previous section, we disabled **Use Gravity** on the shooting balls. We did this in anticipation of changing the balls from being bouncy balls to balls of fire. Let's make that magic happen now. We will use the Particle System to render it instead of mesh geometry.

There are a lot of ways to get particle effects into your Unity project. If you recall, in Chapter 4, *Gaze-Based Control*, we added a water hose, spark emitter, and explosion effects from the `Unity Standard Assets` package. Here, we'll build our own, but use one of the materials, `ParticleFireCloud`, provided with the package. In the Unity Asset Store, you can find many offerings of particle effects and system enhancements too.

First, make a new prefab derived from ShooterBall, named `FireBall`, as follows:

1. Drag a copy of `ShooterBall` prefab from the `Project` folder into **Hierarchy**
2. Rename it FireBall
3. Drag **FireBall** into the `Project` *Prefabs* folder to create a new prefab
4. Select the `GameController` from **Hierarchy**
5. Drag the `FireBall` prefab from `Project` *Prefabs* folder onto the **Object Pooler Prefab** slot

OK, now we can add the particle system:

1. Select the **FireBall** from **Hierarchy**
2. Disable its **Mesh Renderer**, as we will render it with particles instead
3. Right-click **FireBall** and select **Create** | **Effects** | **Particle System**
4. Rename it Fireball Particle System

There are a lot of details in working with particles, many options and configuration parameters. As we step through this quick implementation of fireballs, observe the effects of each change as we make them one at a time. Note that you can preview the particle effects in the **Scene** window. Feel free to experiment on your own.

1. First, at the bottom of the Particle System **Inspector**, find the **Renderer** panel. In its **Material** slot, click the **doughnut icon** and choose the **ParticleFireCloud** material (located in `Standard Assets/Particle Systems/Materials`. If not present, you may need to import it using **Assets** | **Import Package** | **ParticleSystems**).
2. Near the top of the Particle System inspector, find the **Shape** panel. Select **Shape: Sphere**, and set its **Radius** to `0.1`.
3. Find the **Emission** panel, and set **Rate of Time** to `15`.
4. At the top of the inspector, set **Duration**: `2.00`.
5. **Start Lifetime**: `1`.
6. **Start Speed**: `0`.
7. **Start Size**: `0.5`.

8. For **Start Rotation**, click the **selector icon** on the right and choose **Random Between Two Curves**. Then click the slot and scroll to the **Curve Editor** at the bottom of the Inspector. If you're not familiar, the editor can take some getting used to. Choose a full range of values from 180 (at top of graph) to –180 (bottom of graph), as shown:

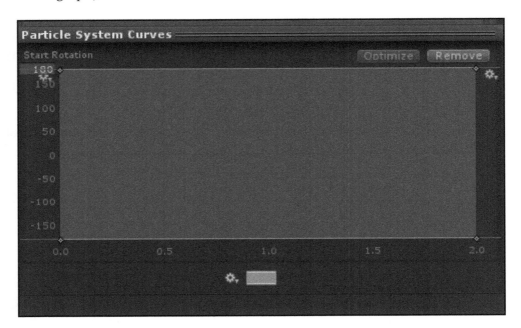

9. Enable **Color Over Lifetime** and click the slot to open its **Gradient Editor**. We want to adjust the **Alpha** curve so it starts at **Alpha** 0 at **Location** 0%, then becomes **Alpha** 255 at 10%, then fades out over time back to **Alpha** 0 at 100%. The editor is shown here:

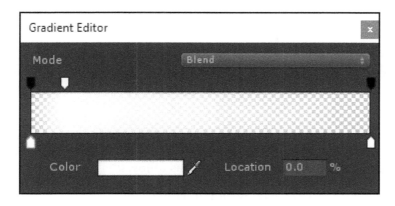

10. Set the **Start Color**, as **Gradient** (right-side selector) and then pick a range of colors such as yellow to red, as shown here:

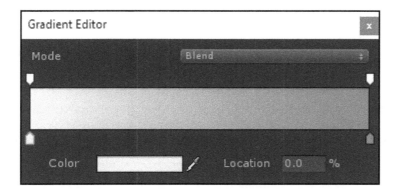

11. Next, set the **Velocity Over Lifetime**, using **Random Between Two Curves**. For each **X, Y, Z**, use the **Curve Editor** to set max and min values of 0.05 and -0.05 respectively. (You can modify the vertical axis of the graph by clicking the axis label and typing a number; you can copy curves, for example, by right-clicking the Z slot, choosing **Copy**, then right-clicking the Y slot and choosing **Paste**.)

At this point, we should adjust the fireball so it's about the same size as our original BouncyBall. To check:

1. Re-enable the FireBall's **Mesh Renderer**. Adjust the particle system by changing the Renderer's **Max Particle Size** to 0.1, or using the **Transform Scale**
2. Save your work by selecting **Apply** at the top of Inspector, to update your prefab

Now when you press **Play**, the Shooters will fire FireBalls. *Oh wow!*

If you'd like to add some sparkle effect to the fireball, we can do that with the **Trail** panel:

1. Enable the **Trail** panel
2. A warning may pop up tell you to add a trails material to the **Renderer**
3. In the **Renderer** panel, select the **doughnut icon** on the **Trail Material** slot, and choose **ParticleFireCloud** as we use for the main fireball

Speaking of trails, if you'd like to also implement trail effects on the fireball, there are several ways to do this too. A quick solution is to duplicate our fireball particle system and modify it to use a Cone shape instead of Sphere, as follows:

1. Select the **Fireball Particle System** in **Hierarchy.**
2. Right-click to **Duplicate**, move the duplicate as a child of Fireball Particle System and name it Trail Particle System.
3. Change its **Shape** to **Cone.**
4. Change its **Velocity Over Lifetime**. The **Z** curve needs a higher value range, such as 0.75 to 0.25.
5. The **X** and **Y** velocity curves should be smaller for some variation, such as 0.2 to −0.2.
6. Set the **Size Over Lifetime** range to 1.0 to 0.5.
7. In its Transform, set **Position** to (0, 0, 0.5) to give it an extra tail.

Here is a screenshot of the gameplay window paddling an incoming fireball!

Special thanks to Tyler Wissler for his instructional video *How To: Basic Fireballs in Unity* (June 2014), which was very helpful is developing this topic (`https://www.youtube.com/watch?v=OWShSR6Tr50`).

# Skull environment

To spice up our game, even more, we should find an exciting environment and scene. Searching the Asset Store, I found the *Skull Platform* free asset (`https://assetstore.unity.com/packages/3d/props/skull-platform-105664`). You can use it too, or find something different.

Assuming you've found and installed the Skull Platform asset, we'll add it to our scene. First, let's render our target as a skull:

1. Drag **Platform_Skull_o1** as a child of **Target** (under `TargetWall`).
2. Set its **Transform Rotation** (`0, 0, 180`) and **Scale** (`0.3, 0.3, 0.3`).
3. Select the **Target** and disable its **Mesh Renderer**.
4. Also, create a new Spotlight (**Create | Light | Spotlight**) to shine on the skull. As a child of Target, I used the following settings: **Position** (`-1, -30, -0.6`), **Rotation** (`-60, 60, 0`), **Range**: `10`, **Spot Angle**: `30`, **Color**: `#FFE5D4FF`, **Intensity**: `3`.

Next, let's add the big platform as a backdrop behind the wall. The quickest way is to merge in the Demoscene they provide:

1. Create an **Empty** game object in the **Hierarchy** root, name it SkullPlatform, reset its transform.
2. Drag a copy of the Skull Platform's demo scene named **Platform** (`Assets/Skull Platform/Demo/` folder) into the **Hierarchy.**
3. Select the Demo's **Scene**, **Lighting,** and **Particles** objects and drag them as children of **SkullPlatform.**
4. Now that we have the assets we want, right-click the **Platform** scene in Hierarchy and choose **Remove Scene**. When prompted, choose **Don't Save.**
5. Set the SkullPlatform **Position** to (`0, -1.5, 0`) so it's just below the ground plane.
6. Select the **GroundPlane** and disable its **Mesh Renderer**.

Now, we'll set up the scene environment lighting:

1. Delete the **Directional Light** from the scene Hierarchy.
2. Open the **Lighting** window. If its not already a tab in your editor, use **Window | Lighting | Settings** and dock it next to the Inspector.
3. Set its **Skybox Material** to **Sky** (provided in the Skull Platform package).
4. In the **Environmental Lighting** section, set **Source: Color** to #141415.
5. Check the **Fog** checkbox (in **Other Settings**), **Color** to #8194A1FF, **Mode: Exponential**, and **Density** to 0.03.

Here is a screen capture of the scene with the skull platform environment and lighting. *Sweet!*

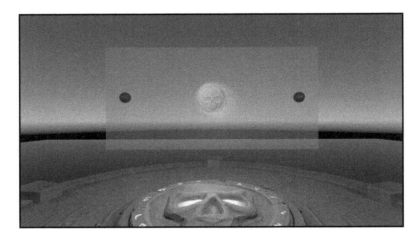

# Audio synchronization

We're almost there building our own version of Audio Shield, we just need to add synchronizing the fireball shots with music!

Unity provides an API for sampling audio source data, including `AudioSource.GetSpectrumData` and `GetOutputData`. Extracting actual beats in the music from this data is not trivial and requires a lot of math and some understanding of how music encoding works.

Fortunately, we found an open source script that does this for us, called Unity-Beat-Detection (`https://github.com/allanpichardo/Unity-Beat-Detection`). It conveniently provides Unity Events for `onBeat`, which we'll use. (It also provides `onSpectrum` events, with music frequency bands per frame, which you could use too, for example, to change the color of the fireball or other things based on frequency bands.)

1. Download the `AudioProcessor.cs` script from GitHub (we've provided a copy with the files for this book for your convenience)
2. Drag the file into your `Scripts` folder (or use **Assets | Import New Asset**)

For your music, find any MP3 or WAV file that has a nice beat, and import it into your project. We looked on SoundCloud NoCopyrightSounds track (`https://soundcloud.com/nocopyrightsounds/tracks`) to find one named *Third Prototype - Dancefloor* (`http://ncs.io/DancefloorNS`).

1. In Project window, create a folder named Audio
2. Drag your music file into the Audio folder (or use **Assets | Import New Asset**)

To implement this feature, we'll make a **MusicController** and then modify the `ShooterBallGame` script to use its beats to fireballs. In Unity, do the following:

1. In **Hierarchy**, create an **Empty** game object and name it MusicController
2. Add the **AudioProcessor** script as a component
3. Note that it automatically adds an **Audio Source** component too
4. Drag your imported music file onto **AudioClip** slot
5. Drag **MusicController** itself onto **Audio Source** slot

 Note the **G Threshold** parameter on **Audio Process**. You can use this to adjust the sensitivity of the beat recognition algorithm.

Now, update the `ShooterBallGame` script on `GameController` as follows:

```
void Start()
{
    if (shootAt == null)
        shootAt = Camera.main.transform;
    pool = GetComponent<ObjectPooler>();

    AudioProcessor processor = FindObjectOfType<AudioProcessor>();
    processor.onBeat.AddListener(onBeatDetected);
}
```

```
void onBeatDetected()
{
    if (Random.value > 0.5f)
    {
        shooterId = 1;
        shooter = shooter1;
    } else
    {
        shooterId = 0;
        shooter = shooter0;
    }
    ShootBall();
}
```

It's very similar to the previous version, but instead of calling ShootBall from Update, based on the time interval, we call it from onBeatDetected. In Start, we add onBeatDetected as an onBeat event listener.

Also, we've decided to randomly decide which shooter to use rather than just alternating back and forth.

Press **Play** and go at it! *Whoohoo,* we have our own version of Audio Shield! A screenshot of active gameplay is shown here:

# Summary

In this chapter, we built a game that uses Unity's Physics Engine and a number of other features. First, we explained in layman's terms the relationship between Rigidbody, Colliders, and Physic Materials, and explored how the physics engine uses these to determine the velocity and collision of objects in the scene.

Then, we considered the life cycle of game objects and implemented an object pooler that helps avoid memory fragmentation and garbage collection, which can lead to performance problems and VR discomfort.

Using what we learned, we implemented several variations of a ball game, first aiming for a target with your head, then using hand paddles. We modified the game so that, instead of serving balls from above-using gravity, we shoot them from in front and apply a velocity vector. Lastly, we juiced up our game, changing the bouncy balls into fireballs, adding a cool level environment, and synchronizing the fireballs to music beats. In the end, we have a good start to making our own version of the Audio Shield VR game.

In the next chapter, we will see another more practical example of a virtual interactive space. We are going to build an interactive art gallery space that you can move through and query the artwork for information and details.

# 9
# Exploring Interactive Spaces

In this chapter, we'll dig a bit more into level design, modeling, rendering, teleporting, and animation; implementing an interactive space you can experience in VR. The scene is a photo gallery, where you design a simple floor plan and use a Blender to extrude it vertically into the walls. Use your own photos.  You can move around the space via teleport or an animated ride through.

In this chapter, we are going to discuss the following topics:

- Using Blender and Unity to build a simplistic art gallery
- Interacting with objects and metadata
- Data structures, lists, and scriptable objects
- Using teleportation
- Creating an animated walkthrough

 Note that the projects in this chapter are separate and not directly required by the other chapters in this book. If you decide to skip any of it or not save your work, that's OK.

## Level design with Blender

For this project, we're going to design an art gallery layout. We just need something simple, a small art gallery exhibit room about 24 by 36 feet. The room is so simple, in fact, it could easily be built within Unity using 3D cube primitives, but we'll take this opportunity to use Blender a little more since we introduced it in Chapter 2, *Content, Objects, and Scale,* keeping it minimal and instructive. If you prefer, you can skip this section and build the floor and walls using Unity cubes. Or, use the Gallery.blend file provided in the files for this chapter.

# Defining the walls

To start, draw a simple floor plan on a piece of paper or use a drawing app. Mine is just an open space with two entrances and interior walls to display artwork (`Gallery-floorplan.jpg`), which looks like the following image:

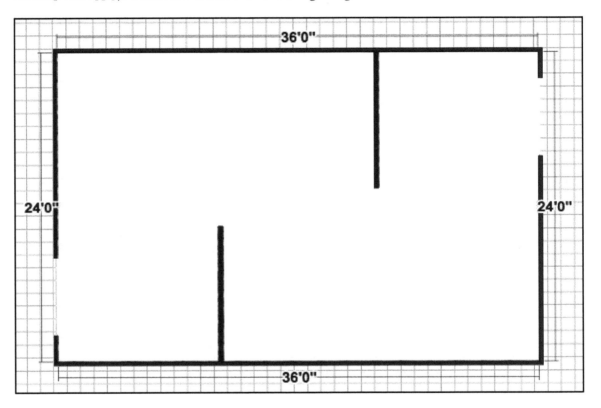

Now, open Blender. We'll use a common technique of starting with a simple object (plane) and then extruding it to make each of the wall segments. To accomplish this, perform the following steps:

1. Start with an empty scene, press the **A** key to select all, and then press the **X** key to delete.

2. Add the floor plan image for reference by pressing the **N** key to open the properties panel. In the **Background Images** pane, select **Add Image**, click on **Open** and select your image (Gallery-floorplan.jpg).
Depending on the size and scale of your floor plan reference image, you'll want to choose a scale factor so that it's correct in the Blender world coordinate space. A scale of 6.25 works for me. Actually, the most important thing is the relative scale of the features in the diagram, since we can always adjust the scale in Unity in the **Import** settings, or even in the **Scene** view itself.

3. In the **Background Images** pane, set **Size** to 6.25. This pane, with the **Size** field highlighted, is shown in the following screenshot:

4. Go to a top-down orthographic view by pressing **7** on the numpad (or navigating to **View** | **Top**) and the orthographic view by pressing **5** (or navigating to **View** | **Persp/Ortho**). Note that the background image only gets drawn when it's in the **top-ortho** view.

5. Now, we'll make a tiny square in one corner of the room that will be extruded into a wall. Add a pane by pressing *Shift + A* and select **Plane.** Then, press *Tab* to go into the **Edit** mode. Press *Z* to toggle from the solid to the **wireframe** view. Press *G* to drag it into a corner, click *Enter* to confirm. Press *S* to scale it to fit the width of the corner of the wall, as shown in the following screenshot (you may recall that you can use the mouse scroll wheel to zoom and *Shift* and click on the middle mouse button to pan):

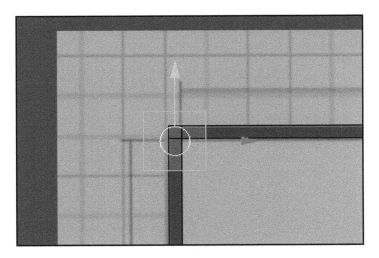

6. Extrude the corner to make the outer walls. Go into the **Edge Select** mode (via the icon shown in the following screenshot), press *A* to unselect all, and then **right-click** on the edge that you want to extrude. Press *E* to begin extruding, press **X** or **Y** to constrain it to that axis, and then press *Enter* to complete the extrusion where you want it:

7. Repeat the previous steps for each outer wall. Create a small square at the corners so that you can extrude in the perpendicular direction. Leave gaps for the doorways. (You may recall that if you need to modify the existing edges, select it with a right-click, *Shift* and right-click to select multiple, and move with *G*. You can also duplicate the selected items.) Also, you can use *Shift* + *D* to duplicate in Object mode.

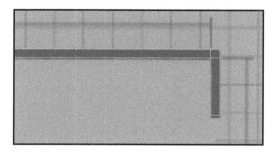

8. To extrude out a face from the middle, we need to add an *edge loop*. With the mouse over the face, press *Ctrl* + *R* and left-click to create the cut. Slide the mouse to position it and left-click again to confirm. Repeat these steps for the width of the wall (making a square cut in the outer wall). Select the edge segment and press **E** to extrude it into the room:

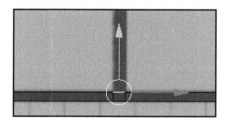

9. Once the floor plan is done, we can extrude it along the z axis to create the walls. Change the view from **Ortho** to **Persp** by pressing *5*. Tilt it back using the middle mouse click and move. Select all by pressing *A*. Extrude with *E*. Begin to extrude with the mouse, press *Z* to constrain, and left-click to confirm.

10. Save the model to a file named `gallery.blend`:

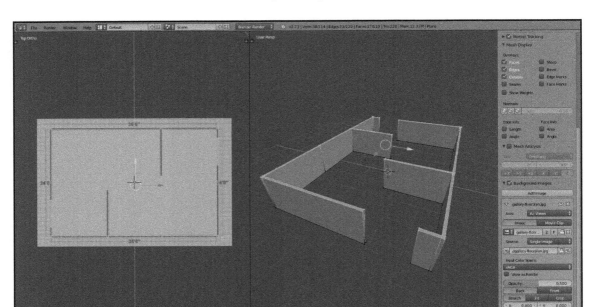

# Adding a ceiling

Now, add a ceiling with two skylights. The ceiling will just be a flat slab build from a single cube. Let's see the steps to add a ceiling:

1. Return to **Object** mode using *Tab*
2. Add a cube using *Shift* + *A* and select **Cube**
3. Position it at the center using *G* and the mouse (*Alt* + *G* resets all its transforms)
4. Scale it along *x* and *y* so that it's size is the same as that of the room using *S* + *X* and *S* + *Y*)
5. Switch to **Front** view using *1*, scale it so that it is flattened using *S* + *Z*, and move it to the top of the walls using *G* + *Z*)

The skylights will be holes cut out of the ceiling using another cube as a modifier, as show in the following screenshot:

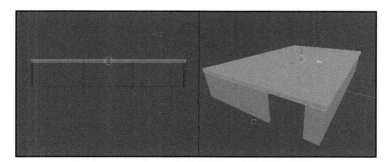

1. Add a cube, using *Shift + A*, scale it to size, and move it to the position where you want the skylight.
2. Position the cube's z axis so that it cuts through the ceiling slab.
3. Duplicate the cube by pressing *Shift + D* and move it to the other skylight's position, as shown in the following screenshot:

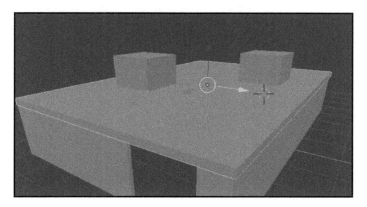

4. Select the ceiling slab with a right-click.
5. In the far right **Properties Editor** panel, select the **wrench-icon**.

6. Then, navigate to **Add Modifier** | **Boolean** and for the **Operation** option, select **Difference**. For the **Object** option, select the first cube (Cube.001):

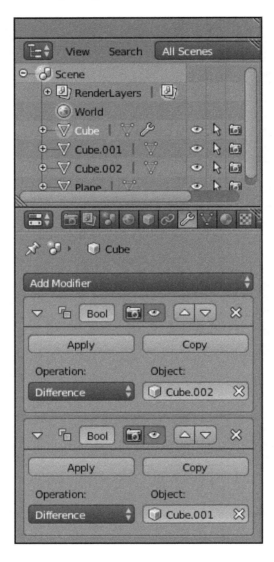

7. Click on **Apply** to make the operation permanent. Then, delete the cube (select it and press **X**).
8. Repeat the process, adding another **Boolean** modifier for the second cube.

If you get stuck, I've included a copy of the finished model with the files for this book. This model is simple enough. You can build it using Unity cubes alone. So much more can, of course, be done to make this a more realistic architectural model, but we're going to move ahead as is:

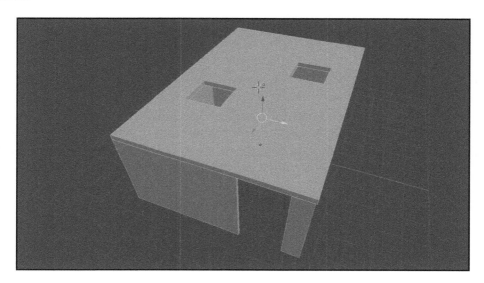

# Assembling the scene in Unity

Now, we can use the gallery room model in Unity and add a floor and a ceiling with skylights. We will apply textures to the walls and add lighting.

We can start a new Unity scene, as follows:

1. Create a new scene by navigating to **File** | **New Scene**. Then, **Save Scene As** and name it Gallery.
2. Drag a copy of your MeMyselfEye prefab into the **Hierarchy**.
3. Delete the default **Main Camera** from **Hierarchy**.

# The gallery room level

First, we'll build the art gallery's room structure by performing the following steps:

1. Create a floor plane by navigating to **GameObject | 3D Object | Plane**. Reset its **Transform** option and rename it to `Floor`.

2. Create the material for the floor and color it brown. **Create | Material**, rename it, set its **Albedo** (70, 25, 5), and drag the material onto the `Floor`.

3. Our room is sized 24 by 36 feet, which in meters is roughly 7.3 by 11. A Unity plane is 10 units square. So, **Scale** it to (0.73, 2, 1.1).

4. Import the gallery model (for instance, `Gallery.blend`). Drag a copy from **Project Assets** into the **Scene**. Reset its **Transform** option.

5. Manually rotate and/or scale it to fit the floor, as needed (mine fits, but its **Rotate Y** value needed to be set to 90). It may help if you first change the **Scene** view to **Top Iso**.

6. It is a good idea to add a collider to the walls so that a character doesn't just walk through them. To accomplish this, navigate to **Add Component | Physics | Mesh Collider**.

Note that when imported, as we defined in Blender, the **Gallery** has separate objects for the walls from the ceiling. A material is created (perhaps named `unnamed`) that has a neutral gray Albedo (204, 204, 204). I like this color for the walls, but I made a new material, all White (255, 255, 255) for the ceiling.

For a good default skybox, we recommend **Wispy Skybox**, a free package on the Asset Store (`https://assetstore.unity.com/packages/2d/textures-materials/sky/wispy-skybox-21737`). Go ahead and download and import it into your project now if you want to use it.

Next, add some sky and sunlight, as follows:

1. If a **Lighting** tab is not visible in your Unity Editor, navigate to **Window | Lighting | Settings**

2. In the **Lighting** pane, select the **Scene** tab

3. For sunlight, in the **Lighting Scene** pane, at the **Sun** input, select the (default) Directional Light from the Hierarchy and drag it onto the Sun Source slot

4. For the sky, if you imported Wispy Skybox (see previously), then in the Lighting Scene tab, select the doughnut icon on the Skybox Material slot and select the material named `WispySkyboxMat`

Since we selected the `Directional Light` for the sun source, you can play with the angle by selecting the Directional Light and modifying its **Rotation**, with the gizmo in the **Scene** window or directly in the **Inspector**, perhaps one that is consistent with the Skybox you chose (such as **Rotation** 60, 175, 0).

> You may consider textured materials for the floor and other surfaces. For example, search the Asset Store for "Floor Materials." There are many free packages as well as paid ones.

# The artwork rig

Now, we can plan the art exhibition. We'll create a reusable artwork rig prefab with a picture frame, lighting, positioning, artist info, and a teleportation viewing position. Then, we'll hang the art on the walls of the gallery. Later, we'll apply the actual images. The artwork rig will consist of a picture frame (cube), a photo plane (quad), and a spotlight, all relative to the artwork's placement on the wall. We will create the first one inside our **Scene**, save it as a `Prefab`, and then place duplicates on the walls throughout the gallery. I suggest doing this in the **Scene** view. Let's get started:

1. Create a container object by navigating to **GameObject | Create Empty**. Name it `ArtworkRig`.
2. Create the frame. With `ArtworkRig` selected, right-click and navigate to **GameObject | 3D Object | Cube**. Name it `ArtFrame`. In **Inspector**, set its **Scale Z** to 0.05. Also, let's assume a 3:4 aspect ratio. So, set its **Scale Y** value to 0.75.
3. Position the rig on a wall (the one facing the entrance at the upper right of the original floor plan). It may help to hide the ceiling child of the `Gallery` object (uncheck its **Enable** checkbox option). Then, change the **Scene** view to **Top and Iso** using **Scene View Gizmo** on the upper right of the **Scene** panel. Click on the green Y icon for the **Top** view and the middle square icon for the **Iso** view.
4. Select `ArtworkRig`, ensure that the **Translate** gizmo is active (the second icon in the top left icon toolbar), and use the *x* and *z* axis arrows to position it. Be sure to select and move the `ArtworkRig`. Leave the frame position at (0,0,0). Set the height at eye level (Y=1.4). The **Transform Position** value that works for me is (2, 1.4, -1.82) and no **Rotation** at (0,0,0), as shown in the screenshot that follows.
5. Make the frame black. Navigate to **Assets | Create | Material**, name it `FrameMaterial`, and set its Albedo color to black. Then in **Hierarchy**, select the **Frame** option and drag the `FrameMaterial` material onto `ArtFrame`.

6. Make the image placeholder. With `ArtFrame` selected in Hierarchy, right-click and navigate to **3D Object | Quad**. Name it to `Image`. Position it just in front of the frame so that it's visible; set **Position** to (0, 0, -0.8) and scale it so that it's slightly smaller than the frame by setting **Scale** to (0.9, 0.9, 1).

7. To better appreciate the current scale and eye level, try inserting a copy of **Ethan** into the scene:

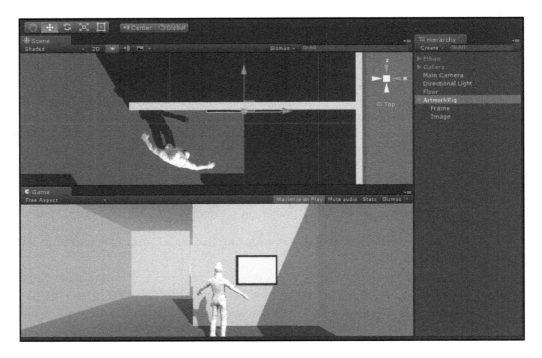

Next, we'll add a spotlight to the rig, as follows:

1. First, put the ceiling back in by checking off the **Enable** checkbox option for the child object of **Gallery**.

2. With `ArtworkRig` selected in **Hierarchy**, right-click, navigate to **Light | Spotlight**, and position it one and half meters away from the wall (**Z**=-1.5) and up near the ceiling. The exact height doesn't matter much since we don't actually have a light fixture. We just have a Vector3 location for the source. I set **Position** to (0, 1.5, -1).

3. Now, adjust the `Spotlight` value so that it appropriately illuminates the artwork. I set **Rotation X** to 2, and adjust the light parameters to your liking, such as **Range** to 5, **Spot Angle** to 45, and **Intensity** to 3. The results are shown in the following screenshot:

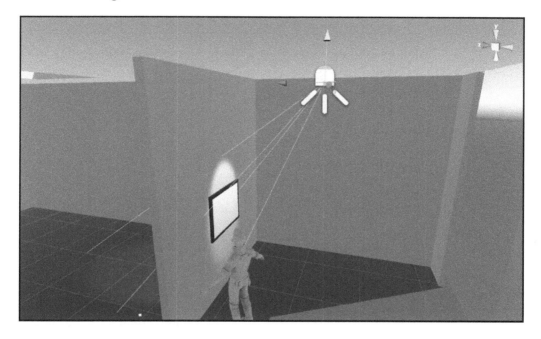

4. Notice the spotlight is passing through the wall, illuminating the floor on the other side. We don't want that. Select the Spotlight and enable shadows via **Shadow Type: Soft Shadows**.

5. To preserve the rig as a prefab, select `ArtworkRig` in **Hierarchy** and drag it into your **Project Assets** Prefabs folder.

Getting to know your Lighting settings can be important. If you see holes in your objects or shadows, for example, try sliding the Directional Light's Normal Bias to 0 and Bias to a low value like 0.1. For more information on shadows and the bias property, see https://docs.unity3d.com/Manual/ShadowOverview.html.

# The exhibition plan

The next step is to duplicate ArtworkRig on each wall where we want to display the images. Position it and rotate as needed. If you follow the plan shown in the following diagram, your exhibition will display ten images, indicated by the stars:

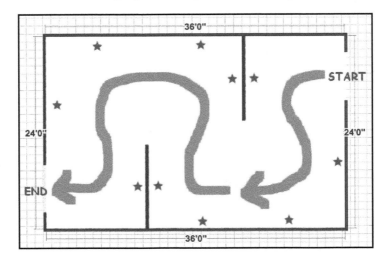

The following are the steps to duplicate ArtworkRig on each wall:

1. As before, it may be easier to hide the ceiling and change the **Scene View** panel to **Top and Iso**.
2. On the top left of the **Scene View** panel, change the **Transform Gizmo** toggles so that the tool handle is placed at the **Pivot** point rather than **Center**.
3. Create a new **Empty** game object, **Reset** its transform, and name it Artworks.
4. Move the existing ArtworkRig so it's a child of Artworks.

For each location, place an artwork in the gallery, as follows:

1. Select an existing ArtworkRig in the **Hierarchy**
2. Duplicate Artworkrig with right-click on **Duplicate**, or press *Ctrl + D*
3. Rotate the rig so that it faces the correct direction by setting **Rotation Y** to 0, 90, 180, or -90
4. Position the rig on the wall

The settings that work for my gallery are provided in the following table (and assume your Artworks transform is reset to the origin):

| | Position X | Position Z | Rotation Y |
|---|---|---|---|
| 0 | 2 | -1.8 | 0 |
| 1 | -1.25 | -5.28 | -180 |
| 2 | -3.45 | -3.5 | -90 |
| 3 | -3.45 | -0.7 | -90 |
| 4 | -2 | 1.6 | 0 |
| 5 | 2 | -1.7 | 180 |
| 6 | 3.5 | 0 | 90 |
| 7 | 3.5 | 3.5 | 90 |
| 8 | 1.25 | 5.15 | 0 |
| 9 | -2 | 1.7 | 180 |

Note that the objects are listed in the same order that we'll use in the animated ride-through of the scene. Place them, as children of `Artworks`, in this order in **Hierarchy**.

# Adding pictures to the gallery

Please find 10 of your favorite photos from your photo library to use and add them to a new **Project Assets** folder named `Photos`. We are going to write a script that, given the list of images, will add them to each of the ArtworkRigs in the scene:

1. To create the photos folder, navigate to **Assets | Create | Folder** and name it `Photos`
2. Import 10 photos by dragging and dropping them from your **File Explorer** into the `Photos` folder that you just created (or navigate to **Assets | ImportNew Asset...**)

Now, we'll write a script to populate **Artworks Images**:

1. In **Hierarchy**, select `Artworks`. Then, in **Inspector**, navigate to **Add Component | New Script** and name it `PopulateArtFrames`.
2. Open the new script for editing.

Write the code for `PopulateArtFrames.cs`, as follows:

```
using UnityEngine;
```

```
public class PopulateArtFrames : MonoBehaviour
{
    public Texture[] images;

    void Start()
    {
        int imageIndex = 0;
        foreach (Transform artwork in transform)
        {
            GameObject art = artwork.Find("ArtFrame/Image").gameObject;
            Renderer rend = art.GetComponent<Renderer>();
            Material material = rend.material;
            material.mainTexture = images[imageIndex];
            imageIndex++;
            if (imageIndex == images.Length)
                break;
        }
    }
}
```

What is going on here? First, we declare a public array of `Textures` named `images`. You will see, this will appear in Inspector so we can specify what photos to include in the scene.

This script is attached to the Artworks container object, which contains as children the ArtworkRigs. When the app starts, in `Start()`, we loop through all `theArtworkRigs`, find the Image object. For each image, we get its Renderer component's Material, and assign a new Texture, that being the next image in the list. We use an `imageIndex` variable to increment through the list, and stop when we've run out of images or run out of ArtworkRigs:

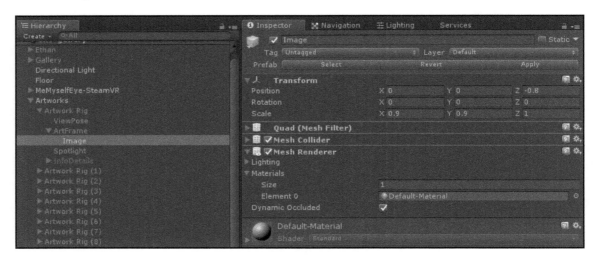

The astute reader may wonder since all the ArtworkRigs use the same Material, and the Default-Material at that, why wouldn't changing the material on any ArtworkRig Image change them all? In fact, Unity takes care of that by cloning the material into a new unique one when you modify its texture (or other attributes) at runtime. So each ArtworkRig's Image gets its own Material with its own Texture, and thus, each picture in our gallery is different.

To finish this up, let's perform the following steps:

1. Save the script and return to the Unity editor
2. With `Artworks` selected in **Hierarchy**, unfold the **Populate Art Frames** script component in **Inspector** and unfold the **Images** parameter
3. Set the **Images Size** value to `10`
4. Find the images you imported in the `Photos` folder under Project Assets and drag them, one at a time, into the **Images** slots as **Element 0** through **Element 9**

When you click on **Play mode**, the artwork in the scene will get populated with the images in the order that you specified:

To view the scene in VR, we can position the MeMyselfEye in front of the first ArtworkRig:

1. Select the `MeMyselfEye` camera rig in **Hierarchy**
2. Set its **Position** to (2, 0, -2.82)

That's pretty nice!

# Managing art info data

We could end here, but suppose we want to track more data than just the images for each artwork, such as artist, title, description, and so on. First, we'll consider several software design patterns to manage the data, including separate lists, data structures, and scriptable objects. Later, we'll update our ArtworkRig to display the info with each framed artwork.

The first two scenarios are for explanation only. We will actually implement the `ScriptableObjects` one last.

# Using lists

One approach could be to add more lists to the `PopulateArtFrames` script for each of the data fields. For example, if the script had the following:

```
public Texture[] images;
public string[] titles;
public string[] artists;
public string[] descriptions;
```

The **Inspector** would show the following (I limited the list to four items for brevity):

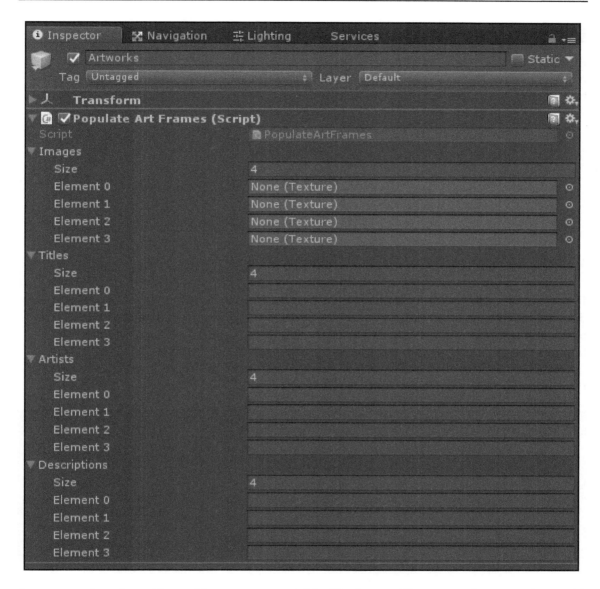

As you can imagine, this could get very unwieldy. To change **Element 3**, for example, you'd have to go to all the lists, which is easily prone to mistakes; things could fatally get very out of sync.

# Using data structures

A better approach could be to write a C# `struct` (or `class`) as a data structure that contains each of the fields we want and then make the list in `PopulateArtFrames` as this type. For example, the script may read as follows:

```
[System.Serializable]
public struct ArtInfo
{
    public Texture image;
    public string title;
    public string artist;
    public string description;
}

public class PopulateArtFrames : MonoBehaviour
{
    public List<ArtInfo> artInfos = new List<ArtInfo>();
```

In this example snippet, we declare a separate data structure named `ArtInfo` defining our data fields. Then, in `PopulateArtFrames` we declare it as a `List` (which must be initialized with the `new List<ArtInfo>()` call). In the script, we'd then reference the textures as `artInfos[i].image`. Likewise, you'd get its size using `artInfos.Count` rather than `Length`. Also, we need to say it's `System.Serializable` so the list appears in the editor **Inspector**, as follows:

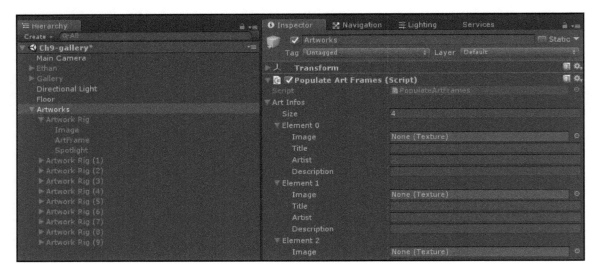

Now we have a list of `ArtInfo` elements that we can fill in, and the data for each element is grouped together.

Another benefit of this structure is it could be more easily populated from an external data source, such as cloud-based JSON data or a CSV (comma separated values) data file.

 If you are interested in loading data from a database there are a number of approaches, outside the scope of this chapter. But briefly, if you do find a source of CSV data, this handy CSV parser (`https://github.com/frozax/fgCSVReader`) is basic but gets the job done. If you are in need of a JSON parser, from a web-based REST API for example, consider the JSON .NET For Unity package (`https://assetstore.unity.com/packages/tools/input-management/json-net-for-unity-11347`) or another similar one.

# Using scriptable objects

In the previous examples, the art info data is maintained on a `GameObject` in the Scene Hierarchy. As a software design, this is not really where the data belongs. Data objects are not game objects and should be managed separately.

In the Scene hierarchy, we define the level design and game behaviors. ArtworkRigs have spatial coordinates (Transform) and renderers (and other potentially necessary runtime components such as colliders and RigidBodies for physics). But other data, still a project asset, can live outside the scene hierarchy. For this, Unity offers *ScriptableObjects*. We first introduced ScriptableObjects in `Chapter 5`, *Handy Interactables*, as a way of sharing input data across game objects. We will use them again here:

1. In the **Project** window, create a new folder under *Assets* named `ScriptableObjects` if not already present
2. In the new folder, right-click and select **Create | C# Script**
3. Name the script `ArtInfo`
4. Then, open the `ArtInfo.cs` script for editing

Create the `ArtInfo.cs` script as follows:

```
using UnityEngine;

[CreateAssetMenu(menuName = "My Objects/Art Info")]
public class ArtInfo : ScriptableObject
{
    public Texture image;
```

```
        public string title;
        public string artist;
        [Multiline]
        public string description;
    }
```

Rather than inheriting from `MonoBehaviour`, we define the class as a `ScriptableCbject`. We added a `Multiline` attribute for description so the input field in **Inspector** will be a text area.

 If you are importing JSON data into your project and want to generate ScriptableObject classes that match the JSON object properties, take a look at this tool: `https://app.quicktype.io/#r=json2csharp`.

At the top, we provide a `CreateAssetMenu` attribute, which generates a menu item in the Unity Editor for our object. Since scriptable objects are not added to the scene Hierarchy, we need a way to create them in the project. Using this attribute makes it easy, as follows:

1. Save the script and return to Unity.
2. In the **Project** window, select your **Photos** folder where you imported your image textures. We'll create the Art Info objects in the same folder.
3. In the Unity editor main menu, navigate to **Assets | Create**.
4. You will see a new item **My Objects** with a submenu with an item Art Info, as directed in the CreateAssetsMenu property attribute in our script.
5. Choose **Art Info** to create an instance. By default, it will be created in the same folder as the defining script (this can be changed in the property attribute options).
6. It maybe be helpful to rename the object similar to your images. For example, if you have **PictureA**, name it `PictureA Info`.
7. Drag the image texture onto the scriptable object's **Image** slot.
8. Add information for the **Title**, **Artist**, and **Description** too.

Here is a screenshot of an ArtInfo object with data filled in:

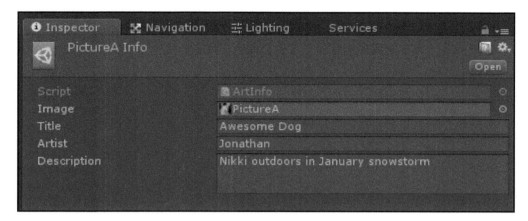

Repeat these steps for all your pictures. When you're done, your art data will be Project assets.

To use the scriptable object assets in the project, we could modify the PopulateArtFrames much like we would have for the `struct` version of the code. We'll do a little bit of refactoring, creating a new component on the ArtworkRig to populate itself with an ArtInfo object, as follows:

1. Select one of the ArtworkRigs in the Hierarchy
2. Add **Component | New Script**, name it `ArtworkController`

Open it for editing and write it as follows:

```
using UnityEngine;

public class ArtworkController : MonoBehaviour {
    public GameObject image;

    public void SetArtInfo(ArtInfo info)
    {
        Renderer rend = image.GetComponent<Renderer>();
        Material material = rend.material;
        material.mainTexture = info.image;
    }
}
```

Save the script and back in Unity, on the `ArtworkRig` where we just added this component:

1. Drag the image child onto the **image** slot
2. Press **Apply** to save the `ArtworkRig` prefab

Now, update the `PopulateArtFrames` to iterate the list of `ArtInfo` and send the object to the `ArtworkRig`, as follows:

```
using System.Collections.Generic;
using UnityEngine;

public class PopulateArtFrames : MonoBehaviour
{
    public List<ArtInfo> artInfos = new List<ArtInfo>();

    void Start()
    {
        int index = 0;
        foreach (Transform artwork in transform)
        {
artwork.GetComponent<ArtworkController>().SetArtInfo(artInfos[index]);

            index++;
            if (index == artInfos.Count || artInfos[index]==null)
                break;
        }
    }
}
```

Now, the Inspector interface is much cleaner and workable. The Artworks' Populate Art Frames component maintains a list of Art Info objects, as shown next. We just need to populate the list and use it. The data the list references are maintained separately as `ScriptableObjects`:

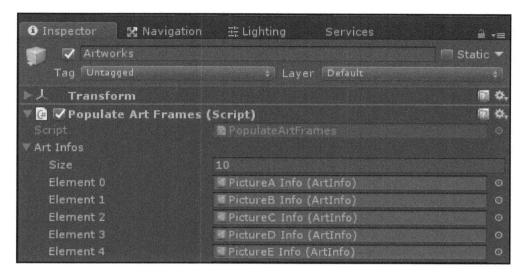

Press **Play**. The artwork images should get loaded during Start, just like before although we've greatly improved the underlying implementation and can now extend our app to include more info about each art picture.

Another advantage of using ScriptableObject in situations like this is once you have a distributable app, you can package these assets into an AssetBundle. This would allow, for example, changing out the gallery pictures, along with all the art info, in the live version.

# Displaying the art info

Now that we have more information on each art piece, we can incorporate that into our project. We will add a UI canvas to the ArtworkRig. First, we'll include an info plaque with each picture. Then we'll make it interactive. If you'd like a reminder introduction to Unity's canvas and UI elements, please look at Chapter 6, *World Space UI*.

# Creating the title plaque

The title plaque will be a small canvas next to each picture, with a title text UI element:

1. Select one of the **ArtworkRig** objects in **Hierarchy.**
2. Add a child canvas, **Create UI | Canvas,** named InfoPlaque.
3. Set its **Render Mode** to **World Space.**
4. Initially reset its position **Pos** to (0, 0, 0).
5. Set the canvas **Width**: 640, **Height**: 480.
6. If you recall, the canvas scaled in world space will be 640 meters wide! Set the **Scale** to 0.0006.
7. Now you can visually adjust the position using the move gizmo, we found this works: **Pos** (0.8, -0.1, -0.01).
8. Next, create a child pane, **Create UI | Panel.**
9. And a sub-child of the panel, create a child text element, **Create UI | Text,** rename it Title.
10. Set some default **text**, like Title title title title.
11. For **Anchor Presets** (the fancy icon in the top-left of the Transform panel), select **Stretch / Stretch**, click and also **Alt-click** it. This will let the text fill the panel area.
12. **Font Size**: 80.
13. **Alignment: Middle, Center.**
14. Set its **Horizontal Overflow:** Wrap, and **Vertical Overflow:** Truncate.

Now, we can modify ArtworkController script to add a new public Text title variable and set its text property to the info.title, as follows:

```
using UnityEngine;
using UnityEngine.UI;

public class ArtworkController : MonoBehaviour {

    public GameObject image;
    public Text title;

    public void SetArtInfo(ArtInfo info)
    {
        Renderer rend = image.GetComponent<Renderer>();
        Material material = rend.material;
        material.mainTexture = info.image;
```

```
        title.text = info.title;
    }
}
```

That was easy. Save the script, and then:

1. Drag the Title element onto the **Text** slot
2. To save the prefab, make sure the ArtworkRig itself is selected in the **Hierarchy**, then press **Apply**

Now when you press **Play**, the picture images and title text will get initialized on Start for each of the artwork rigs. Here's one of my photos with a title plaque:

# Interactive info details

We have more information on each picture that fits on the plaque, so we'll allow the player to click an input controller button to open the detail infobox. Let's create that canvas first, with text for artist and description:

1. As a shortcut, duplicate the **InfoPlaque** and name it DetailsCanvas.
2. Scale and position it, perhaps out front and a slight angle. The following values work for me: **Pos** (0.7, 0, -0.2), **Width Height** (1200, 900), **Rotation** (0, 15, 0).

3. Rename the **Title** text element to `Description`.
4. Duplicate **Description**, rename it `Artist`, set to **Top Alignment.**
5. Press **Apply** to save the prefab.

The `ArtworkController` can now populate the details fields too:

```
public Text artist;
public Text description;
public GameObject detailsCanvas;
```

And in the `SetArtInfo` function:

```
artist.text = info.artist;
description.text = info.description;
```

Then, we'll add an `Update` handler to check for user input and display (or hide) the details canvas. And ensure the canvas starts out disabled in `Start`.

```
void Start()
{
    detailsCanvas.SetActive(false);
}

void Update()
{
    if (Input.GetButtonDown("Fire1"))
    {
        detailsCanvas.SetActive(true);
    }
    if (Input.GetButtonUp("Fire1"))
    {
        detailsCanvas.SetActive(false);
    }
}
```

For Daydream on Android, you would call `GvrControllerInput.ClickButtonDown` and `ClickButtonUp`.

Save the script.

1. Drag the **Artist** and **Description** elements onto the corresponding slots
2. Drag the **InfoDetails** canvas onto the **Details Canvas** slot
3. Press **Apply** on the **ArtworkRig** to save the prefab changes

Now, when you **Play** and press the Fire1 button on your input controller, the details canvas will show, as follows:

If you would like to implement a different button, such as the finger trigger, or are using a device without a Fire1 mapping (Daydream), please refer to Chapter 5, *Handy Interactables*, for implementation options and handling input events.

As implemented, all the details canvases will appear when you press the button. If you want to control one canvas at a time, you could add a UI button to the **InfoPlaque**, for example, and then use click events on that to trigger the canvas visibility, using gaze-based look and click, or laser pointer & click interactions. Reference Chapter 6, *World Space UI*, for implementation ideas.

# Adjusting for image aspect ratio

You probably noticed that some of your pictures appear squished since our framed image is shown at a fixed size and aspect ratio. What we really would like is for the frame and image to adjust themselves depending on the dimensions of the image.

When Unity imports a texture, it prepares it (by default) for GPU rendering as an object material texture, which includes resizing it to a square power of two (for example, 1024 x 1024, 2048 x 2048, and so on). If you adapt your project to read images at runtime, for example, from the Resources directory, the device's photo stream, or over the web, then you will have access to the image file's metadata header that includes its pixel width and height. In lieu of that, since we're using imported textures, we can change the Advanced import settings for the images we're using:

1. From your **Assets Photos** folder, select an image texture
2. In **Inspector**, under **Advanced**, change **Non Power of 2** to **None**
3. Press **Apply**

Repeat this for each image in the project. Note that this also decompresses the image, so what might start out as a 400k `.jpg` file becomes a 3 MB, 24-bit image in the project, so be cautious of the width and height of the source images you choose to use.

 Not scaling textures to a power of two is really bad for performance. If you have more than a few images, you should avoid this. One approach would be to add the image aspect ratio as another field of the ArtInfo, and manually set the value in the corresponding scripted objects. Then, change ArtworkController to use this value instead of calculating it.

In `ArtworkController.cs`, add the following helper function, which returns a normalized scale of a texture. The larger dimension will be 1.0 and the smaller one will be a fraction. For example, an image that is 1024w x 768h will get a scale of (1.0, 0.75). It also maintains the current relative scale of the picture using the Z scale value, since that's not changed by our aspect ratio calculation, but will be changed by the Scale tool!

Modify `ArtworkController` first by adding a private function `TextureToScale` which normalizes the image scale to 1.0 for the larger of width or height, and sets the other dimension to the aspect ratio, as follows:

```
private Vector3 TextureToScale(Texture texture, float depth)
{
    Vector3 scale = Vector3.one;
    scale.z = depth;
    if (texture.width > texture.height)
```

```
    {
        scale.y = (float)texture.height / (float)texture.width;
    } else
    {
        scale.x = (float)texture.width / (float)texture.height;
    }
    return scale;
}
```

The function also preserves the frame depth in the returned scale vector. Now, we can use this in SetArtInfo function. Add a new public variable for the frame:

```
public Transform frame;
```

And then, add this line to set the frame's scale:

```
frame.localScale = TextureToScale(info.image, frame.localScale.z);
```

Save the updates script. Then, in Unity:

1. Drag the **ArtFrame** onto the Frame slot in the component
2. Press **Apply** to save the prefab

Now when you play, the framed images are scaled with the correct aspect ratio, like the one shown here:

# Moving around the gallery

We've done so much, and yet have not discussed moving about the gallery level. In Chapter 7, *Locomotion and Comfort,* we examined various ways of implementing locomotion and teleportation. Let's now consider setting up specific teleportation spawn points that provide an optimal viewing pose for each artwork picture in the gallery.

## Teleporting between pictures

I suppose a good viewing position is about one meter back from the picture. We can add a ViewPose object at that location, within the ArtworkRig. We'll place its origin on the floor. Let's add that now:

1. Select a **ArtworkRig** in **Hierarchy**
2. Create a child **Empty** game object, name it `ViewPose`
3. **Reset** the ViewPose transform
4. Set its **Position** to (`0, -1.4, -1.5`)

In Chapter 7, *Locomotion and Comfort*, we examined various ways of implementing locomotion and teleportation, including our own home-grown scripts as well as higher-level toolkits. Here, we'll use teleportation toolkits for SteamVR and Daydream. For a more general introduction to these toolkits, or alternative solutions, please refer back to that chapter.

## Teleporting with SteamVR Interaction System

To use the SteamVR Interaction System, we start with their Player prefab and add the components we want to use:

1. Locate the **Player** prefab in `SteamVR/InteractionSystem/Core/Prefabs`
2. Drag it as a child of `MeMyselfEye` in your scene **Hierarchy**
3. Delete or disable the `[CameraRig]` object
4. Drag a copy of **Teleporting** prefab from Project `Assets/SteamVR/InteractionSystem/Teleport/Prefabs` as a child of MeMyselfEye (this controller can actually go anywhere in the scene)
5. Select the **Player** in **Hierarchy**, and drag its parent `MeMyselfEye` onto its **Tracking Origin Transform** slot

6. Select the **ViewPose** object in the **ArtworkRig**
7. Drag a copy of the **TeleportPoint** prefab from
   Project `Assets/SteamVR/InteractionSystem/Teleport/Prefabs` into the
   Hierarchy as a child of ViewPose
8. Select the ArtworkRig and **Apply** to save the prefab changes

That's it! Press **Play**. The teleport points do not show until you press the button on your controller, then they glow, a dashed laser arc lets you choose one, and you go there. Here is a screenshot of the Scene view while the teleport points are activated:

# Teleporting with Daydream Elements

The Daydream Elements toolkit is more granular so it takes a little more to get this working. By default, the TeleportController lets you teleport to any horizontal surface on the scene (provided it has a collider). To limit it to our teleport stations we'll restrict the search to a specific layer, named `Teleport`.

1. In an ArtworkRig in Hierarchy, select its **ViewPose** object and create a child cylinder (**Create** | **3D Object** | **Cylinder**) and name it `TeleportPod`.
2. Set its **Scale** to (`0.5, 0.5, 0.01`). You may choose to decorate its material, for example, with transparency.
3. Put it on **Layer** `"Teleport"` (If there is no layer named Teleport, from the **Layers** select list choose **Add Layer...** first).
4. Select the parent **ArtworkRig** and **Apply** to save the prefab changes.

Now, we add the Daydream Elements teleport controller:

1. Drag the **TeleportController** prefab into your **Hierarchy** as child of **Player** (for us, `MeMyselfEye` / `GVRCameraRig` / `Player`)
2. Reset its **Transform**, if necessary
3. Drag the `MeMyselfEye` object onto the `TeleportController` component's **Player** transform slot
4. Drag **GvrControllerPointer** (or whichever controller game object you're using) onto the **Controller** transform slot
5. On the TeleportController's **Valid Teleport Layers**, select **Teleport** (so both **Default, Teleport** are selected)
6. On **Raycast Mask**, we want only Teleport, so select **Nothing** (to deselect all), then select **Teleport**. The layer settings are shown in the screen capture here:

Press Play. When the controller pointer's arc touches a teleport pod, it will glow highlight. If you click, you will be teleported to that spot.

# Room-scale considerations

The gallery level layout we have designed works best in seated, standing, or non-positionally tracked VR. Our use of the zig-zag partitions, for example, is not a good idea in room scale VR unless you take care to not allow the player's play space (chaperone boundaries) to cross these walls. This can be done, but you would need to make the overall space larger, perhaps adaptive to the actual play space size, and add conditions to the teleportation feature that we implement later in the chapter, complicating our examples. See `Chapter 7`, *Locomotion and Comfort* for more about room-scale considerations.

The following image is a depiction of an initial position for MeMyselfEye for a room scale OpenVR camera rig, showing the guardian boundaries fit neatly within the gallery viewing space for the first ArtworkRig. It may not fit so easily at the other viewing situations, so you'd need to make adjustments to discourage the player from walking through walls (or through Ethan!). Also, whereas this is the default length and width, the player's actual space will vary to their configuration requirements. To fully accommodate these possibilities, it may be necessary to go to a procedurally generated level layout, where the position and scale of the walls are determined at runtime based on the player settings.

# Animating a ride-through

If you can be certain the player will be seated or at least standing in one place, they might enjoy a ride-through guided tour of the gallery.

In conventional games, first-person animation is often used for a cut-scene, that is, a canned fly-through animation as a transition from one level to another. In VR, it's somewhat different. Walkthroughs can really be the VR experience itself. Head tracking is still active. So, it's not simply a prerecorded video. You can look around and experience it, and it is more like an amusement park ride. This is often called an on-the-rails VR experience.

Be cautious using ride-through animations in your VR apps. It can cause motion sickness. If you do, give your players as much control as possible. For example, we're animating the MeMyselfEye rig, allowing users to continue to look around. Placing the user in a cockpit or vehicle with stationary surfaces in the foreground can also reduce the tendency for sickness. On the other hand, if you're a thrill seeker, techniques similar to those here can be used for making roller-coaster rides on a track that moves in three dimensions!

In this topic, we are scripting the animations ourselves. In a later chapter, we will dive more deeply into other Unity animation and cinematic tools. We create a RidethroughController that animates the first-person character (MeMyselfEye) **Transform** position, and rotation over time. It works by defining the key-frame transforms, using the Unity AnimationCurve class (https://docs.unity3d.com/ScriptReference/AnimationCurve.html). As the name suggests, for key-frame animation, we define the player's location at specific key times in the ride. The in-between frames are calculated automatically.

1. At the root of Hierarchy, create a new **Empty** game object and name it RidethroughController
2. Add a new C# script component and name it RidethroughController
3. Open the script for editing

First, we'll define some variables we will need:

```
public Transform playerRoot;
public GameObject artWorks;
public float startDelay = 3f;
public float transitionTime = 5f;

private AnimationCurve xCurve, zCurve, rCurve;
```

`playerRoot` is the player transform we will animate (`MeMyselfEye`). `artWorks` is the container of the **ArtworkRigs**. We've included an option to specify an initial delay and the transition time between pictures. The setup function will generate three curves, for position (*x* and *z*) and rotation (about the *y* axis).

Next, we write a `SetupCurves` function that generates the animation curves, using each of **ArtworkRig**'s **ViewPose** as nodes in the curve. We do this concurrently for the *x*, *z*, and rotation curves as follows:

```
private void SetupCurves()
{
    int count = artWorks.transform.childCount + 1;
    Keyframe[] xKeys = new Keyframe[count];
    Keyframe[] zKeys = new Keyframe[count];
    Keyframe[] rKeys = new Keyframe[count];

    int i = 0;
    float time = startDelay;
    xKeys[0] = new Keyframe(time, playerRoot.position.x);
    zKeys[0] = new Keyframe(time, playerRoot.position.z);
    rKeys[0] = new Keyframe(time, playerRoot.rotation.y);

    foreach (Transform artwork in artWorks.transform)
    {
        i++;
        time += transitionTime;
        Transform pose = artwork.Find("ViewPose");
        xKeys[i] = new Keyframe(time, pose.position.x);
        zKeys[i] = new Keyframe(time, pose.position.z);
        rKeys[i] = new Keyframe(time, pose.rotation.y);
    }
    xCurve = new AnimationCurve(xKeys);
    zCurve = new AnimationCurve(zKeys);
    rCurve = new AnimationCurve(rKeys);
}
```

We will define the `RidethroughController` to start animating when the game object is enabled:

```
void OnEnable()
{
    SetupCurves();
}
```

On each Update, we evaluate the X and Z curves to set the player's current position. And, we evaluate the rotation curve to set the player's current rotation. We use the native `Quaternion` representation of rotations since we're interpolating between two angles we do not want use Euler coordinates:

```
void Update()
{
    playerRoot.position = new Vector3(
            xCurve.Evaluate(Time.time),
            playerRoot.position.y,
            zCurve.Evaluate(Time.time));

    Quaternion rot = playerRoot.rotation;
    rot.y = rCurve.Evaluate(Time.time);
    playerRoot.rotation = rot;

    // done?
    if (Time.time >= xCurve[xCurve.length - 1].time)
        gameObject.SetActive(false);
}
```

Lastly, we check whether we've completed the animation by comparing the current time with the time of the last node in the curve. If so, we disable the game object.

In this script, I used the `transform.rotation` Quaternion y value directly. It's usually not recommended to manipulate Quaternion's value directly, but since we're consistently changing only a single axis, it is safe. For more information on Quaternion versus Euler angles, see https://docs.unity3d.com/Manual/QuaternionAndEulerRotationsInUnity.html.

As written, if/when the **RidethroughController** game object is enabled, the animation will play. You can save your scene with it enabled, and it will play when the app begins. We'll leave it up to you to modify it to be trigged by a player's option such as a *Start Ride* button within the app!

Save the script and then perform the following steps:

1. From **Hierarchy**, drag MeMyselfEye onto the **Player Root** slot
2. Drag the Artworks (which contains all ArtworkRigs) onto the **Artworks** slot

When you **Play** the scene, you get a nice easy ride through the art gallery, with a slight pause to view each photo. That's real nice! Hopefully, you picked images that can be shown by you to all your friends and family!

# Summary

In this chapter, we built an art gallery scene from scratch, starting with a 2D plan drawing and going into Blender to construct a 3D architectural structure. We imported the model into Unity and added some environmental lighting. Then, we built an artwork rig consisting of an image, a picture frame, and a spotlight, and placed instances of the rig on various walls throughout the gallery. Next, we imported a bunch of personal photos and wrote a script that populates the art frames at runtime. Adding more detailed data about each artwork, we explored several ways of managing lists of non-graphical data. Finally, we added the ability to move around within the art gallery level, via teleportation and an automated first-person walkthrough of the scene.

In the next chapter, we will take a look at a different kind of VR experience using pre-recorded 360-degree media. You will build and learn about photospheres, equirectangular projections, and infographics.

# 10
# Using All 360 Degrees

360-degree photos and videos are a different way of using virtual reality that is accessible to consumers today, both in terms of experiencing them as well as producing and publishing them. Viewing prerecorded images requires much less compute power than rendering full 3D scenes, and this works very well on mobile phone-based VR in particular. In this chapter, we will explore the following topics:

- Understanding 360-degree media and formats
- Using textures to view globes, photo spheres, and skyboxes
- Adding 360-degree video to your Unity projects
- Writing and using custom shaders
- Capturing 360-degree images and video from within your Unity app

 Note that the projects in this chapter are separate and not directly required by the other chapters in this book. If you decided to skip any of it or not save your work, that's okay.

## 360-degree media

The terms 360-degree and *virtual reality* are tossed around a lot lately, often in the same sentence. Consumers may be led to believe that it's all the same thing, it's all figured out, and it's all very easy to produce, when in fact it is not so simple.

Generally, the term 360-degree refers to viewing of prerecorded photos or videos in a manner that allows you to rotate your view's direction to reveal content that was just outside your field of view.

Non-VR 360-degree media has become relatively common. For example, many real-estate listing sites provide panoramic previews with a web-based player that lets you interactively pan around to view the space. Similarly, Facebook and YouTube support uploading and playback of 360-degree videos and provides a player with interactive controls to look around during the playback. Google Maps lets you upload 360-degree still photosphere images, much like their Street View that you can create with an Android or iOS app or a consumer camera (for more information, visit `https://www.google.com/maps/about/contribute/photosphere/`). The internet is teeming with 360-degree media!

With a VR headset, viewing 360-degree media is surprisingly immersive, even just still photos. You're standing at the center of a sphere with an image projected onto the inside surface, but you feel like you're really there in the captured scene. Simply turn your head to look around. It's one of those things that gets people interested in VR the first time they see it, and it is a popular application for Google Cardboard and Gear VR, having jump-started the consumer VR revolution for a lot of people.

# Equirectangular projections

Ever since it was discovered that the Earth is round, cartographers and mariners have struggled with how to project the spherical globe onto a two-dimensional chart. The variations are plentiful and the history is fascinating (if you're fascinated by that sort of thing!) The result is an inevitable distortion of some areas of the globe.

 To learn more about map projections and spherical distortions, visit `http://en.wikipedia.org/wiki/Map_projection`.

As a computer graphics designer, it's perhaps a little less mysterious than it was to ancient mariners because we know about *UV Texture mapping*.

3D computer models in Unity are defined by *meshes*-a set of Vector3 points connected with edges, forming triangular-shaped facets. You can unwrap a mesh (in Blender, for instance) into a flattened 2D configuration to define the mapping of texture pixels to the corresponding areas on the mesh surface (UV coordinates). A globe of the Earth, when unwrapped, will be distorted, as defined by the unwrapped mesh. The resulting image is called a **UV Texture image**.

In computer graphic modeling, this UV mapping can be arbitrary and depends on the artistic requirements at hand. However, for 360-degree media, this typically is done using an *equirectangular* (or a Meridian) projection (for more information, visit `http://en.wikipedia.org/wiki/Equirectangular_projection`), where the sphere is unraveled into a cylindrical projection, stretching the texture as you progress towards the north and south poles while keeping the meridians as equidistant vertical straight lines. The following *Tissot's indicatrix* (visit `http://en.wikipedia.org/wiki/Tissot%27s_indicatrix` for more information) shows a globe with strategically arranged identical circles (illustration by Stefan Kühn):

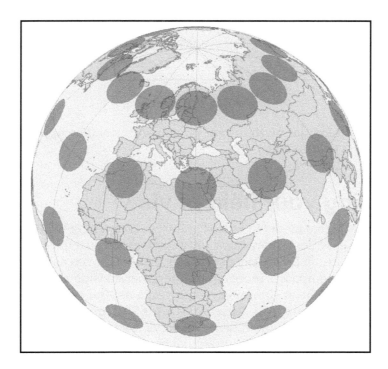

The following image shows the globe unwrapped with an equirectangular projection:

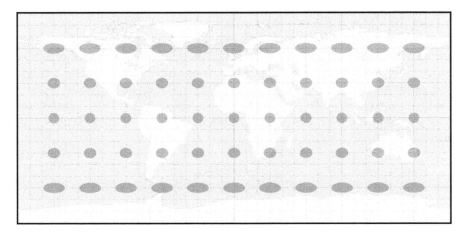

Illustration by Eric Gaba - Wikimedia Commons user: Sting

We will use an equirectangular mesh for our photo spheres and an appropriately projected (warped) image for its texture map.

# VR is hacking your field of view

OK, but why are 360-degree media in virtual reality so compelling? There's a huge difference in how we experience viewing a 360-degree video on a flat screen versus inside a VR headset. For example, an IMAX cinema theater with larger screens than that of the conventional cinema encompasses more of your peripheral vision and has a wider **field of view** (**FOV**). A mobile phone or computer monitor, at a natural viewing distance, is about a 26-degree FOV; a movie theatre is 54 degrees (IMAX is 70 degrees). Oculus Rift and HTC VIVE are about 120 degrees. In human vision, one eye is about 160 degrees, both eyes combined provides about a 200-degree horizontal field of view.

 For more information about FOV adjustments in conventional video games, read the excellent article *All about* FOV (July 18, 2014) by visiting http://steamcommunity.com/sharedfiles/filedetails/?id=287241027.

In VR, you're not so obviously limited by the FOV and physical dimensions of the screen because you can easily move your head to change your view direction at any time. This provides a fully immersive view, horizontal 360 degrees, as you look side to side and up and down by 180 degrees. In VR, with your head still, the field of view is only significant with regard to the outer reaches of your peripheral vision and eyeball movement. But move your head (at the neck and/or full body); the software detects the change in head pose (viewing direction) and updates the display. The result is you believe to have an uninterrupted view of the 360-degree image.

# 180-degree media

I sometimes joke that taking pictures and videos with my consumer 360-degree camera is like shooting a landscape and a selfie at the same time! Especially if you're holding the camera when taking the pictures, you are always in it. But really, when you take a photo, you're most likely already facing the action, and so when viewing the photo the user is also facing the action. So maybe all you need is 180 degrees. Furthermore, it can be tedious to look all the way behind you. As the name implies, a 180-degree image is half a 360 one, projected onto a hemisphere.

In 2017, Google introduced a standard for 180-degree media intended for VR (`https://vr.google.com/vr180/`). In addition to offering equirectangular projection, the cameras have two lenses for capturing stereographic, one for each eye. It works pretty well for a 180-degree view because while you can move left-right to look around, the actual movement needed is relatively small (human peripheral vision is about 200-degree horizontal anyway). Stereo 360 is more challenging.

# Stereo 360-degree media

To capture monoscopic 360-degree media, you can use a consumer 360-degree camera. These cameras typically have a couple of back-to-back super wide angle lenses and corresponding image sensors. The resulting image captures are stitched together, using clever algorithms to avoid seams, and the result is processed into an equirectangular projection. Viewing it in VR, each eye sees the same 360 photo. For landscapes, such as mountain views or other large areas, where the subject is more than 20 meters from your viewing position, it is fine because there is no parallax. Each eye sees pretty much from the same viewing angle. But if the photo includes objects closer to you, it will look incorrect, or at least artificially flattened, because you expect parallax where each eye has a slightly different view.

What about true 360-degree stereo? Shouldn't each eye have its own photo sphere offset from the other eye's position?

To capture *stereo* 360-degree media, it cannot simply be photographed by two 360 cameras from two viewpoints but can be constructed by stitching together images from a rotating stereo pair. The distance between camera image captures simulates a human's separation between eyes (IPD, interpupillary distance). There is a new generation of consumer cameras (such as *Fuze Camera,* https://vuze.camera/ with eight cameras), and high-end professional camera rigs, such as *Google Jump* (https://vr.google.com/jump/), which arranges sixteen separate cameras in a cylindrical array. Advanced image processing software then constructs stereographic views.

Google has introduced an advanced file format for stereo 360-degree video: *omni-directional stereo,* or ODS. It is a variant of conventional equirectangular projections with the advantages of avoiding bad seams or dead zones, it is pre-rendered for faster playback, and video uses conventional encoding so you can edit using conventional tools. And Unity supports ODS in their Panoramic Skybox shaders (see the topic later in this chapter).

 For a more detailed explanation of the challenges and geometry of stereo 360 media captures, see the Google whitepaper *Rendering Omni-directional Stereo Content* (https://developers.google.com/vr/jump/rendering-ods-content.pdf). Also, check out the article *Stereographic 3D Panoramic Images* by Paul Bourke (May 2002) by visiting http://paulbourke.net/stereographics/stereopanoramic/.

# Fun with photo globes

To begin exploring these concepts, let's have a little fun as we apply an ordinary (rectangular) image as a texture to a sphere, just to see what it does and how bad it looks. Then, we'll use a properly distorted equirectangular photosphere texture.

## Crystal balls

*Auntie Em! Auntie Em!* cried Dorothy in the Wizard of Oz, as she gazed into a crystal ball seeking help from the Wicked Witch. Let's consider making a crystal ball using Unity, *my little pretty!*

First, set up a new scene for this chapter by performing the following steps:

1. Create a new scene by navigating to **File** | **New Scene**. Then, navigate to **File** | **Save Scene As...** and name it 360Degrees.
2. Create a new plane by navigating to **GameObject** | **3D Object** | **Plane** and reset its transformation using the **Transform** component's *gear* icon | **Reset**.
3. Set the Main Camera **Position** to (0, 0, −1)

You can choose to use the MeMyselfEye camera rig we've been using throughout the book, but it is not necessary in this project. The Main Camera will implement the VR camera based on the SDK you've selected in Player Settings. We will not be using device-specific input or other features.

Now, create the first sphere and write a rotator script while we're at it. I'm using the EthanSkull.png image that was provided with this book (drag and drop it into your **Project Assets Textures** folder).

Then, perform the following steps:

1. Create a new sphere by navigating to **GameObject** | **3D Object** | **Sphere**, reset its transformation using the **Transform** component's *gear* icon | **Reset**, and name it CrystalBall.
2. Set its **Position** to (0, 1.5, 0).
3. Drag and drop the texture named EthanSkull (you can use any photo that you want) onto the sphere.
4. Create a new script by navigating to **Add Component** | **New Script** and name it Rotator.

Note that dropping the texture onto the game object will automatically create a corresponding Material named EthanSkull.mat in your Materials/ folder, with this texture in the **Albedo** texture map slot.

Open the rotator.cs script and write it, as follows:

```
using UnityEngine;

public class Rotator : MonoBehaviour
{
    [Tooltip("Rotation rate in degrees per second")]
    public Vector3 rate;

    void Update()
    {
```

```
        transform.Rotate(rate * Time.deltaTime);
    }
}
```

Note that we added a `Tooltip` attribute for the Unity Editor that gives the developer more detail how to use the `rate` values.

Then, set the rotation rate so that it spins around the *y* axis 20 degrees per second, as follows:

1. On the **Rotator Script** component, set **Rate** for **X**, **Y**, **Z** as (0, 20, 0).
2. Save the scene. Try it in VR.

*Is that scary or what?* No worries. The projected image may be distorted, but it looks wicked cool. For some applications, a little distortion is the artistic intent, and you don't need to worry about it.

Careful editing such as smudging the edges of the photo can help avoid seams in the texture map.

While we're at it, lets try making the ball look more like crystal glass by adjusting the shader properties:

1. Select `CrystalBall` in **Inspector**
2. Set its **Metallic** value to `0.75`
3. Set its **Smoothness** value to `0.75`
4. Open the **Albedo** color (click the color swatch), and adjust the **Alpha** (A) value to `100`

That looks better. Add more objects with various textures into your scene to visualize the transparency and specular highlights.

If you're interested in more realistic glass simulation for your crystal balls, here are some suggestions:

- Consider adding a reflection probe to the scene (`https://docs.unity3d.com/Manual/class-ReflectionProbe.html`) so the surface seems to reflect other objects in the scene.
- For transparency and refraction, a `GlassRefractive` material is provided in the **Standard Assets Effects** package.
- Try a custom shader in your material. An example of a Simple Glass shader is given in the Unity ShaderLab documentation (`https://docs.unity3d.com/Manual/SL-CullAndDepth.html`).
- Also consider third-party materials and shaders that simulate glass with refraction, distortions, glass surface patterns, and colors (search the Asset Store, `https://assetstore.unity.com/search?q=category%3A121q=glass`).
- Note that transparency should be used sparingly in VR applications as it requires additional rendering passes per pixel, potentially slowing your frame generation and causing unwanted latency.

# Globes

Next, we'll make another sphere and add a texture, like we just did, but this time use a texture with an equirectangular (photosphere) distortion.

Import the `Tissot_euirectangular.png` image, which is included with this book (and available on Wikipedia at `https://en.wikipedia.org/wiki/Tissot%27s_indicatrix#/media/File:Tissot_behrmann.png`), into your Texture folder and perform the following steps:

1. Create a new sphere and name it `Globe`. Add the `Rotator` script if you want.
2. Drag the texture named `Tissot_equirectangular` onto the sphere.
3. Try it in VR. Take a close look at the globe, as shown in the following image:

Note that unfortunately the Tissot circles are oval, not circular, except along the equator. It turns out that the default sphere provided in Unity does not mesh well for equirectangular texture maps. Instead, I have provided one designed specifically for this purpose, `PhotoSphere.fbx` (which happens to be the default sphere model in 3D Studio Max). Let's try it:

1. Import the `PhotoSphere.fbx` file by dragging it into your **Project Assets Models** folder (or through the menu: **Assets | Import New Asset...**).
2. Create a new equirectangular sphere by dragging the `PhotoSphere` model from **Project Assets** into **Scene**.
3. Set its position and name it `Globe2`. Add the `Rotator` script if you want.
4. Drag the texture named `Tissot_equirectangular` onto the sphere.

Try it in VR. *Much better.* You can see the texture is correctly mapped now; the circles are round (and the underlying mesh grid is more regular):

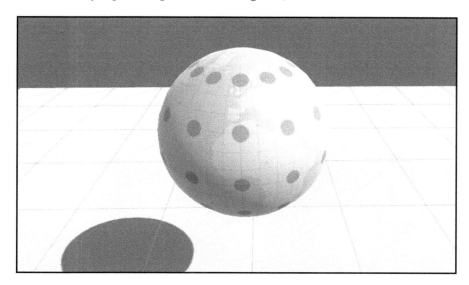

Now you can apply any 360 degree photo to the globe, creating your own *photo-globes* or virtual Christmas tree ornaments!

Expanding upon this topic further, you could build a nice model of the Solar System. Equirectangular texture maps of each of the planets and moons can be downloaded free from Solar System Scope (`https://www.solarsystemscope.com/`). Data regarding the rate of rotation (day/night) and orbit (around the sun) can be found on the NASA site (`https://nssdc.gsfc.nasa.gov/planetary/factsheet/index.html`). A complete Unity tutorial project can be found in the book *Augmented Reality for Developers* (`https://www.amazon.com/Augmented-Reality-Developers-Jonathan-Linowes/dp/1787286436`).

Another idea is that photo globes have been used as a teleportation mechanism in VR games-- as a player, you grab a globe depicting another scene, put it on your face and you are teleported into that world. See the topic on *Capturing 360-degree media* for how to capture a 360-degree photo of your Unity scenes.

# Rendering photospheres

The inverse of a globe is a photosphere. Where a globe maps an equirectangular texture onto the outside surface of a sphere, a photosphere would map the texture onto the inside surface, and you view it from the inside so it surrounds you.

For our examples, I'm using the `Farmhouse.png` image which is provided with this book, as shown below. Feel free to use your own 360-degree photo, whether you have a 360-degree camera such as the Ricoh Theta or other brand, use a photo stitching app for Android or iOS, or download one from any number of photo sources on the web.

As we've seen, Unity ordinarily renders only the outward-facing surfaces of objects. This is determined, mathematically, as the *normal* direction vector of each facet of its surface mesh. A Plane is the simplest example. Back in `Chapter 2`, *Content, Objects, and Scale*, we created a big screen image plane with the Grand Canyon on it. When you are facing the plane, you see the image. But if you move around behind the plane, it is not rendered, as if it were not in the scene at all. Similarly, suppose there is a cube or sphere in front of you; you will see it rendered, lit, and shaded. But if you put your head inside the object, it seems to disappear, because you're now looking at the inside faces of the object's mesh. This is all handled by the shader. And since we want to change it, we need to use a different shader.

# Writing a custom Inward shader

We are going to write a custom shader to render our texture on the inside of the sphere mesh.

Shaders are a critical part of the Unity rendering pipeline, and it's where a lot of the magic of computer graphics and virtual reality actually occurs. Unity provides an impressive set of built-in shaders, as you've likely noticed just by opening the **Shader** select list on any object's Material in the Inspector. Many asset packages you import may also include shaders that implement custom effects, including some we've already used in previous chapters, such as TextMeshPro and TiltBrush. The VR toolkits from Oculus, Google Daydream, and SteamVR also include shaders that provide an extra kick in performance and optimization of the rendering pipeline.

Writing shaders is an advanced topic in computer graphics and Unity development. Nonetheless, Unity provides tools to facilitate the programming of shaders (see `https://docs.unity3d.com/Manual/SL-Reference.html`), including a declarative language called *ShaderLab*, a lot of documentation and tutorials, and example shaders to work from. We are not going to go very deep here but many find it a very interesting and valuable skill to learn.

To create a new shader, begin as follows:

1. Navigate to **Create** | **Shader** | **Unlit Shader** and name it `MyInwardShader`
2. Double-click the new shader file to open it for editing

To turn the shader into an inside shader, all you need to do is add the line `Cull Front`, for example, immediately after the `Tags` line as follows:

```
...
Tags { "RenderType"="Opaque" }
Cull Front
...
```

The `Cull` command tell the shader whether to ignore front or back facing surfaces. The default is Back; we're changing it to cull the front ones and render the back ones. (For details on this, see `https://docs.unity3d.com/Manual/SL-CullAndDepth.html`.)

Save the file. Now we can use it in our project.

Notice that the top line of the shader file names it `Shader "Unlit/MyInwardShader"`, which means you'll find it in the select **Shader** | **Unlit** submenu, or you can modify it without the submenu to `Shader "MyInwardShader"`.

Since we're inverting the texture, it may appear mirrored backwards. We will fix that by setting its **X Tiling** to –1, as we will see.

An alternative approach is to invert the vertex normals within the shader. We used that technique in the first edition of this book, and it is shown here:

```
Shader "MyInwardNormalsShader" {
    Properties {
        _MainTex ("Base (RGB)", 2D) = "white" {}
    }
    SubShader {
        Tags { "RenderType" = "Opaque" }
        Cull Off

        CGPROGRAM
        #pragma surface surf Lambert vertex:vert
        sampler2D _MainTex;

        struct Input {
            float2 uv_MainTex;
            float4 color : COLOR;
        };

        void vert(inout appdata_full v) {
            v.normal.xyz = v.normal * -1;
        }

        void surf (Input IN, inout SurfaceOutput o) {
            fixed3 result = tex2D(_MainTex, IN.uv_MainTex);
            o.Albedo = result.rgb;
            o.Alpha = 1;
        }
        ENDCG
    }
    Fallback "Diffuse"
}
```

Briefly, this shader script declares the following:

- Lets you supply both a texture and a color property
- Does no culling of surfaces (the texture will be visible both inside and out)
- Uses a simple Lambert diffuse lighting algorithm (versus unlit or the Standard Unity physically-based lighting)

- The `vert` function inverts the mesh vertices (by multiplying the normal vector by −1)
- The `surf` renderer copies the texture pixel and also lets you tint it with an Albedo color (but forces Alpha to be opaque)

You can use this shader instead of the quick one we wrote previously.

 Consider what would happen if you used an Alpha channel in your shader settings and set up a cutout mask. It would allow photospheres with some areas completely transparent. This opens the possibility of nesting multiple photospheres to create visual layers of 360 activity within your scene!

# Magic orbs

Before we do full 360-photo viewing, for fun let's first consider a special case, *magic orbs*. For this example, we'll look at the sphere from the inside, mapping a 360-degree image onto its inside surface. Then, we'll put a solid colored *shell* around the outside. So, you really have to stick your head into the sphere to see what's there, or grab the sphere and "put it on your eyes!"

To build it, follow these steps:

1. Create a new material by navigating to **Assets** | **Create** | **Material** and name it `FarmhouseInward`.
2. In **Inspector,** use the **Shader** selector and choose **Unlit** | **MyInwardShader**, the one we just created.
3. Locate the `Farmhouse` texture image and drag it onto the shader component's **Albedo** texture. If needed, set **Tiling X** to −1 to compensate for mirroring.
4. Add a new sphere to the scene, dragging the `PhotoSphere.fbx` from your *Models* folder introduced before, and name it "MagicOrb."
5. Drag the `FarmhouseInward` material onto the sphere.

We'll encase it in a solid colored orb by performing the following steps:

1. Select the `MagicOrb` object in **Hierarchy**, right-click, and navigate to **3D Object** | **Sphere** so that the new sphere is a child.

2. Set its **Scale** to something a little bigger than the inner sphere, such as (1.02, 1.02, 1.02)
3. Disable its **Sphere Collider** component by unchecking it.
4. Find a solid material, such as the one we made in a previous chapter named RedMaterial, and drag it onto the new sphere.

Try it in VR. From the outside, it looks like a solid ball, but lean into it and there's a whole new little world in there! The following image is a capture of what I see. It's like peering into an egg shell!

For non-positionally tracked mobile VR devices, you may not be able to do this in VR, but you can manually drag the camera rig in the Scene view while playing the scene in the Editor. Or, add some locomotion as described in Chapter 7, *Locomotion and Comfort*. Or, make the orb grab-able, so the player can pick it up and move it very close to their face, using techniques described in Chapter 5, *Handy Interactables*.

If you want to dive deeper into shaders, as an exercise, try and see how you could modify InwardShader to take an additional Color parameter that is used to render the outward facing surface, while the texture is used to render the inward facing ones.

# Photospheres

*Yes sir, it's all the rage these days. It's better than panoramas. It's better than selfies. It may be even better than Snapchat! We're finally getting to the moment that you've been waiting for! It's 360-degree photospheres!*

We covered a lot of topics in this chapter, which will now make it fairly easy to talk about 360-degree photospheres. To build one, we'll just make a very big sphere with the `MyInwardShader` shader.

Start with a new empty scene:

1. Create a new scene by navigating to **File | New Scene**. Then, **File | Save Scene** and name it `PhotoSphere`. Delete the default Main Camera.
2. Add the `MyMyselfEye` prefab and reset its **Transform Position** to (0, 0, 0).
3. Create an equirectangular sphere by dragging the `PhotoSphere` model from the `Project Models` folder into the scene (as imported from `PhotoSphere.fbx` in the previous example).
4. Reset its **Transform** (*gear* icon | **Reset) and** set its **Scale** to (10, 10, 10).
5. Create a material (**Create | Material**) and name it to `PhotoSphere Material`.
6. Navigate to **Shader | Unlit | MyInwardShader** (as created earlier in this chapter).
7. Drag the `Photosphere` Material onto the `Photosphere` game object.
8. If there will be other objects in the Scene, you may need to disable shadows. On the Photosphere game object, in its **Mesh Renderer** component, uncheck the **Receive Shadows** checkbox.

Now, to add the photo:

1. Import the photo that you want to use; ours is named `FarmHouse.jpg`.
2. With `PhotoSphere` selected (or the `PhotoSphere Material` itself), drag the `FarmHouse` texture onto the **Albedo** texture tile.
3. Set the **Tiling X** value to −1 to compensate for the mirror inversion, if necessary.

Press **Play**. You should now see the photosphere surrounding you in the scene.

If you are using a device with positional tracking, such as the Oculus Rift, we need to disable it. Create a new script on `MemMyselfEye` as follows:

```
public class DisablePositionalTracking : MonoBehaviour
{
    void Start()
    {
        UnityEngine.XR.InputTracking.disablePositionalTracking = true;
    }
}
```

You may find that the default texture resolution and/or compression are not high enough quality for your taste. To modify the resolution, follow these steps:

1. Select the texture (Farmhouse.png)
2. In **Inspector**, change the **Max Size** to `4096` or `8192`
3. Press **Apply** to re-import the texture

Note the file size (at bottom of **Inspector**) can grow exponentially, affecting the final size of your app, load times, and runtime performance. Also try the other compression settings, including the new Crunch Compression (`https://blogs.unity3d.com/2017/11/15/updated-crunch-texture-compression-library/`). You can configure these settings on a per-platform basis.

To switch images, repeat the last two steps: import the asset and assign it to the **Albedo** texture of the `Photosphere Mataterial`. If you want to do this in-game, you can do this in a script (for example, by using `Material.mainTexture()`).

# Playing 360-degree videos

The steps for adding a 360-degree video are pretty much the same as adding a regular rectangular one to your project (see `https://docs.unity3d.com/Manual/class-MovieTexture.html`). To play a 360-degree video, you use a `Video Player` to render the video on a `Render Texture`. If you do not have a 360-degree video handy, search the web free downloads and pick one that's not too long and a limited file size.

 Depending on the format of your video, you may need to install QuickTime on your system first before you can import it into Unity, for the conversion codec.

If you would like, start a new scene and reset the MyMyselfEye **Transform** to the origin. Then, import a 360 video into your **Project Assets.** Note its dimensions (for example, a 4K video is 4096 x 2048). You can see it in **Inspector,** if you're not sure.

Add a video player to your project as follows:

1. Create an **Empty** named "VideoPlayer"
2. **Add Component | Video Player**
3. Drag your video file onto its **Video Clip** slot
4. Check the **Play On Awake** checkbox and the **Loop** checkbox
5. Ensure **Render Mode** is set to **Render Texture**

Now, we will create a Render Texture, a special Unity texture that will be rendered at runtime by the video player:

1. In your **Project Assets, Create | Render Texture**, name it "Video Render Texture"
2. Set the **Size** to exactly the size of your video, (such as 4096 x 2048).
3. Setting **Anti aliasing** to **2 samples** is recommended.
4. You can set **Depth Buffer** to **No Depth Buffer**
5. Select **VideoPlayer** in Hierarchy and drag VideoRenderTexture onto its **Target Texture** slot

Now, create your photosphere:

1. Create a new 3D **Sphere** and name it "VideoSphere"
2. Reset its **Transform**, so its **Position** is (0, 0, 0), then set its **Scale** to (10, 10, 10)
3. Drag **Video Render Texture** onto the sphere and make a new Material (or you could have separately created this material first)
4. Change the Material **Shader** to **MyInwardShader**

A resulting VideoPlayer in Inspector is shown here:

Press **Play**. You now have a basic 360 video player built with Unity.

To review, the sphere uses a material with an inward shader. The shader renders an equirectangular texture on the inside of the sphere. The video player modifies that texture each update with the next video frame.

> When building for Android and iOS, you must put your video file (such as MP4) into a folder named *StreamingAssets* in your Project Assets. For more information on this and other considerations for Video Player and codecs, see the Unity documentation at `https://docs.unity3d.com/ScriptReference/Video.VideoPlayer.html`.

If the video has audio, we can make the video an **Audio Source** as follows:

- Select the **VideoPlayer** and **Add Component** | **Audio Source**
- Drag `VideoPlayer` itself onto its Video Player component's **Audio Source** slot

As with all Unity components, the video player has an API and can be controlled via scripting. For example, to simply pause the video with a button click, you could add this script to the `VideoPlayer`:

```
using UnityEngine;
using UnityEngine.Video;

public class PlayPause : MonoBehaviour {
    private VideoPlayer player;

    void Start() {
        player = GetComponent<VideoPlayer>();
    }

    void Update() {
        if (Input.GetButtonDown("Fire1"))
        {
            if (player.isPlaying)
            {
                player.Pause();
            }
            else
            {
                player.Play();
            }
        }
    }
}
```

For additional tips, also check out the tutorial from Unity *Getting started in interactive 360 video: Download our sample project* at `https://blogs.unity3d.com/2018/01/19/getting-started-in-interactive-360-video-download-our-sample-project/`.

# Using Unity skyboxes

Back in the olden days, or at least before 360 photos, we simply referred to *skyboxes* as the way to create background imagery in computer graphics. Skyboxes depict what's far on the horizon, may contribute to the ambient lighting of the scene, be used for rendering reflections on object surfaces, and are not interactable. Unity supports skyboxes as part of the Lighting Environment for each scene. We used skyboxes already in a few of the previous chapters' projects (including Wispy Sky and Skull Platform ones).

Common sources of skyboxes are cylindrical panorama, spherical panorama (360 images), and a six-sided cube. We won't consider the cylindrical one, since it's less useful for VR.

# Six-sided or cubemap skyboxes

A skybox can be represented by a six sides of a cube, where each side is akin to a camera capturing its view pointing in each of the six directions, as illustrated here:

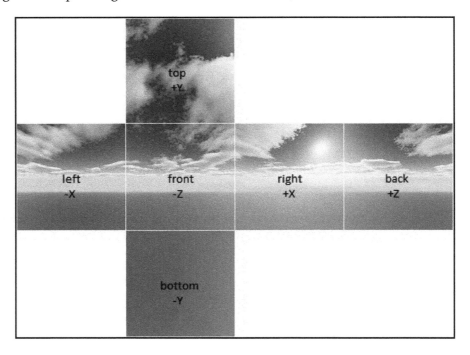

Given these six images, as textures, you'd create a *six-sided* skybox material like the one shown next for the WispySky cubemap. And then, set it in the Lighting window as the Skybox Material for the scene:

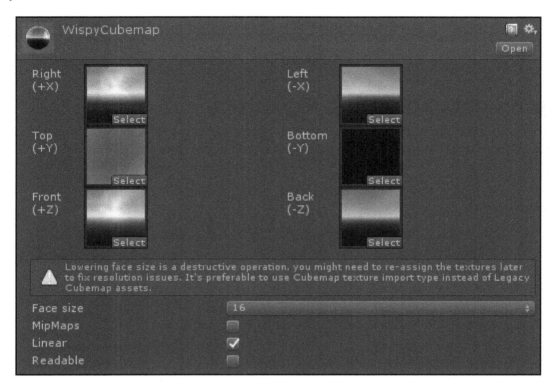

Alternatively, you could combine the six images into a single *cubemap* image, laid out similarly.

Cubemaps have an advantage because equirectangular textures waste pixels where the image is stretched at the top and bottom poles of the spherical projection. On the other hand, care must be taken to properly design images so they'll smoothly stitch together and not cause seams or other visual artifacts.

A variant over traditional cubemaps is the **Equi-Angular Cubemap** (**EAC**). EAC strives to have even more uniform pixel sizes and "equal angle pixel distribution in 3D." (See `https://blog.google/products/google-vr/bringing-pixels-front-and-center-vr-video/`.)

But most 360 media today, especially coming from consumer cameras, use equirectangular projections, aka spherical panoramas.

# Spherical panoramic skyboxes

Using a 360 photo for a skybox is referred to a *spherical panoramic*. Earlier in this chapter we used a spherical game object to render an equirectangular texture and placed the player camera dead-center inside it. Now, we'll now use the same image in a skybox. (Note, this will also work for 180-degree content.)

Start with a new empty scene:

1. Create a new scene by navigating to **File | New Scene**. Then, **File | Save Scene** and name it `Skybox`. Replace the `Main Camera` with the `MyMyselfEye` prefab.
2. Assuming you're using the `Farmhouse.jpg` image as earlier, create a new `Material` and name it `Farmhouse Skybox`.
3. For the material's **Shader**, choose **Skybox | Panoramic**.
4. Drag your 360 image (`Farmhouse.jpg`) onto the **Spherical** texture area.
5. Set the **Mapping** to **Latitude Longitude Layout**.
6. Set the **Image Type** to **360 Degrees**.

The Material settings are shown here:

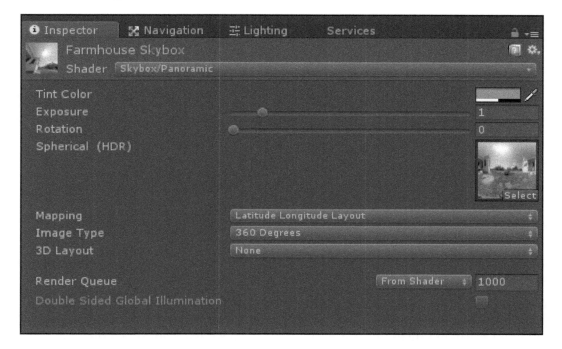

Now to use it in your scene:

1. Open the **Lighting** window tab (if not in your Editor, navigate to **Window** | **Lighting**)
2. Drag your `Farmhouse Skybox` material onto the **Skybox Material** slot

The **Lighting Environment** settings are shown here:

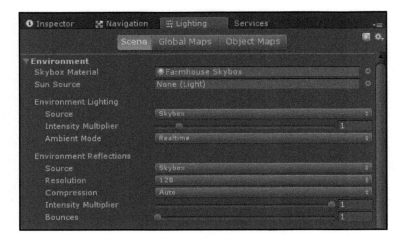

Press **Play**. *Voila!* You should now see the photosphere surrounding you in the scene. That was almost too easy. Thank goodness!

One thing that's interesting is, since skyboxes are always rendered as if at a very far distance away, the camera will always be at the center of the photosphere. Thus, we don't need to set the camera rig at the origin, and we don't need to disable positional tracking, as we did for the spherical game object version of this project. Wherever you move, the skybox will surround you just the same. If your 360 image contains content (people or objects) that are relatively near, this may feel very unnatural, as if the objects are projected or flattened against the spherical projection (which they are!). This is why skyboxes are generally used for landscapes and wide open spaces. (Later, we'll see how this can be solved using *stereo* skyboxes.)

At this point, you can add more content to your scene. After all, we're in Unity and not just making an generic 360 photo viewer. Enhance your lovely outdoor scene by adding falling snow or leaves (for example, see the *Falling Leaves* particle package, `https://assetstore.unity.com/packages/3d/falling-leaves-54725`).

A common application is to use a 360 image in a lobby scene, and add an interactive menu panel for launching other apps or scenes. The Google Daydream lobby comes to mind.

Another application is to make the 360 image more interactive by add UI canvases to label content in the photo. It may take some thoughtful work to align the labels with the photosphere. Then, using a camera raycast, you can dynamically highlight what the player is looking at (see `Chapter 4`, *Gaze-Based Control* for coding tips).

# 360 video skyboxes

Turning your skybox into a 360 degree video player is nearly identical to the steps outlined previously for the spherical game object version. We won't repeat everything again, but briefly it goes as follows:

1. Set up a `Video Player` to play back the video source to a `Render Texture`
2. Set up a `Skybox Material` that will receive the `Render Texture`
3. Set the scene to use the `Skybox Material`

Note, according to Unity, equirectangular videos should have an aspect ratio of exactly 2:1 (or for 180-degree content, 1:1) for the skybox shader. Also, many desktop hardware video decoders are limited to 4K resolutions and mobile hardware video decoders are often limited to 2K or less, limiting the resolution that can be played back in real time on those platforms.

# 3D stereo skyboxes

If you have a 360 image or video with stereo views, for each of the left and right eyes, Unity can now use that too. As of Unity 2017.3, the Panoramic Skybox material supports 3D textures in with a 3D layout. You can specify **Side by side** or **Over under**, as shown here:

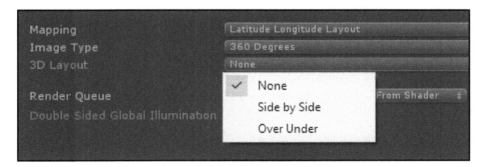

An example 3D stereographic equirectangular over-under image is given in the next topic, where we discuss capturing 360 media within your Unity project.

# Capturing 360-degrees in Unity

We've talked about using 360-degree media captured using 360 cameras. But what if you wanted to capture a 360 image or video from within your Unity app and share it on the internet? This could be useful for marketing and promoting your VR apps, or just simply using Unity as a content generation tool but using 360 video as the final distribution medium.

## Capturing cubemaps and reflection probes

Unity includes support for capturing scene views as part of its lighting engine. A call to `camera.RenderToCubemap()` will bake a static cubemap of your scene, using the camera's current position and other settings.

The example script given in the Unity documentation, `https://docs.unity3d.com/Documentation/ScriptReference/Camera.RenderToCubemap.html`, implements an editor wizard for capturing a cubemap of your scene directly in the Editor, and is included here:

```
using UnityEngine;
using UnityEditor;
using System.Collections;

public class RenderCubemapWizard : ScriptableWizard
{
    public Transform renderFromPosition;
    public Cubemap cubemap;

    void OnWizardUpdate()
    {
        string helpString = "Select transform to render from and cubemap to
render into";
        bool isValid = (renderFromPosition != null) && (cubemap != null);
    }

    void OnWizardCreate()
    {
        // create temporary camera for rendering
        GameObject go = new GameObject("CubemapCamera");
        go.AddComponent<Camera>();
```

```
        // place it on the object
        go.transform.position = renderFromPosition.position;
        go.transform.rotation = Quaternion.identity;
        // render into cubemap
        go.GetComponent<Camera>().RenderToCubemap(cubemap);

        // destroy temporary camera
        DestroyImmediate(go);
    }

    [MenuItem("GameObject/Render into Cubemap")]
    static void RenderCubemap()
    {
        ScriptableWizard.DisplayWizard<RenderCubemapWizard>(
            "Render cubemap", "Render!");
    }
}
```

To run the wizard:

1. Create an **Empty** game object for the camera position to capture from
2. Create a cubemap to render into (**Assets | Create | Legacy | Cubemap**)
3. Set **Face size** to a high resolution, such as `2048`
4. Check the **Readable** checkbox
5. Run the wizard (**GameObject | Render into Cubemap**)
6. Drag the position object into the **Render From Position** slot
7. Drag cubemap into the **Cubemap** slot
8. Press **Render!**

This `.cubemap` file can now be used in a Skybox Cubemap material.

A similar but different approach is to use Reflection probes. They're normally used by objects with reflective materials to render realistic surface reflections (see `https://docs.unity3d.com/Manual/class-ReflectionProbe.html`). A reflection probe captures a spherical view of its surroundings and is then stored as a cubemap. Scene designers will strategically place multiple reflection probes in a scene to provide more realistic rendering. You can repurpose a reflection probe as a 360 image capture of your scene! Since they're intended for reflection lighting, they're usually low resolution.

Unity chooses where to store the reflection probe lightmap file (`.exr`) depending on your lighting settings. To save it under your *Assets* folder (rather than the GI cache), go to the **Lighting** tab, disable **Realtime Global Illumination**, and disable **Auto Generate**. This will generate the refection probe `.exr` file in a folder with the same name as your scene.

Try adding one to your scene by navigating to **GameObject | Light | Reflection Probe**. Set **Resolution** to a high value, like `2048`. Then, press **Bake**. You can then assign this `.exr` file to a Skybox Cubemap material, making a quick and easy 360 scene-shot.

# Using a third-party package for 360 image capture

There are a number of packages that provide the ability to capture 360 images and video in Unity, including:

- 360 Panorama Capture from eVRydayVR (free) (`https://assetstore.unity.com/packages/tools/camera/360-panorama-capture-38755`)
- VR Panorama 360 PRO from OliVR ($49) (`https://assetstore.unity.com/packages/tools/video/vr-panorama-360-pro-renderer-35102`)
- Oculus 360-Capture-SDK (free), includes a sample Unity project (`https://github.com/facebook/360-Capture-SDK`)

Each of these packages support mono and stereoscopic capture, sequenced captures for video encoding, and possibly other features for color conversion, antialiasing, camera image effects, and 3D spatialized audio.

Using the 360 Panorama Capture script from eVRydayVR, for example, to capture a single 360 image, open a scene you want to capture, then:

1. Create an **Empty** game object, named `CapturePanorama`, positioned where you want to make the capture
2. Add the **Capture Panorama** script as a component
3. Press **Play**, then press *P* on the keyboard

The screen will fade to black, and an image will be captured and saved to your project root directory. The component options are shown here:

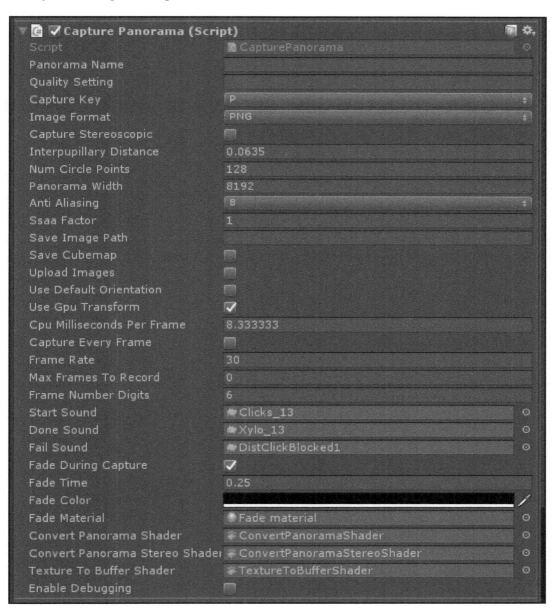

To capture video, you would enable the **Capture Every Frame** checkbox. It recommends the open source *ffmpeg* tool (`https://www.ffmpeg.org/`) to assemble the frames and encode the video. See the README file for details.

Of course, this component can also be controlled via scripts, and can be built into your runtime game, not just used in the Editor.

# Unity built-in stereo 360 image and video capture

As of Unity 2018.1, Unity includes an integrated stereo 360 image and video capture capability. The feature is based on Google's omni-directional stereo (ODS), described at the beginning of this chapter. Details in this section summarize the Unity Blogs post from January, 2018 (`https://blogs.unity3d.com/2018/01/26/stereo-360-image-and-video-capture/`), which explains how to capture ODS stereo cubemaps and convert them to stereo equirectangular textures.

To capture a scene in Editor or standalone player, call `camera.RenderToCubemap()` once per eye. We used this function earlier; there is a variant that takes a `stereoEye` parameter, for example:

```
camera.stereoSeparation = 0.064; // Eye separation (IPD) of 64mm.
camera.RenderToCubemap(cubemapLeftEye, 63,
        Camera.MonoOrStereoscopicEye.Left);
camera.RenderToCubemap(cubemapRightEye, 63,
        Camera.MonoOrStereoscopicEye.Right);
```

To convert cubemaps to stereo equirectangular maps, call `RenderTexture.ConvertToEquirect()` as follows:

```
cubemapLeftEye.ConvertToEquirect(equirect,
        Camera.MonoOrStereoscopicEye.Left);
cubemapRightEye.ConvertToEquirect(equirect,
        Camera.MonoOrStereoscopicEye.Right);
```

Using the Unity frame recorder (`https://github.com/Unity-Technologies/GenericFrameRecorder`), a sequence of these images can be captured as frames of a stereo 360 video.

To capture in the PC standalone build, you need to enable the **360 Stereo Capture** in the **Build Settings**, as shown here, so Unity generates the shader variants required by this feature:

Here is an example of a resulting stereo equirectangular video capture (from the Unity blog, `https://blogs.unity3d.com/wp-content/uploads/2018/01/image5-2.gif`):

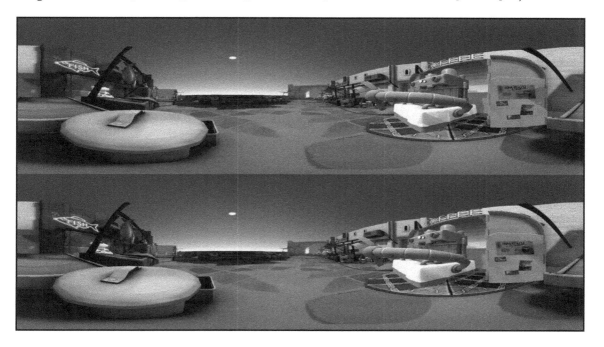

# Summary

360-degree media is compelling because VR hacks your field of view (FOV). The view you see is updated in real time as you move your head around, making it seem to have no edges. We started this chapter by describing what 360-degree images are, and how the surface of a sphere would be flattened (projected) into a 2D image, and equirectangular projections in particular. Stereo 3D media includes separate equirectangular views for the left and right eyes.

We began exploring this in Unity by simply mapping a regular image on the outside of a sphere, and were perhaps frightened by the distortions. Then, we saw how an equirectangular texture covers the sphere evenly. Next, we inverted the sphere with a custom shader, mapping the image inside the sphere, making it a 360 photosphere viewer. And, we added video.

Then, we looked at using skyboxes instead of a game object for rendering 360 media. We saw how Unity supports cubemaps and spherical panoramas, video skyboxes, and 3D stereo skyboxes too. Lastly, we explored capturing 360 media from within your Unity scenes using third-party packages and Unity's built-in API.

In the next chapter, we consider an important application of virtual reality, for storytelling. Using the animation and cinematic editing feature of Unity, we build a short VR cinematic experience.

# Animation and VR Storytelling

# 11

The stories we tell, and how we tell them, say a lot about who we are and what we will become. Storytelling between humans is as primal as any human activity, the basis of interpersonal communications, mythology, historical record, entertainment, and all of the arts. VR is emerging as one of the newest, and potentially most profound, storytelling media formats.

In the previous chapter, we looked at 360-degree media, which itself is becoming its own form of VR storytelling, especially for nonfictional documentary, capable of transmitting human experience and creating immersive empathy for humanitarian crises. Many of the tools and lessons we cover in this chapter can also be used with 360 media, but we're going to focus on 3D computer graphics and animation here.

For this project, we are going to create a little VR experience, a simplistic story about a bird who gains its wings and learns to fly.

In this chapter, we are going to learn about the following topics:

- Importing and using external models and animations
- Using Unity Timelines to activate and animate objects
- Using the Animation editor window for editing property keyframes
- Controlling Animation Clips with an Animation Controller
- Making the story interactive

# Composing our story

*You start in a dark scene and notice a small sapling in the ground in front of you. It starts to grow into a tree. As dawn breaks, a bird's nest appears, and we notice it has an egg in it. The egg begins to shake, and then hatches. A baby bird emerges, hops around, grows, and tests its wings. Finally, in daylight, it flies away to freedom.*

Our story is about birth, growth, spreading your wings (literally and figuratively), and moving on. We will start with a music soundtrack and animate our graphics based on its parts.

We are using free, off-the-shelf assets. Of course, you can use your own music and graphics, but we'll assume you're following along using the ones we have selected, which are all available online for free (links are given). As an instructive project, it's minimalistic and not embellished with effects that one might expect of a polished product. But you'd be very proud of your 9-year old cousin or nephew if they made it!

The soundtrack we will use is a rendition of The Beatles and Paul McCartney song, "Blackbird". (A download link is in the next section, and a copy is included with the files for this chapter for convenience.) Based on our mp3 recording of the song, we sketched out a rough timeline plan of our VR experience on a chart, shown here:

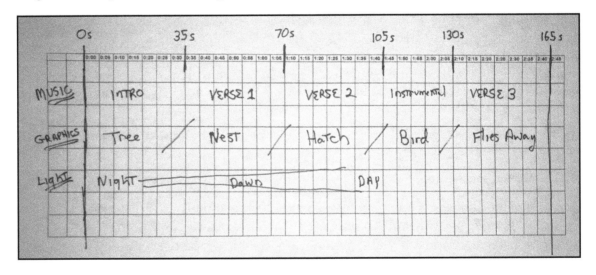

As indicated, the entire song is 165 seconds (2:45). It starts with a 35-second instrumental intro, then verse one and verse two (also 35 seconds), a 25-second instrumental, and then verse three is 35 seconds. We'll use this to divide our story into five segments.

Plenty of other features ought to be planned out as well. The scene lighting, for example, will start in the dark of night and gradually lighten the sky into dawn and then daytime.

# Gathering the assets

As mentioned, we're going to build our story from a variety of sources of free and simplistic assets. I recommend you download and install each of them now (or your own substitutions) so they're accessible as we work:

- Music: The Beatles and Paul McCartney song, "Blackbird" performed by guitarist Salvatore Manalo. Mp3 download: `http://mp3freeget4.online/play/the-beatles-paul-mccartney-blackbird-cover/chSrubUUdwc.html`
- Scene and tree: Nature Starter Kit, `https://assetstore.unity.com/packages/3d/environments/nature-starter-kit-1-49962`
- Nest and egg: Use the `NestAndEgg` prefab file provided with this book (source: tutorial using Cinema 4D: `https://www.youtube.com/watch?v=jzoNZslTQfI`, .c4d file download, `https://yadi.sk/d/ZQep-K-AMKAc8`)
- Living Birds: `https://assetstore.unity.com/packages/3d/characters/animals/living-birds-15649`
- Wispy Skybox: `https://assetstore.unity.com/packages/2d/textures-materials/sky/wispy-skybox-21737`

Note that the nest and egg object we are using is modified from the one found online. That was in `.c4d` format, and we have converted it to `.fbx`, packaged them into a prefab, and made a few other changes.

# Creating the initial scene

We're going to make a simple, minimalist scene using a plane for the ground and some rocks from the Nature Starter Kit, a bird's nest with an egg, and a bird:

1. Create a new scene (**File** | **New Scene**) and name it "Blackbird" (**File** | **Save Scene As**)
2. Create a 3D **Plane** named `GroundPlane`, reset its **Transform**, then **Scale** it to (`10, 10, 10`)
3. Create a new **Material** named `GroundMaterial`, set its **Albedo** color to an earthy brown (such as `#251906ff`), and drag the material onto the plane
4. Set the **Main Camera Position** to (`0, 2, -3`)

You can replace `Main Camera` with the `MeMyselfEye` camera rig we've been using throughout the book, but it is not necessary in this project as we will not be using device-specific input or other features. The `Main Camera` will provide a sufficient VR camera based on the SDK you've selected in **Player Settings**.

 We are using a simple ground plane, as it gives the aesthetic we want. But this could be a good opportunity for you to explore the Unity Terrain system. This is another rich and very powerful topic, where you can "paint" complex landscapes with trees and grasses. See the manual at `https://docs.unity3d.com/Manual/script-Terrain.html`.

Now, add a tree and some rocks:

1. From the `Assets/NatureStarterKit/Models/` folder, drag the **Tree** into the scene. Reset its **Transform**, so it's at the origin.
2. Add a few rocks near the tree, move them so they're partially buried below the ground. You might put these under an **Empty** game object named `Environment`.
3. Add a Wind Zone (**Create | 3D Object | WindZone**) , so the Tree object responds to wind and rustles its leaves.

The rocks in my scene are placed as follows (all at **Scale** `100`):

| Prefab | Position |
|--------|----------|
| rock03 | (2.9, -0.6, -0.26) |
| rock03 | (2.6, -0.7, -3.6) |
| rock04 | (2.1, -0.65, -3.1) |
| rock01 | (-6, -3.4, -0.6) |
| rock04 | (-5, -0.7, 3.8) |

Next, we'll add the nest:

1. Drag a copy of the **NestAndEgg** model into the scene.
2. **Scale** and **Position** it on the ground so it's in easy view, near the tree, and not too small. We chose **Position** (`0.5, 0.36, -1.2`) and **Scale** (`0.2, 0.2, 0.2`).

And add a bird. The Living Birds package doesn't have a blackbird, but it does have a bluejay, which is close enough:

1. From the **Project** Assets/living birds/resources/ folder, drag the lb_blueJayHQ prefab into the **Hierarchy**. For convenience, rename it Bluejay.

2. **Scale** and **Position** it so it appears full grown and perched on the edge of the nest. We chose **Scale** (8, 8, 8), **Position** (0.75, 0.4, -1.25), and **Rotation** (0, 0, 0).

The bird is inserted into the scene in a T pose. It has animations attached, which we'll control later in this project. Like most character animations, it runs an Idle animation initially. (Note, don't rotate the bird object, it messes up the flying animations.)

Remember to press **Play** and check how it looks in VR. It's always much different within VR than the view you see on the flat screen. Our scene and hierarchy is shown in the following screen capture. You many also want to adjust the Main Camera position now:

# Timelines and Audio tracks

Earlier, we planned out our movie using a graph paper timeline. Unity provides the tools to implement that almost directly. This Timeline feature was introduced with Unity 2017.

Timelines consist of one or more tracks that play over time. It's like an Animation (which controls the properties of a single game object), but Timelines work with many different objects and different types of tracks. As we'll see and explain later, Timelines can have Audio Tracks, Activation Tracks, Animation Tracks, and Control Tracks.

Timelines are a type of Unity *Playable*. Playables are runtime objects that "play" over time, updating each frame based on its prescribed behavior. Animations are playables too. For more details, see `https://docs.unity3d.com/ScriptReference/Playables.Playable.html`.

Presently we'll add a Timeline to the project and add an Audio Track. To create the Timeline object and open it in the Timeline Editor window, do the following steps:

1. In **Hierarchy**, create an **Empty** game object and name it `BlackbirdDirector`.
2. Open the **Timeline Editor** (**Window | Timeline**).
3. In the window you will see a message "*To begin a new timeline with BlackbirdTimeline, create a Director component and a Timeline asset*" with a **Create** button.
4. Press the **Create** button.
5. You are then prompted to save a new Playable asset in your **Project** *Assets* folder. Name it `BlackbirdTimeline`. Press **Save**.

At this point, you may have noticed a few important things just happened:

- The `BlackbirdTimeline` asset was created in the `Asset` folder you specified
- A `Playable Director` component was added to the `BlackbirdDirector` game object, associating it with that `BlackbirdTimeline`
- The `Timeline Editor` window is opened for the `BlackbirdTimeline`

The next screenshot shows the `BlackbirdDirector` inspector with its `Playable Director` component. A Playable Director component controls when and how a Timeline instance plays, including whether to **Play On Awake**, and **Wrap Mode** (what to do when the Timeline is done playing: **Hold**, **Loop**, or **None**):

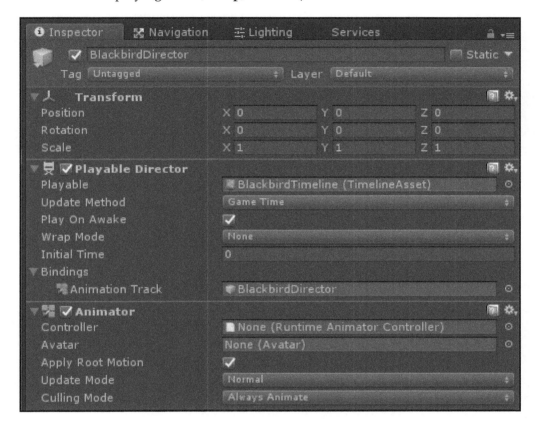

Here is the **Timeline Editor** window for the `BlackbirdTimeline`:

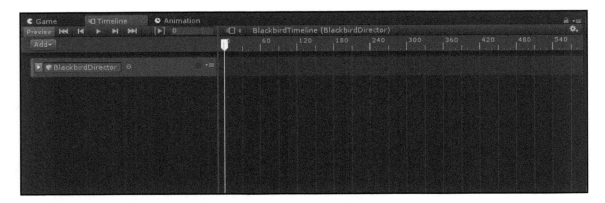

Let's now add an **Audio Track** to the timeline, with our Beatles song:

1. Locate the mp3 file in your **Project Assets**, and drag it directly onto the **Timeline Editor**
2. Press **Play** to play your scene as normal and now the music should start playing as well

Here is the **Timeline Editor** now containing the **Audio Track**:

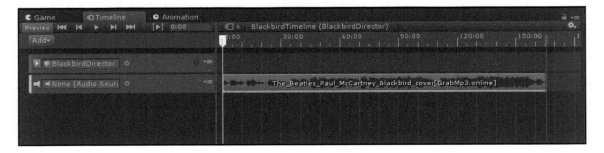

The white vertical cursor, or *Playhead*, indicates the current time frame. The default scale is **Frames**, but in the previous screenshot we have already changed it to **Seconds** (using the gear-icon in the upper right). You can see this clip is set start at 0 and continues to about 165 seconds.

> You can scale the view using the scroll wheel on your mouse. View all by pressing "A" on the keyboard. When the Timeline contains multiple tracks, you can focus on a specific clip by pressing "F" on the keyboard.

You may notice in the upper left of the Timeline Editor are preview controls. These let you play a preview of the Timeline itself, rather than the whole scene using the usual Editor Play button.

> Unfortunately, at the time of this writing, the Timeline preview play mode does not play audio clips. You need to use the Editor Play mode for audio.

> In this scene, we decided to make the music to be ambient audio. The audio will play in 2D mode if no audio source is selected. If you want to play it as spatial audio, emanating from a specific location in the scene, you should create an audio source and put that in the timeline track instead.

# Using a Timeline to activate objects

We just added an **Audio Track** to the Timeline. Another type of Timeline track is an **Activation Track**. Associated with a specific game object, an **Activation Track** with enable or disable that game object at the specified times.

According to our plan, when the timeline starts, the bird's nest will be hidden (NestAndEgg object). At the 35-second mark, it becomes enabled. Also, when the nest is first enabled, it should have the WholeEgg. Then at the 80-second mark, it is hidden and the HatchedEgg is enabled instead.

The `NestAndEgg` game object hierarchy, as shown here, contains the `Nest` itself, a `WholeEgg` object, and a `HatchedEgg` (which has the two eggshell halves):

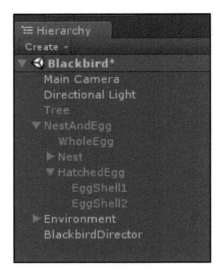

Let's add the activation sequence to the Timeline now:

1. With `BlackbirdDirector` selected in **Hierarchy**, drag the `NestAndEgg` object from **Hierarchy** into the **Timeline Editor** window.
2. A menu pops up, asking what type of track to add; choose **Activation Track.**
3. A small rectangular track marker is added to the track. Click and drag it into place.
4. Position and size the track to start at `35:00` and end at`165:00`.

Now for the eggs. Although the egg models are children of NestAndEgg, they can be activated separately from the parent (of course, only when the parent itself is already enabled):

1. Drag the `WholeEgg` object from **Hierarchy** onto the **Timeline** as an **Activation Track**
2. Position it to start at `35:00` and end at `60:00`
3. Drag the `HatchedEgg` object from **Hierarchy** onto the **Timeline** as an **Activation Track**
4. Position it to start at `60:00` and end at `165:00`

Similarly, activate the bird when the egg hatches, at the 60-second mark:

1. Drag the `Bluejay` object from **Hierarchy** onto the **Timeline** as an **Activation Track**
2. Position it to start at `35:00` and end at `60:00`
3. Drag the `HatchedEgg` object from **Hierarchy** onto the **Timeline** as an **Activation Track**
4. Position it to start at `60:00` and end at `165:00`

The **Timeline** with **Activate Tracks** now looks like the following. You can see, on the left, each track has an object slot containing the game object being controlled by the track.

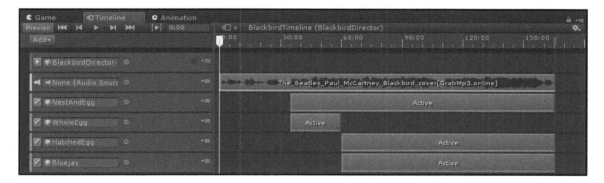

Using **Preview Play** (control icons in the upper left of the **Timeline Editor**) you can play and review these tracks. You can scrub through the time frames by dragging the white Playhead cursor. You will see the nest, eggs, and bird activate and deactivate as specified.

# Recording an Animation Track

As you would expect, in addition to audio and activation tracks, Timelines can include animation tracks. Unity's animation features have evolved over the years and Timeline greatly simplifies basic animation capabilities within Unity. You can create and edit animations directly within Timeline without having to create separate Animation Clips and Animator Controllers. These we will get to later in this chapter. For now, we will start simple, animating just a few Transform parameters on the tree and the nest.

# A growing tree

We want to add an animation of the tree growing from small (scale 0.1) to full size, from 0 to 30 seconds in the Timeline. We do this by adding an Animation Track for the Tree, and then recording the parameter values at each keyframe time:

1. Ensure `BlackbirdDirector` is selected in **Hierarchy** and the **Timeline Editor** window is open
2. Drag the `Tree` from **Hierarchy** into the **Timeline** window
3. Select **Animation Track** as the type of Track we are adding

Now, we can begin recording the keyframes:

1. Ensure the **Playhead** cursor is set to 0:00
2. Press the red **Record** button on the Tree track in Timeline to begin recording
3. Select the `Tree` in **Hierarchy**
4. Set its **Scale** to (0.1, 0.1, 0.1)
5. Slide the Playhead to the 30-second mark
6. With Tree still selected in Hierarchy, set its **Scale** to (1, 1, 1)
7. Press the blinking red **Record** button again to stop recording
8. Click the small graph icon to reveal the animation curve, as shown here:

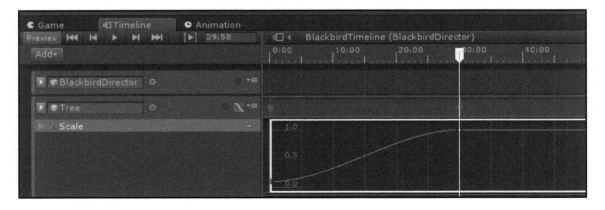

You can see, our Timeline now has an **Animation Track** that references the `Tree` game object. It has two keyframes, starting at 0 and ending at 30 seconds. Unity fits a gentle curve to ease in and ease out the transition between the polemic key values.

When you grab and slide the **Playhead** cursor across the timeline curve, you can see the tree change size in your **Scene** window. If you press the **Preview Play** icon, you can play the animation.

# A growing bird

Repeat the previous exercise, this time growing the Bluejay. Scale it from a baby bird (**Scale** = 1) to full size (**Scale** = 8), for 10 seconds between the 60 and 70-second marks.

# Using the Animation editor

Next, we'll create another animation track, to animate the nest so it starts positioned in the grown tree and then drifts slowly to the ground, wafting like a falling leaf. We want it to exhibit a gentle rocking motion. This is a little more complicated than the simple two-keyframe animation we just did, so we'll do our work in a separate Animation Window instead of the narrow track band on the Timeline Editor. It will animate from 0:35 to 0:45.

Animations are based on Keyframes. To animate a property, you create a Keyframe and define the property values for that frame in time. In the previous example, we had just two Keyframes, for the start and end Scale values. Unity fills in-between values with a nice curve. You can insert additional Keyframes, and edit the curve shape.

# A wafting nest

Let's assume your scene already has the nest positioned on the ground, where we want it to end up with the following steps:

1. Drag the NestAndEgg object from **Hierarchy** into the **Timeline** window.
2. Select **Animation Track** as the type of track.
3. Set the **Playhead** cursor to 35:00.
4. Note that the **Record** icon will be disabled when the object is inactive. The **Playhead** must be within the object's **Activation track**'s **Active** range.
5. Press the **Record** icon for the NestAndEgg **Animation Track** to begin recording.
6. Select the NestAndEgg object in **Hierarchy**.
7. Copy the current **Transform** values to the clipboard (in **Inspector**, select the **gear-icon** on the Transform component, and **Copy Component**).
8. In the **Scene** window, ensure the **Move gizmo** is presently selected.

9. Reposition the nest up in the Tree. **Position Y** = 5 works for me.

10. Slide the **Playhead** to 45:00.

11. In the NestAndEgg **Inspector**, click the Transform's **gear icon** and **Paste Component Values.**

12. Press the blinking red **Record** button again to stop recording.

Having defined an initial Animation recording, we can now work on it in an Animation editor window:

1. On the track, click the little **menu icon** in its upper right

2. Select **Edit in Animation Window**, as shown here:

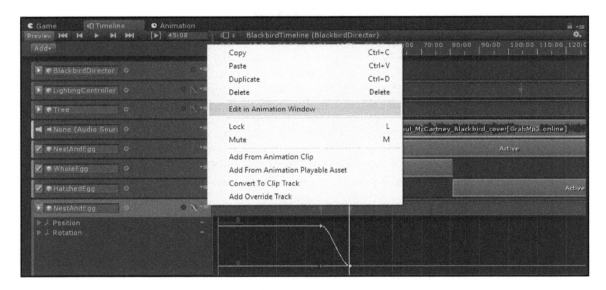

The **Animation Window** has two view modes: **Dopesheet** and **Curves**. The **Dopesheet** view lets you focus on the Keyframes for each property. The **Curves** view lets you focus on the transitions between Keyframes.

The goal is to animate a subtle floating action, where the Nest rocks from side to side (X and Z axes) and rotates lightly on each of the axes. To do this, first we'll "anchor" the Nest at the beginning, middle and end of the fall. (We already have the begin and end positions.) Then, we'll add a couple more keyframes with arbitrary values to implement the gentle motion.

Using the **Dopesheet** view, we're first going to ensure we have keyframes at the start and end times, and one in between. Add keyframes at 35, 40, and 45 seconds as follows:

1. If not present, add **Rotation** properties too (**Add Property | Transform | Rotation | "+"**)
2. Position the **Playhead** at the start of our animation (35:00)
3. Click the **Add Keyframe icon** in control bar atop the properties list (highlighted in the screen capture below)
4. Move the **Playhead** about halfway, to the 40 second mark
5. Click **Add Keyframe icon**
6. And again, make sure there's Keyframe markers at the end (45:00)

You can use hotkeys to move between Keyframes. Press "Alt+." (Alt+period) for next Keyframe. Press "Alt+," (Alt+comma) for previous Keyframe, and "Shift+," (Shift+comma) for first Keyframe.

Now, we'll add a Keyframe at 37.5:

1. Move the **Playhead** to **37.5**
2. Click the **Add Keyframe icon**
3. Click the red **Record** icon in the upper left to capture new values
4. Select the NestAndEgg object in **Hierarchy**
5. In the **Scene** view, using the **Move Tool** gizmo, move the nest a little bit along the X and Z axes (about 0.4 units)
6. Using the **Rotate Tool**, rotate the nest gently on any combination of axes (up to 10 degrees)
7. Move the **Playhead** to 42.5 and repeat steps 2-6

The resulting **Animation Window** in **Dopesheet** view, with its **Position** and **Rotation** property values, is shown here at Keyframe 37.5. The **Add Keyframe icon** is identified for the reader:

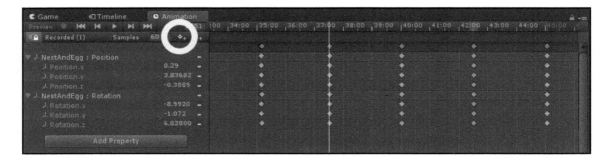

The **Curves** view lets you focus on the transitions between Keyframes, and provides the ability to adjust the values and shape the curve splines. My current Curves view is shown here:

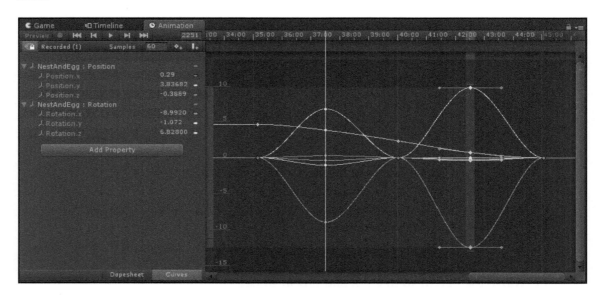

The length of the scrollbars in the Animation Window indicate the current zoom view. The oval ends of each scrollbar are grab-able controls that let you directly adjust the zoom as well as position of the view.

Go back to the TImeline Editor window. You can slide the **Playhead** cursor to see animations in your **Scene** window, or press the **Preview Play** icon to play them.

# Animating other properties

In our story, we want the lighting to start at night and progress through dawn to daylight. We'll do it by manipulating the Directional Light, Skybox Material, and a Spot Light.

# Animating lights

For dramatic effect, let's make the scene slowly fade from night to daytime. We will turn off the Directional Light at the start and slowly increase its Intensity:

1. Select `BlackbirdController` in **Hierarchy** and open the **Timeline Editor** window
2. Drag the `Directional Light` object from **Hierarchy** onto the **Timeline**
3. Press its **Record** button
4. Ensure the **Playhead** is at `0:00`
5. Select the `Directional Light` in **Hierarchy** and change its **Intensity** parameter to `0`
6. Move the **Playhead** to the `40:00` second mark
7. Set the **Intensity** to `1`

The Directional Light's Animation Track with the Intensity parameter curve is shown here:

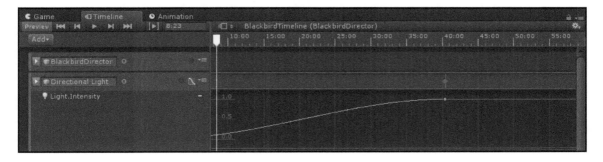

Other parameters of the light could also be animated, including its Color and the Transform Rotation angles. Just imagine the possibilities!

Let's also add a Point Light. For dramatic effect, position it at the same location as the Nest resting position. This will illuminate the baby tree at first, and focus the user's attention on the egg in the nest once the nest settles onto the ground:

1. **Create | Light | Point Light**
2. In **Scene** view, use the **Move Tool** gizmo to position it inside the Nest at the Nest's ground position
3. Select `BlackbirdDirector` and open the **Timeline Editor**
4. Drag the `Point Light` onto the **Timeline Editor**
5. Choose **Activation Track**
6. Enable the light from 0s to about 95s, sometime after the egg hatches

Things are looking pretty good!

Our Timeline is starting to get a little crowded. Let's move the lights into a **Track Group**:

1. In **Timeline**, choose **Add | Track Group**
2. Click its label and name it "Lights"
3. Drag each of the light tracks into the group

 Use Group Tracks to organize your Timeline in a nested tree structure

# Animating a scripted component property

As we're seeing, you can animate just about any GameObject property that you can modify in the Inspector. This includes your own C# script component's serialized properties.

We want to fade the environmental lighting from night to day. There are several ways to achieve this (see the discussion of photospheres in the previous chapter). We've decided to do it by modifying the Skybox Material's Exposure value (0 is off, 1 is all the way on). But Timeline can only animate GameObject properties, and this is not one. So what we'll do is create an empty LightingController GameObject and write a script that controls the Skybox Material.

Let's add our own Skybox Material to the scene. You can use any skybox texture you like. We will grab one from the WispySkybox package, `WispyCubemap2`, that we imported earlier:

1. Create a new **Material** (**Assets** | **Create** | **Material**), name it `BlackbirdSkyMaterial`
2. In **Inspector**, for its **Shader**, select **Skybox/Cubemap**
3. Click **Select** in its **Cubemap** texture chip, and select `WispyCubemap2`
4. Open the **Lighting** window (if not already in the Editor, choose **Window** | **Lighting** | **Settings**)
5. Drag the `BlackbirdSkyMaterial` from **Project Assets** onto the **Skybox Material** slot
6. Uncheck the **Mixed Lighting Baked Global Illumination** checkbox

We don't want to bake any of the environment lighting since we're going to modify its settings at runtime.

Selecting the `BlackbirdSkyMaterial` again, see what happens when you slide the **Exposure** value between 1 and 0. It fades the brightness of the skybox. We will animate this value to modify the ambient light in our scene. But Animations can only modify GameObject parameters, so we'll write a script:

1. Create a new C# script and name it `SkyboxMaterialExposureControl`.
2. Open the script and write it as follows:

```
public class SkyboxMaterialExposureControl : MonoBehaviour
{
    public Material skyboxMaterial;
    public float exp = 1.0f;

    private void Update()
    {
        SetExposure(exp);
    }

    public void SetExposure(float value)
    {
        skyboxMaterial.SetFloat("_Exposure", value);
    }
}
```

Save the file. In Unity, lets make a LightingController object that uses the script as follows:

1. Create a **Empty** object in **Hierarchy**, named "LightingController"
2. Add the `SkyboxMaterialExposureControl` to this object
3. Drag the `BlackbirdSkyMaterial` onto its **Skybox Material** slot

Now, let's animate this parameter:

1. Select `BlackbirdController` in **Hierarchy** and open the **Timeline Editor** window
2. Drag the `LightingController` object from **Hierarchy** onto the **Timeline**
3. Press its **Record** button
4. Ensure the **Playhead** is at `0:00`
5. Select the `LightingController` in **Hierarchy**, and change its **Exp** parameter to `0`
6. Move the **Playhead** to the `100:00` second mark
7. Set the **Exp** to `1`

The Timeline Editor window with a **SkyboxMaterialExposureControl** track is shown here:

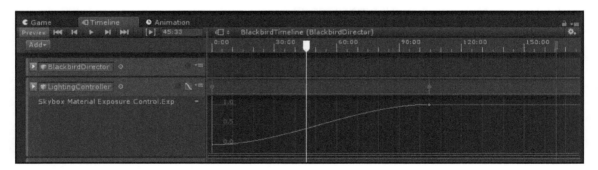

Press **Play**, and the scene lighting will fade from night to day as the skybox material's Exposure animates from 0 to 1. (Note it's not available in the Timeline preview Play, just the Editor Play). Here is a screenshot of the scene playing at about 45 seconds:

# Controlling particle systems

You could continue to improve the scene with other effects. We'd like to include falling leaves, which can be implemented using particle systems and played using a **Control Track**.

 Unfortunately, we cannot recommend a specific free "falling leaves" asset as all the ones we found in the Asset Store are paid ones. There's an out-of-date free Sky FX package (https://assetstore.unity.com/packages/vfx/particles/environment/sky-fx-pack-19242), from which we borrowed the textures and made our own particle system prefab, included with this book.

Assuming you have a FallingLeaves particle system, we can add it to the project now:

1. Drag a copy of the FallingLeaves prefab into the scene.
2. In the **Timeline Editor** window (with BlackbirdDirector selected), click **Add** and choose **Control Track.**
3. In the Control Track's menu icon, choose **Add Control Playable Asset Clip.**
4. This creates a small rectangle for the clip on the track. Select it.
5. In **Inspector**, drag the FallingLeaves game object from **Hierarchy** onto the **Source Game Object** slot.
6. Going back to the Timeline window, grab and slide the rectangle to the 120-second position, then stretch its right edge to the end of the timeline (165s).

The playable asset's **Inspector** is shown here:

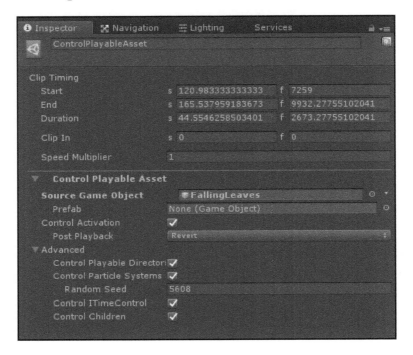

And the Timeline with this **Control Track** is as follows:

Likewise, if you have multiple Timelines in a scene, you can control them from another Timeline using a Control Track (via game objects with `PlayableDirector` components). In our app, we're using a single Timeline, with **Play On Awake**, so it starts at the beginning of the app and plays through. However, with multiple Timelines in a scene, you can play them on demand.

You can write your own custom Timeline track classes too. For example, using a Control Track for playing Particle Systems is limited. Here (https://github.com/keijiro/TimelineParticleControl) is a custom track class, ParticleSystemControlTrack, that offers control of emission rate, velocity, and other functionality. And if you look into their .cs code, it provides a good example of how to write a custom track class.

Separate Animation Clips are another Playable asset you can add and sequence in Timeline tracks. We look at that next.

# Using Animation clips

For the next animation example, we'll get the egg to rattle and shake before it hatches. We will create a simple animation and make it loop for its duration. To illustrate, we'll make an Animation Clip of the WholeEgg rattling and then add it to the Timeline on an Animation Clip Track.

## Shaking an egg

To create a new Animation Clip on the WholeEgg object, follow these steps:

1. In Hierarchy, select the WholeEgg object (child of NestAndEgg)
2. Open the Animation Window (**Window** | **Animation**)
3. You should see a message, **To begin animating WhileEgg, create an Animation Clip** and a Create button
4. Press **Create**
5. When prompted for a file name, save it to EggShaker.anim

We've seen the Animation Window earlier in this chapter. We're going to make a very short, 2-second animation that rotates the egg on the X axis and Z axis by manipulating the animation curves:

1. Show the Curves view using the Curves button on the bottom of the window.
2. Press Add Property and **WholeEgg** | **Transform** | **Rotation** | + to add the Rotation properties.
3. Select the **WholeEgg: Rotation** property group on the left.

4. Press *A* on the keyboard to zoom all; you should see three flat lines, one for each X, Y, Z rotation axes.

5. Click the Add Keyframe icon in the upper right of the control bar.

6. There may already be a Keyframe at one second (1:00) by default. If not, move the Playhead and click Add Keyframe.

7. Scroll out (middle scroll wheel on mouse, or using the horizontal scrollbar oval-end handles) so you can see the 2:00-second marker.

8. Move the Playhead to 2 seconds and Add Keyframe.

9. Move the Playhead back to the 1 second mark.

Now, we'll edit the animation spline curves. If you're familiar with spline editing, there is a line at each node representing the tangent of the curve at that point, and handles at the ends of the line for editing the curve. (You also modify the operation of this gizmo by right-clicking the node.)

1. Click the 1:00s node for the Rotation.X property, then grab one of the handles to make a smooth S-curve. Not too steep, something between 30 and 45 degrees

2. Repeat this for the Y and Z axes, with some variation, as shown here:

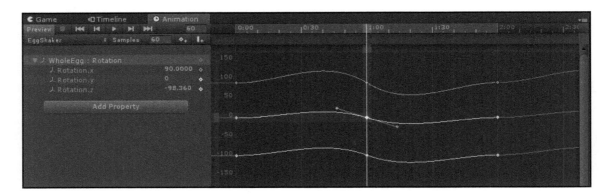

For one or two of the axes, add an extra Keyframe to make the curves look a little more random. My final curves are shown here.

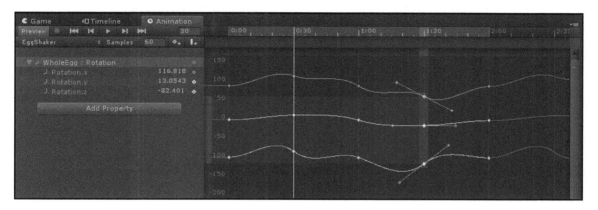

With that done (the curves can be edited and refined later), select **BlackbirdDirector,** open the Timeline window, and perform the following steps:

1. Select **Add** and choose **Animation Track**
2. Drag the `WholeEgg` object from **Hierarchy** onto the **Timeline**
3. Choose **Animation Track**

This time, instead of recording we'll use the one we just created, and make it animate back and forth as follows:

1. Using the menu-icon on the track, choose **Add From Animation Clip.**
2. A small rectangle is added to the track. Slide it to about 50 seconds, when the nest is on the ground but the chick has not yet hatched.
3. In **Inspector,** we now have more clip options. Under **Animation Extrapolation,** choose **Post-Extrapolate: Ping Pong.**

Animation Clips with Timeline can be quite flexible. You can add multiple Animation Clips to an Animation Track, and blend between them by sliding them into one another. If you need even more control, you'd use an Animator Controller instead.

# Using Animator Controllers

While recording animations as Timeline tracks is very convenient, it does have limitations. Those animations "live" in the Timeline. But, sometimes you want to treat animations as assets in their own right. For example, you would use Animation Clips if you want an animation to loop repeatedly, or transition between animations, or blend their actions, or apply the same set of animation curves to other objects.

We will take a look at a couple of existing examples of Animators and then use the existing birds one to make our Bluejay fly.

# Definitions for Animation and Animator

**Animators** have been the standard way of managing *Animation Clips* in Unity, before Timeline. It uses an **Animator Component**, an **Animator Controller**, and an **Animation Clip**. Fortunately, if you create a new Animation Clip on an object, Unity creates each of these items for you. But it's important to understand how they fit together.

Briefly, from the Unity manual (`https://docs.unity3d.com/Manual/animeditor-CreatingANewAnimationClip.html`):

> *"To animate GameObjects in Unity, the object or objects need an **Animator Component** attached. This Animator Component must reference an **Animator Controller**, which in turn contains references to one or more **Animation Clips**."*

These objects originate from the Mecanim animation system folded into Unity a few versions back (you may still see references to Mecanim in the Unity Manual and web searches). This animation system is especially tailored for humanoid character animations (see `https://docs.unity3d.com/Manual/AnimationOverview.html`). The terminology can seem redundant and confusing. The following definitions may help (or not!). Pay especially close attention to the use of "animator" versus "animation":

- *Animation Clips*: Describes how an object's properties change over time.
- *Animator Controller*: Organizes clips in a state machine flowchart, keeps track which clip should currently be playing, when animations should change or blend together. References the clips it uses.

- *Animator component*: Brings together Animation Clips, the Animation Controller, and the Avatar if used.
- Do not use *legacy Animation components* : Animation component is legacy but Animation window is not!
- *Animation window*: Used to create/edit individual Animation Clips, and can animate any property you can edit in the inspector. Shows a **timeline** but is not the same as the Timeline window. Offers Dopesheet versus Curves view.
- *Animator window*: Organizes existing animation clip assets into a flowchart-like state machine graph.

 Actually, Timeline animation recordings also use Animation Clips, you just don't need to explicitly create them. Each recorded Animation Track in a Timeline has a corresponding animation playable file (named "Recorded (n)") in your Assets folder.

# ThirdPersonController Animator

The `ThirdPersonController` character prefab we used for Ethan in previous chapters uses an animator controller to manage humanoid animation clips on the rigged model. For curiosity, let's examine it now (although we will not use it in this scene):

1. Temporarily drag a copy of the `ThirdPersonController` prefab from your **Project** `Assets/Standard Assets/Characters/ThirdPersonCharacter/Prefabs/` folder into the scene.
2. Notice in **Inspector**, it has an **Animator** component and the **Controller** slot references `ThirPersonAnimatorController`. Click on that.
3. This will highlight the controller asset (in `Assets/.../ThirdPersonCharacter/Animator`).
4. Double-click`ThirdPersonAnimatorController` to open it in an **Animator** window.

The Animator graph for Ethan is shown next. You can see that when the character is activated (Entry), it initializes to the Grounded state. The oval boxes are **States**; the lines between them are **Transitions**. On the left is the list of state **Properties** that the Animator can use. When Crouch is true, for example, the animation transitions to Crouching, plays that, then transitions back (and clears the Crouch state flag):

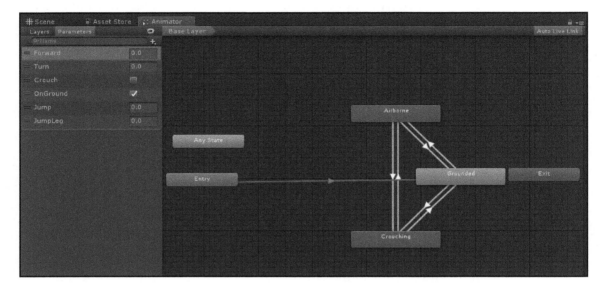

If you open the Grounded state (double-click), you can see a **Blend Tree** with an impressive collection of **Animation Clips** for standing idle, walking, turning, and so on. These will be activated and combined (blended) based on user input.

Next, let's look at another example, the BirdAnimatorController used by our Bluejay.

You can now delete the ThirdPersonController object from the scene.

# Living Birds Animator

The Living Birds package comes with a lot of animation clips. You can actually open the FBX models in Blender or another animation application and examine how the models and animations are defined. These have been combined into a BirdAnimationController. Examine the Animator using the following steps:

1. Select the Bluejay in **Hierarchy**.

2. Notice in **Inspector**, it has an **Animator** component, and the **Controller** slot references `BirdAnimatorController`. Click on that.

3. In **Project Assets**, double-click the `ThirdPersonAnimatorController` to open it in an **Animator** window.

The Animator graph is shown here:

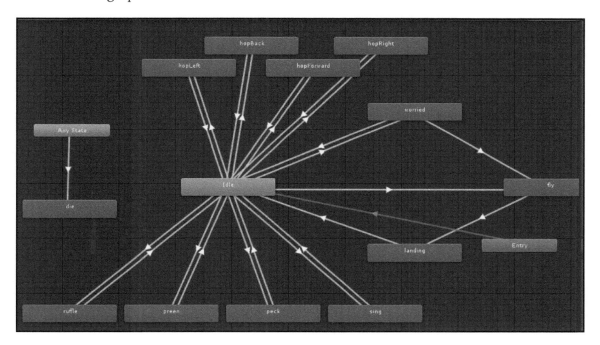

You can see that almost all the animations readily transition to and from the Idle one, whether Preen, Peck, Sing, or HopLeft, HopRight, HopForward, and so on. Also, note the Idle -> Fly -> Landing -> Idle loop, as we're going to use that.

The Bluejay also has a C# script, `lb_Bird`, which invokes the Animator behaviors. It's not the cleanest code, but it is useful. The most pertinent functions are `OnGroundBehaviors` and `FlyToTarget`:

- `OnGroundBehaviors` randomly chooses and plays one of the idle animations every 3 seconds
- `FlyToTarget`, will cause the bird to fly to a given position, including takeoff and landing and random fluttering around; it looks reasonably natural

So in our project, rather than recording the Keyframe position details of the bird's animation path like we did the falling nest, we'll define specific targets and let the `lb_Bird` script actually control the bird transforms. This is a lot like using a **Navmesh** to direct Ethan's movement as we did in Chapter 4, *Gaze-Based Control*. We will use Timeline to select one target position to the next, over time.

# Learning to fly

First, let's create a `BirdController` and specify a list of locations where the bird should fly between. Then, we'll add this to the Timeline:

1. In **Hierarchy**, create an **Empty** game object named `BirdController` and reset its **Transform.**
2. Create a child **Empty** object, named `Location1`. Move it to be just atop the rock closest to the Nest .
3. Create another **Empty**, named `Location2`, positioned back near the Nest but not in it this time.
4. Continue creating location markers. The values I used, based on my scene and rock locations, are shown in the following table.
5. The last location should be far away. The bird will head there at the end of the video.

| Name | Position | Description |
| --- | --- | --- |
| Location0 | (0.75, 0.4, -1.25) | Start position of the Bluejay |
| Location1 | (3, 0.8, 0) | Atop nearest rock |
| Location2 | (1.2, 0.2, -1.7) | Ground near Nest but not in it |
| Location3 | (2.5, 0.8, -3.4) | Atop next nearest rock |
| Location4 | (-5.85, 0.8, -0.3) | Next rock |
| Location5 | (-5, 0.33, 3.5) | Last rock |
| Location6 | (45, 11, 45) | In the distance |

Create a new C# script on the `BirdController`, named `BirdController`, and write it as follows:

```
using System.Collections;
using System.Collections.Generic;
using UnityEngine;
```

```
public class BirdController : MonoBehaviour
{
    public GameObject bird;
    public List<GameObject> targets = new List<GameObject>();
    public int animIndex;

    public bool collideWithObjects = false;
    public float birdScale = 1.0f;

    private int prevIndex;

    void Start()
    {
        prevIndex = 0;
    }

    void Update()
    {
        if (animIndex != prevIndex &&
            index > 0 &&
            index < targets.Count)
        {
            prevIndex = animIndex;
            bird.gameObject.SendMessage("FlyToTarget",
targets[index].transform.position);
        }
    }
}
}
```

There are a number of things going on here. We'll explain.

BirdController has a reference to the bird, and a list of location targets. We'll populate this list in the Unity Editor. Each location is identified by an index value between 0 and the size of the list. An integer, animIndex, will be the parameter controlled by the Timeline, telling the controller which location the bird should fly to.

On each Update, we check whether the animIndex has changed. If so, and it's within the range for our list, it calls FlyToTarget on the bird. (We use SendMessage, not a best practice way of triggering functions in another object, but it's the least disruptive given the existing scripts provided with the Living Birds package.)

The extra two variables, collideWithObjects and birdScale, are not used but are required by the lb_Bird.cs script on the Bluejay.

Save the script. Now, in Unity:

1. Drag the `BirdController` script onto the `BirdController` object as a component
2. Drag `Bluejay` onto the **Bird** slot
3. Unfold the **Targets** list and set **Size** to 7
4. Drag `Location0` onto **Element 0**, `Location1` onto **Element 1**, and so on

The Hierarchy with the BirdController component is shown here:

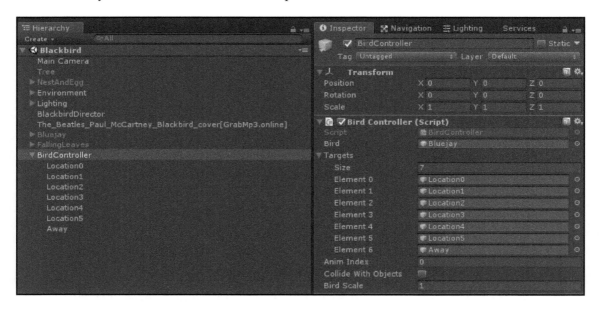

# Hacking the birds

Unfortunately, like a lot of code you'll find on the internet, the Living Birds code works for its own purposes but not necessarily ours. In this case, the package is designed for generating a flock of various birds that fly and land randomly, avoid collisions and can even be killed. We have just one bird and want more control over the landing locations, so we'll make a change to use our `BirdController` rather than the `lb_BirdController` in the package.

Open the `lb_Bird.cs` file (attached to `Bluejay`) and modify it as follows:

Replace the definition of `controller` to be our `BirdController`:

```
// lb_BirdController controller; // removed
public BirdController controller; // added
```

Comment out or remove the `SetController` function:

```
// remove this
// void SetController(lb_BirdController cont){
//      controller = cont;
// }
```

Save it. In Unity, drag the `BirdController` object onto the **Bluejay**'s **LB_Bird Controller** slot.

# Fly away!

Now, we'll add the BirdController as an Animation Track in our Timeline. The AnimIndex parameter is an integer value that will step up in value along the timeline. We want to Bluejay to start learning to fly around 80 seconds, and jump from location to location about 10 seconds apart (80, 90, 100, 110, 120, and away at 130).

1. Open the **Timeline Editor** window for the `BlackbirdDirector`.
2. Drag the `BirdController` object from **Hierarchy** onto the **Timeline**, adding a new **Animation Track**.
3. Press its red **Record** button.
4. Select the `BirdController` in **Hierarchy**.
5. Move the **Playhead** to `80`, and in **Inspector**, set **Anim Index** to `1`.
6. Move the **Playhead** to `90` and set **Anim Index** to `2`.
7. Continue for the other indexes `3` through `6`.
8. Press the red **Record** button again to stop recording.
9. Preview the curve. If it doesn't start at 0 (prior to 80s), use **Edit in Animation Window** and add another Keyframe with value `0`.

The **Animation Track** curve for the **Anim Index** parameter is shown here, simply incrementing by one at each keyframe:

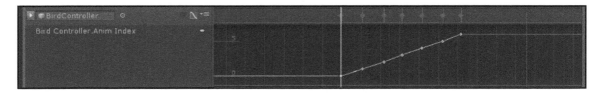

**Play** it through. Wow! The bird flies from rock to rock, and eventually flies away!

You can adjust the bird's path and timing between landings by moving the location objects and the animation curve keyframes, respectively. You could also try animating the BirdController's **Bird Scale** parameter to make the bird increasingly more bold and strong as it learns to fly. A screen capture is given here with the bird flying and leaves falling:

We have a completed story. To wrap this up, let's add a little bit of interactivity, so the player can control when the story begins playing.

# Making the story interactive

So far, we used the Timeline to drive our entire VR story experience from start to finish. But in fact, Timelines are a playable asset like others in Unity. For example, if you select the BlackbirdDirector object and look in Inspector at its Playable Director, you'll see it has a Play On Awake checkbox, and it's presently checked. What we're going to do now is not play on awake, but rather start playing on a user event, namely looking directly at the small tree for a few seconds. And when the story ends, it resets itself.

## Look to play

First, we'll add a LookAtTarget encasing the small tree and then use that to trigger playing the timeline:

1. Select the `BlackbirdDirector` and uncheck the **Play On Awake** checkbox
2. For reference, set the Tree game object Scale to its starting keyframe Scale (`0.1, 0.1, 0.1`)
3. In **Hierarchy**, create a cube (**Create | 3D Object | Cube**) and name it `LookAtTarget`
4. Scale and place it to encase the small tree, **Scale** (`0.4, 0.5, 0.4`), **Position** (`0, 0.3, 0`)
5. Disable its **Mesh Renderer**, but keep its **Box Collider**
6. Create a new C# script on the cube, named `LookAtToStart`, and write it as follows:

```
using System.Collections;
using System.Collections.Generic;
using UnityEngine;
using UnityEngine.Playables;

public class LookAtToStart : MonoBehaviour
{
    public PlayableDirector timeline;
    public float timeToSelect = 2f;
    private float countDown;

    void Start()
    {
        countDown = timeToSelect;
    }
```

```
    void Update()
    {
        // Do nothing if already playing
        if (timeline.state == PlayState.Playing)
            return;

        // Is user looking here?
        Transform camera = Camera.main.transform;
        Ray ray = new Ray(camera.position, camera.rotation *
Vector3.forward);
        RaycastHit hit;
        if (Physics.Raycast(ray, out hit) &&
            (hit.collider.gameObject == gameObject))
        {
            if (countDown > 0f)
            {
                countDown -= Time.deltaTime;
            }
            else
            {
                // go!
                timeline.Play();
            }
        }
        else
        {
            // reset timer
            countDown = timeToSelect;
        }
    }
}
```

The script is similar to ones we wrote in Chapter 4. We use the main camera and determine the direction it is looking. Using the physics engine, we call `Physics.Raycast` to cast a ray in the view direction and determine if it hit this object. If so, we start or continue a countdown timer and then play the timeline. Meanwhile, if you look away, we reset the timer.

Try it now. The Timeline will not start playing until you look at the cube for a few seconds.

# Resetting the initial scene setup

You probably noticed, unfortunately, that the default start scene is not necessary the same state we have for the beginning of the timeline. You could fix this by manually ensuring that every object in the scene Hierarchy has the same initial state as the start of the timeline. Instead, we'll add a little hack that plays the timeline for a brief 0.1 seconds to reset the objects.

We will implement this using a coroutine. Modify the LookAtToStart script as follows. Add a new variable, resetSetup, and initialize it to true:

```
private bool resetSetup;

void Start()
{
    countDown = timeToSelect;
    resetSetup = true;
}
```

Add a PlayToSetup function that will be run as a coroutine. Coroutines are a way to run a function, let Unity do other stuff momentarily, and then resume where you left off (via the yield statement). Here, we start playing the timeline, go away for 0.1 seconds, and then tell it to stop playing:

```
IEnumerator PlayToSetup()
{
    timeline.Play();
    yield return new WaitForSeconds(0.1f);
    timeline.Stop();
}
```

Call the coroutine from Update when we want to reset the setup:

```
void Update()
{
    if (timeline.state == PlayState.Playing)
    {
        return;
    }
    if (resetSetup)
    {
        StartCoroutine("PlayToSetup");
        resetSetup = false;
    }
```

We also want the scene to reset after the timeline plays all the way through, so we set `resetSetup` as soon as the timeline starts playing. It'll be recognized once `timeline.state` is no longer playing:

```
    . . .
        // go!
        timeline.Play();
        resetSetup = true;
    }
```

Press Play. Look at the tree. Enjoy the experience. When it ends, you're reset to the beginning and can look at the tree again to replay.

# More interactivity ideas

We're going to stop developing now. Some suggestions on how to improve the interactivity and user experience include:

- Add a particle effect around the tree to indicate that it's a trigger
- Highlight the tree as feedback when you're looking at it
- Display a countdown cursor to indicate the timer has started and when the story will begin playing

Here are other suggestions for interactable objects you could add to the story:

- Look at the egg in the nest causes it to hatch sooner than its default timing
- When you look at the bird while it's idle, it will turn to look back at you
- If you poke the bird with your hand controller, it jumps out of the way
- You can pick up a rock and throw it to kill the bird (nooo, just kidding!)

# Summary

In this chapter, we built an animated VR story. We began by deciding what we want to do, planning out the timeline, music track, graphic assets, animation sequences, and lighting. We imported our assets and placed them in the scene, then created a Timeline and roughed out when specific objects are enabled and disabled using an Activation Track. Next, we animated several objects, including growing the tree, floating the nest, and rumbling the egg. We also animated the lighting, learning how to animate game object parameters other than Transforms.

We also used Animation Clips and an Animator Controller, using animations imported from a third-party package. We reviewed a script that calls into the Animator and wrote a controller on top of that, to fly the bird from location to location. Lastly, we added interactions to the story, using gaze-based control to start and replay the experience.

In the next chapter, we go social as we look at ways to add multi-user networking to Unity VR projects and how to add scenes to the emerging metaverse. Multiplayer games are familiar to most of us, but when combined with virtual reality, it provides a social experience that is unparalleled by any other technology. We will learn about networking technology using the Unity Networking features.

# 12
# Social VR Metaverse

*That's me, Linojon, the guy with a baseball cap in front, to the left!* Momentously, the following photo was captured during the eve of the metaverse on December 21, 2014 at a live VRChat session. I had built a seasonally-themed world named GingerLand and invited my chatroom friends to visit during one of the weekly meetups. Then, someone suggested, "Hey, let's take a group picture!" So, we all assembled on the front porch of my wintry cabin and said "Cheese!" The rest is history:

For many people, the visceral experience of socially interacting live with other people in VR is at least as dramatic as the difference between using Facebook versus browsing a static website, or sharing Snapchats versus viewing an online photo album. It's very personal and alive. If you've tried it out yourself, you know exactly what I mean. We're now going to look at how social VR experiences can be implemented using Unity. There are many approaches, from building it from scratch to plugging into an existing social VR platform. In this chapter, we will discuss the following topics:

- An introduction to how multiplayer networking works
- Implementing a multiplayer scene that runs in VR using the Unity Networking engine
- Using Oculus personalized avatars
- Building and sharing a custom VRChat room

Note that the projects in this chapter are separate and not directly required by the other chapters in this book. If you decide to skip any of it or not save your work, that's OK.

# Multiplayer networking

Before we begin any implementation, let's take a look at what multiplayer networking is all about and define some terms.

## Networking services

Consider a situation where you are running a VR application that is connected over the internet to other players running the same application on their own VR rigs at the same time. When you move your first person view within the game, shoot things, or otherwise interact with the virtual environment, you expect the other players to see that, too. Their version of the game stays in sync with yours and vice versa. How does this work?

One instance of the running game acts as a host or server. Other players are concurrently connected to the same. When you move, your character's new position is shared with each of the other connections, which then updates your avatar's position in their own views. Similarly, when your game receives a changed position of another character, it is updated in your view. The faster, the better. That is, the shorter the delay (latency) between the *send* and *receive* messages and the corresponding screen updates, the more live, or real-time, the interaction feels.

Multiplayer services should help you manage the sharing of the game's state between all active clients, the spawning of new players and objects, security considerations, as well as the management of low-level network connections, protocols, and quality of service (such as data rate and performance).

Networking is built as a series of API layers, where the low-level functions deal with details of the data transport and would be agnostic to the content of the data. Middle and higher layers provide increasingly aggregated features that also may be more directly helpful for the networking application. In our case, this is multiplayer gaming and social VR. Ideally, the high-level layer will provide all you need to implement multiplayer features into your games with minimal custom scripting, while offering access to other layers through a clean API in case you have special requirements.

There are a number of multiplayer services available, including Photon from Exit Games and platforms from Google, Facebook/Oculus, Apple, Microsoft, Amazon, and more.

- The popular Photon Cloud service can be easily added using their free **Photon Unity Networking** (**PUN**) package from the Unity Asset Store (for more information, visit `https://www.assetstore.unity3d.com/#/content/1786`). If you are interested in trying Photon with Unity, take a look their documentation and tutorial pages (`https://doc.photonengine.com/en-us/pun/current/demos-and-tutorials/photon-unity-and-networking-links`).

- Unity has its own built-in networking system, **Unity Networking** (**UNet**), which reduces the need for custom scripting and provides a feature-rich set of components and API that tightly integrate with Unity. There is a whole tutorial series on the Unity website (`https://unity3d.com/learn/tutorials/s/multiplayer-networking`), and it's what we will use in this chapter's project.

# The network architecture

A key to networking is the client-server system architecture. We see this all around us in today's world; your web browser is a client and websites are hosted on a server. Your favorite music listening app is a client and its streaming service is a server. Similarly, each instance of your game, when connected to a network, is a client. It talks to a server, which communicates the status and control information between all the other game clients.

I say *server*, but it doesn't necessarily need to be a separate physical computer somewhere. It could be, but it's probably not. It's best to think of a client and server as *processes*: instances of a program or an application running somewhere. A **cloud server** is a virtual process that is accessible via the internet as a service.

A single app can sometimes act as both a client and a server at the same time. This latter case, where the server and client are one, is said to be running as a host. With Unity networking, games can be run as a client, a server, and/or as a host.

Even so, a public **IP** (**Internet Protocol**) address is needed for game instances to talk to one another. A lightweight relay server can provide this service with minimal resources.

# Local versus server

In Unity, you can use scripting to create, or instantiate, new objects during gameplay. In a multiplayer situation, these objects need to be activated, or spawned, locally as well as on the network so that all the clients will know about it. A spawning system manages objects across all the clients.

 It is important to make a distinction between objects that are local player *objects* versus network ones. Local player objects are controlled by actions in your playing version of the game, on your client, rather than remotely.

For example, in a first-person experience, you are the camera whereas other players see you as your avatar, and you would want security precautions; for example, to prevent others from hacking a game and changing your avatar.

Local player objects have local authority, that is, the player object is responsible for controlling itself, such as its own movement. Otherwise, when the creation, movement, and destruction of objects are not controlled by any player, the authority should reside on a server. Local authority is needed when individual players are driving gameplay.

On the other hand, server authority is needed when game logic and random events are driving the gameplay. For example, when a game creates enemies at random locations, you'd want all the clients to get the same random locations. When a new player joins an ongoing game, the server helps create and set up objects that are active in the current gameplay. You wouldn't want an object to show up in its default position and then jump to a different current position as it's syncing with the other clients.

The following image from Unity documentation shows ways in which actions are performed across the network. The server makes **remote procedure calls** (**RPC**) to the client to spawn or update objects. The client sends **commands** to the server and affects actions, which then are communicated to all the remote clients:

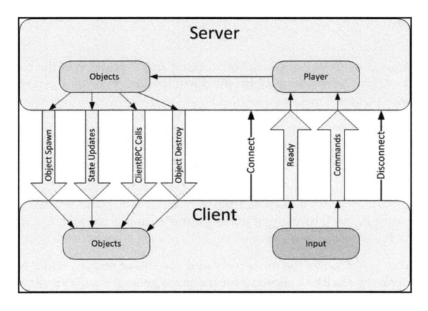

Image source: https://docs.unity3d.com/Manual/class-NetworkBehaviour.html

Real-time networking is an engineering discipline. Layered network architectures aim to simplify and shield you from brutally arcane details.

It all comes down to performance, security, and reliability. If you need to debug or optimize any of these in your multiplayer game, you may need to dig in your heels and gain a better understanding of what's going on under the hood. Refer to the next chapter, Chapter 13, *Optimizing for Performance and Comfort*, for suggestions.

# The Unity networking system

The **Unity Networking** engine (**UNet**) includes a robust set of high-level component scripts that make it easy to add multiplayer capabilities to your games. Some of the more important components include *Network Identity, Network Behavior, Network Transform,* and *Network Manager.*

 A good overview of Unity Networking and exposition of the concepts is the Unity Networking Concepts document (http://docs.unity3d.com/ Manual/UNetConcepts.html).

The **Network Identity** component is required on each game object prefab that may be spawned (created) on clients. Internally, it provides a universally unique asset ID, and other parameters, so that objects can be unambiguously identified and spawned across the network.

The NetworkBehaviour class is derived from MonoBehaviour and provides network functionality to scripts. We'll be using it in the examples in this chapter. Details are documented at http://docs.unity3d.com/Manual/class-NetworkBehaviour.html.

When you want to synchronize the movement and physics of objects, add a **Network Transform** component. It's like a shortcut for the more general SyncVar variable synchronization with additional intelligent interpolation for smoother movement between updates.

The **Network Manager** component is the glue that puts it all together. It handles the managing of connections, the spawning of objects across the network, and configuration.

When new player objects are spawned, you can specify a spawn position in the Network Manager component. Alternatively, you can add game objects to your scene and give them a *Network Start Position* component, which can be used by the spawning system.

Nonplayer objects that can get spawned can also be set in the Network Manager spawn list. Additionally, the Network Manager component handles scene changes and provides debugging information.

Related to the Network Manager component is the matchmaking functionality, using Unity Cloud Services, which can be configured to match up players to make them come together and start a game at the same time-a multiplayer lobby manager where players can set themselves as ready for the game to start, among other useful features.

# Setting up a simple scene

Let's jump right in and make our own multiplayer demo project. For instructional purposes, we'll start out with a very simple scene with a standard first-person camera and get the networking implemented. Then, we'll synchronize multiple players' avatars over the network. And then we'll share a game object, a bouncy ball, between players to play a game.

# Creating a scene environment

To get set up, we will make a new scene with a ground plane and a cube and create a basic first-person character. Perform the following steps:

1. Create a new scene by navigating to **File** | **New Scene**. Then, **File** | **Save Scene As...** and name the scene `MultiPlayer`.

2. Remove the `Main Camera` and insert a copy of your `MeMyselfEye` prefab. Reset its **Transform** so it's positioned at the origin.

3. Create a new plane by navigating to **GameObject** | **3D Object** | **Plane**, rename it `GroundPlane`, and reset its **Transform** using the **Transform** component's *gear* icon | **Reset**. Make the plane bigger by setting **Scale** to (`10, 1, 10`).

4. Make `GroundPlane` easier on the eyes. Drag your `Ground Material` onto the plane. If you need to create one, navigate to **Assets** | **Create** | **Material**, name it `Ground Material`, click on its **Albedo** color chip, and select a neutral color.

5. To provide some context and orientation, we'll just add a cube. Navigate to **GameObject** | **3D Object** | **Cube**, reset its **Transform**, and set its **Position** to the side, such as (`-2, 0.75, 1`).

6. Give the cube some color. Drag your `Red Material` onto the cube. If you need to create one, Navigate to **Assets** | **Create** | **Material**, name it `Red Material`, click on its **Albedo** color chip, and select a nice red, such as RGB (`240, 115, 115`).

# Creating an Avatar head

Next, you'll need an avatar to represent yourself and your friends. Again, I'm going to keep this super simple so that we can focus on the fundamentals. Forget about a body for now. Just make a floating head with a face. Here's what I did. Your mileage may vary. Just be sure that it's facing forward (the positive Z direction):

1. Create an avatar container. Navigate to **GameObject | Create Empty**, rename it Avatar, reset its **Transform,** and set its Position to the eye level, such as (0, 1.4, 0).

2. Create a sphere under the Avatar for the head (**3D Object | Sphere**), rename it Head, reset its transformation, and set **Scale** to (0.5, 0.5, 0.5).

3. Give the head some color. Navigate to **Assets | Create | Material**, name it Avatar Head Material, click on its **Albedo** color chip, and select a nice red, such as RGB (115, 115, 240). Drag the Avatar Head Material onto the Head.

4. The dude has got to be cool (and bald headed). We'll borrow a pair of Ethan's glasses and put them on the head. Navigate to **GameObject | Create Empty**, as a child of Avatar, rename it Glasses, reset its **Transform,** and set its **Position** to (0, -5.6, 0.1) and **Scale** (4, 4, 4).

5. Then, while Glasses is selected, go to the Project pane, drill down into the Assets/Standard Assets/Characters/ThirdPersonCharacter/ Models folder, unfold the Ethan prefab, find the EthanGlasses.fbx file (the mesh file), and drag it into the **Inspector** panel. Be sure to select the fbx version of EthanGlasses, not the prefab.

6. It has a mesh, but it needs a material. While Glasses is selected, go to the **Project** pane, find the Assets/Standard Assets/Characters/ThirdPersonCharacter/Materials/ folder, find EthanWhite, and drag it into the Inspector.

The following screenshot shows a version of mine (which also includes a mouth):

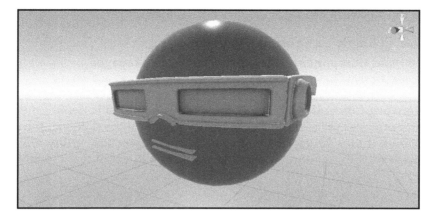

When running as multiplayer, an instance of the avatar will get spawned for each connected player. So, we must first save the object as a prefab and remove it from the scene, as follows:

1. With Avatar selected in the **Hierarchy**, drag it into your **Project** Assets/Prefabs folder

2. Select Avatar again from the **Hierarchy** and delete it

3. Save the scene

OK, now we should be ready to add multiplayer networking.

# Adding multiplayer networking

To make the scene run as multiplayer, we need at a minimum a Network Manager component and we need to identify any objects that will get spawned using the Network Identity component.

# Network Manager and HUD

First, we'll add the Network Manager component, as follows:

1. Create an **Empty** game object and name it `NetworkController`
2. Select **Add Component** | **Network** | **Network Manager**
3. Select **Add Component** | **Network** | **Network Manager HUD**

We added a **Network Controller HUD** which displays a simplistic default menu, in screen space, that Unity offers to select the runtime networking options (you can see it in the images that follow). It's for development. In a real project, you'll probably replace the default HUD with something more interesting. And for VR, you'll want to make yours in world space.

# Network Identity and sync Transform

Next, add a Network Identity to the `Avatar` prefab. We will also add a Network Transform, which instructs the networking system to synchronize the player's **Transform** values to the avatar instances on each client, as follows:

1. In **Project Assets**, select the `Avatar` prefab
2. Navigate to **Add Component** | **Network** | **Network Identity**
3. Ensure the **Local Player Authority** checkbox is checked

We will now tell the `Avatar` to sync its **Transform** properties with all other players over the network, by adding an `Network Transform` component:

1. Navigate to **Add Component** | **Network** | **Network Transform**
2. Ensure that **Transform Sync Mode** is set to **Sync Transform**
3. And **Rotation Axis** is set to **XYZ (full 3D)**

The Network Transform component is configured to share the actual Transform values with other player's instances of this object, including the full XYZ rotations.

Now, tell the `Network Manager` that our `Avatar` prefab represents players:

1. In **Hierarchy**, select `NetworkController`
2. In **Inspector**, unfold the **Network Manager Spawn Info** parameters so that you can see the **Player Prefab** slot

3. Drag the `Avatar` prefab from Project Assets onto the **Player Prefab** slot
4. Save the scene

# Running as a host

Click on the Play mode. As shown in the following screenshot, the screen comes up with the HUD start menu, which lets you select whether you wish to run and connect this game:

Choose **LAN Host** (press *H* on keyboard). This will initiate a server (default port `7777` on `localhost`) and spawn an `Avatar`. The avatar is positioned at a default location, (`0, 0, 0`). Also, it's not connected to the camera. So, it is more like a third-person view. As mentioned above, for VR you'll eventually want to modify this default HUD to run in World Space.

The next thing to do is run a second instance of the game and see two spawned avatars in the scene. However, we wouldn't want them to overlap as both are positioned at the origin, so first we define a couple of spawn positions.

# Adding spawn positions

To add a spawn position, you just need a game object with a Network Start Position component:

1. Navigate to **GameObject** | **Create Empty**, rename it `Spawn1`, and set its **Position** to (0, 1.4, 1)
2. Navigate to **Add Component** | **Network** | **Network Start Position**
3. Duplicate the object (**Ctrl-D**), rename it `Spawn2`, and set its **Position** to (0, 1.4, -1)
4. In Hierarchy, select `NetworkController`. In **Inspector, Network Manager** | **Spawn Info** | **Player Spawn Method**, select **Round Robin**

We now have two different spawn locations. The Network Manager will choose one or the other when a new player joins the game.

# Running two instances of the game

A reasonable way to run two copies of the game on the same machine (`localhost`) is to build and run one instance as a separate executable and the other instance from the Unity Editor (the Play mode). Unfortunately, we cannot run both in VR. (Ordinarily, you can only run one VR device on a PC at a time, and one VR app on that device). So, we'll build one without VR, using a non-VR first-person controller, and run the editor version with VR enabled.

Add a standard first-person character to the scene, as follows:

1. If you do not have the standard **Characters** assets package loaded, navigate to **Assets** | **Import Package** | **Characters** and choose **Import**
2. Find the `FPSController` in the **Project** `Assets /Standard Assets/Characters/FirstPersonCharacter/Prefabs/` folder and drag it into the scene
3. Reset its **Transform**, and set it looking at the front of objects. Set **Position** to eye level, (0, 1.4, 0)

4. With `FPSController` selected, in the **Inspector**, on the **First Person Controller** component, set **Walk Speed** to `1`
5. Disable `MeMyselfEye`

> It can also be helpful to modify the **XR Settings** in **Player Settings**, by adding the SDK named `None` to the top of this list. This will cause projects to build and run without VR hardware even if you forget to uncheck the **Virtual Reality Supported** checkbox.

Build the executable as usual. For standalone Windows:

1. Navigate to **File | Build Settings....**
2. Ensure that the current scene is the only one checked in **Scenes In Build**. If it's not present, click on **Add Open Scenes**.
3. Open**Player Settings....**
4. Under **XR Settings**, uncheck the **Virtual Reality Supported** checkbox.
5. Under **Resolution and Presentation**, check the **Run In Background** checkbox as true.
6. Select **Build and Run**, give it a name. Subsequently, you can launch the game by double-clicking after it's built.

Enabling the **Run In Background** will permit the user input controls (keyboard and mouse) in each window when running the executables.

To run the game in Unity Editor, we need to reverse some of these settings:

1. In **Hierarchy**, disable `FPSController` and enable `MeMyselfEye`
2. In **Player Settings**, check the **Virtual Reality Supported** checkbox and move your **SDK** to the top of the list

In one of your game windows, click on the Play mode and select **LAN Host (H)**, like we did previously. Then, in the other window, select **LAN Client (C)**. In each game, you should now see two instances of the avatar, one for each player, as shown in the following screenshot:

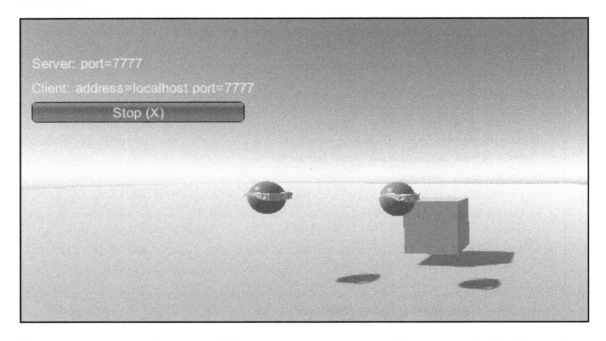

If you want to run an instance of the game on a separate machine, enter the IP address of the host machine into the **Client** input field (for instance, 10.0.1.14 on my LAN) instead of localhost. If each machine has its own VR device, they can each run the corresponding MeMyselfEye prefab as applicable.

If you're running multiple instances of the project on a single machine, just set the LAN Client address to localhost. If you want to run on other machines on your network (including mobile devices), note the IP address of the LAN host machine and enter that value on the Client connections (for example, mine is 10.0.1.14). A default value for this can even be added to your project's **Network Manager** component's **Network Info | Network Address** parameter.

# Associating Avatar with the first-person character

It's not very interesting if the avatars don't move. That's the next piece of this puzzle.

You might think that we should have parented the avatar object under the player camera, (MeMyselfEye or FPSController ) and saved it as a Prefab, and then told the Network Manager to use that for spawns. But then, you'd end up with multiple cameras in the scene and controller scripts listening on user input. Not good.

We must have only one active player in the scene. Other players' avatars get spawned but are not controlled here. In other words, when the local player (and only the local player) gets spawned, its avatar should become a child of the camera. To achieve this, we will write a script:

1. In **Project Assets**, select Avatar, navigate to **Add Component** | **New Script**, and name it AvatarMultiplayer
2. Open and edit the AvatarMultiplayer.cs script, as follows:

```
using UnityEngine;
using UnityEngine.Networking;

public class AvatarMultiplayer : NetworkBehaviour
{
  public override void OnStartLocalPlayer ()
  {
    GameObject camera = Camera.main.gameObject;
    transform.parent = camera.transform;
    transform.localPosition = Vector3.zero;
  }
}
```

The first thing you'll notice is that we need to include the using UnityEngine.Networking namespace to access the networking API. Then, the class AvatarMultiplayer is derived from NetworkBehaviour, which internally is derived from MonoBehaviour.

NetworkBehaviour provides additional callback functions. We are going to use OnStartLocalPlayer, which gets called whenever the local player object is spawned. However, it is not called when the remote player objects are spawned. Its declaration requires the override keyword.

`OnStartLocalPlayer` is exactly what we want because only when a local player is spawned do we want to parent it to the camera. We access the current main camera object and make it the avatar's parent (`transform.parent = camera.transform`). We also reset the avatar's transform so that it's centered at the camera's position.

> Consider improving the script to specify the actual game object you want to parent your avatar.

Run two instances of the game: **Build & Run** to execute one, and use the Play mode for the other. Control the player in one window, and it moves the avatar in the other. Wow! You can even launch more executables and have a party!

> Depending on the size and local position of your avatar, its model objects (such as eye glasses) may be visible from the first person camera and obstruct the view. You can hide them by disabling the child graphics. But then, for example, you wont see your own shadow (which I like). Another option is to shift the avatar graphics backwards to ensure they don't obstruct the camera's view. Either way, this can be done in this `AvatarMultiplayer` script. Likewise, if your game gives each avatar a body, or chair, or whatnot, the current player's instance may not need or want all those graphic detail to be following them around.

# Adding a matchmaking lobby

So far, connecting two or more players over the network requires you to know the IP address of the host instance of the game that is running, or simply `localhost` if they're all running on the same machine.

Unity Networking and Cloud Services includes a built-in networking lobby manager for matchmaking between online players. It lets you create and join online "rooms," limited to a maximum number of players. Using the lobby feature is as easy as choosing **Enable Match Maker** in the Network HUD in your app. But first, you must subscribe to Unity Multiplayer cloud services (free, with limits for the number of concurrent users, based on your Unity license).

To use it, first enable Unity Cloud Services for your app:

1. Above **Inspector**, select the **Cloud icon** (indicated in the following screenshot) to open the **Services** window
2. Create or choose a **Unity Project ID** for this project. To create an ID, click **Select Organization** and choose your organization, and then click **Create**.
3. Choose **Multiplayer** to open the multiplayer services panel
4. From there, open the web-based dashboard, where you're asked to specify the **Max Players Per Room**. Enter 4 and press **Save**

A configured **Multiplayer Services** panel is shown here, with the **Cloud** services icon highlighted for your reference:

After enabling the services in your project, you may need to rebuild the executable (**File** | **Build And Run**) and then, in the first instance of the game:

1. From the HUD menu choose **Enable Match Maker (M)**
2. Type in a name for your room
3. Choose **Create Internet Match**

In the second instance of the game:

1. From the HUD menu, also choose **Find Internet Match**
2. Your room should appear as a new button
3. Choose the **Join:** button for your room

You can now run the multiplayer game across the internet, letting Unity Services negotiate the IP addresses and maximum connections per room.

This will get you started. Of course, you have full control of the networking lobby matchmaking, like other Unity Networking services. And you most likely will want to make your own GUI. For documentation, see the NetworkManager API (`https://docs.unity3d.com/ScriptReference/Networking.NetworkManager.html`).

Consider starting with the example Network Lobby free asset from Unity (`https://assetstore.unity.com/packages/essentials/network-lobby-41836`). Unfortunately this asset is out of date and has bugs, but you can get it to work (read the comments). Or at least, reference it as an example when writing your own UI. Also, it is a screen space UI; for VR, you would need to modify it to be a world space canvas.

An example of HUD code that seems up to date can be found in this forum comment: `https://forum.unity.com/threads/networkmanagerhud-source.333482/#post-3308400`

# Syncing objects and properties

Let's play ball! Back in `Chapter 8`, *Playing With Physics And Fire*, we implemented various ball games in VR. Now, we have the means to make a multiplayer one. We will make a game similar to the *Headshot* game, which uses your head as the paddle. But after this exercise, feel free to go and build multiplayer versions of the *Paddle Ball* and/or *Shooter Ball* games, which use a hand controller to hold and move a paddle to hit or deflect the ball.

Also, since the objective here is to focus on the multiplayer networking considerations, we will leave out some details covered in the earlier chapter, such as sound effects, particles, and object pooling.

# Setting up the headshot ball game

First, we'll add the cube paddle to the Avatar head as the one and only Collider on the Avatar:

1. Drag a copy of the `Avatar` prefab into your **Hierarchy** for editing
2. For each of its children (`Head, Glasses`), disable the **Collider** if present
3. Create a new cube child of `Avatar` (**Create** | **3D Object** | **Cube**) and name it `CubePaddle`
4. Reset its **Transform** and set its **Scale** to (`0.5, 0.5, 0.5`)
5. Disable the Cube's **Mesh Renderer**
6. Apply the Avatar changes back to its prefab (click **Apply** in Inspector)
7. Delete it from **Hierarchy**

Now, we'll add a `GameController` object and a script that serves balls to the avatar at fixed intervals:

1. Create an **Empty** game object at the **Hierarchy** root named `GameController`, and reset its **Transform**
2. **Add Component** | **New Script** and name it `BallServer`

Open the script and write it as follows:

```
using System.Collections;
using System.Collections.Generic;
using UnityEngine;

public class BallServer : MonoBehaviour
{
    public GameObject ballPrefab;
    public float startHeight = 10f;
    public float interval = 5f;
    public List<Color> colors = new List<Color>();

    [SerializeField] private int colorId;
    private Transform player;

    void Start()
```

```
    {
        colorId = Random.Range(0, colors.Count);
        player = Camera.main.transform;
        StartCoroutine("DropBall");
    }

    IEnumerator DropBall()
    {
        while (true)
        {
            Vector3 position = new Vector3(player.position.x,
                                    startHeight, player.position.z);
            GameObject ball = Instantiate(ballPrefab, position,
                                    Quaternion.identity);
            ball.GetComponent<Renderer>().material.color =
                                            colors[colorId];
            // (network spawn will go here)

            Destroy(ball, interval * 5);

            yield return new WaitForSeconds(interval);
        }
    }
}
```

In this script, we play a new ball every 5 seconds. Each ball remains in the scene for 25 seconds (`interval * 5`). We use a coroutine, with `yield return new WaitForSeconds(interval)` to instantiate a new ball each interval.

We also create a list of `colors` and randomly choose one for this player when the game starts. All balls instantiated by this player will be this color. Create the list of colors to pick from:

1. On **Ball Server** component, unfold the **Colors** parameter
2. Set **Size** to 4 or higher
3. Define unique colors for each of the **Element n** color slots

The **GameController** component will look similar to this in **Inspector**:

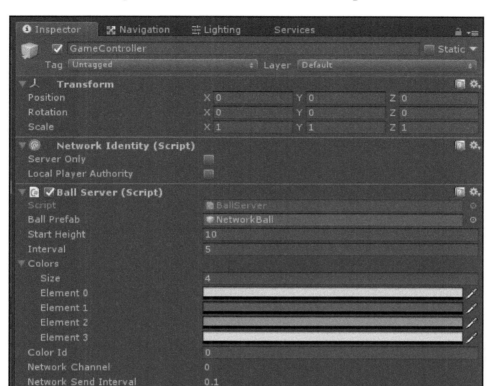

Create a bouncy ball. We'll name it NetworkBall because in the next section we will share it across the network:

1. Create **3D Object | Sphere**, name it NetworkBall, and **Scale** (0.5, 0.5, 0.5)
2. On its **Sphere Collider**, assign the Bouncy physic material to the **Material** slot
3. Add a Rigidbody component (**Add Component | Physics | Rigidbody**)
4. Drag NetworkBall into your **Project Assets** *Prefabs* folder to create a prefab, and delete the object from **Hierarchy**
5. Drag a NetworkBall from *Prefabs* onto **Ball Prefab** slot of the GameController's **BallServer**

Press **Play**. Locally, you'll get served balls from above, and you can deflect them with your head, just like we did in `Chapter 8`, *Playing with Physics and Fire*.

# Spawning the ball over the network

Other players in our networked game need to see the same balls you do. There are several steps to getting this going:

- First, when we instantiate a ball locally, we need to tell the network to also spawn it for all the players
- When the ball moves, is bounced or hit, its Transform must be updated for all the players
- When the ball's life is done, it must be destroyed for all the players

In our present single-player version of the game, we instantiate new balls in the `BallServer` script. Let's make it networked:

1. Open the `BallServer` script for editing
2. Add `using UnityEngine.Networking;` namespace at the top
3. Add a call to `NetworkServer.Spawn(ball);` once we have an instance created

Then, we must register the `NetworkBall` prefab with the `NetworkManager` to inform it the prefab is spawnable:

1. Select `NetworkController` in **Hierarchy**
2. In **Inspector**, unfold the **Spawn Info** parameters
3. Click + in the **Registered Spawnable Prefabs** list
4. Drag a copy of `NetworkBall` onto the spawnable prefab **Game Object** slot

The **Network Manager** component now looks like the following:

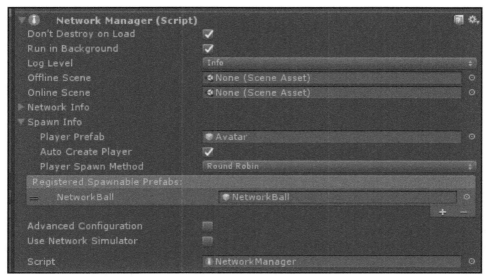

There's one other thing that we did not handle yet: destroying ball instances. In the standalone version, we called `Destroy(ball, interval*5)` to destroy the ball after the given time. For network spawned objects, you will call `Network.Destroy(ball)` instead. However, there is not an equivalent version with a timer argument. You could write a countdown timer for it in BallServer, or use some other strategy for determining when its life cycle is complete and it can be destroyed (such as a DestroySelf script on the ball prefab itself) that runs locally.

# Synchronizing the ball transform

Unity Networking has a component to share this data between players, `Network Transform`, which we used earlier for syncing the Avatar head. Now, we'll use it for the ball:

1. Select the `NetworkBall` prefab in **Project Assets.**
2. **Add Component | Network Transform.**
3. Ensure the **Transform Sync Mode** is set to **Sync Rigidbody/3D.**
4. Adding Network Transform will add a **Network Identity** for you. Check its **Local Player Authority** checkbox.

The Network Transform parameters for `NetworkBall` are shown here:

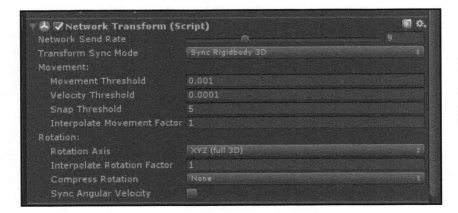

Run two copies of your project now. *Voila!* When you connect the games on the network, the player's balls will be visible to all other players (*nsfw? Keep it clean guys*). The movement of each ball in the local game will control its transform on all the other game instances.

Note that Unity is providing optimizations to limit the amount of data and frequency of updates while ensuring each player continues to see the same thing. For example, in the Network Transform, while you can sync an object's Transform position and rotation each update, you can also specify movement and velocity thresholds that signal when a sync is required. Perhaps more significant, you can choose what to sync. Instead of the Transform values themselves, you can sync changes in the Rigidbody physics (velocity, angular velocity, and so on), which happen much less often, and let each player's local game calculate the corresponding new Transform. This is the option we chose for the NetworkBall.

# State variable synchronization

When we spawn an object over the network, it uses the prefab object we registered with the Network Manager. So the spawned balls all have the default color, not the one we set locally when the object was instantiated in BallServer. We'll use this as an opportunity to show how to synchronize other properties.

The example is a little contrived, but let's say we want the object color to be a state variable. (You could add others too, such as power, health, magic and so on.) We will write a script that tells the network to sync the properties across the network, if and when its value is changed.

The compiler [SyncVar] attribute identifies the property we want to sync and sets up an *observer*. If we include a hook, that function will be called by the observer when the value changes.

On the NetworkBall prefab, create a new script named StateVariables and write it as follows:

```
using UnityEngine;
using UnityEngine.Networking;

public class StateVariables : NetworkBehaviour
{
    [SyncVar(hook = "OnColorChanged")]
    public Color color;

    public void SetColor(Color changedColor)
    {
        color = changedColor;
        GetComponent<Renderer>().material.color = color;
    }

    void OnColorChanged(Color networkColor)
    {
        GetComponent<Renderer>().material.color = networkColor;
    }
}
```

The class derives from NetworkBehaviour. We declare color with a SyncVar attribute. We provide a public setter function, SetColor, that can be called from other game objects as normal. Likewise, when the color variable is changed, it will be synchronized over the network. Remote copies running your game will call OnColorChanged to change that instance of the object too.

Now, we just need to modify the BallServer to set the color using this interface rather than modifying the material color directly. Modify the loop in the DropBall function to read as follows:

```
IEnumerator DropBall()
{
    while (true)
    {
        Vector3 position = new Vector3(player.position.x, startHeight,
player.position.z);
        GameObject ball = Instantiate(ballPrefab, position,
Quaternion.identity);
        NetworkServer.Spawn(ball);
```

```
ball.GetComponent<StateVariables>().SetColor( colors[colorId] );
Destroy(ball, interval * 5);

yield return new WaitForSeconds(interval);
    }
  }
```

Now the server will not just spawn balls on the clients, but will then send its color property setting as well.

Here is a screenshot of live two-player HeadShot gameplay on our makeshift game court:

Using this basic pattern, you could extend this script to set and sync other variables representing the state of individual objects (heath, power, and so on) or the game itself (score, who's turn it is to serve, and so on).

# Advanced networking topics

We have only touched the surface of what you can do with networking. If this interests you, I recommend you look closely at the Unity manual and go through their tutorials too. As we mentioned at the beginning of this chapter, a good place to start is the Unity Networking Concepts document (http://docs.unity3d.com/Manual/UNetConcepts.html).

It's important to understand Peer-to-Peer versus Client-Server versus Dedicated Server networking architecture. As we've seen, by default Unity Networking is Client-Server, with a player as the host Server (the player is also its own Client). You also have the option of setting up with a dedicated server running Unity as a standalone player in headless mode.

Some other networking topics and issues include:

- Synchronizing other serializable state variables (`https://docs.unity3d.com/Manual/UNetStateSync.html`)
- Client custom spawn functions (`https://docs.unity3d.com/Manual/UNetCustomSpawning.html`)
- Spawning and controlling non-player characters (NPC) from a server
- Further understanding when to use local player authority versus server authority (`https://answers.unity.com/questions/1440902/unet-local-player-authority.html`)
- Calling Commands (client to server) versus Remote Procedure Call (RPC) (server to client) (`https://docs.unity3d.com/Manual/UNetActions.html`)
- Building your own multiplayer lobby (`https://docs.unity3d.com/Manual/UNetLobby.html`)
- Testing, debugging, and simulating networking conditions (`https://docs.unity3d.com/Manual/UNetManager.html`)

Networking is not specifically a VR topic, but if you do embark on building a multiplayer networked VR application, you should spend time gaining an understanding of how data, messages, and commands are exchanged between client and server. VR includes its own unique networking challenges. The immediate, immersive experience of VR can amplify problems of latency, synchronization, and realism. We will also address some of these issues in the next chapter.

# Options for voice chat

Once you have two or more people in the same VR space, it is natural to want to speak with one another. Almost all VR devices have headphones and microphones so the hardware support is ubiquitous.

Presently, Unity Networking does not support voice chat (VoIP). But there are other solutions:

- Third-party packages such as *Dissonance Voice Chat* (`https://assetstore.unity.com/packages/tools/audio/dissonance-voice-chat-70078`) add voice chat over your existing network connection.
- *Photon Voice* (`https://assetstore.unity.com/packages/tools/audio/photon-voice-45848`). If you are already using **Photon Unity Networking** (**PUN**), this is the go-to package to use. If you are using Unity Network (UNet), then Photon Voice is not a great choice, or at least you'd need to establish separate connections for voice on the Photon network from your other networking.
- *Oculus VoIP* (`https://developer.oculus.com/documentation/platform/latest/concepts/dg-cc-voip/`). If you are using the Oculus OVR Utilities for Unity (see next topic), you can add the Oculus VoIP SDK and its sister package, Oculus Lipsync.

# Using Oculus platform and avatars

It is worthwhile, and fun, to mention at this point the rich platform networking tools provided by Oculus for their VR devices. As a Facebook organization, Oculus obviously has a keen interest in making VR an engaging social experience. With Oculus Platform SDK (`https://developer.oculus.com/documentation/platform/latest/concepts/book-plat-sdk-intro/`), each user can create and use a personalized identity and avatar across Oculus games and apps, and find and connect with friends, all with a respectable degree of security and authentication.

- Oculus Platform SDK Intro (`https://developer.oculus.com/documentation/platform/latest/concepts/book-plat-sdk-intro/`)
- Oculus Platform Getting Started Guide (`https://developer.oculus.com/documentation/platform/latest/concepts/book-pgsg/`)
- Oculus Avatar Getting Started Guide (`https://developer.oculus.com/documentation/avatarsdk/latest/concepts/avatars-gsg-intro/`)

Along with the basic Unity integration SDK, the Oculus development ecosystem includes Oculus Rooms with match-making, 3D ambisonic audio, voice chat, lip sync, and their integrated Oculus Avatar system.

In `Chapter 3`, *VR Build and Run*, we included a section on *Building for Oculus Rift*, where you may have set up your scene to include the following:

- Add `Oculus` SDK to the **Virtual Reality SDKs** in **Player Settings**
- Import the *Oculus Integration package* from the Asset Store, which installs an OVR folder in your Project Assets (`https://assetstore.unity.com/packages/tools/integration/oculus-integration-82022`)
- Use the `OVRCameraRig` prefab instead of `Main Camera` in `MeMyselfEye`

# Oculus platform entitlement check

To use the Oculus platform and cloud services, your app needs to be registered with Oculus.

Register your app in the Developer Center in order to obtain an App ID, as follows:

1. In your browser, go to `https://dashboard.oculus.com/`
2. Select **Create New App** and choose the device, **GearVR** or **Oculus Rift**
3. Make a note of the **App ID** (copy into your clipboard), required to initialize the Platform SDK (if you need to revisit this page, it's located at **Manage | your organization | your app | Getting Started API**)
4. Create a Test User by navigating to **Manage | your organization | Settings | Test Users**, and **Add Test User**

Now in Unity, we need to configure your settings so it will pass the entitlement checks:

1. Select **Oculus Platform | Edit Settings** from the main menu
2. Paste your **App ID** into the corresponding slot in Inspector
3. Under the **Unity Editor Settings**, check the **Use Standalone Platform** checkbox, and enter the **Test User Email** and **Password** generated by Add Test User previously

Setting **Use Standalone Platform** will bypass your credential's entitlement checks on the Oculus server when running in the Unity Editor. But otherwise, you need to add code for this to your project, as follows:

1. On an object in your **Hierarchy**, such as GameController, create a script named OculusEntitlementCheck
2. Write it as follows (derived from the Oculus docs):

```
using UnityEngine;
using Oculus.Platform;

public class OculusEntitlementCheck : MonoBehaviour
{
    void Awake()
    {
        try
        {
            Core.AsyncInitialize();
Entitlements.IsUserEntitledToApplication().OnComplete(EntitlementCallback);
        }
        catch (UnityException e)
        {
            Debug.LogError("Oculus Platform failed to initialize due to
                                                exception.");
            Debug.LogException(e);
            // Immediately quit the application
            UnityEngine.Application.Quit();
        }
    }

    void EntitlementCallback(Message msg)
    {
        if (msg.IsError)
        {
            Debug.LogError("Oculus entitlement check FAILED.");
            UnityEngine.Application.Quit();
        }
        else
        {
            Debug.Log("Oculus entitlement passed.");
        }
    }
}
```

# Adding a local avatar

Now, we'll add the Oculus Avatar to the scene for the local player. There are two avatar prefabs in the **Project** `Assets/OvrAvatar` folder: one for the local user, which may show just the player's hands in first-person view, and one for the remote players. Note that the Oculus avatars will not appear in your Unity Scene window until you press play, as they are procedurally generated and (ordinarily) require a connection to the Oculus cloud server:

1. In **Hierarchy**, locate and unfold your `OVRCameraRig`. Notice it contains a child `TrackingSpace`
2. From the **Project Assets** `OvrAvatar/Content/Prefabs/` folder, drag the `LocalAvatar` into the **Hierarchy** as a child of `TrackingSpace`
3. In Inspector, check the **Start With Controllers** checkbox
4. Check the **Show First Person** checkbox

Press **Play**. You can now see your hands and controllers.

# Adding remote avatars

The Avatar SDK also uses the Oculus cloud services to get specific player's avatar settings and preferences. Set the **App ID** for the Avatar SDK, as follows:

1. Select **Oculus Avatars | Edit Settings** from the main menu
2. Paste your **App ID** into the corresponding slot in Inspector

This may not really be necessary right now if you're OK with the default "blue" avatar, but we'll need it for multiplayer networking. According to the Oculus docs:

*Note: You may ignore any **No Oculus Rift App ID** warnings you see during development. While an App ID is required to retrieve Oculus avatars for specific users, you can prototype and test experiences that make use of Touch and Avatars with just the default blue avatar.*

To add other player's avatars, we'll use the Oculus RemoteAvatar prefab. We need to set it up for Unity Networking like we did previously with our handmade one, including a Network Identity and Network Transform.

1. In the **Project Assets** `OvrAvatar/Content/Prefabs/` folder, select the `RemoteAvatar` prefab
2. Choose **Add Component** | **Network** | **Network Identity**
3. Ensure the **Local Player Authority** checkbox is checked
4. Choose **Add Component** | **Network** | **Network Transform**
5. Set **Transform Sync Mode** to **Sync Transform**
6. Set **Rotation Axis** to **XYZ (full 3D)**
7. Select `Network Manager` in **Hierarchy**
8. Drag the `RemoteAvatar` onto the Network Manager's **Player Prefab** slot

We can also modify the `AvatarMultiplayer` script we wrote previously, which moves the local player's avatar under the player camera. In the present case, we don't really want to render the remote avatar but we do want other players to sync its Transform values, so we'll disable the rendering as follows:

```
using UnityEngine;
using UnityEngine.Networking;

public class AvatarMultiplayer : NetworkBehaviour
{
    public override void OnStartLocalPlayer()
    {
        GameObject camera = Camera.main.gameObject;
        transform.parent = camera.transform;
        transform.localPosition = Vector3.zero;

        GetComponent<OvrAvatar>().enabled = false;
    }
}
```

Now, when two or more players join the same room, the players should be tracked and synchronized over the network. Here is a screen capture of an Oculus Avatar playing ball in our scene:

# Building and sharing custom VRChat rooms

If your goal is simpler, to build a virtual reality world and share it with others as a shared social experience, you can use one of a number of existing social VR platforms that provide the infrastructure and allow customization. Among the best, VRChat is the only one that lets you create custom worlds and personalized avatar rigs using Unity.

VRChat is built with Unity, and you can use Unity to make custom worlds and avatars. If you haven't tried it, download a copy of the client from Steam (`http://store.steampowered.com/app/438100/VRChat/`) and play around with it.

 As of this writing, VRChat requires the older Unity 5.6.3p1 version. (Download at `https://unity3d.com/unity/qa/patch-releases/5.6.3p1`.) Copy your project into a new folder before attempting to open it in an older version of Unity. You may get warnings, but go ahead. They're mostly pertaining to scripts and we will not be exporting scripts to VRChat.

To develop for VRChat requires you have an account on their site (not the same as your Steam account). Go to `https://www.vrchat.net/register` to register.

# Preparing and building the world

Before we begin, decide a scene to use in VRChat. Pick any Unity scene you want. It could be the `Diorama` playground that we used earlier in this book, the PhotoGallery from Chapter 9, *Making Interactive Spaces*, or something else.

1. Open the scene in Unity that you want to export.
2. Save a copy to a new name, such as `VRChatRoom`

Download the VRChat SDK from `http://www.vrchat.net/download/sdk` and check the documentation at `https://docs.vrchat.com/` for the latest instructions:

1. Import the VRChat SDK package. Navigate to **Assets** | **Import Package** | **Custom Package...**, find your downloaded copy of `VRCSDK-*.package`, click on **Open**, and select **Import**
2. **Delete** the camera object (`Main Camera`, or `MeMyselfEye`, or whatever it is named)
3. From the **Project** `Assets/VRCSDK/Prefabs/World/` folder, add the `VRCWorld` prefab into the scene

Spawn points define where players enter the scene. `VRCWorld`, by default, acts as a spawn point itself, so you can just position this object in the scene. Or, create other **Empty** game objects, position them where you like, and add them to the **Spawns** list in the `VRCWorld` **VRC_SceneDescriptor** component.

Take a look at the other **VRC_SceneDescriptor** parameters. Explanations can be found in the documentation at `https://docs.vrchat.com/docs/vrc_scenedescriptor`. The **VRC_SceneDescriptor** inspector is shown here:

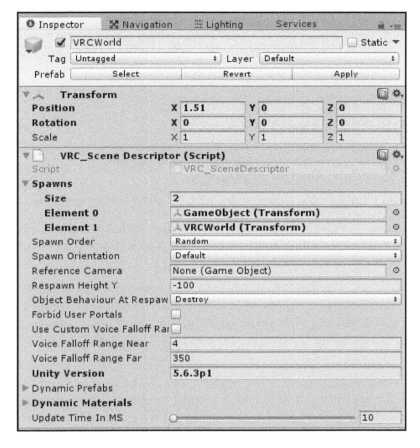

Continue to prepare your scene for VRChat as follows:

1. Log in to your VRChat account, via **VRChat SDK | Settings**
2. Navigate to **VRChat SDK | Show Build Control Panel** and review the options there.
3. Click the **Setup Layers** button, if present, to add the layers required by VRChat
4. Click the **Setup Collision Layer Matrix** button, if present
5. Click the **Enable 3D Spatialization** button

When you're ready, you can test your world:

1. Click the **Test | New Build** button to begin building a new test world
2. A local version of VRChat will open in a window

When you're ready to publish the world in cyberspace:

1. Click the **Publish | New Build** button
2. When prompted, enter the name, player capacity, description, and other information requested in the **Game** window in Unity
3. The world will be uploaded to VRChat
4. You can manage your uploads via **VRChat SDK | Manage Uploaded Content**

Your uploaded world will be private. You can use it in VRChat and invite others to join you, but otherwise it is not public. To go public with your uploaded content, you must email a request to support@vrchat.net.

The VRC SDK provides a toolbox of components you can add to your scene, including pedestals, mirror reflections, YouTube videos, and even a combat system. To make your scene interactive, you can add your own scripts to objects with basic actions triggered by events in the world, including OnSpawn, OnPickup, OnDrop, and OnAvatarHit, to name just a few.

VRChat is one of the original social VR platforms and has proven itself with a strong community and longevity. It is a little rough around the edges but as an indie project, we have a great deal of respect and offer a lot of kudos! It is a good stable implementation that is community driven and welcomes user contributions of content.

# Summary

In this chapter, we learned about networking concepts and architecture and used some of the many features of Unity's own multiplayer networking system. We built a simple scene and an avatar, keeping in mind that the intent is to allow the avatar's head movement to be synchronized with the player's head-mounted display.

We then converted the scene to multiplayer, adding the Unity Network components, which simplifies the multiplayer implementation to just a handful of clicks. Having proven we can build a shared multiplayer experience with the avatars, we added a bouncy ball game object shared between players, providing the fundamentals for building a multiplayer networked game.

Next, we took a quick spin of the Oculus Avatar SDKs, replacing our spherical avatars with full bodied personalized ones from the Oculus Platform ecosystem. Finally, we stepped through how easy it is to create a virtual room in VRChat by exporting a scene that you can share almost instantly.

In the next chapter, we will dive into the technical details of optimizing your VR projects to run smoothly and comfortably in VR. We will consider the different areas that affect performance and latency, from model polygon count, to Unity scripting, to bottlenecks on the CPU and GPU processors.

# Optimizing for Performance and Comfort

# 13

As we've mentioned throughout these chapters, the success of your VR app will be negatively impacted by any discomfort your users feel. It is a fact that VR can cause motion sickness.

The symptoms of motion sickness are nausea, sweating, headaches, even vomiting. It can take hours, perhaps an overnight sleep, to recover. In real life, humans are susceptible to motion sickness: riding a roller coaster, a bumpy airplane, a rocking boat. It's caused when one part of the balance-sensing system thinks your body is moving but other parts don't.

In VR, this could occur when the eyes see motion but your body doesn't sense it. We've considered ways you can design your VR apps to avoid this. With locomotion, always give the user control over their first person movement. Try to avoid riding-the-rails experiences and especially avoid free-falling. Include using a horizon line or dashboard in the foreground so at least the player feels they're grounded in a cockpit if not on solid ground.

The opposite is also true: when you body feels motion but your eyes don't see it. Even very subtle discord can have a bad effect. In VR, a major culprit is latency. If you move your head but the view you see doesn't keep up with the movement, that can cause nausea.

Although this chapter is at the end of this book, we do not mean to suggest that performance issues be left for the end of your project implementation. The old adage "first get it to work, then get it to work faster" doesn't necessarily apply to VR development. You need to pay attention to performance and comfort throughout your development process, which we will address as the main topics in this chapter:

- Optimizing your artwork and 3D models
- Optimizing your scene and lighting
- Optimizing your code
- Optimizing the rendering with shaders and settings

Key tools in analyzing and diagnosing performance issues are the built-in Unity Profiler and Stats windows. We will start with a quick introduction to these.

# Using the Unity Profiler and Stats

Optimizing can be a lot of work, and there is a learning curve to get the hang of it. The good news is that it can be accomplished incrementally. Tackle the more obvious, bigger bang-for-the-buck things first. You can accomplish a lot with little or no visual degradation after a bit of experimentation.

The Unity **Editor** includes two built-in tools to assess performance: the **Stats** window and the **Profiler** window.

## The Stats window

The **Stats** window shows real-time rendering statistics when you press **Play** in the Unity Editor. Reviewing and understanding these statistics is your first line in evaluating and improving the performance of your app, and can help you decide which optimization strategies, including those covered in this chapter, to tackle first.

In the **Game** window, enable **Stats** by pressing the **Stats** button. A screenshot is shown here:

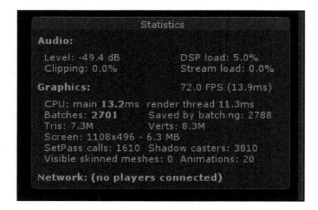

The actual statistics displayed will vary depending on your current build target (see http://docs.unity3d.com/Manual/RenderingStatistics.html), including:

- Graphics FPS (frames per seconds) and time per frame
- CPU time per frame
- Tris (triangles)/Verts (vertices)
- Batches

In VR, you want to pay close attention to the frames per second. The minimum acceptable rate varies depending on your target device, but generally for desktop devices you should keep it at or above 90 FPS, while 60 FPS (or 75 FPS) is considered an absolute minimum. The Sony PlayStation VR accepts 60 FPS but uses hardware to automatically double the rate to 120 FPS to compensate. Windows Mixed Reality HMD will throttle the frame rate between 90 and 60 depending on the graphics processor hardware on your computer, allowing laptops with slower mobile GPU to run VR. Phone-based mobile VR devices can target 60 FPS.

 When in Editor **Play** mode, the FPS is not necessarily the same as you'd experience running a built executable in your device, so it should be used as an indicator, not necessarily an actual value. But, thankfully, it does not include any editor-only processing such as drawing the **Scene** view.

Examining the **CPU** time per frame and comparing that with the overall graphics time per frame will tell you whether your game is CPU bound or GPU bound. That is, which process is the bottleneck, slowing you down the most. The CPU is used for physics calculations, geometry culling, and other operations that prepare the data for rendering in the GPU. The GPU runs the shaders and actually generates the pixel values for display. Knowing if you're CPU or GPU bound can help dictate where to focus your optimization efforts to improve your game performance.

The **Tris** (triangles) and **Verts** (vertices) values show the size of your geometric models' meshes that are drawn. Only the visible faces of your meshes are counted, so your scene could include much more. That is, the values in **Stats** are the geometry the camera is looking at, not including any vertices outside the view, and after any occluded surfaces have been removed. As you move the camera or as objects in the scene move, the numbers will change. As we'll see in the next topic, reducing the poly count of your models can lead to significant gains in performance.

The **Batches** value is an indicator of how hard your GPU is working. The more batches, the more rendering the GPU must perform each frame. The number of batches, not the size of a batch, is the bottleneck. You can reduce batches by reducing the geometry in your scene. Since it's faster to have fewer (albeit larger) batches than lots of small ones, you can tell Unity to optimize the graphics by combining more geometry into larger batches, and pump that through the GPU pipeline.

> When profiling and optimizing, write down (or take screenshots of) the stats and label them, perhaps in a spreadsheet, to log your progress and measure the effectiveness of each technique that you try.

# Overview of the Profiler

The Unity **Profiler** is a performance instrumentation tool that reports how much processing time is spent in various areas of your game, including rendering and scripts. It records the statistics over time during gameplay and shows them in a timeline graph. Clicking lets you drill down into the details. See `http://docs.unity3d.com/Manual/Profiler.html` and the following screenshot:

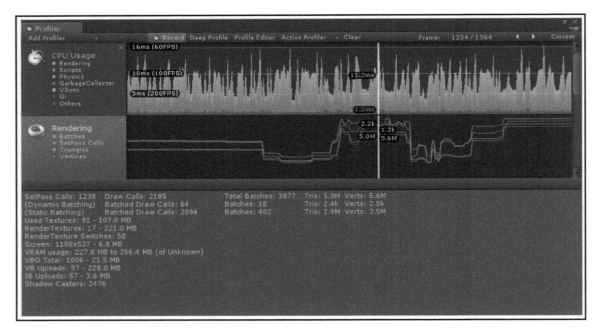

The **Profiler** compacts a lot of information into a small space, so you should recognize its various parts to understand better what you're seeing. Along the top of the window is the Profiler controls toolbar, which enables you to turn profiling on and off (**Record**) and navigate through profiled frames. The white vertical line in the profile Tracks is the playhead, indicating the current frame being examined.

The **Deep Profile** button lets you drill down into more detail, recording all function calls in your scripts. This can be useful to see exactly where time is spent in your game code. Note that deep profiling incurs a lot of overhead and causes your game to run very slowly.

Underneath the toolbar are the profile tracks. Scroll down the Tracks pane to reveal more. You can add and remove tracks using the **Add Profiler** select list.

Each track includes stats for many parameters pertaining to that category of processing. For example, **CPU Usage** includes **Scripts** and **Physics**; the **Rendering** one include **Batches** and **Triangles**. The visual graph allows you to readily detect anomalies. When troubleshooting, look for stretches and spikes where the data exceeds your expected thresholds.

You can profile your game running in the Unity Editor, or remote profile your game running in a separate player, such as a mobile device.

# Optimizing your art

Some decisions that impact performance the most are your intentionally creative ones. Maybe you want hyper-realistic graphics with high-fidelity sound because *its gotta be so awesome!* Realizing you must dial that down may constitute a difficult design compromise. However, it's also likely that with a little creative *outside-the-box* thinking and experimentation, you can achieve (nearly) identical visual results with much better performance. The one thing that you have most control over in your project is the content of your scenes.

Quality is not only how it looks, but also how it feels. Optimizing for user experience is as fundamental a design decision as any.

In general, try to minimize the number of vertices and faces in your model's meshes. Avoid complex meshes. Remove faces that will never be seen, such as the ones inside of solid objects. Clean up duplicate vertices and remove doubles. This will most likely be done in the same 3D modeling application you used to create them in the first place. For example, Blender has the tools for this. Also, there are third-party tools that you can purchase to simplify model meshes.

 Be sure to check out Unity's Import Settings for your FBX models. There are option to compress and optimize your meshes, for example. See `https://docs.unity3d.com/Manual/FBXImporter-Model.html`.

Let's demonstrate what we mean. We are going to set up a scene with a high polygon count model, replicate that model 1000 times, examine it in the Profiler, and try some optimization techniques.

# Setting up the scene

To begin, we'll need a high-poly model. We found one of a pair of sunglasses on Turbosquid with over 5,800 triangles, and which includes a transparent material for the lenses (`https://www.turbosquid.com/3d-models/3ds-sunglasses-blender/764082`). Please download the FBX file now. A copy is also included with the files for this book, for convenience. We will refer to this as `Sunglasses-original.fbx` to distinguish it from other versions we'll modify along the way.

Then, go into Unity, as follows:

1. Create a new scene (**File | New Scene**), then save it (**File | Save Scene As**) and name it `Optimization`
2. Import the model into your **Project** `Assets Models` folder (**Assets | Import New Asset**)
3. Create a ground plane for reference (**Create | 3D Object | Plane**), named `Ground Plane`, reset its **Transform**, and create or assign it a material with a neutral color (such as our `Ground Material` with **Albedo** #908070FF)
4. Create a cube (**Create | 3D Object | Cube**), **Positioned** at (−1, 1, 1), and give it a colored material (such as our `Red Material` with **Albedo** #E52A2AFF)
5. Move the `Main Camera` to **Position** (0, 0.5, −2)

Now add a copy of the sunglasses:

1. Drag a copy of the `Sunglasses-original` model into the scene
2. Set its **Position** (`0, 1, 0`), **Rotation** (`90, 180, 15`), and **Scale** (`10, 10, 10`)

As a baseline, let's look at its Stats and Profile, and make a note of the values:

1. In the **Game** window, press **Stats**
2. Also, open the Profiler window (**Window | Profile**)
3. Press **Play**

The **Game** window has the following scene and Stats window, showing the graphics hovering around 420 FPS, CPU main 2.4ms, with 22.6k Tris:

The corresponding Profiler window is shown next. You can see in the Rendering timeline where I moved the HMD around:

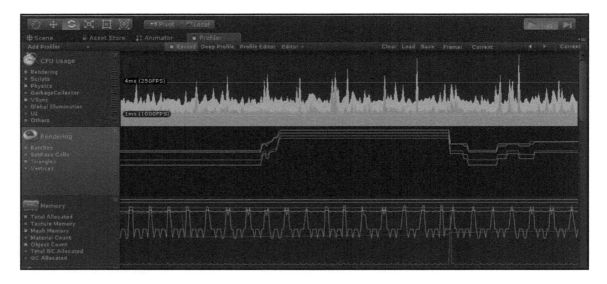

This scene is too simple to gather much in the way of meaningful statistics. Let's create 1000 copies of the sunglasses in the scene; follow these steps:

1. Create an **Empty** game object and name it SunglassesReplicator
2. Create a new C# script on it, named SunglassesReplicator, and write it as follows:

```csharp
using UnityEngine;

public class SunglassesReplicator : MonoBehaviour
{
    public GameObject prefab;
    public Vector3Int dup = new Vector3Int(10, 10, 10);
    public Vector3 delta = new Vector3(2, 2, 2);

    void Start()
    {
        Vector3 position = transform.position;
        for (int ix = 0; ix < dup.x; ix++)
        {
            for (int iy = 0; iy < dup.y; iy++)
            {
                for (int iz = 0; iz < dup.z; iz++)
```

```
        {
            position.x = transform.position.x + ix * delta.x;
            position.y = transform.position.y + iy * delta.y;
            position.z = transform.position.z + iz * delta.z;
            GameObject glasses = Instantiate(prefab);
            glasses.transform.position = position;
        }
      }
    }
  }
}
```

The script takes a `prefab` object and instantiates it the `dup` number of times (10) in each of the X, Y, and Z axes, offsetting each by `delta` units (2), generating a total of 1000 instances of the prefab.

Save the script, then back in Unity, set up and assign the replicator parameters as follows:

1. Make a prefab of your sunglasses. Drag the `Sunglasses-original` from **Hierarchy** into your **Project** `Assets prefabs` folder
2. Select the `SunglassesReplicator` in **Hierarchy** again and drag the prefab from **Project Assets** onto its **Prefab** slot
3. Set the `SunglassesReplicator` **Position** to (–10, 1, 0) as the origin of our stack of sunglasses

Press **Play** and the generated sunglasses Borg is shown in the **Scene** window:

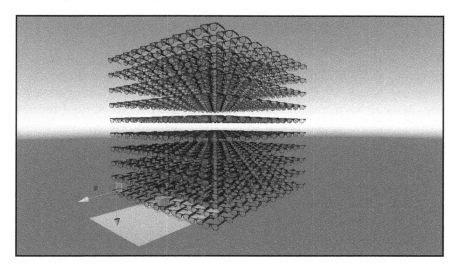

The Stats now report over 36 million tris and a frame rate under 60 FPS. Ugh! The corresponding Profiler timeline is shown here:

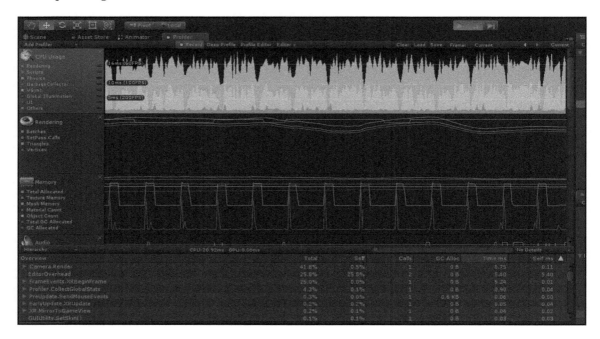

OK, now that we have a poorly performing scene, let's see what we can do about it.

# Decimating models

One thing we can do is try to simplify the models that we imported into Unity. If you select the `SunGlasses-original` object in your **Project Assets**, you can see it consists of two meshes: the `Frame` with 4176 tris, and the `Lens` with 1664 tris. We should reduce the number of faces on the mesh, or *decimate* the model. Presently, we will use the separate free and open source Blender application (`https://www.blender.org/`).

 Note that the original FBX file of this model downloaded from Turbosquid is in FBX 6 ASCII format, which is not compatible with Blender 2.7+. The version of the file provided with this book was converted using Autodesk FBX Converter 2013 (`http://usa.autodesk.com/adsk/servlet/pc/item?siteID=123112id=22694909`).

Follow these steps to decimate the model in Blender:

1. Open Blender, and delete all to clear the default scene (keyboard **A** | **A** again | **X** | **Delete**)
2. Import the source Sunglasses fbx file (**File** | **Import** | **FBX**)
3. Select the sunglasses' frame model mesh (right-click)
4. On the right, choose the **Modify** tool (wrench icon)
5. Select **Add Modifier** | **Decimate**
6. Set **Ratio** to 0.1, as shown here:

7. Then, press **Apply**
8. Select the sunglass' lens model mesh (right-click)
9. Decimate it also to **Ratio** 0.1 and **Apply**
10. Delete the camera, light, and background objects (select with mouse, keyboard **X** to delete)
11. Export as FBX (**File** | **Export** | **FBX**) and give it a new name, such as SunGlasses-decimated.fbx

Now back in Unity, import the model and use it in our replicator as follows:

1. Import the new SunGlasses-decimated.fbx file (**Assets** | **Import New Asset**) into your Models folder
2. Drag a copy of this model, SunGlasses-decimated, into the scene
3. Copy/paste the transform from the original (using Transform **Copy Component** from the original, and **Paste Component Values** on the decimated version)

4. Save this as a prefab (drag `SunGlasses-decimated` from **Hierarchy** into your **Project** `Assets Prefabs` folder)

5. Set this one in the `SunglassesReplicator` (drag the prefab from **Project Assets** onto the replicator's **Prefab** slot)

Press **Play** and as expected, we are now running about 3.4M tris, about 10% of what we had before, and we've boosted the FPS some, consistently more than 60 FPS. Better, but not good enough.

# Transparent materials

Another killer of graphics processing and frame rate is the use of transparency and other rendering techniques that require each pixel to be rendered multiple times. For the sunglasses lens to appear transparent, Unity will render the solid objects behind it first, then render the semi-transparent lens pixels on top, effectively merging the pixel values. Possibly dozens of lenses stacked in front of one another causes a considerable amount of processing work.

Let's see what happens when we replace the transparent lens material with an opaque one:

1. In your **Project** `Assets Materials` folder, create a new **Material** and name it `Lens_Opaque`

2. For its **Albedo** color, choose an opaque gray, such as `#333333FF`

3. Drag a copy of `Sunglasses-source` to **Hierarchy** and rename it `Sunglasses-opaque`

4. Unfold it and select the `Lens` child object

5. Drag the `Lens_Opaque` material onto the Lens

6. Select the `Sunglasses-opaque` and drag it into the `Prefabs` folder, creating a new prefab

7. With `SunglassesReplicator` selected, drag the `Sunglasses-opaque` prefab onto its **Prefab** slot

When you press **Play** now, we have 1000 of the opaque sunglasses and we get a much better frame rate, about 80 FPS.

What happens if we combine these two techniques? Let's use the opaque material on the decimated lenses. Like we just did, create another version of the prefab, named `Sunglasses-decimated-opaque`, as follows:

1. Drag a copy of `Sunglasses-decimated` to Hierarchy and rename it `Sunglasses-decimated-opaque`
2. Unfold it and select the `Lens` child object
3. Drag the `Lens_Opaque` material onto the Lens
4. Select the `Sunglasses-decimated-opaque` and drag it into the `Prefabs` folder, creating a new prefab with the opaque lenses
5. With `SunglassesReplicator` selected, drag the `Sunglasses-decimated-opaque` prefab onto its **Prefab** slot

Pressing **Play** we consistently get about 100 FPS, as shown in the **Profiler** timeline:

Terrific! We have the frame rate we want. But... that's not the look we want either. We have opaque lenses, but we expect translucent ones. And, disappointingly, the low poly versions of the glasses look... low poly. That's just not acceptable. Perhaps there's a compromise.

# Levels of detail

Reviewing our scene, we realize that the high-poly sunglasses are really only needed for the ones closest to you. As they recede further into the distance, the low-poly version is just fine. Likewise, the transparency on the lenses is really mostly needed on the ones near you. The sunglasses in the distance, and those occluded by other glasses, do not really need transparency. Unity understands this and provides a component to automatically manage levels of detail, called **LOD Group** (see `https://docs.unity3d.com/Manual/LevelOfDetail.html`).

Let's use this now. We'll create a group of sunglasses, with each of our versions for levels of detail:

1. In **Hierarchy**, create an **Empty** game object, name it `SunglassesLOD`, and reset its **Transform**
2. Drag a copy of the `Sunglasses-original` prefab as a child of `SunglassesLOD`
3. Drag a copy of the `Sunglasses-decimated` prefab as a child also
4. And drag a copy of the `Sunglasses-decimated-opaque` too
5. Select the parent `Sunglasses` object and **Add Component | LOD Group**

Look at the LOD Group component in Inspector. Notice it has several ranges for when to use each model based on camera distance, labeled **LOD0**, **LOD1**, and **LOD2**. The range is a percentage of the object's bounding box height relative to the screen height. When closest, the LOD0 objects are active. Further away, those will be deactivated and the LOD1 ones will be active, and so on.

Let's assign the LOD groups now:

1. Select **LOD0**
2. Drag the `Sunglasses-original` game object from **Hierarchy** onto the **Add** button
3. Select **LOD1**
4. Drag the `Sunglasses-decimated` game object onto the **Add** button
5. Select **LOD2**
6. Drag the `Sunglasses-decimated-opaque` object onto **Add** also

A screen capture of the **Inspector** is shown here:

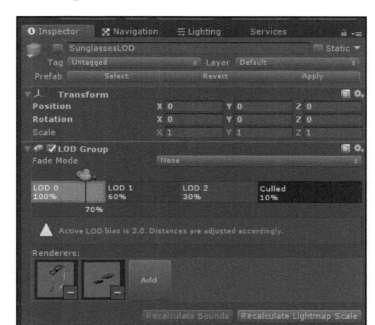

Notice there is a little camera icon on the top edge of the LODn groups. You can select and slide it across to preview the LOD activations based on camera distance. You can also configure the active range of each LOD (percentage) by sliding the edge of each area box.

Now, let's try it in our scene:

1. Drag the `SunglassesLOD` object into your **Project Prefabs** folder
2. Select `SunglassesReplicator` in **Hierarchy** and drag the `SunglassesLOD` prefab onto its **Prefab** slot

Press **Play**. The **Profiler** timeline is shown next. There's essentially no difference from our most optimized version, but we get the high-poly models and transparent lenses when we need them:

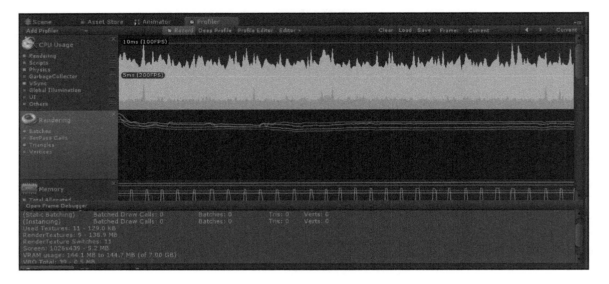

Next is a screen capture of the Game view using SunglassesLOD. Closest to us are the high-poly glasses. The middle are low-poly, but with transparent lenses. Further away are low-poly and opaque versions of the model:

There are a number LOD tools available in the Unity Asset Store to help manage levels of detail and even generate decimated meshes from your models. Unity itself is toying with such a tool, AutoLOD, available free on GitHub (`https://blogs.unity3d.com/2018/01/12/unity-labs-autolod-experimenting-with-automatic-performance-improvements/`).

# Optimizing your scene with static objects

In addition to your art objects, the next step in optimization might be how your scene itself is organized. If we tell Unity that specific objects will not move in the scene, it can precompute a lot of the rendering in advance rather than at runtime. We do this by defining these game objects as *static*, and then *baking* them into specific contexts.

We used static objects in `Chapter 4`, *Gazed-Based Control*, when we set up a `Navmesh` for Ethan to run through. His walkable *nav* area was defined by the flat ground plane minus any large static objects that might get in his way, baked into a *navmesh*.

Statics can also be used to help precompute the scene rendering. Baked lightmaps and shadowmaps precompute lighting and shadows. Baked occlusions divide the scene into static volumes that can be readily culled when out of view, saving processing by possibly eliminating many objects from consideration at once. Let's try some examples.

## Setting up the scene

To demonstrate the use of static game objects, we cannot use the dynamically instantiated sunglasses by `SunglassesReplicator`. But given we have this script, we'll use it to our advantage now:

1. In **Hierarchy**, select `SunglassesReplicator` and drag the `Sunglasses-original` prefab from **Project Assets** onto its **Prefab** slot
2. Press **Play**
3. While playing, in the **Hierarchy**, select all the `Sunglasses-original(Clone)` objects (there's 1000 of them!). Right-click and select **Copy**
4. Stop the play mode
5. In **Hierarchy**, create an **Empty** game object and name it `SunglassesBorg`.
6. Paste the cloned sunglasses as children of `SunglassesBorg`
7. Disable the `SunglassesReplicator` object, as we no longer want to use it

If you had the need to do this more than once, you could write an *Editor Script*. For example, maybe you need a BorgMaker menu option in the Editor's main menubar. It could prompt you with a dialog box asking for the prefab object, duplication counts, and offset parameters, much like our `SunglassesReplicator`. Writing scripts that customize and extend the Unity Editor is common practice. If you're interested, see the *Manual: Extending the Editor* (`https://docs.unity3d.com/Manual/ExtendingTheEditor.html`) and the *Editor Scripting Intro* tutorial (`https://unity3d.com/learn/tutorials/topics/scripting/editor-scripting-intro`).

# Lighting and baking

The use of lights in your scene affects frame rate. You have a great deal of control over the number of lights, types of lights, their placement, and settings. Read up on it in the Unity manual, which can be found at `http://docs.unity3d.com/Manual/LightPerformance.html`.

Use baked lightmaps whenever possible, which precalculates the lighting effects into a separate image rather than at runtime. Use real-time shadows sparingly. When an object casts shadows, a shadow map is generated, which will be used to render the other objects that might receive shadows. Shadows have a high rendering overhead and generally require high-end GPU hardware.

Let's see the impact of using baked lightmaps on our scene:

1. Select `SunglassesBorg` and click its **Static** checkbox in the upper right of **Inspector**
2. When prompted, answer **Yes, change children**

If you get an error, "Mesh doesn't have UVs suitable for lightmapping," select the imported fbx model in your Project window, choose **Generate Lightmap UVs**, and **Apply**.

Depending on your Lighting settings, the lightmaps may begin generating right away. Review and modify the lightmap settings as follows:

1. Open the **Lighting** window (**Window | Lighting**)
2. With **Auto Generate** checked, it will start generating lightmaps any time your scene changes

3. Or, uncheck it and click **Generate Lighting** to build them manually

Here is a screen capture of the Game window running with 1000 high-poly Sunglasses with transparency. We're getting 90 FPS now, and as I move the non-static red cube around, it still renders with transparency and shadows present:

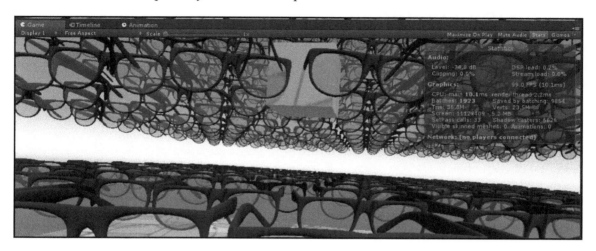

In the **Lighting** window, there are also settings for **Realtime Lighting** (enabled by default), **Baked Global Illumination** (enabled by default), **Lightmapper** subsystem (**Enlighten** by default), and **Fog** effects (disabled by default), all of which affect the quality and performance of your scene.

Here are some more tips when dealing with lighting:

- Avoid dynamic shadows, just use a "blurry blob" underneath moving things by using a Projector (see https://docs.unity3d.com/Manual/class-Projector. html).
- Check your project's **Quality Settings** (**Edit** | **Project Settings** | **Quality**). Use fewer **Pixel Lights** (on mobile, limit to 1 or 2). Use **High Resolution** on **Hard and Soft Shadows**.
- You can have as many baked lights as you want. Baked lighting produces high quality results, whereas real-time shadows can appear blocky.
- When baking, you can improve lightmap quality by increasing the baked resolution (a 40-100 pixel resolution is reasonable).
- Use light probes with baked lighting to illuminate dynamic objects.
- Use reflection probes for reflective surfaces. These can be static (baked) or dynamic (real-time).

Light probes (either real-time or baked) and the choice of shaders (and the shader options), can make your scene look really amazing. However, they can also have a significant effect on the performance. Balancing aesthetics and graphics performance is an art and a science.

# Occlusion culling

As we've seen, the more you try to reduce the number of objects that need to be rendered, the better. Whether or not you are using high- or low-poly models, Unity still needs to figure out which faces are in view. When there are a lot of objects, perhaps we could help Unity out by giving it some clues.

Occlusion culling disables the rendering of objects when they are not seen by the camera because they are obscured (occluded) by other objects. (See http://docs.unity3d.com/Manual/OcclusionCulling.html.) It examines your scene and, using the bounding boxes (extents) of each object, divides the world space into a hierarchy of cubes. When Unity needs to determine if an object is within view, it will throw away any objects who's culling box is obviously outside of the view, and continue through the hierarchy.

To demonstrate, we'll replicate a few copies of our SunglassesBorg and set up occlusion culling:

1. In **Hierarchy**, select SunglassesBorg, right-click, then **Duplicate** three times
2. For the first copy, set the **Y-Rotation** to 90, then move it off to **Position X** = 20
3. For the second copy, set **Y-Rotation** to -90 and move it to **Position X** = -20
4. For the third copy, set **Y-Rotation** to 180 and move it **Position Z** = -20

When I press **Play**, with so many objects, we are down to about a 50 FPS frame rate.

Now, with the following changes, we can address our performance problem:

1. All four Borgs are already **Static**, but verify that the **Static: Occluder** and **Occludee** are checked (inspect the **Static** drop-down list)
2. Open the **Occlusion Culling** window (**Window | Occlusion Culling**)
3. Click **Bake**

Note that we could have, but didn't, distinguish Occludees versus Occluders in our scene. Occludees are objects that get occluded. Ocluders are ones that may be in front, occluding the others. Translucent objects that do not occlude should be marked as Occludees, but not Occluders.

---

This may take a while. Here is a top-down Scene view with the generated culling volumes:

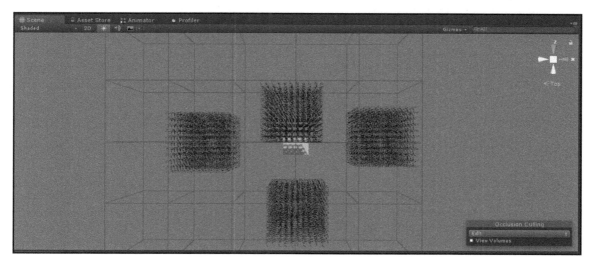

Now when I press Play, the performance is back up to 90 FPS again (more or less, depending on where you're looking, as a user in the scene).

 Another way to reduce the details in a scene is by using Global Fog, which is based on distance. Objects further away than the fog limits will not be drawn.

# Optimizing your code

Another area prone to performance problems and ripe for optimization is your script code. Throughout this book, we have used various coding best practices, without necessarily explaining why. (On the other hand, some examples in this book are not necessarily efficient, in favor of simplicity and explanation.) In Chapter 8, *Playing with Physics and Fire*, for example, we implemented an object pool memory manager to avoid repeatedly instantiating and destroying game objects that causes memory **garbage collection** (**GC**) issues, which in turn slows down your app.

In general, try to avoid code that repeats a lot of computation over and over. Try to pre-compute as much work as you can and store the partial results in variables.

At some point, you may have to use a profiling tool to see how your code is performing under the hood. If the **Profiler** indicates that a large amount of time is spent in the scripts that you've written, you should consider another way to refactor the code so that it's more efficient. Often, this is related to memory management, but it could be math or physics. (See `http://docs.unity3d.com/Manual/`
`MobileOptimizationPracticalScriptingOptimizations.html`.)

 Please follow coding best practices, but otherwise avoid going out of your way with premature optimization. One mistake people make is putting too much effort into optimizing areas of their code that don't need it, sacrificing readability and maintainability in the process. Use the Profiler to analyze where the performance bottlenecks are and focus your optimization efforts there first.

# Understanding the Unity life cycle

Like all video game engines, when your game runs, Unity is executing a giant loop, repeating over and over each frame update. Unity provides many *hooks* to tap into events at just about every step in the game loop. Depicted below is the life cycle flowchart, taken from the Unity Manual page Execution Order of Event Functions (`https://docs.unity3d.com/Manual/ExecutionOrder.html`). The two event functions you are most familiar with, `Start` and `Update`, are highlighted with the red arrows. The green dots highlight a number of other events we'll reference in this conversation:

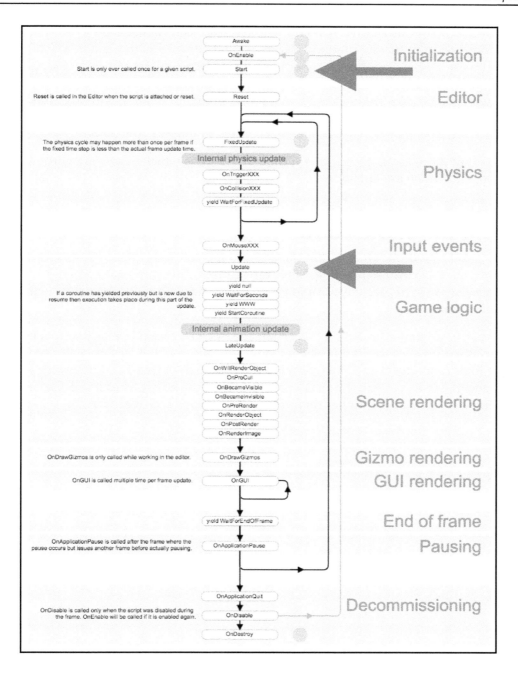

Starting at the top of this chart, when your game starts, each GameObject's component, which is derived from the `MonoBehaviour` class, will be woke with a call to `Awake`. Unless you need to use `Awake` or `OnEnable`, we typically initialize objects in `Start`. Skipping down to the Game Logic section, `Update` is called on each frame iteration. Note the loop line/arrows. (The physics engine has its own loop timing, for dealing with RigidBodies, which may be more frequent than the frame updates. You hook into it with `FixedUpdate`.) The `OnDestroy` event is called to decommission the object.

For the current discussion, the important thing to notice is which events are within the game loop, and which are outside.

# Writing efficient code

We want to keep all of the code within the game loop (such as`FixedUpdate`, `Update`, and `LateUpdate`) as lean as possible. Move any initialization into `Awake`, `OnEnable`, or `Start`. We also want to precompute and cache any computationally expensive work in the initialization functions.

For example, a call to `GetComponent` is expensive. As we've seen in many scripts in this book, it is a best practice to get references to any components that Update will need, outside the game logic loop, in `Start`. The following code, used in Chapter 7, *Locomotion and Comfort*, gets the `CharacterController` component in `Start`, caches it in a variable, and then references it in `Update`, rather than calling `GetComponent` every frame:

```
public class GlideLocomotion : MonoBehaviour
{
    private Camera camera;
    private CharacterController controller;

    void Start ()
    {
        camera = Camera.main;
        character = GetComponent<CharacterController>();
    }

    void Update()
    {
        character.SimpleMove(camera.transform.forward * 0.4f);
    }
}
```

Any time you declare an `Update()` function in your script (or any other event function), Unity will call it, even if it's empty. Therefore, you should remove any unused `Updates` even though they're part of the default template when you create a new C# `MonoBehaviour` script.

Likewise, if you have code in `Update` that does not need to be called every frame, turn off the calculations using a state variable (and an `if` statement) when they are not needed, for example:

```
public bool isWalking;

void Update()
{
    if (isWalking)
    {
        character.SimpleMove(camera.transform.forward * 0.4f);
    }
}
```

# Avoiding expensive API calls

Other than moving expensive API calls out of Update into an initialization function, there are some APIs that should be avoided altogether if possible. Here are a few.

Avoid `Object.Find()`. To obtain a reference to a game object in your scene, do not call `Find`. Not only is `Find` by name expensive, as it must search the Hierarchy tree, but it is brittle (might break) if you rename the object it is looking for. If you can, define a `public` variable to reference the object and associate it in the Editor Inspector. If you must find the object at runtime, use Tags or perhaps Layers to limit the search to a known fixed set of candidates.

Avoid `SendMessage()`. The legacy use of `SendMessage` is computationally expensive (because it makes use of runtime *reflection*). To trigger functions in another object, use Unity **Events** instead.

Avoid fragmenting memory and garbage collection. Temporary allocations of data and objects may cause memory to fragment. Unity will periodically go through the memory heap to consolidate free blocks, but this is expensive and can cause frames to skip in your app.

For more suggestions and a deeper discussion, see the Unity best practices guide, *Understanding Optimization in Unity* (`https://docs.unity3d.com/Manual/BestPracticeUnderstandingPerformanceInUnity.html`).

Another area of optimization is Unity Physics. In previous chapters, we briefly mentioned using layers for ray casting, to limit the objects Unity needs to search, for example, for gaze-based selection in VR. Likewise, physics collision detection can be limited to objects on specific layers by defining a Layer Collision Matrix. See the manual page on Optimizing Physics Performance (`https://docs.unity3d.com/Manual/iphone-Optimizing-Physics.html`) and the Physics Best Practices tutorial (`https://unity3d.com/learn/tutorials/topics/physics/physics-best-practices`).

# Optimizing the rendering

There are a number of important performance considerations that are specific to how Unity does its rendering. Some of these may be common for any graphics engine. Some recommendations may change as newer versions of Unity emerge, the technology advances, and algorithms get replaced.

There are many articles offering recommendations for which setting to use to optimize your VR apps, and it's not unusual for one's advice to contradict another's. Here are some good ones:

- Use the **Forward Rendering** path. This is the default in **Graphics Settings**.
- Use 4X **MSAA** (multi-sampling anti-aliasing). This is a low-cost anti-aliasing technique that helps remove jagged edges and shimmering effects in **Quality Settings**.
- Use **Single Pass Stereo Rendering**. It performs efficient rendering of parallax perspective for each eye in a single pass in **Player Settings**.
- Enable **Static Batching** and **Dynamic Batching** in **Player Settings**. These are discussed later.

Note that some rendering settings are device- or platform-specific, and found in the **Player Settings** (**Edit | Project Settings | Player**). Others have been abstracted by Unity into project **Quality Settings** (**Edit | Project Settings | Quality**). Still others are in the **Graphics Settings** (**Edit | Project Settings | Graphics**).

The phrase *Player Settings* in Unity does not refer to the user (player) nor a first-person character (player rig). Rather it's referring to the platform executable that *plays* your app. More like a media player, such as a video player that plays mp4s, the Unity *player* runs your game after it has been compiled. The Player Settings configure the generated executable.

# Life's a batch

Perhaps, the biggest bang for the buck is a feature in Unity that groups different meshes into a single batch, which is then shoveled into the graphics hardware all at once. This is much faster than sending the meshes separately. Meshes are actually first compiled into an OpenGL vertex buffer object, or VBO, but that's a low-level detail of the rendering pipeline.

Each batch takes one draw call. Reducing the number of draw calls in a scene is more significant than the actual number of vertices or triangles. For mobile VR, for example, stay around 50 (up to 100) draw calls.

There are two types of batching, **static batching** and **dynamic batching**, enabled in **Player Settings**.

For static batching, simply mark the objects as static by checking off the **Static** checkbox in the Unity **Inspector** for each object in the scene. Marking an object static tells Unity that it will never move, animate, or scale. Unity will automatically batch together the meshes that share the same material into a single, large mesh.

The caveat here is meshes must share the same Material settings: the same texture, shader, shader parameters, and the material pointer object. How can this be? They're different objects! This can be done by combining multiple textures into a single macro-texture file or **TextureAtlas** and then UV-mapping as many models as will fit. It's a lot like a sprite image used for 2D and web graphics. There are third-party tools that help you build these.

A useful analytic tool for checking resources in your scene, including active textures, materials and meshes, is the Unity Resource Checker, found here: `https://github.com/handcircus/Unity-Resource-Checker`.

Dynamic batching is similar to static batching. For objects that are not marked **Static**, Unity will still try to batch them, albeit it will be a slower process since it needs to think about it frame by frame (the CPU cost). The shared Material requirement still holds, as well as other restrictions such as vertex count (less than 300 vertices) and uniform **Transform Scale** rules. (See `http://docs.unity3d.com/Manual/DrawCallBatching.html`.)

When managing textures in scripts, use `Renderer.sharedMaterial` rather than `Renderer.material` to avoid creating duplicate materials. Objects receiving a duplicate material will opt out of the batch.

Currently, only **Mesh Renderers** and **Particle Systems** are batched. This means that skinned meshes, cloth, trail renderers, and other types of rendering components are not.

# Multipass pixel filling

Another concern in the rendering pipeline is sometimes referred to as the pixel fill-rate. If you think about it, the ultimate goal of rendering is to fill each pixel on the display device with the correct color value. If it has to paint any pixels more than once, that's more costly. For example, watch out for transparent particle effects, such as smoke, that touch many pixels with mostly transparent quads.

For VR, Unity paints into a frame buffer memory that is larger than the physical display dimensions, which is then post-processed for ocular distortion correction (barrel effect) and chromatic aberration correction (color separation), before getting tossed onto the HMD display. In fact, there may be multiple overlay buffers that get composited before the post-processing.

This multipass pixel filling is how some advanced renderers work, including lighting and material effects such as multiple lights, dynamic shadows, and transparency (**Transparent** and **Fade Render** modes) - the Unity Standard Shader as well. Basically, all the good stuff!

VBO batches with materials that require multipass pixel filling get submitted multiple times, thus increasing the net number of draw calls. Depending on your project, you may choose to either optimize the heck out of it and avoid multipass pixel filling altogether, or carefully curate the scenes with an understanding of what should have a high performance and what should have a high fidelity.

You can use **Light Probes** to inexpensively simulate dynamic lighting of your dynamic objects. Light probes are baked cubemaps that store information about direct, indirect, and even emissive light at various points in your scene. As a dynamic object moves, it interpolates samples of the nearby light probes to approximate the lighting at that specific position. This is a cheap way of simulating realistic lighting on dynamic objects without using expensive real-time lights.
(See `http://docs.unity3d.com/Manual/LightProbes.html`.)

Unity 2018 introduces a new Scriptable Render Pipeline, providing a way of configuring and controlling rendering from C# scripts. Unity 2018 includes alternative built-in pipelines for lightweight rendering (such as for mobile and VR apps), and high definition rendering (such as for high fidelity physically based renders), and there's an opportunity for the community to build and share more. Use of these pipelines may supersede information and recommendations made here.

# VR-optimized shaders

Shaders are small programs that are compiled to run in the GPU. They process your 3D vectors and polygons (triangles), prepared by the game engine on the CPU, along with lighting information, texture maps, and other parameters, to generate pixels on the display.

Unity comes with a rich set of shaders. The Default Surface Shader is a powerful and optimized one that supports textures, normal maps, height maps, occlusion maps, emission map, specular highlights, reflections, and more.

Unity also includes a set of mobile optimized shaders that are popular for mobile (and desktop) VR development. While they may not provide as high-quality lighting and rendering support, they are designed to perform well on mobile devices and should be considered in any developer's toolbox, even on desktop VR apps.

VR device manufacturers and developers have released their own custom shaders that optimize graphics processing in ways they see fit.

**Daydream Renderer** (https://developers.google.com/vr/develop/unity/renderer) is a Unity package designed for high-quality rendering optimized for the Daydream platform. It supports normal maps, specular highlights with up to eight dynamic lights, "hero shadows" with significant performance improvements over Unity's standard shaders.

Valve (Steam) released the VR shaders used in their impressive demo project, *The Lab*, as a Unity Package (https://assetstore.unity.com/packages/tools/the-lab-renderer-63141). It supports up to 18 dynamic shadowing lights in a single pass with MSAA.

The Oculus OVRPlugin, included with Unity, contains a number of Oculus-specific shaders, used by their prefabs and script components.

Third-party developers also provide shaders with their tools and utilities. As mentioned in Chapter 2, *Content, Objects, and Scale*, the Google Poly Toolkit for Unity include shaders for models downloaded from Poly, including artwork created with TiltBrush.

And you can experiment and write your own shader. In `Chapter 10`, *Using All 360 Degrees,* we looked at the Unity **ShaderLab** language when we wrote our own inward shader. Unity 2018 introduces a new **Shader Graph** tool for visually building shaders instead of using code. It's intended to be "simple enough that new users can become involved in shader creation."

# Runtime performance and debugging

Graphics hardware architectures continue to evolve towards performance that benefits rendering pipelines of virtual reality (and augmented reality). VR introduces requirements that weren't so important for traditional video gaming. Latency and dropped frames (where rendering a frame takes longer than the refresh rate) took a back seat to high-fidelity AAA rendering capabilities. VR needs to render each frame in time and do it twice: once for each eye. Driven by the requirements of this emerging industry, semiconductor and hardware manufacturers are building new and improved devices, which will inevitably impact how content developers think about optimization.

That said, most likely you should develop and optimize for the lower specs that you want to target. If such optimizations necessitate undesirable compromises, consider separate versions of the game for high- versus low-end platforms. VR device manufacturers have started publishing minimum/recommended hardware specifications, which take much of the guesswork out of it. Start with the recommended Unity settings of your target device and adjust as needed.

For instance, for mobile VR, it is recommended that you tune for CPU-bound rather than GPU-bound usage. Some games will make the CPU work harder, others will impact the GPU. Normally, you should favor CPU over GPU. The Oculus Mobile SDK (GearVR) has an API that is used to throttle the CPU and GPU to control heat and battery drain.

Running in the editor is not the same as running on a mobile device. But, you can still use the Profiler while running in the device.

It can be useful to have a developer mode in your app that shows a heads up display (HUD) with current **frames per second** (**FPS**) and other vital statistics at runtime. To make your how FPS HUD display, add a UI Canvas to your scene with a child Text object. The following script updates the text string with the FPS value:

```
public class FramesPerSecondText : MonoBehaviour
{
    private float updateInterval = 0.5f;
    private int framesCount;
```

```
    private float famesTime;
    private Text text;

    void Start()
    {
        text = GetComponent<Text>();
    }
    void Update()
    {
        framesCount++;
        framesTime += Time.unscaledDeltaTime;
        if (framesTime > updateInterval)
        {
            float fps = framesCount / framesTime;
            text.text = string.Format("{0:F2} FPS", fps);
            framesCount = 0;
            framesTime = 0;
        }
    }
}
```

Some VR devices also provide their own tools, which we will look at next.

# Daydream

Daydream developer options include the GvrInstalPreviewMain prefab that lets you use your Daydream device with the Unity Editor Play mode.

The *Daydream Performance HUD* (https://developers.google.com/vr/develop/unity/perfhud) is built into Android. To enable it:

1. Launch the Daydream application on your phone
2. Tap the gear icon on the top right of the screen
3. Tab **Build Version** six times to make the **Developer Options** item appear
4. Select **Developer Options** | **Enable performance heads-up display**

Then, run a VR app and you will see the performance overlay.

# Oculus

Oculus offers a suite of performance analysis and optimization tools (`https://developer.oculus.com/documentation/pcsdk/latest/concepts/dg-performance/`), which includes extensive documentation and a workflow guide for developers. Good stuff! It also includes an Oculus Debug Tool, Lost Frame Capture Tool, Performance Profiler, and a Performance Head-Up Display (`https://developer.oculus.com/documentation/pcsdk/latest/concepts/dg-hud/`).

To activate the Performance Head-Up Display, you run it from the Oculus Debug Tool as follows:

1. Go to `Program Files\Oculus\Support\oculus-diagnostics\`.
2. Double-click `OculusDebugTool.exe`.
3. They recommend you first turn off Asynchronous Spacewarp (ASW) to get a good sense of your app's performance without ASW. Find **Asynchronous Spacewarp** and choose **Disabled** from the select list.
4. Find **Visible HUD** and choose the type you'd like to see: **Performance**, **Stereo Debug**, **Layer**, or **None**.

# Summary

Latency and low frames-per-second rates are not acceptable and can cause motion sickness in VR. We are bound by the capabilities and limitations of the hardware devices we run on and their SDKs. In this chapter, we dove into some of the more technical aspects of making great VR, considering four separate areas that affect performance: the artwork, the scene, the code, and the rendering pipeline.

We started the chapter by introducing the built-in Unity Profiler and Stats windows, our primary weapons in this battle. To illustrate the impacts of designing models and materials, we built a scene with 1000 high-poly Sunglasses with transparent lenses, examined the performance stats, and then tried several ways to improve the frame rate: decimating the models (making them low poly), removing transparency in the materials, and managing level of detail (LOD) in the scene. Then, we considered things we can do at the scene level, using static objects, baked lightmaps, and occlusion culling.

Next, we looked at basic practices for optimizing your C# scripts. A key to this is understanding the Unity life cycle, game loop, and expensive API functions, encouraging you to make the frame `Update` processing as lean as possible. Then, we looked at the rendering pipeline, gaining some insight into how it works and how to use recommended **Quality**, **Graphics** and **Player** settings, VR optimized shaders, and runtime tools to analyze and improve performance.

It should be abundantly clear by now that developing for VR has many facets (pun intended). You work hard to create an awesome scene with beautiful models, textures, and lighting. You try to provide a thrilling interactive experience for your visitors. At the same time, you should also be thinking about the requirements of your target platform, rendering performance, frames per second, latency, and motion sickness. It's never too early to focus on performance. It's a mistake to start too late. Follow recommended best practices that are easy to implement, while keeping your code and object hierarchy clean and maintainable. However, take a thoughtful, scientific approach to troubleshooting and performance tuning, using the Profiler and other tools to analyze your project so you can zero in on the root causes rather than spend time on areas that may yield little net effect.

> *We developers rapidly become immune to all but the most obvious rendering errors, and as a result we are the worst people at testing our own code. It introduces a new and exciting variation of the coder's defense that "it works on my machine" - in this case, "it works for my brain." -Tom Forsyth, Oculus*

Developing for VR is a moving target. The platform hardware, software SDKs, and the Unity 3D engine itself are all changing and improving rapidly. Books, blog posts, and YouTube videos can be readily superseded as products improve and new developer insights emerge. On the other hand, great strides have already been made to establish best practices, preferred Unity settings, and optimized device SDKs that address the needs of VR developers.

As VR goes mainstream, it is coming into its own as a new medium for expression, communication, education, problem solving, and storytelling. Your grandparents needed to learn to type and read. Your parents needed to learn PowerPoint and browse the web. Your children will build castles and teleport between virtual spaces. VR will not replace the real world and our humanity; it will enhance it.

# Other Books You May Enjoy

If you enjoyed this book, you may be interested in these other books by Packt:

**Getting Started with Unity 2018 - Third Edition**
Dr. Edward Lavieri

ISBN: 978-1-78883-010-2

- Set up your Unity development environment and navigate its tools
- Import and use custom assets and asset packages to add characters to your game
- Build a 3D game world with a custom terrain, water, sky, mountains, and trees
- Animate game characters, using animation controllers, and scripting
- Apply audio and particle effects to the game
- Create intuitive game menus and interface elements
- Customize your game with sound effects, shadows, lighting effects, and rendering options
- Debug code and provide smooth error handling

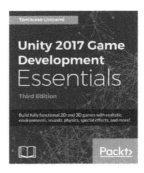

**Unity 2017 Game Development Essentials - Third Edition**
Tommaso Lintrami

ISBN: 978-1-78646-939-7

- Script games using C#
- Build your very first 2D and 3D games
- Work through the key concepts in game development such as animations, physics, and scripting
- Test and optimize your games to attain great performance
- Create fully functional menus, HUDs, and UI
- Create player character interactions with AI and NPC

## Augmented Reality for Developers
Jonathan Linowes, Krystian Babilinski

ISBN: 978-1-78728-643-6

- Build Augmented Reality applications through a step-by-step, tutorial-style project approach
- Use the Unity 3D game engine with the Vuforia AR platform, open source ARToolKit, Microsoft's Mixed Reality Toolkit, Apple ARKit, and Google ARCore, via the C# programming language
- Implement practical demo applications of AR including education, games, business marketing, and industrial training
- Employ a variety of AR recognition modes, including target images, markers, objects, and spatial mapping
- Target a variety of AR devices including phones, tablets, and wearable smartglasses, for Android, iOS, and Windows HoloLens
- Develop expertise with Unity 3D graphics, UIs, physics, and event systems
- Explore and utilize AR best practices and software design patterns

# Leave a review - let other readers know what you think

Please share your thoughts on this book with others by leaving a review on the site that you bought it from. If you purchased the book from Amazon, please leave us an honest review on this book's Amazon page. This is vital so that other potential readers can see and use your unbiased opinion to make purchasing decisions, we can understand what our customers think about our products, and our authors can see your feedback on the title that they have worked with Packt to create. It will only take a few minutes of your time, but is valuable to other potential customers, our authors, and Packt. Thank you!

# Index